Bristol Studies in International Theory series

Series Editors: **Felix Berenskötter**, SOAS, University of London, UK, **Neta C. Crawford**, Boston University, USA and **Stefano Guzzini**, Uppsala University, Sweden, PUC-Rio de Janeiro, Brazil

---

This series provides a platform for theoretically innovative scholarship that advances our understanding of the world and formulates new visions of, and solutions for, world politics.

Guided by an open mind about what innovation entails, and against the backdrop of various intellectual turns, interrogations of established paradigms, and a world facing complex political challenges, books in the series aim to provoke and deepen theoretical conversations in the field of International Relations and demonstrate their relevance.

Also available

The Idea of Civilization and the Making of the Global Order

Andrew Linklater

Find out more at

bristoluniversitypress.co.uk/
bristol-studies-in-international-theory

Bristol Studies in International Theory series

Series Editors: **Felix Berenskötter**, SOAS, University of London, UK, **Neta C. Crawford**, Boston University, USA and **Stefano Guzzini**, Uppsala University, Sweden, PUC-Rio de Janeiro, Brazil

---

International advisory board

Claudia Aradau, King's College London
Jens Bartelson, Lund University
Pinar Bilgin, Bilkent University
Toni Erskine, Australian National University
Matthew Evangelista, Cornell University
Karin Fierke, University of St Andrews
Kimberly Hutchings, Queen Mary University of London
Peter Katzenstein, Cornell University
Gilbert Khadiagala, University of the Witwatersrand
Anna Leander, University of Geneva
Sheryl Lightfoot, The University of British Columbia
Cecelia Lynch, University of California Irvine
Jonathan Mercer, University of Washington
Heikki Patomäki, University of Helsinki
Sergei Prozorov, University of Jyväskylä
Yaqing Qin, China Foreign Affairs University
Fiona Robinson, Carleton University
Justin Rosenberg, University of Sussex
Chih-Yu Shih, National Taiwan University
Jennifer Sterling-Folker, University of Connecticut

Find out more at
bristoluniversitypress.co.uk/
bristol-studies-in-international-theory

WHAT IN THE WORLD?

Understanding Global Social Change

Edited by
Mathias Albert and Tobias Werron

First published in Great Britain in 2022 by

Bristol University Press
University of Bristol
1-9 Old Park Hill
Bristol
BS2 8BB
UK
t: +44 (0)117 374 6645
e: bup-info@bristol.ac.uk

Details of international sales and distribution partners are available at bristoluniversitypress.co.uk

© Bristol University Press 2022

British Library Cataloguing in Publication Data
A catalogue record for this book is available from the British Library

ISBN 978-1-5292-1331-7 hardcover
ISBN 978-1-5292-1332-4 paperback
ISBN 978-1-5292-1331-1 ePub
ISBN 978-1-5292-1334-8 ePdf

The rights of Mathias Albert and Tobias Werron to be identified as editors of this work has been asserted by them in accordance with the Copyright, Designs and Patents Act 1988.

All rights reserved: no part of this publication may be reproduced, stored in a retrieval system, or transmitted in any form or by any means, electronic, mechanical, photocopying, recording, or otherwise without the prior permission of Bristol University Press.

Every reasonable effort has been made to obtain permission to reproduce copyrighted material. If, however, anyone knows of an oversight, please contact the publisher.

The statements and opinions contained within this publication are solely those of the editors and contributors and not of the University of Bristol or Bristol University Press. The University of Bristol and Bristol University Press disclaim responsibility for any injury to persons or property resulting from any material published in this publication.

Bristol University Press works to counter discrimination on grounds of gender, race, disability, age and sexuality.

Cover design: blu inc, Bristol
Front cover image: istock/Maxiphoto

Contents

List of Figures and Tables		vii
Notes on Contributors		viii
Acknowledgements		xii
1	Introduction: World Society and Its Histories – The Sociology and Global History of Global Social Change *Mathias Albert and Tobias Werron*	1
2	*Every Epoch, Time Frame or Date that Is Solid Melts into Air.* Does It? The Entanglements of Global History and World Society *Mathias Albert*	25
3	Periodization in Global History: The Productive Power of Comparing *Angelika Epple*	43
4	Communication, Differentiation and the Evolution of World Society *Boris Holzer*	63
5	Field Theory and Global Transformations in the Long Twentieth Century *Julian Go*	81
6	Organization(s) of the World *Martin Koch*	99
7	Particularly Universal Encounters: Ethnographic Explorations into a Laboratory of World Society *Teresa Koloma Beck*	117
8	From the First Sino-Roman War (That Never Happened) to Modern International-cum-Imperial Relations: Observing International Politics from an Evolution Theory Perspective *Stephan Stetter*	139

9	Nationalism as a Global Institution: A Historical-Sociological View *Tobias Werron*	157
10	States and Markets: A Global Historical Sociology of Capitalist Governance *George Lawson*	177
11	The Impact of Communications in Global History *Heidi Tworek*	195
12	The 'Long Twentieth Century' and the Making of World Trade Law *James Stafford*	211
13	Third-Party Actors, Transparency and Global Military Affairs *Thomas Müller*	227
14	Technical Internationalism and Global Social Change: A Critical Look at the Historiography of the United Nations *Daniel Speich Chassé*	243

References	265
Index	299

List of Figures and Tables

Figures

5.1	Number of first anticolonial nationalist events in colonies, 1850–1990	91
5.2	Imperial and colonial political fields	93

Tables

5.1	Inter-imperial versus interstate global fields	86
6.1	Typology of world organization	111

Notes on Contributors

Mathias Albert is Professor of Political Science at Bielefeld University. He has published widely on world society, globalization, IR theory, youth studies and polar research. His latest book publications include: *A Theory of World Politics* (2016); *The Politics of International Political Theory* (with A.F. Lang, 2019); *Jugend 2019. 18. Shell Jugendstudie* (with K. Hurrelmann et al, 2019).

Angelika Epple is Professor of Modern History at Bielefeld University. She has published widely on the history of globalization/s, theory of history, and historiography. Her latest publications in English include: *Practices of Comparing: Towards a New Understanding of a Fundamental Human Practice* (with W. Erhart and J. Grave, 2020); 'Comparing Europe and the Americas: The Dispute of the New World Between the Sixteenth and Nineteenth Centuries', in W. Steinmetz (ed) *The Force of Comparisons: A New Perspective on Modern European History and the Contemporary World* (2019); 'Calling for a Practice Turn in Global History', *History and Theory*, 57(3) (2018): 390–406.

Julian Go is Professor of Sociology at the University of Chicago. His most recent books include *Postcolonial Thought and Social Theory* (2016) and *Global Historical Sociology* (with G. Lawson, 2017).

Boris Holzer is Professor of General Sociology and Macrosociology at the University of Konstanz. He has written on globalization and modernization theory, social networks and conflicts between protest groups and transnational corporations. His current research focuses on political and economic sociology, social networks and globalization. Recent book publications include: *From Globalization to World Society* (ed with F. Kastner and T. Werron, 2015); *Schlüsselwerke der Netzwerkforschung* (ed with C. Stegbauer, 2019).

Martin Koch is Senior Lecturer in Political Science at Bielefeld University. His research interests include international organizations, international relations theory and world society studies. He is currently working on the role of the G20 in world politics, on inter-organizational relations and world order, and on the IOM as a world organization. His recent publications are *Internationale Organisationen in der Weltgesellschaft* (2017); (with M. Geiger) 'World Organizations in Migration Politics', *Journal of International Organization Studies*, 8(1) (2018): 25–44; (with A. Kaasch and K. Martens) 'Exploring Theoretical Approaches to Global Social Policy Research: Learning from International Relations and Inter-organizational Theory', *Global Social Policy*, 19(1) (2019): 87–104.

Teresa Koloma Beck is Professor for the Sociology of Globalisation at Bundeswehr University Munich. Her work focuses on the everyday dynamics of violence, armed conflict and globalization. She has undertaken ethnographic field research in Angola, Mozambique and Afghanistan. Among her publications are *The Normality of Civil War* (2012); (with T. Werron) 'Violent Conflictition: Armed Conflicts and Global Competition for Attention and Legitimacy', *International Journal of Politics, Culture, and Society*, 31(3) (2018): 275–96.

George Lawson is Professor of International Relations at ANU, having previously taught at LSE and Goldsmiths. He works on the relationship between history and theory, with a particular interest in historical sociology and revolutions. On the latter, he has published *Anatomies of Revolution* (2019) and *Negotiated Revolutions* (2005). On the former, he has published *Global Historical Sociology* (ed with J. Go, 2017), *The Global Transformation* (with B. Buzan, 2015), and *The Global 1989* (ed with C. Armbruster and M. Cox, 2010).

Thomas Müller is a postdoctoral researcher at Bielefeld University. His research interests centre on hierarchies, the politics of comparison and quantification in world politics. In the Collaborative Research Centre 1288 'Practices of Comparing', he explores how state and non-state actors produce and use comparative knowledge on military expenditures, capabilities and power in global security politics. His most recent articles are: 'The Variety of Institutionalised Inequalities: Stratificatory Interlinkages in Interwar International Society', *Review of International Studies*, 45(4) (2019): 669–88 and 'Institutional Reforms and the

Politics of Inequality Reproduction: The Case of the League of Nations' Council Crisis in 1926', *Global Society* 34(3) (2020): 304–17.

Daniel Speich Chassé is Professor of Global History at the University of Lucerne. His research focuses on the history of knowledge in international relations. He has published a monograph on the invention of the Gross Domestic Product: *Erfindung des Bruttosozialprodukts* (2013) and several articles on the historical unfolding of comparative statistics of nations since the late eighteenth century. His latest contribution is 'In Search of a Global Centre of Calculation: The Washington Statistical Conferences of 1947', in Willibald Steinmetz (ed) *The Force of Comparison* (2019), pp 266–87.

James Stafford is a postdoctoral researcher in the DFG-funded Research Training Group (Graduate College) 'World Politics' at Bielefeld University. A historian of international legal, political and economic thought, he is currently completing his first book, *Ruling Ireland: Empire and Political Economy, 1776–1848*.

Stephan Stetter is Professor of International Politics and Conflict Studies at the Bundeswehr University Munich. He has published widely on historical and sociological approaches to international relations, theories of world society and world politics, Middle East conflicts and society as well as EU foreign affairs. His latest books are *Middle East Christianity: Local Practices, World Societal Entanglements* (ed with M. Moussa Nabo, 2020), and *Modern Subjectivities in World Society: Global Structures and Local Practices* (with D. Jung, 2018).

Heidi Tworek is Associate Professor of History and Public Policy at the University of British Columbia, Vancouver. Her latest book is *News from Germany: The Competition to Control World Communications, 1900–1945* (2019), which received the Wiener Holocaust Library Fraenkel Prize and the Ralph Gomory Prize from the Business History Conference. Along with two edited volumes on the history of media and global business, she has published widely on the history of media, communications, and health. She is co-editor of *Journal of Global History*.

Tobias Werron is Professor of Sociological Theory at Bielefeld University. His main research interests include competition, nationalism and globalization. Among his recent publications are: (with J. Brankovic and L. Ringel) 'How Rankings Produce Competition: The Case of Global University Rankings', *Zeitschrift für Soziologie*, 47(4) (2018): 270–88; (with T. Koloma Beck) 'Violent Conflictition: Armed Conflicts and Global Competition for Attention and Legitimacy', *International Journal of Politics, Culture, and Society*, 31(3) (2018): 275–96; *Der globale Nationalismus* (2018).

Acknowledgements

Earlier versions of the chapters of this book were discussed at two workshops, one held in the Bavarian Alps in Osterhofen (Bayrischzell) in June 2018, and one in Bielefeld in March 2019. We would like to thank the Institute for World Society Studies of Bielefeld University for organizing and supporting both workshops.

Special thanks go to Stephen Curtis, who undertook thorough language editing of those chapters whose authors' mother tongue is not English. At Bielefeld University, we would like to thank Felix Maximilian Bathon for providing assistance in preparing the original manuscript, and Helga Volkening, Ellen Hegewaldt and Antonia Stüwe for providing assistance in preparing the final typescript.

1

Introduction: World Society and Its Histories – The Sociology and Global History of Global Social Change

Mathias Albert and Tobias Werron

Global social change: asking old questions anew

The aim of the present book is to prise open pertinent questions that need to be addressed when thinking about global social change. It assembles scholars from three disciplines: sociology, International Relations (IR) and history. We have not attempted to propose a single theoretical framework for analysing global social change, nonetheless we are convinced that we have reached a juncture in terms of thinking about global issues and their dynamics so that the time has come to seek cross-fertilizations between the various branches of global history, world society theories, global historical sociology, postcolonial studies, theories of International Relations and so forth. All these branches have emerged in criticism of disciplinary traditions, particularly in criticism of a 'methodological nationalism' not seen as fit for a comprehensive understanding of historical and contemporary global social orders and their dynamics. However, while they may have effectively delegitimized many old certainties and world views, they have been less successful in establishing a new paradigm.

The argument to be pursued in this book is that such a paradigm is most likely to emerge out of cross-disciplinary debates that make use of the empirical knowledge accumulated in globalization scholarship of recent decades; the book also re-examines the theoretical standpoints that guide the empirical work in different disciplines. All this requires openness to the knowledge and concepts that other disciplines bring to the table and consideration of varying traditions of thought and disciplinary contexts. Against this background, the aim of the book is to lay open some of the main questions (or problems) and issues (or topics) that have emerged as key entry points to the discussion about global social change in a vast body of scholarship. Many of the key questions of globalization research, such as periodization and 'epochal' change, or the meanings and implications of modernity, are by no means new. Quite the contrary. They are at the core most notably of history and sociology as academic disciplines. In addition, the field of IR, at the centre of its theoretical debates, has arguably always pondered on how to conceptualize change in world politics. It is reflection on precisely these core issues that promises to reveal the extent of work still to be done in seeking to reorient lines of thought that emerged in a decidedly national and colonial world to a global perspective.

Global social change is, admittedly, a big subject. In fact, it might be argued that every piece of social science or historical research that does not operate with a decided limitation in scale or scope is, explicitly or implicitly, dealing with it. However, things are not that easy. It might appear that social theories, with their universal claims about the social world, offer well-tested tools for the development of theories of global social change. Nonetheless, their limitations are well known. Social theories of Western European origin have hardly worked as a bulwark against pervasive 'methodological nationalism' – the equation of nation state and society and the imagery of nation state societies as quasi-natural 'containers' – in much of the social sciences.[1] Moreover, a wealth of postcolonial critical literature has pointed out that social theories, as well as the analyses that use them, often fail to systematically account for the power and knowledge relations characteristic for the formation of the contemporary world in a truly global perspective. Starting from the classical period of sociology (ca 1880–1920), sociologists have taken an interest in the world mainly in comparative terms, particularly, for the purpose of understanding the uniqueness of Western civilization, in comparing the distinct historical developments of the 'East' and the 'West'. While it can be argued, therefore, that global comparisons were already very much present in classical sociology, there was less interest in actual global connections, which at the time manifested itself, for instance, in the reception and use of Western conceptions of modernity by 'Eastern' intellectuals and politicians (see Robertson, 1993; Hill, 2008). In other words, while the outlook of sociologists has been global for a long time, the perspective has often been Eurocentric, guided by an interest in European-style modernity. Globalization and world society theories as well as global history approaches, at least programmatically, have sought to redress such issues insofar as they were inherent in more traditional approaches to international or world history. They have sought to develop not only a global outlook on the world, but also a truly global perspective that 'provincializes Europe' (Chakrabarty, 2000) in order to analyse European modernity not (just) as the centre but (also) as the product of global developments. It is this particular interest in global social change that is shared by all contributors to this volume.

The aim of our project is not to arrive at one theory of global social change, let alone to engage in the philosophical intricacies associated with such a theory (such as questions of a purpose or goal of history – which is not to say that there are no philosophy of history issues lurking around the corner). Our aim is to engage disciplines and to bring together a range of theoretical approaches, analytical takes and substantive research areas that, in combination, offer promising vistas for understanding change in a comprehensive fashion. By 'bringing together' we are deliberately not implying anything like a 'merger', as such an attempt would invariably lead back to (sub)disciplinary turf wars. Cross-disciplinary fertilization is the most that can be aimed for, and is hard enough to practice. We attempt it in the shared interest of understanding global social change. Our guiding image is that of different disciplines, theories, approaches, concepts and questions all moving along something that might be taken for a broad avenue – yet one that soon turns out not flat, but rocky; not straight, but winding; not lined by rows of trees, but ill-defined at the edges. Our goal, seemingly modest but actually rather ambitious, is to bring together and synchronize some of these journeys, and make those trotting along the highway think about the way they are going in the light of, and in conversation with, others who are travelling in the same direction. Not establishing what global social change 'is', but outlining some of the most important devices for understanding and further studying it is the common 'rest area' along the route that we aim to arrive at.

To facilitate the common journey, we first identify a range of basic problems and questions that present themselves when dealing with issues of global social change. As mentioned before, it would be presumptuous to assume that dealing with them in a combined fashion would lead to a somehow unified or integrated account. Quite to the contrary. Possibly the most that can be hoped for is to establish more clearly the various assumptions concerning, and the explicit or implicit constructions underlying, what the 'global' is that is the subject of change. The very title of this volume, *What in the World?*, seeks to emphasize that different theoretical and disciplinary perspectives are often not about differences between the dynamics and forms of change (for example, about accounts of change as evolutionary as opposed to accounts of change as revolutionary), but rather more about what the 'world' is that is changing. It is in this sense that we look first at the broad and, certainly to some degree, stylized differences between the disciplines contributing to this volume, namely history, sociology, and IR and discuss their particularities. Using the issue of Eurocentrism as an outstanding, yet by no means singular, case, we then briefly outline the pitfalls associated with any kind of master narrative or indeed counter-master narrative in accounting for global social change. From there we turn to the issue of the reflective forms that underlie images of change, most notably periodizations and the identification of epochs – as much as their critical questioning – that allow us to think about change without subscribing to one specific 'grand' narrative, before following up with a brief discussion of the fact that, despite all due methodological and theoretical caution, some empirical trajectories of change certainly do appear to be more 'grand' than others. This chapter concludes by giving an overview of the chapters that follow and by highlighting some of the most pertinent and promising issues that have emerged from our collaboration.

The global from different disciplinary points of view

It barely seems worth discussing why sociology, history, and International Relations should make almost 'natural' companions in what we see as a 'searching move' to analyse social change. Each of them, in a sense, brings to the table a vast array of theoretical tools and methodological traditions of 'thinking big' (see Albert and Buzan, 2013, 2017). What is more difficult is identifying the specific approaches and aspects of these disciplines that can be put to use, and motivated to talk to each other, in the present context. In fact, it seems that, given the vast array of things now covered by any given discipline, those approaches and aspects most important here can only be defined in a negative sense on the basis of what they are *not* in relation to other parts of their respective disciplines: they are, for example, not about sociological approaches that, implicitly or explicitly, treat national societies as an almost natural starting point, to which 'globalization' might or might not happen to various degrees; they are not about history as a conglomerate of national historiography and classical international history; and they are not about International Relations which takes an interstate system as a given in an analytical space thin in historical and social context. Put differently, we are interested in those parts of history, sociology and IR that are cognitively open despite being rooted in their disciplines and, in particular, are interested in devising a global horizon for their analyses (or, indeed, actively inquiring about the characteristics of that horizon).

Put in more positive terms, while being open to a range of approaches from the three disciplines, the main theoretical dialogue pursued here is between sociological theories of world society on the one hand and global history on the other. It is true that such a dialogue will in itself always be stylized to some degree, given the number of different voices involved. On the one hand, theories of world society broadly fall into two categories: those oriented towards a systems approach, with a strong social evolutionary take on social change; and those oriented towards a 'world culture' or 'world polity' approach, with a more institutionalist take (on the dialogue between the two see the contributions in Holzer et al, 2015a). On the global history side of things, a bifurcation seems to have taken place between what might be called 'big' global history and 'micro' global history: global histories of world regions and their mutual entanglements, or of large-scale periods/epochs, on the one hand, and global histories of developments at a micro level that look at global entanglements 'from the bottom up', so to speak, on the other. The latter often seem to come with both an empirical concentration on small-scale stories about specific localities and local practices and a certain aversion to theory-building. While both world society theories and global history approaches could be construed as belonging to separate, albeit internally diverse, disciplinary fields, such a disciplinary duality is easily broken up when approaches from neighbouring fields are brought in. This leads on to the third research field represented in this volume, that of International Relations. Although traditionally pretty good at developing self-referential inner-disciplinary theory discourses, IR has in recent years also emerged as an important interlocutor for both sociology and history, whether in terms of the mutual reception of theories and approaches, or of the proposed research programmatic of a 'global historical sociology' (Go and Lawson, 2017a).

While many of the disciplinary takes on (global) social change often borrow from multiple different theories and utilize a whole range of concepts, four conceptual clusters seem to stand out. First is the conceptualization of world society as a single social system that is internally differentiated into many social systems and their subsystems.

The main question here has to do with the emergence of a global social realm and the historical evolution of forms of social differentiation. Second is the emergence and transformation of (global) social fields. This is inimical in particular to theories of social differentiation. Seeing the world in terms of fields focuses less on social change as (systemic) social evolution, while putting considerably more emphasis on practices, agency and struggle. Third is the institutionalization of global models (the neo-institutional approach to world society). While mostly, if often only implicitly, accepting the existence of differentiated social systems or fields as both historically contingent and constructed boundary conditions, the world polity approach emphasizes the historical proliferation and institutionalization of Western forms of rational actorhood and rationality as underlying basic generalized expectations in (world) society. Fourth, the notion of (global) entanglements pursues a research strategy of openly asking about historical relations between social spaces often treated as separate (and autonomous) in history. It is arguably the least theoretical of the four approaches. Because of that, it could also, in an optimistic reading, be seen as the one most open for dialogue with different bodies of theory.

By identifying these four clusters, we have of course already made a selection within the respective disciplines. While this is not the place to provide a systematic overview of (at least three) disciplinary states of affairs and the internal differentiation of fields, substantive areas and methodologies, it is safe to say that these four clusters identify the most vibrantly active disciplinary playing fields when it comes to thinking about global social change over recent years – but that is not to claim that these are the only playing fields.

What unites all scholars based in these disciplinary fields and working from these theoretical perspectives is the idea that there is something global that can be subject to change. However, the question as to what constitutes global social change, as opposed to the locally, nationally or regionally limited kind, is open to debate. Is there a global entity, one that could perhaps be described in terms of a world society, which is changing? If so, since when has this entity existed? Which were the main structural features or historical causes that led to its emergence? Has there been a trend towards increasing global integration over the last centuries that has led to the emergence of such a global social entity or that plays out within it? Or should we think of global social change as a more fragmented process that mainly occurs in specific locales or particular social fields, or in the form of entanglements between different locales and fields? To what degree can we think of the global as a product of intentional social action, as being organized, for example, in international governmental and non-governmental organizations? To what degree should we see it as a by-product of contingent social interaction and evolution? How do global interaction and entanglements, on the one hand, and global observation and comparisons, on the other, work together in the creation of global events and structures? Whatever its disciplinary background or theoretical preferences, scholarship on global social change starts with an interest in such questions.

That being said, it is the *questions* that form the bond that unites the chapters in this volume. Even more – admittedly stylizing this argument to quite a considerable degree – they are about establishing an interdisciplinary dialogue about the substance of change more than the nature of change. Conceptualizing change, in other words, does not necessarily have to involve theorizing change in fundamental ways. Thus, while in conversations about global social change it is more than fair to reflect on whether individual takes adhere more to evolutionary theories, to eschatological or teleological motives, to linear or cyclical views of history, or to some substantive motive underpinning a specific philosophy of history, this is not a book about theories and the philosophy of (necessarily historical) social change. It might, however, be seen as a kind of prelude to such a still-to-be-written book, in that one important starting point here is the fact that while all of the clusters mentioned previously are seen as needing to establish a conversation with one another, many of their specific weaknesses result not from a lack of conversation, but from persistent issues they have with their underlying explicit or, more often, implicit theories of change. This issue is not taken up at any length here, as in Chapter 2 Mathias Albert directly addresses it in relation to global history and world society approaches in sociology.

Distortions: modernity, coloniality, Eurocentrism, postcoloniality (and the 'Eurocentrisms' of world society)

Raising the question of global social change requires taking a range of approaches, disciplinary backgrounds and theoretical perspectives into account. The goal is to formulate questions and pathways for substantive research agendas, not a unified theory of global social change. While such an intrinsically dialogical path of inquiry should not shy away from enlisting what might qualify as 'grand theories', such as, for example, world society theory in the systems theory tradition, such a dialogical process can only be successful if it critically questions 'grand narratives' of change. More often than not, motives that attribute meaning to history itself (*Geschichtsphilosophie*) lurk behind such narratives. Yet it is possible to engage with the substantive issues that are the subject of grand narratives in a constructive, yet critical, multi-perspectival fashion, without buying into any kind of 'grand' equals 'master' narrative. A case in point would be the concept of global modernity. Modernity (or 'modernities' in the plural) is an important, almost all-pervasive process and condition that is both a driver and a result of global social change, besides being the starting point and a useful point of reference for both substantive and methodological engagements with global social change. However, just as there is no single process of modernization, there can be no overarching master narrative of modernity. Multiple temporalities and their various meanings can and should be addressed as such. What is interesting is their relation to one another, and analysing that relation is something different from collapsing all those temporalities into one.

The same holds true for the 'master narrative' of 'Eurocentrism' and increasingly also for the master 'counter-narrative' of postcolonialism. Eurocentrism is an important and thorny issue, and one that can only with great difficulty be accounted for analytically when one thinks about global social change. The Eurocentrism of historical accounts is both inevitable and has been successfully transcended. Following Reinhard (2015), it seems possible to account for this strangely paradoxical situation of simultaneous endurance and transcendence as a three-step move.

The first step involves the historical origins of global history: 'Because it is incontestable that the decisive impulses of this prehistory [of a unified world] came from Europe, the question is predisposed to be Eurocentric in and of itself regardless of the stance of individual historians' (Reinhard, 2015: 4). The second results from the first step turning on itself reflexively in a kind of 'enlightened Eurocentrism' that acknowledges 'how much European development owes to the Jewish and Islamic world above all, and that later other cultures also made their independent contribution to the modern world' (Reinhard, 2015: 4). In a third step, enlightened Eurocentrism 'transcends itself, by switching from the historical navel-gazing of the West to self-referential histories of other cultures, despite being well aware that even the formulation 'other cultures' is an intrinsic feature of an ineluctably Eurocentric mode of discourse' (Reinhard, 2015: 45).

This three-step view highlights what we take to be a basic ambiguity built into 'global' accounts of all sorts: there is still a significant chunk of cognitive and even normative Eurocentrism in accounts of global history and global social change. Even though this Eurocentrism has been thoroughly criticized in a wealth of postcolonial literature, it still is extremely entrenched and widespread. If as influential and comprehensive a book on global history as *Empires and Encounters: 1350–1750* can state in 2015 that it 'is still impossible to effect without further ado' that 'the histories of the still extremely diverse areas of the world existing in the period treated in this volume be written exclusively by citizens of the cultures in question' (Reinhard, 2015: 5), then this diagnosis stands for itself (ironically, it does so whether true or not).

There is a 'structural' Eurocentrism that probably can never be discarded given the historical unfolding of events. The very practice of social-scientific research, for instance, is deeply rooted in a Western European tradition of knowledge production and will never be able to completely disconnect from those roots. The same tradition, on the other hand, puts social scientists worldwide into the position to develop a universalistic outlook on the world. It is the constant task of people inquiring into global social change to reflect upon how much of that inquiry actually accounts for this structural dimension and is thus unavoidable, and how much of it subscribes to rather outdated cognitive and normative claims that are not necessarily related to it. Another constant task is to challenge these cognitive and normative claims, particularly how they impact on substantive accounts of change. While those performing this latter task can now draw on a wealth of postcolonial literature, any account of global social change also needs to inquire into what is excluded by the 'Eurocentrism/colonialism–postcolonialism' pattern. Internally, for example, it still seems to be heavily tilted towards the British Empire, with structures and experiences relating to other empires being relatively underrepresented. Regarding the analysis of global social change in the twentieth century, this pattern seems to have pasted itself very strongly on distinctions between the First and Third worlds, or 'developed' and 'underdeveloped' countries, with the rather strange exclusion, for the most part, of the 'Second World' from accounts of global social change (see, however, recent attempts to develop a global perspective on the Cold War in, for example, Duara, 2011 and Westad, 2017).

It is in this sense that engaging with global social change requires actively engaging with and utilizing a range of rather 'big' reflective devices, which will be addressed in the following section – nevertheless, one would still be well advised to remain sceptical when convincing narratives claim precedence. The motto in analysing global social change should be to take all those narratives into account, but always under the condition of asking what they exclude.

Reflective devices: periodization, epochs and orders

Acknowledging the fact that there are no master narratives, there are still concepts that can hardly be avoided in thinking about global social change over a long time. The rationales for periodization and the identification of 'epochs' do not point to questions that could reasonably be settled, but provide invaluable reflective devices. They do so not only in terms of thinking about change itself, but also, on another level, by providing useful ordering devices in reconstructing how historians and social scientists think about, or have thought about, that change. While periodization and epochs are important reflective devices, it seems noteworthy that they merely stand out as prominent markers for thinking about the temporal dimension of change more generally in terms of synchronicities and asynchronicities in social evolution.

There are no naturally given 'epochs' in history, irrespective of time and place, as well as irrespective of analytical interest. What exists is an understanding that histories have never unfolded in synchronicity, yet that much of what is commonly known as 'globalization' in its broadest sense can be reconstructed as partial synchronizations of asynchronous processes. Telling the story of a 'modern' world society or writing a 'modern' global history always faces more than the already daunting task of identifying spatial reference points as both the (often fuzzy) 'containers' of history and, ultimately, as the enablers of interaction and contact. It faces the multiple tasks of identifying relevant epochs as 'containers of time' for specific purposes. It faces the task of identifying the temporal boundaries of the central dynamics that made the global-modern world: while the 'long nineteenth century' has become the almost consensual shorthand for this, a 'long twentieth century' has also been proposed as the time of fulfilment of a global modernity that was only conceived in the long nineteenth century. It faces the task of asking when and where to locate the precursors of the global-modern world. Is this ultimately a story of large spatial 'empires' or civilizational containers developing more or less independently from each other and laying the seeds of a globalized world? Or is it ultimately the story of European expansion that subdued, yet did not fully eliminate, the histories of these containers? Last but not least, what makes all of this not only an emergence of globality but also of modernity (either in its singular form or in plural forms of 'multiple modernities')? This is an issue that cannot and must not be seen as settled, but can be seen as continuing to provide an important reflective device for thinking about global social change.

One of the productive heuristic implications of periodization is that it urges us to think about whether, and to what degree, the drivers of global social change might have changed over time too. What have been the primary driving forces of global social change? Was it the economy, as Wallersteinian world systems theory would suggest for the history of the modern world economy since the fifteenth century? Was it the enlightenment *Sattelzeit* in Europe around 1800 (pointing to the global significance of a 'long nineteenth century')? Or can we attribute equally important roles to communication technologies, the nation state system or international organizations, roles which might have gained in importance particularly since the mid-to-late nineteenth century (pointing to the significance of a 'long twentieth century')?

Enlisting the reflective devices of periodization and epochs should not obscure the fact that, although this might lead to a theoretically open analysis of global social change, it does not lead to complete empirical openness. There remain large-scale substantive shifts over the long run that are established in the sense that they can barely be avoided as both *explanans* and *explanandum* in any theoretical account of global social change. In this sense, if there is one central running theme that has characterized thought about global social change over the past three centuries, it is the succession of or relation between the orders of empire and the orders of the nation state. While it seems next to impossible to simply add to that literature, the question of how these orders relate to each other can still serve as a powerful analytical tool in and of itself – and even more so if put into a wider, truly global context. Nation state and empire never were successors on a 'single' track of successive forms of organizing political authority, on which they may have coexisted for only some time. They were never either completely distinct and unrelated forms of organizing political authority, or interwoven to such a degree as to be completely indistinguishable in the mazes of their historical origins. They need to be seen, in addition to their well-established definitions in distinction to one another, as two important forms, yet *only two*, in a maze of different forms of organizing political authority that were always interwoven in competitive, conflictive, subsidiary, complementary or parasitic relations with each other. The establishment of a global political order in the form of *one* single system of world politics always crucially depended on the double, unsynchronized movement of nationalization and globalization-through-colonialism. Moreover, paying close attention to historical relationships between imperial and national forms of political organization points to changes in the legitimacy of these forms which shaped both the (partial) demise of imperial orders and the rise of nationalism and the nation state between the nineteenth and the twenty-first century.

Again, the main purpose of these considerations is heuristic – to raise a series of closely connected questions. In what sense, and to what degree, can we actually speak of the demise of imperial orders? What were the main historical prerequisites for the delegitimization of empires, on the one hand, and the increasing legitimacy and diffusion of nationalism and the nation state, on the other? How did nationalism turn into a global model – that is, a political imaginary that was considered as universally applicable and copied by nationalist movements around the world? And which alternative, less prominent forms of political organization tend to be neglected as a result of our focus on imperial and national orders?

Problematizing social change in a global perspective

The problem of global social change has proven to be a multifaceted one. It presupposes the idea of 'the global' as something that can be subject to change; it involves an interest in concepts of modernity, coloniality/postcoloniality and globality/universality as both scientific and historical terms; it raises fundamental questions regarding the periodization of global history and the primary drivers of change; and it draws attention to the persistence of 'empire' as well as its complex relationship to the formation of the nation state system.

The more we think about these fundamental problems, the more we have to acknowledge that the very idea of social change turns out to be problematic too: identifying change requires distinguishing between things that change and others that remain the same. And the one valuable insight that we owe to the discussion of social change in social theory of recent decades is that stability, persistence and continuity are just as much in need of explanation as change, transformation and discontinuity. There is no guarantee that existing structures will persist for the same reasons that brought them into existence; the persistence of social structures depends on social mechanisms that *make* them persist, just as their transformation depends on mechanisms of change.

While the task at hand is thus always to think about *both* change and continuity, this task is not made easier by the fact that arguably most narratives of change in most disciplines tend to favour the expansion and intensification of the new, while underemphasizing the decline and disappearance of the old. That the latter is mostly seen as something intrinsic to the former, while in fact one may be dealing with two quite distinguishable processes, is, however, not a given, but rather an expression of the knowledge order of modernity with its orientation towards progress and the novel. This pertains to any part of social analysis as much as it pertains to the study of global social change. The latter has to be anchored in the study of global social continuity and vice versa. Thinking about the problems enumerated earlier, therefore, also requires constant thinking about the conditions of stability *and* change, continuity *and* discontinuity, persistence *and* transformation.

A laboratory of thinking about global change: the individual chapters

It is in this sense that the following chapters are best understood as a laboratory for thinking about global social change from theoretical and disciplinary perspectives that are all different, yet all in productive dialogue with each other. While they cannot touch on every possibly interesting issue in this respect, we are fairly confident that we have been able to include quite a wide range of the most important ones. The interventions are roughly ordered from the more theoretical to the more empirical, and the more 'macro' to the more 'micro'. The 'roughly' is important here. Much of the present volume, as well as of its individual contributions, is about undermining established distinctions as possible obstacles to thinking fruitfully about global social change. While they are so entrenched in our thought and our academic traditions that they cannot be simply wished away, nor should they be, the structure of this book is not intended to reproduce them more than is necessary.[2]

In his chapter *'Every Epoch, Time Frame or Date that is Solid Melts into Air. Does It? The Entanglements of Global History and World Society'*, Mathias Albert (IR) explores the possibilities of a fruitful exchange between world society theory and global history approaches. He does so by examining the use of 'turning' points in their accounts. What is the quality of significant change in each, and can these accounts of significant change be linked to one another? Both global history and world society theory are united in rejecting any obvious 'telos' of history. In global history, this rejection takes the form of a narrative in which history unfolds as nothing but a transformation of complexity ('entanglements'), while in world society theory it takes the form of a theory of social evolution. Against this common background, the chapter discusses possible substantive overlaps between the two endeavours, focusing on three distinct aspects: (1) large-scale, 'epochal' change; (2) the role of the 'long nineteenth century'; and (3) the role of single 'big' events or 'turning points'.

Angelika Epple (history), in her chapter 'Periodization in Global History: The Productive Power of Comparing', develops a new perspective on fundamental problems of periodization. Going beyond postcolonial criticism, she argues that Eurocentrism is merely a symptom of an even more fundamental challenge in periodization: it relies on comparisons. These comparisons, even if they reject a 'telos' of history, depend on 'narrative objectives' to distinguish important from less important historical movements, as well as to identify directions, velocities and standstills in these movements. Based on these insights, Epple looks into what scholars actually do when they cut history up into epochs, showing that from the heyday of Eurocentrism in nineteenth-century historicism (Leopold von Ranke, Johann Gustav Droysen) to current global and world history writing (Jürgen Osterhammel, Christopher Bayly, Jane Burbank and Frederick Cooper), epoch making has always been based on comparing different velocities and drivers of change based on various 'narrative objectives'. Eurocentrism, then, is caused not only by universalized time concepts, but also by justifications of periodization based on comparative operations. It follows that historians should make the objectives of the narratives that guide these comparisons explicit – at least if they want to escape Eurocentrism and other shortcomings in global history.

The chapter 'Communication, Differentiation and the Evolution of World Society' by Boris Holzer (sociology) uses a systems theory perspective in order to examine how the globalization processes of the nineteenth and twentieth centuries affected social contacts, societal groups and the form of social change itself. As far as these three aspects are concerned, a closer look at the developments and changes that took place in the nineteenth century points to both continuities and ruptures with earlier epochs and their further consolidation and elaboration throughout the twentieth century. A sociological perspective on such a 'long twentieth century' is primarily interested in whether we can discern transformations of the social world that provided the foundation for a global modernity and popularized the aspiration towards it – implying an interest in fundamental sociological concepts such as communication, differentiation and evolution. On this basis, Holzer argues that, even if we cannot observe a fundamental or sudden societal revolution during that period, the long-term transformation of which it forms an integral part is great enough to warrant closer inspection.

Julian Go (sociology), in his chapter 'Field Theory and Global Transformations in the Long Twentieth Century', explores how Bourdieusian field theory might be deployed to make sense of global dynamics. There is only minimal guidance in existing scholarship.

IR scholars have enlisted Bourdieu in their analyses and applied his work to international issues, but from his larger theoretical conceptual apparatus they take only certain concepts such as habitus and practice. This has left Bourdieu's field theory largely unattended. Only recently have some sociological works tried to apply Bourdieu's field theory to global processes. Go builds on these efforts in order to analyse three transformative processes (or macro-historical turning points): the expansion of colonial empires during the phase of 'high imperialism' (around the late nineteenth and early twentieth century), the two world wars (1914–45), and the post-war end of formal colonial empires heralding the rise to dominance of the modern nation state (1946–present). This, in turn, leads him to map the points of differentiation between field theory approaches and other approaches discussed in this volume.

The chapter 'Organization(s) of the World', written by Martin Koch (IR), takes a closer look at the emergence of the idea of international organization in the nineteenth century. It argues that the perception of some kind of organization for the world accompanied the foundation of states from the very beginning. The emergence of states is not a precondition for international organization(s); rather, states and international organization are co-constitutive. Thus the period between the Congress of Vienna and World War I is not the period of 'preparation for international organization' (Inis Claude), it should rather be seen as the founding period of world organization, the phase when the idea of organizing and organizations as such emerged in almost all fields of society. The chapter shows that (1) the idea of organizing, that is establishing order, is deeply rooted in debates among legal scholars in the nineteenth century; (2) in that period, the idea of world organization was not limited to a world of states, but contained a more comprehensive and encompassing understanding of the world; (3) organizing the world took place in different forms that are still relevant today or have been reinvigorated in recent years.

Teresa Koloma Beck (sociology), in 'Particularly Universal Encounters: Ethnographic Explorations into a Laboratory of World Society', explores an experimental setting that is of major relevance in world politics: international military and humanitarian interventions in armed conflicts. Societies subject to intervention are 'laboratories of world society'. In these laboratories an abstract and global epistemic, normative and political order comes to be enacted, stabilized and made negotiable in human interaction, which makes them productive fields for the study of social change in world society. Koloma Beck sketches the potential of such an approach based on her own ethnographic research into the intervention in Afghanistan. She focuses on one field of interventionist politics that has attracted particular attention and controversy: policies to empower women. As embodied actors in their day-to-day lives come to be invested in the enactment of, and struggle over, allegedly universal ideals of gender equality, interactions take place not as encounters between people from different (parochial) contexts, such as, for example, between 'Americans' and 'Afghans'. They take the form of encounters between 'the universal' and 'the particular', between 'the global' and 'the local'. Yet, at the same time, they challenge and subvert exactly these distinctions as embodied actors in lifeworld interactions cannot strip themselves of their experiences and their personal and collective histories.

Stephan Stetter's chapter, 'From the First Sino-Roman War (That Never Happened) to Modern International-cum-Imperial Relations: Observing International Politics from an Evolution Theory Perspective', asks how, in global modernity, a thing called the 'international political system' was eventually established – a system of global reach, that is to say, within which struggles over collectively binding decisions are played out. Drawing on historically oriented scholarship in IR and global historical sociology – while being theoretically anchored in the world society approaches of modern systems theory – Stetter studies some central dynamics that have shaped the evolution of international politics and its imperial underpinnings, arguing that this approach allows for a better understanding of what happened after the modern international political system became firmly established as a distinct and recognizable social field than one based on conventional IR theories. However, he also argues that this system and its field-specific power constellations are anything but static; they were the result of social evolution and have been subject to ongoing transformations ever since.

Tobias Werron (sociology), in his chapter 'Nationalism as a Global Institution: A Historical-Sociological View', argues that nationalism has long been underestimated in both sociological theory and globalization studies. While sociological theorists have rarely theorized the role of nationalism in modernity, the globalization literature tends to see globalization and nationalism as being in a zero-sum relationship, with more globalization implying less nationalism and more nationalism implying less globalization. These views make us prone to being surprised by the resilience of nationalism over and over again. The chapter therefore aims to develop a historical-sociological perspective on the nationalism–globalization nexus which allows nationalism to be studied as a global institution: a largely taken-for-granted feature of the modern world that has been woven into the very fabric of global modernity. For this purpose, it connects recent insights into inconspicuous 'banal' (Michael Billig) forms of nationalism to insights from globalization studies. Werron puts particular emphasis on two types of nationalism, which he calls 'institutionalized nationalism' and 'scarcity nationalism', and shows how they have been reinforced by globalization dynamics – facilitated by the emergence of a global media system – since the mid-to-late nineteenth century.

George Lawson (IR), in his chapter 'States and Markets: A Global Historical Sociology of Capitalist Governance', examines the relationship between states and markets over the last century and a half. The chapter both builds upon and extends insights from global history into IR and historical sociology. It borrows a key concept from global history, entanglements, but shows how entanglements are patterned through power relations. The result is both a differentiation between, and a sequencing of, state–market complexes. On this basis, Lawson identifies four main phases in the modern relationship between states and markets: the first, running from the third quarter of the nineteenth century to World War I, was marked by high flows of capital and finance; the second, during the inter-war years, was marked by capital controls and, as a result, a reduction in global transactions; the third, from 1945 to 1973, saw a gradual relaxation of capital controls and the partial recovery of financial and capital flows; the fourth, from the early 1970s until the present day, has been one of relatively unconstrained controls and, therefore, high capital mobility.

The chapter written by Heidi Tworek (history), 'The Impact of Communications in Global History', aims to show how understanding the impact of communications can help the interdisciplinary thrust to integrate sociology with history and International Relations. A global history of how communications affected populations around the world shows why they played a key role in differentiation, for example. Communications did not cause colonialism, but helped to entrench imperial rule for decades before anticolonial activists used some Western communications systems in their favour. The historical record, then, is not simple. Rather, there are multiple, overlapping impacts that can function differently in different times and places. This point can provide a basis for assessing our contemporary situation, where American-owned social media companies appeared to be the drivers of democratic social change during the Arab Spring of 2011, but now seem to foster conspiracy-theory-driven violence and the rise of strongman leaders around the world. Tworek presents nine different forms of impact, subdivided into four clusters (cultural, economic, political and environmental), to illustrate the myriad uneven global effects of communications over time and space, while tracing out some concrete examples of the interaction between communications and broader societal change.

James Stafford's 'The "Long Twentieth Century" and the Making of World Trade Law' develops a new narrative of the emergence of a global 'system' of trade law since the mid-nineteenth century. He argues that, while the extent, depth and nature of global economic integration may have dramatically varied over this period, we can identify a continuous attempt to establish and elaborate systems of inter-polity law designed to regulate economic exchanges on a global scale. This, Stafford argues, should be seen as a central feature of global social change in the 'long twentieth century' understood in terms of the elaboration of global communicative infrastructures. The rise of world trade law enabled, and was encouraged by, the expansion and growing status of a transnational body of trade diplomats, consuls, economists and economic lawyers. Projects of international economic law were often associated with liberal ideals of 'free trade', but they were pliable instruments, which could also support regionalist or protectionist ambitions. Stafford concludes that the development of fundamental institutions of global economic order – commercial treaty systems, consular jurisdiction and international organizations – should be analysed as part of 'world politics' as well as the 'world economy'.

In his chapter 'Third Party Actors, Transparency and Global Military Affairs', Thomas Müller (IR) explores the history and effects of third-party actors in global military affairs. He starts with the observation that, since the second half of the nineteenth century, transnational and international organizations have collected, produced and published comparative data on a variety of aspects of world politics, creating a complex global system of ongoing quantified observation and evaluation of patterns, trends and problems in world politics and also in other parts of world society. Müller makes two arguments, one about the scope and one about the impact of these third-party actors. First, global military affairs have been no exception to the rise of third-party actors over the last one and half centuries. The group of third-party actors here notably includes the United Nations (UN), the International Institute for Strategic Studies (IISS) and the Stockholm International Peace Research Institute (SIPRI). Second, while the emergence of third-party actors has fundamentally changed the system of observation and comparison in global military affairs, it has (so far) not changed the underlying dynamics of military competition. On the whole, third-party actors constitute commentators on, rather than shapers of, the military competition in world politics. Global military affairs in this sense provide insights into the conditions that hamper the impact of third-party actors.

Finally, Daniel Speich Chassé's chapter 'Technical Internationalism and Global Statistics: A Critical Look at the Historiography of the United Nations', ventures into the technical basis of global sociability from a historical perspective. Such a view renders the nation an effect of global communication rather than an agent. The argument is that global numerical statistics on territories, populations and economic potentials over the past centuries have created a vast political space in which the nation features as a result, not as a prime mover. Numbers rule the world in manifold comparative frameworks by setting norms and designing communicative devices such as balance sheets for companies and states and comparative sets of statistics on territory, population and economic potential. Speich Chassé suggests the notion of technical internationalism as a general framework for the analysis of these governing organs. He argues that these structural processes of a more anonymous nature constitute a global communicative convergence concerning the aims of social change and were agents of change in their own right.

Conclusion: follow-up questions for future research

All contributions to this volume grapple with the challenge of how to make sense of global social change in a non-teleological manner. Some deal with it directly on a theoretical level; others try to meet it in empirical studies. In so doing, the chapters produce significant overlaps in topics, problems, concepts and propositions that transcend their respective disciplines, while they still argue from their respective disciplinary perspectives. The volume thus demonstrates the benefits of interdisciplinary dialogue in an ideal manner: not by attempting to 'merge' the disciplines but by allowing disciplines to change and develop in reaction to what is going on in other disciplines, and by raising research questions that become clearer when approached from different disciplinary angles. In conclusion to this introduction, there are a number of open research questions that seem to be immediate products of this interdisciplinary dialogue.

First, the contributions raise new questions revolving around problems of periodization. There is significant overlap in this volume not just between global history and world society theories, as Albert argues in his chapter, but also between Epple's and Albert's ways of looking at periodization: While Epple points to the 'productive power of comparing' and to the role of 'narrative objectives' in epoch making by historians, Albert's chapter compares the ways in which historians and social scientists look at 'epochal' change – raising the question whether both ways of looking at comparisons can be combined. Could comparisons between how historians and social scientists use comparisons to identify 'epochs', 'ruptures' or 'turning points' help us to better understand the functions and limits of periodization? What might systematic comparisons of such comparisons look like? Epple's and Albert's chapters, then, open an interdisciplinary discussion on what might be called the methodology of periodization, based on the idea that our understanding of globalization will benefit from comparisons of comparisons used to justify distinctions between historical periods.

Other chapters complement the methodological questions raised by Epple and Albert by addressing questions of periodization more directly. An interesting thread that emerges from these chapters is their repeated references to a 'long twentieth century' (see the chapters by Holzer, Go, Werron, Lawson, Tworek and Stafford). In some chapters, this interest appears largely theory-driven, as in Holzer's outline of a communication-based approach to globalization or Go's analysis of transformations in the global field, while in others it is a by-product of empirical studies of phenomena such as capitalist governance (Lawson), trade negotiations (Stafford), communication technologies (Tworek) or nationalism (Werron). In all cases this interest in a 'post-mid-nineteenth century' period is based not on ideas about American hegemony (as Giovanni Arrighi would have it), but on the observation that telecommunication technologies since the mid-to-late nineteenth century have played an increasing role in the production of global connections, comparisons and power relationships. For future discussions it should be noted, therefore, that focusing on this period of globalization, irrespective of the discipline involved, seems to depend on an interest in communication or in accelerated communication dynamics. Following Epple's methodological arguments on periodization, however, one might then raise the question of whether there are implicit 'narrative objectives' at play here – not of increasing worldwide integration perhaps, but of increasing global communication, interaction and observation – that call attention to some phenomena while neglecting others.

Second, a number of chapters point to the important, though perhaps still underrated, role of organization(s) in globalization processes over the last two centuries. As Koch points out in his chapter, 'organization' has a double meaning in this context, referring to ambitions of all kinds to 'organize the world', as well as to what sociologists understand as 'formal organizations', that is social entities with names, formal membership and formal rules such as universities, companies, governments or sport associations. Koch, Stafford, Tworek, Speich Chassé and Müller show in their respective chapters how (formal) organizations have in fact contributed to 'organizing', or at least shaping, the world as we know it, by forming as international bodies (Koch), negotiating or regulating trade treaties (Stafford), regulating global communications (Tworek) or collecting, interpreting and publishing statistics (Speich Chassé, Müller). These studies point to a multitude of 'organizing' activities that are interesting not just in and of themselves, but also as a causal force driving globalization processes of all kinds. It is suggested understanding this as a reminder that organization(s) can and should play a more prominent role in globalization studies, both as a topic of theorizing and an object of historical study – and irrespective of card-carrying membership in any academic discipline.

Third, there is an implicit thread running through this volume which might usefully be made explicit. While some chapters argue at a general level of analysis, deploying abstract arguments about the differentiation and evolution of world society (Holzer, Stetter and Go) and discussing meta-theoretical questions of periodization (Epple, Albert), others aim to discover the effects of globalization 'on the ground', using ethnographic methods (Koloma Beck), while others again may be said to occupy some sort of middle ground, dealing with particular institutions (Koch, Stafford, Werron), technologies (Tworek), practices of data collection, interpretation and publication (Speich Chassé, Müller) or the interplay between entanglement and power relationships (Lawson). Future studies could aim at bridging and connecting these different approaches, not just by asking how different theoretical approaches, for instance systems and field theory, can inform one another, but also by trying to switch between levels of abstraction and specificity. How, for instance, could abstract claims about differentiation and evolution in world society be 'grounded' in, and questioned by, ethnographical studies of the sort suggested in Koloma Beck's chapter? This volume has only just begun to meet the challenge of finding the right level of abstraction to ground theories of world society empirically while informing historical studies theoretically; further attempts are urgently needed.

Fourth and finally, the theme of 'comparing' and 'comparisons' looms large in this volume. It appears that the significance of what Epple calls the 'productive power of comparing' is not limited to periodization but constitutes a type of social practice that is too often taken for granted. It is, in fact, hard to think of a 'global' topic that cannot be expected to benefit from taking a closer look at the role of comparisons in the creation of global connections, structures or institutions, ranging from the production of symbolic capital (Go's chapter), to worldviews implied by international statistics (Speich Chassé), the institutionalization of national differences and nation states (Werron), the roles and possible impact of third-party actors in international politics (Müller), the identity and roles of (international) organizations (Koch, Speich Chassé, Müller), and the discovery, in encounters during local interventions, of particularities against the background of universalities (Koloma Beck). Comparing can mean both comparing oneself with others and being compared by – an increasing number of – further others; it can also mean both of these forms coming and playing together. Moreover, our discussion of periodization indicates that the heuristic benefits of looking at practices of comparing might also affect how we look at our own disciplinary practices, both as historians and social scientists (see Epple et al, 2020).

These follow-up questions prove that the interdisciplinary dialogue organized in this volume – and in the workshops preceding it – has not only affected the thinking of its contributors, it may also inspire future research in the disciplines involved and, hopefully, encourage future collaborations of this sort. For the editors of as well as the contributors to this book, at least, it was a worthwhile endeavour.

Postscript

We are putting the finishing touches on this volume in May 2020, in the middle of the COVID-19 pandemic. In fact, experts tell us that we are still at the beginning of the epidemic. The illness caused by the virus known as Sars-CoV-2 has put matters of public health at the centre of governance, public debates and private concerns in (almost) all countries of the world, capturing worldwide attention like few events have before. We have resisted the urge to add late changes to the chapters, which were written and revised before the scale of the virus' impact on society became apparent. However, given that this is a book about global social change, and given that there is growing speculation about how the world will be different after the pandemic is over, we would like to sneak in an additional thought on the question: How could scholars of global social change approach the task of studying the effects of a pandemic which they are living through themselves?

Any answer to this question must start with the acknowledgement that we simply cannot know yet what kind of change, and how much of it, the pandemic will bring about. Rather than speculating about future effects, then, we might be studying the pandemic as an emergent event (cf Werron and Ringel 2020): An on-going collection of micro-occurrences that together form and define 'the pandemic' as a one-time social occurrence with potential, but not yet knowable, structural effects. Accepting that what we are dealing with is indeed a unique and unpredictable event may be the best way towards understanding the change that may come out of it. Rather than producing largely predictable descriptions, predictions and critiques based on pre-existing structural theories, we could accept the radical contingency of the emergent event and let it speak to us empirically. And rather than brushing over its eventful elements, we could observe in detail what is going on during the pandemic, hopefully arriving at new ideas about what may happen after it. Global change may follow or not. Rather than speculating about it, we should study it in the making.

Notes

[1] It should be noted that methodological nationalism, that is the taken-for-granted equation of the concept of society with the nation state, was the result of fairly recent developments during the mid-to-late twentieth century. There is not much of it to be found in classical sociological authors like Karl Marx and Max Weber (see Chernilo, 2006).

[2] A confession is in order here. We initially structured the volume in three parts, roughly following a macro–meso–micro progression. However, more than one reader of the book proposal suggested dropping that order.

2

Every Epoch, Time Frame or Date that Is Solid Melts into Air. Does It? The Entanglements of Global History and World Society

Mathias Albert

Introduction

The starting point of this chapter is the suspicion that, while global history identifies a range of quite large-scale patterns and even structures, it remains somewhat reluctant to engage with large-scale theoretical accounts (or 'narratives') of long-term historical change. World society theory, on the other hand, provides exactly this kind of account, yet, at least in terms of the global unfolding of events, seems to lag behind when it comes to substantiating its claims in historical terms. Global history and world society theory are strong candidates when it comes to effecting an engagement between approaches from history and sociology on the subject in hand. But they are certainly not the only ones out there. Nevertheless, as the chapter will seek to argue, they promise to foster a productive dialogue when both traditions' strengths are put to good use in reciprocally addressing one another's shortcomings. In that sense, although the chapter provides what is admittedly a parochial reading of both traditions, it does so with the programmatic purpose of stimulating common research agendas.

So, the present chapter attempts a rather bold *tour d'horizon* that seeks to establish the possibilities for a fruitful exchange between world society theory and global history approaches. It will do so by inspecting the use of 'turning' points in their accounts. What is the quality of significant change in both, and can these accounts of significant change be linked to one another? Posing this question means focusing on possible substantive overlaps. It explicitly does not mean asking for commonalities grounded in a common motive from *Geschichtsphilosophie* (the philosophy of history). Quite the contrary. The argument proceeds on the basis of an acknowledgement that global history and world society theory are probably united in standing quite firm in rejecting any motive from *Geschichtsphilosophie* (although, as will be argued later, in one respect the latter probably cannot be completely dispensed with when it comes to an epochal view of history). In global history this rejection takes the form of a narrative in which history unfolds as nothing but a transformation of complexity ('entanglements'); in world society theory it takes the form of a theory of social evolution.

The chapter will begin by providing fairly specific readings of global history and world society theory in general. In the former case, the approach is that of a highly interested reader who is, nonetheless, an 'outsider' in the field. In the latter, it is based on previous work. The second part of the chapter will then focus on how global history and world society theory conceive of change in three different manifestations: (1) large-scale, 'epochal' change; (2) the role of the 'long nineteenth century'; and (3) the role of single 'big' events or 'turning points'.

The present chapter is meant to be provocative insofar as it stylizes arguments and positions and makes a couple of what are, without doubt, rather rash generalizations that do not do justice to many individual contributions and authors. It is driven, however, by the conviction that bringing out, even in so general a fashion, some of the ideas underlying how world society theory and global history think about global historical change will stimulate discussion and collaborative agendas within and between both fields.

A reading of global history

This is not the place to recount many of the well-known attributes of 'global history' – its increasing prominence, its relation to, and distance from, other kinds of historical research, and quite simply the impressive amount and scope of work done under its aegis. In the present context, the chapter will focus on two main issues that seem to directly impact on the possibilities of establishing a conversation with approaches from the social sciences – in particular, with world society theory – and on the way in which this might be done. The first of these relates to the 'object' of study, that is the scope of the terms 'global' and 'history'. The second relates to the quality of the social relations studied.

While there are obviously a range of possible ways in which global history contributions could be structured – for example, on the basis of the exact time period, the functional realm or the geographic area that is the specific focus of study – it seems safe to say that there is a characteristic bifurcation into what seems like a distinction between the micro and the macro. The uniting bond is the 'global', which is usually defined by at least one negative and at least one positive reference. The negative reference is that the processes in question cannot be understood in the context of a historical environment that is limited to the territorial borders of a (nation) state (the 'container model'). The positive reference is that the relevant environment is usually more than that of a specific territorial state, or that state and the territorial state spaces immediately surrounding it. Instead it is planetary in scale or at least transregional in character (although a 'universal' reference to *every* part of the globe – part usually meaning 'continent' – is usually not a requirement for qualifying as 'global' in this respect). With this shared background, the subject of global history can be many things: it can range from analysis of the entangled histories of all parts of the globe during the 'long' nineteenth century (Bayly, 2004; Osterhammel, 2014), via histories of colonial entanglements (Anghie, 2007), to histories of the global relations and embedding of a specific chocolate manufacturer (Epple, 2010). In that sense there has been a tendency in global history to interpret the global as a reference that functions irrespective of whether the prime interest is in issues that are conventionally filed under 'micro-' or 'macro-' (or possibly even 'meso-') history.[1] Against this background, the global as a reference can be characterized as operating in relation to both scope and quality.

As hinted at already, regarding the *scope* of the global there is no clear or shared definition of the specific degree of geographic extension necessary for relevant connections to count as 'global', nor is there any 'requirement' for one. In a sense, the purview of global history comprehends anything that is not strictly limited to processes taking place within territorial-cum-national containers and possibly to intra-regional processes as well (although, of course, what counts as 'regional' in this context is another issue; Albert and Stetter, 2015). Whatever lies beyond that is another matter then: 'globality' definitely remains a somewhat underspecified concept in terms of its scope. Most writings that self-identify as contributions to global history will usually *not* touch upon issues that are 'global' in terms of having a geographic scope that extends to all continents (but see later on the quality of the global in this respect). Indeed, the most important part of understanding globality here might be the negative definition partly alluded to already: 'global' history is not a history of national spaces, or the sum of them, but an effort to 'make visible cross-connections and points of contact that remain invisible in the usual representations' (Conrad and Osterhammel, 2016: 32; translated by MA). The second pillar in this respect is probably the motive of not telling the more or less linear history of the worldwide 'expansion' of an essentially European international society (Bull and Watson, 1984; see also Dunne and Reus-Smit, 2017), but 'de-coupl[ing] the history of the international political system and the specific path of developments in Europe (Westphalian Peace, Atlantic Revolution, modernity, etc)' (Aydin, 2016: 59).

Though the two are related, it is necessary to distinguish between the *quality* of the global in global history and its scope. Not to put a too fine point on it, the vast majority of contributions to global history do not explicitly reflect on these issues. However, they do seem to share a basic common denominator regarding the quality of the global. This common denominator, it could be argued, is that global references require a minimum of structure (and indeed this common denominator is what lies behind the prominent, but notoriously underspecified – let alone undertheorized – notion of 'entanglement' in this context). The 'minimum of structure' here means that different regions and cultural-political spaces develop with a marked primacy of self-references, even though other-directed references and repeated interactions with other regions and cultural political spaces exist. This, in a nutshell, is a process that only changes, gradually yet markedly, with the global expansion of European empires (see Reinhard, 2016), although this is, and needs to be, a far cry from seeing the world before European colonialism as a world of distinct, politically and culturally completely self-enclosed *worlds* (see Reinhard, 2015).

A 'minimum of structure' suggests that a purely phenomenological quality of the global, even in a rather wide sense, is *not* sufficient for something to qualify as a central subject of global history. A 'phenomenological quality' here refers to global processes and relations – global, that is, in their scope in the sense described earlier – being present within the horizon of meaning. Social relations and communications of any kind, even if very limited in scope, can be 'global' in this sense if they take place against the background knowledge of such a horizon. This would basically be the phenomenological notion of the 'world' in the concept of 'world society'. It is quite possible that one of the reasons why global history eschews the notion of 'world', in addition to marking a difference between itself and 'world history', lies precisely in a desire to avoid a purely phenomenological understanding of world/global.[2] While the global in global history is certainly not conceived as the mere addition of international interactions to national spaces, it is, nonetheless, almost unanimously treated as an increase in, or the establishment of, some kind of recurrent interaction (interdependence, 'entanglement'). Exceptions here seem to confirm the rule: in one of the, thus far, rare encounters of global historians with world society theory, Jürgen Osterhammel (2017) acknowledges that the 'bottom-up' account of globality needs to be complemented by a view of the social differentiation of world society that accounts for the global (re)production of local and regional contexts as well. However, upon closer inspection this seems more like an issue of including previously neglected structurally relevant levels into global history accounts and does not seem to refer to the distinction between the structural and phenomenological dimensions of the global inherent in the 'world' of world society theory.

One important caveat needs to be added at this point: the rendition of global history in the preceding paragraphs is not only stylized to some degree, it also probably does not reflect what most people who work under this label actually 'do'. Most global historians do not write 'big brick' books about entire centuries, epochs, global entanglements and so on (such as Osterhammel, 2014, or, most notably, the volumes in the 'A History of the World' series by Harvard University Press). However, while most global historians do far more 'small-scale' history, the 'big bricks' have arguably become the foci and common reference points for an otherwise extremely diverse field.

A reading of world society theory

World society theories come in different guises, yet the most widely used are varieties of systems theory and of sociological neo-institutionalism. It seems noteworthy that the notion of the world in this context is not unambiguous at all. Quite the opposite. One can safely say that, particularly in the systems theory version, 'world' in world society is used in two different senses, a phenomenological one and a structural one. Moreover, noting these two different uses is of more than purely theoretical interest. Not only has there been a development over the years in which the structural sense has become more prominent, this structural sense also marks the most significant point of overlap between the systems theory and neo-institutionalist accounts. Furthermore, this development points to different ways in which world-society-based analysis can (or should) relate to historical analysis.

Phenomenologically speaking, the 'world' in world society theory has to do with the observation of what constitutes the horizon of meaning for communication.[3] In simple terms, this horizon is the present knowledge of the boundaries of the social world. There can have been – and historically there actually have been – *many* world societies on one single planet, the Earth, as long as they existed in absolute ignorance of each other. Whatever the exact historical date might be, it seems safe to say that, except for some pockets of very remote and isolated civilizations, only one world society has existed on Earth for the last 500 years or so. Meaning in society is processed against the background of knowledge of that single world society, and it is therefore a structural possibility that communication can relate to all other communication. This is, it needs to be emphasized, a 'systemic integration' view of society – that is, a society integrated through the internal differentiation of communication. This view starkly contrasts with the 'classical' sociological view of society as something 'socially integrated' (through some form of community, values, norms, or a collective identity). It does, however, offer the possibility of arriving at a description of the modern world as a world society characterized by both internal differentiation and a build-up of structural complexity. This is a decidedly non-methodologically nationalist way of viewing the social world, and this is where the perspective fully overlaps with the leitmotif of global history – although in the latter case the emphasis is clearly on structural complexity rather than social differentiation. The neo-institutionalist version of world society theory is probably closer to global history in this respect, although it would also seem to be quite close to the 'expansion' narrative alluded to in the previous section when it comes to the formal copying and global spread of quintessentially Western motives and models of rationality, bureaucracy and organizing. With 'world culture' as the symbolic repository of world society and the source of its reproduction, the 'Stanford School' version of world society theory includes an emergent level that is mostly absent from, or possibly only implicit in, global history accounts. Even so this does not necessarily bring it too close to the systems theory version of world society theory in this respect, as the concept of social differentiation in particular is arguably of a more residual character in the neo-institutionalist account (see Thomas, 2013).

Focusing on the systems theory side of things, the history of world society is the history of its initial establishment as a social system and, thereafter, of the internal differentiation and structural complexity of that system. It shares with sociological neo-institutionalism the view that the modern nation state is not the (analytically or ontologically) prior constitutive unit in terms of which international and global affairs constitute some kind of 'beyond'. Rather, the modern territorial-cum-nation state seems to be the first instance of political globalization in world society – in terms of the theory of differentiation, the expression of the internal segmentation of a functionally differentiated political system of world society. 'Globalization' in this sense refers to emergent and constitutive characteristics of social systems as well as to their further structural development; 'globalization' in common post-1990 parlance in this sense refers mainly to an intensification of such structural developments.

While systems theory is full of historical references, and there is a strong tradition of studying the development of, and the link between, social structure and historical semantics, it remains a theory of society, not a theory of history. It should be noted, however, that it has a quite well-developed theory of change as social evolution. This theory usually features far less prominently than theories of social differentiation and the theory of social systems in the narrower sense. However, it allows for change to be conceptualized as contingent and non-teleological. As its sole and main point is to analyse how communication continues in the medium of meaning, it is an understanding of evolution quite distinct from theories of natural evolution.[4] The suspicion here (see later) is that this understanding of change as social evolution might provide an important discussion and meeting point for theoretical work and accounts from history.

The history of world society would thus seem to consist of at least three main threads: the history of the emergence of world society; the history of the evolution of world society in terms of its internal differentiation; and the history of the structural complexity of specific social systems within world society. It seems safe to say that world society research in the systems theory tradition has largely focused on the second and third of these threads, and the neo-institutionalist tradition mostly on the third; both tend to neglect the first. The result is only sparsely developed narratives of historical change, which is exactly the possible point of entry and contact for and with global history. However, rather than trying to make an oversimplifying argument that would identify the strengths of one approach as the weaknesses of the other, and vice versa, and come to quick conclusions about synergy effects, the following argument will tread more cautiously by exploring some central issues that mark differences before perhaps allowing possibilities for a more systematic engagement between world society theory and global history to be identified.

Large-scale 'epochal' change

Both the global history and world society approaches talk a lot about changes, but the concept of change itself receives scant attention in both, at least as far as an explicit treatment is concerned. Similarly, both types of account, particularly the global history one, contain numerous identifications of *drivers* of change at different levels of abstraction, yet change as a concept remains undertheorized. While on the global history side in particular one might reasonably suspect an inherent urge not to be associated with any kind of *Geschichtsphilosophie*, a quite significant motive from the latter does seem to linger hereabouts, namely the motive of *epochal* change. Both global history and world society approaches conceive of history as divided into (staggered) epochs. However, and seemingly paradoxically, this is shown at its clearest in the fact that there seems to be little agreement on where to locate the relevant epochal shifts (see also Chapter 3 by Angelika Epple in this volume).

In world society theory this issue mostly focuses on the distinction between modernity and a 'before' modernity. Given the largely sociological origins of world society theory this comes as little surprise, since the invention of sociology as a discipline basically runs alongside the emergence of modern society, part of which is the degree of reflexivity that is expressed in the formation of the discipline. In both its systems theory and its neo-institutionalist variant, world society theory identifies its main subject matter – world society – as primarily characterized by features that also distinguish it from 'before' modern society (or societies in the plural): the establishment of the primacy of functional differentiation in contrast particularly to stratification as the main form of social differentiation on the one hand; and the global spread of the Western model of rationality, embedded in bureaucratic rationality and the sole legitimacy of rational actorhood, on the other. Most accounts of world society theory arguably leave it at that. Besides numerous single treatments of the historical origins or forerunners of the characteristics of modern society, there is a clear sense that a 'before' stage of modern society existed, although the latter's establishment is invariably seen not as a single event, but as a process drawn out at least over the period between the sixteenth and nineteenth centuries. Nonetheless, the 'before' remains mostly that: a 'before' identified *ex negativo*, that is *in contrast to* modernity. References to the Middle

Ages or antiquity exist, but largely remain singular: they do not occur, that is to say, in the context of a sequencing of historical epochs. The clearest account is probably the one that presents the unfolding of social differentiation in the systems theory version of world society theory: there is a common sense that segmentation, stratification and functional differentiation arrived in exactly that historical order – although without the later forms of social differentiation ever fully replacing the earlier ones.

In global history, approaches to the concept of epochal change are arguably far more ambiguous on the one hand, yet far less implicit on the other. The latter is not very surprising given that debates about the concept of epochs and characterizations of epochal change are probably written into the DNA of every historian. The issue is complicated by the fact that references to a 'global' are in a sense the *sine qua non* of any kind of global history, yet, while these references might not always be completely global in a structural sense, they at least pertain to regional histories that are already somewhat influenced by global connections and in terms of their history take place in the shadow of the global – so that in a sense 'epochal asynchronicity' is a built-in challenge. Like the discussions in sociology, the concept of epochs and epochal change in (global) history has been, and continues to be, the subject of intense argument (albeit it remains firmly entrenched institutionally in university departments, learned societies, journals and so forth). Whether the lines – or better the blurred zones – between epochs are placed here or there ultimately depends on the specific criteria applied. However, if global history stands out in any respect, it is probably in terms of its almost unequivocal view that the relevant markers here are complex and consist in more than 'only' one thing (for example, industrialization, enlightenment or suchlike). It always expresses complex shifts in comprehensive orders of power and knowledge that are not entirely self-enclosed in space but entangled to varying degrees. One could, in a sense, argue that one of the distinctive contributions and features of the global history perspective is its avoidance of having to choose between narratives of one (invariably European/Western) modernity and narratives of multiple modernities (whether 'multiple' is defined in spatial terms or in terms of functional temporal trajectories). Epochal shifts do play a role in global history, but global history accounts are complex and bifurcated. Most particularly, they do not 'add up' to a single narrative of epochal change. This seems to make them markedly different from world society accounts, although possibly the difference is only marginal. What unites the two is that they remain largely unconcerned with the history of the pre-world/pre-global world. Global historians would probably shy away from the huge distance that world society approaches put between *modern* world society and everything that went before. However, the pre-global world is woven into the world of global history, but less through being part of an unfolding and continuing narrative and more through the latter containing more singular references to specific historical trajectories. In its large-scale, 'epochal' view of history, global history is more synchronic than diachronic, even if the synchronic layers themselves cover a few centuries. Applying the term 'synchronic' in such a way will, admittedly, appear counterintuitive to most historians. What it seeks to establish is nothing less, but also nothing more, than the observation that, like world society theory, global history is a view with a strong focus on the modern past and the modern present.

Jürgen Osterhammel, in his seminal *The Transformation of the World*, has a chapter entitled 'Time: When Was the Nineteenth Century' (Osterhammel, 2014: 45–76) that provides an excellent general discussion of this subject. Geared towards identifying some kind of coherence in the long nineteenth century (see next section), it demonstrates that, while the difficulties of agreeing on periodizations and constructing epochs are tremendous with respect to single (generally European or Atlantic) regions, 'how much more difficult is it to agree on a periodisation for the world' (Osterhammel, 2014: 53). Osterhammel's – and global history's – solution to the difficulties of periodization and identifying epochs, apart from some theoretical reflections on the issue, is to abstain from any explicit attempts to solve the puzzle formally, but to make a substantive argument about specific characteristics of a particular period that characterize it as a specific complex agglomeration of distinct yet related, simultaneous yet not necessarily synchronized, pre-global to global trajectories.

It is in this sense that epochal shifts are not usually the subject of extended debates in either global history or world society approaches. Accounts of them may be even less prevalent in world society approaches, although arguably they are identified more clearly there in cases where epochal change is taken to be represented in the emergence of, or the relations between, forms of social differentiation. This is also to say that what probably matters most, and why it is important to address questions of epochal change in discussions between the world society theory and global history approaches, is that reflections on epochal changes prompt discussions about changes in substantive orders – and to serve that particular purpose there is little need to actually settle for one specific account of epochal change, or to engage too intensively with the endless theoretical debates about what epochal change actually means.

All that, in and of itself, would not matter much. However, when taken together with some of the issues to be discussed in the following pages, it plays quite fundamentally into general views, or implicit assumptions, about change as such. It is only for this purpose that it possibly makes sense to scrutinize both perspectives in this way, unless one aims to simply rehearse the seemingly endless debates about the concepts of the epoch and epochal change in history. As far as *substantive* accounts of epochal change in global history and world society theory are concerned, it seems useful to compare them not in abstract terms, but rather in relation to their readings of *the* epochal change that in a sense constitutes the *raison d'être* for both: namely the period and its characteristics that justify adding 'global' and 'world' to 'history' and 'society' respectively. This is where the 'long nineteenth century' comes into play.

The 'long nineteenth century'

The so-called 'long nineteenth century', usually taken to start around the time of the American and French revolutions in the 1770s and 1780s and to end with (the beginning or end of) World War I, has almost become a fixed reference point when it comes to identifying a pivotal historical change of some kind that led from a vaguely premodern to a vaguely contemporary order. The point of reference for whichever order is at stake in this respect varies between different markers of social order in general, the order of modern society (or societies in the plural), world order and so on. In a sense, the only thing that is unanimously agreed upon is that a range of specific developments emerged, intensified and became entangled during that period – although not necessarily synchronously and often with different starting points or as results of different processes that were not necessarily even closely linked.

Within his particular use of the concept of world society, Osterhammel observes that all the global entanglements visible during the late eighteenth and at the beginning of the nineteenth century 'do not add up to an integrative boost to world society' (Osterhammel, 2016b: 722; translation MA). It was only the colonial expansion of the mid-nineteenth century that led to an 'end' of closed societies. Their permeation was required by, and a result of, the adaptive pressure exerted by transnational capitalist structures and intensified forms of imperial rule (that both underpinned and were supported by an expansion in communication and transport infrastructures) during the second half of the nineteenth century and global migratory flows at the turn of the twentieth century that led to a more integrated world society. 'The dominant *world* societal mode of integration around 1900 was the mass migration reaching its quantitative apex by then' (Osterhammel, 2016b: 728, translated MA). In fact, seen from the perspective of a social integration of world society, the nineteenth century would seem to have been a rather short one, not beginning until around the 1850s.

Needless to say, many proposals with regard to both the defining characteristics of the long nineteenth century and its delimitations can be found. They all vary in at least two dimensions: first, the main factor or factors taken as underpinning social change – industrialization, the emergence of nationalism, colonialization and so on; second, the accounts of change and the main dynamics and milestones with respect to these factors. Indeed, so great does the variety along these two dimensions seem to be that in the end one sometimes cannot help feeling that, if there is one unifying narrative that exceeds mere reference to the arbitrary numbers of calendar years, it pertains to the speed and the degree of radicality of change – but then any extended study of analyses of so-called 'long' centuries (twentieth, eighteenth, seventeenth, sixteenth or whichever) quickly puts that narrative into the perspective of how difficult it is to *compare* degrees of change.

Approaching the issue from a meta-perspective, it is clear that whatever a comprehensive account of the long nineteenth century might look like, it would be an account of different and overlapping, often mutually disturbing temporalities of change, forms of social differentiation and their associated ordering principles, and the particularities of their spatial expressions. 'Below' such a comprehensive account, one is bound to find emphases on specific aspects within this cacophony of processes. Paraphrasing Robert Cox that '[t]heory is always *for* someone and *for* some purpose' (Cox, 1981: 128), one could say that accounts of the long nineteenth century too are always from someone, for some purpose. And, whatever their differences in many respects, world society and global history approaches are not 'merely' accounts of the long nineteenth century as the maturing period of the capitalist world system (Wallerstein, 1974–89), they are not 'merely' accounts of it as the pivot period of a long age of structurally similar revolutions (see Skocpol, 1979), and they are not 'merely' accounts of it as an age of arts, sciences, education and so forth: they are all of those, and more. They do, however, give pride of place to the overarching motive of the long nineteenth century as the age of globality: in terms of interwoven entanglements, the expansion, diffusion and subjugation of political, economic and knowledge orders, and in terms of the evolution of social systems as expressions of an internal differentiation of world society.

'Big' events and 'turning points'

The delimitation of periods is not a natural given. However, as was discussed in the previous section, there are many good reasons why specific periods can be designated as relatively more important than others in specific respects and always in retrospect. Whether the 'making' of a global world is really something that the telegraph, the emergence of a global public, or colonialism effected during a 'long nineteenth century', or whether the reach of globality to every household with television and the world wide web during a 'long twentieth century' was not the more fundamental transformation in that respect is a question that probably will not be able to be addressed adequately for some time to come. However, there can be no doubt that reflections on and debates about appropriate delimitations of periods for specific purposes are a crucial heuristic device for making sense of historical processes.

The same arguably holds true for the signifying function of identifying key or 'benchmark' dates. In the realm of world politics, it is not very difficult to spot them: 1648 probably stands out as the imagined birthdate of modern international relations, closely followed, in varying order, by 1815, 1914, 1945 and 1989. Barry Buzan and George Lawson (2014a) have explicitly criticized the function of such benchmark dates, particularly the fact that they focus on major wars, which tends to obscure many change processes that are not directly related to war.

It is certainly possible to agree with Buzan and Lawson that a concentration on benchmark dates has too much of a distorting effect on historical reconstructions of the emergence of modern world politics. However, such an agreement does not require sharing their conclusion, which is to focus on years in which, seemingly, little or 'nothing' happened. Something is always happening. It might be both a truism and an illustration of the gigantic scale of the task of thinking about global social change, that there are always myriads of processes going on whose trajectories might be linked to varying degrees and in various forms at different times. The identification of different processes – synchronicity and asynchronicity, benchmark dates or crystallizing events – is an important analytical task when one is trying to make sense of change. However, this does not mean that 'anything goes' here. Even without an underlying philosophy of history, global social change does not simply meander along. This is the point where social evolution does not really differ from natural evolution: both might experiment with the strangest solutions, but the elephant no more starts to fly from one day to the next than a small African state becomes the core of a global empire overnight.

Before turning to the limits and possibilities of evolutionary accounts in this context, it seems worth reconstructing the possibilities of a history of events in accounting for global social change. As Buzan and Lawson (2014a) point out, much of international relations (IR) utilizes a narrative that is structured by big events and benchmark dates: 1648, 1815, 1945 and so on are taken to be wholesale markers for quite substantial periods that are seen as characterized by specific forms of international order. Such accounts tend to be rather static, and they are not in fact 'event' histories in any meaningful sense. Stylized representations of specific events are taken to represent specific forms of order. Historical accounts of these events in their contemporary contexts usually do not completely support the burden put on them in retrospect. An event history, as most notably proposed by Sewell (2005), takes historical events as a starting point and weaves around them the trajectories that emerged from or led to them in order to establish their central role in important historical developments. Common to both versions is that contemporaries shared some sense of the importance of the event. This is what might be called a minimum requirement of actor awareness: a little-noted event that is recognized as a major turning point only decades or even centuries later might thus be an important point of reference in any history of events, but cannot be a central node or starting point.

What benchmark date history and event history share is that they are not histories of events in the sense of idiographic history, in which many single events are put together like pearls on a string (or many strings, in more complex versions). Both are inherently process accounts, though of vastly different degrees of complexity, with the benchmark date version allowing for comparatively little historical change: it might be quite radical, but it doesn't happen very often. There are variations in how important the events are in the process, and this can be open to debate, but it is always possible to *start* from an event that includes its past and its future (the double move of protention and retention), and start to unweave trajectories that begin or end with it, or that criss-cross and culminate in it. Historical research in this sense invariably resembles the frustrating annual experience of trying to untangle last year's 800-piece chain of fairy lights as the festive season comes around again: you simply have to start somewhere. An important thought in this respect is provided by Buzan and Lawson (2014a) when they criticize benchmark-date-focused IR accounts and ventilate the idea of focusing on the seemingly unimportant years, the years in which, in a sense, little happened. However, the important point here lies probably not in the insight that, when abstracting from the retroactive ascription of turning point status to specific years (that were not usually so marked until quite some time after their occurrence), and refocusing on specific historical processes in the 'unremarkable' years, one gets a clearer view of processes of change. It is rather that in this sense history is also being read as a history of events as variations that 'failed to turn'.

Beyond arbitrariness: differentiation as heuristic, evolution as theory?

At first glance, the previous observations might, quite appropriately, be read as suggesting two things. First, 'anything goes' to some extent. Where one locates epochal change depends on one's point of view and the criteria applied. The 'long nineteenth' century has something to do with the years between 1800 and 1900, but its beginnings and endings are subject to an extremely wide variation of interpretations and, when turning to historical events, it seems possible to start from almost anywhere.[5] Second, the more one progresses from the seemingly 'big' picture of epochal change to the 'smaller' web of entangled events, the more the perspective of world society theory with its grand tale of social differentiation seems to recede into the background.

Both interpretations are plausible at first sight, yet they miss one important link that actually can and does tie the global history and world society perspectives together in all of the three areas discussed earlier, that contains few mutual restrictions on inquiry and conceptualization (yet does not open the door to complete arbitrariness). The key probably is in the conceptualization of change as social evolution that underlies world society theory, yet is not often brought to the fore at the expense of, for example, systems-theory-based accounts. Accounting for change in terms of communicative variation, selection and restabilization (see Brunkhorst, 2014) allows for a reconstruction of various entangled trajectories rich in historical detail, as well as the avoidance of any trait of a philosophy of history. Most important for practical analytical purposes, it basically permits one to start anywhere, although it does not permit one to go everywhere. In principle, an evolutionary account can start anywhere and follow on with every variation and choice: to storm the Bastille or not, to conclude a treaty with the East India company or try and oppose it, and so on. Yet starting anywhere often does not make very much sense: there is such a thing as the benefit of hindsight, and the transformative impact of some events may simply not have been clear to contemporaries.

The important point is that social evolution continues without direction or meaning – there is no *Geschichtsphilosophie* behind it. It cannot continue in a completely arbitrary fashion, however. Abstractly speaking, at any particular time there are boundary conditions that influence the likelihood of some variation being selected or not. It is at this point that world society theory has a direct contribution to make through the analysis of the emergence and interplay of different forms of social differentiation. It is exactly these forms of social differentiation and their expression in normative orders that condition the likelihood of selections. The analysis of social differentiation easily links to the thorny problem of epochal change: while the latter can roughly be told in terms of an increasing prominence of specific forms of social differentiation, most notably functional differentiation as the characteristic of modernity, a nuanced analysis of forms of social differentiation also helps to illuminate the intrinsic difficulties of accounts of epochal change: the key here lies in mapping the varied and complex interplay of different forms of social differentiation, as well as the multiple temporalities and regionally varied asynchronicities that go along with this complexity.

Conceptualizations of global social change on a large scale are always linked to explicit or implicit accounts of why some periodizations are to be preferred over others, and why some dates and turning points (or 'non-dates', as argued by Buzan and Lawson (2014a)) deserve more attention than others. It is one of the main merits of the renewed attention being paid to conceptualizing large-scale change in global history, sociology and IR that almost 'naturalized' distinctions and viewpoints have given way to more nuanced accounts of change. While the distinction between medieval times and modernity might still be a largely unquestioned organizing principle for history departments in universities, in the analysis of global social change it is a guiding question that enriches through the *variety* of its many possible conceptualizations, rather than through attempts to identify the 'most important' turning points of all. While the history of international relations might still be imagined as a history of nation states in many IR textbooks, it is precisely the historical reconstruction of the complexities of the relative rise, demise, transformation and interplay of various forms of organizing political authority that has enriched our understanding of the various processes of global social change that have led to our contemporary world order.

Conclusion: evolving together

What should have become clear from the previous observations is that global history and world society approaches have an important role to play in these perspectives on global social change. Global history contributes a nuanced understanding of the various entanglements between different processes and actors that takes full advantage of the possibility of basically starting 'from anywhere': distinct regions, 'levels' of analysis and forms of connection. Global history is a programme of dense, yet multi-perspectival reconstructions. World society theories, on the other hand, provide theoretically coherent research programmes that still need to weather some of the challenges posed both by the accounts given by global history and any possible ensuing adaptations of their theoretical formulae. Bringing them together remains a challenge – with possible rewards, yet also facing two major possible pitfalls. The first of these is an essentialist account of global social change. This is the pitfall of *Geschichtsphilosophie*, mentioned at the beginning of this chapter, namely the idea that ultimately history has a form, a purpose, or a goal in its 'globality', manifest in formal motives of teleology or cyclical change or substantive eschatological or emancipatory accounts. The second pitfall is that of a completely arbitrary 'anything goes'. While a plurality of approaches is called for by a plurality of time scales, processes and trajectories, a completely arbitrary plurality adds little to an understanding of global social change. Quite the contrary. Being completely unchecked, an arbitrary plurality of accounts might actually provoke recourse to what seems to remain the only underlying certainty: some 'pure' history of events.

The trick is to allow for a plurality of historical accounts on various levels, with different timescales, and perspectives on and from different regions, while at the same time enabling a comprehensive account of social change that describes a 'unity' that can only appear as such because of its internal differentiation and diversity, and not because of its integration into a coherent whole. It is in this sense that global history and world society theory can, and should, come together at their respective 'cores': for both, neither the 'global' nor the 'world' is – or should be treated as – a given, but something in need of being explained.

Notes

1. At this point, I should like to mention, but without taking it further, that (as in many of the social sciences) there is an open issue here with respect to clarification of the relation between the micro/macro-dimensional distinction and the distinction between the analytical and/or structural levels, a clarification that is largely absent.
2. It should be noted that the distinction between a phenomenological and a structural concept of 'world' used here was not shared by some of the other contributors to this volume during discussions of draft chapters. This has to do with the fact that they apply this distinction to the concept of 'world society', in which case the phenomenological dimension pertains to the 'world' and the structural dimension to 'society'. By contrast, I take it that some kind of social structure – that is 'society' – is always historically given and the distinction between a phenomenological and a structural dimension pertains to the concept of 'world': the distinction then, one might say, is rather one between the potentialities and the realizations of world society.
3. The *concept* of world society plays an important role in other bodies of thought as well, without making these into world society theories. The increasing interest in the concept of world society in the context of the so-called 'English School' of international relations is quite remarkable. It is a matter of what it seems difficult to call anything other than intra-disciplinary ignorance, that the concept of world society here is usually discussed without so much as an acknowledgement of the existence of world society theory(ies).
4. See generally Luhmann (2012/13), and on this point Brunkhorst (2014).
5. While probably only few historians would explicitly support such a view, they quite often implicitly express this attitude in terms of a stylistic tool, when they start by citing a seemingly small event that then leads to the unfolding of the larger story.

3

Periodization in Global History: The Productive Power of Comparing

Angelika Epple

Still, the problem of dealing with periodisation remains critical for anyone attempting to write contemporary world history. (Bayly, 2018: 324)

Introduction

Periodization in global history is difficult. Since nineteenth-century historicism and for far too long, European epoch concepts have been generalized without any further ado. Eurocentrism is merely a symptom of an even more fundamental challenge of periodization, however: it relies on comparisons. Comparing, this chapter argues, is a far from innocent activity. On the contrary, comparing has a productive power. The aim of this chapter is to show what scholars actually do when they cut history up into epochs, and why they should make the objective of their narrative explicit – at least if they want to escape Eurocentrism and other shortcomings in global history.[1]

After modernization theory lost its power of persuasion in the 1970s and 1980s, historians developed a strong dislike for theories of historical change. This seems to apply particularly to those doing global history. Nonetheless, historians, and global historians in particular, *do* deliver interpretations of historical change. What is often quite revealing in this respect are book titles such as *Remaking the Modern World (1900–2015)*

(Bayly, 2018), *The Transformation of the World* (Osterhammel, 2014), or *The Origins of Globalisation* (de Zwart and van Zanden, 2018). If a book's title refers to space instead of historical change, as in *A History of Southeast Asia* (Reid, 2015) or *The World in the Long Twentieth Century* (Dickinson, 2018), then it will be chapter headings that interpret specific time periods as periods of historical change, such as 'Becoming a Tropical Plantation, 1780–1900' (Reid, 2015: 196–212) or 'Population Explosion, 1800–2000' (Dickinson, 2018: 9–19). Historians cannot do without periodization. If they do not mention distinct periodizations – epochs or periods that are given distinct names, for example – they at least apply weak periodizations such as explanations for the periods of study or sequence of caesurae they have chosen. Since a sequence of periods with clear-cut boundaries between epochs has gone out of fashion, scholars of global history currently tend to work with overlapping time periods, sometimes even transforming them into thematically differing processes during a given period (Dickinson, 2018). Interestingly enough, the thematic order often becomes prominent in the final summarizing chapters (Bayly, 2018; de Zwart and van Zanden, 2018). Periodizations are definitely more than just an indication of the time spans covered; they are pointed interpretations of historical and social change.

Generally speaking, social or political scientists have fewer difficulties interpreting historical change with clear-cut periodizations. In *The Global Transformation*, for example, Barry Buzan and George Lawson (2015: 318) suggest three stages of historical change: 'Western-colonial' (1800–1945), 'Western global' (1945–2008), and 'decentered globalism'. Apart from the question of whether this periodization is meaningful or not, current global historians are more reluctant than their colleagues from the social sciences when it comes to periodization. Why do they shy away from such explicit interpretations?

Global historians (and also universal or world historians) usually have a comprehensive understanding of history that extends beyond a single world-societal subfield such as international relations. If they speak of 'change' at all – and not simply of 'shifts' like, for instance, Burbank and Cooper (2010: 17) – global historians prefer the term 'historical' to 'social' change. Historical change includes transformations other than social change: environmental change, for example, or, closely connected to environmental issues, change in the availability of resources. Because it has become difficult to identify single processes that embrace all historical changes worldwide, periodization has become a very difficult task for global historians. Their comprehensive understanding of history contrasts with their empirical findings that are often contradictory, multiple and diverse. Historical change in a region, society or group seems to be too specific to be generalized. Frequently, developments in two neighbouring regions point in different directions. But however diverse the different approaches to global history may be, they all challenge conventional Eurocentric chronologies and aim instead to outline the multipolar dynamics at work (Stanziani, 2018: 6–7).

World or universal historians usually have a different understanding of historical processes than global historians. Of course, the labels 'world', 'universal' and 'global historian' are not registered trademarks. However, universal or world historians generally stick to the idea that history has a telos towards which the world as a whole is moving. This is different with global historians. They are far more doubtful and sceptical when it comes to overarching processes. It is therefore not surprising to global historians that Christopher Bayly, in his latest book, devoted a short subchapter of the introduction to the theme 'The Challenges to Global History: Historians and Their Doubts' (Bayly, 2018: 4–6). This will be discussed in more detail later.

To global historians, overlapping chronological orders seem an attractive way out of the dilemma. Overlapping periods enable them to distinguish different processes that take place simultaneously, such as economic growth, growing income equality, the expansion of human knowledge, proliferation of communication, secularization and religion, and so forth. They can, for instance, demonstrate that the economy might grow while political freedom is being restricted, that infrastructure is being improved while specific regions become new peripheries, and so forth.

Frederik Cooper, an expert in African history, is one of the prominent sceptics regarding the question of whether the term globalization describes a period in global history. In order for a periodization to be meaningful in global history, it has to describe a development that applies to all world regions. African countries, however, were far less connected to other world regions in the nineteenth and twentieth centuries than they had been in earlier times. Cooper thus denies the existence of a process leading to a more integrated world society. According to him, the most 'global' feature of the nineteenth century was humanitarian language, not the actual structure of economic and political interaction (Cooper, 2005: 104). 'There are two problems with the concept of globalisation' – so goes his often-quoted criticism – 'first the "global" and second the "-isation"' (Cooper, 2005: 91). Similarly, Stanziani points out that 'globalisation as a category is now playing the role that modernisation played during the decolonisation period'

(Stanziani, 2018: 10). Should we throw overarching periodizations overboard then?

Even though Cooper's objection points to an important reason why 'periodisation remains critical' (Bayly, 2018), we need to take a closer look at the challenges and shortcomings of periodization as well as at possible alternatives. Postcolonial and other critics of specific process concepts have identified Eurocentrism as the major problem when it comes to periodization issues. More often than not, European epochs have been used universally: antiquity (including the Greek and Roman empires), the Middle Ages (from the migration of people in late antiquity to the 'discovery' of the Americas), early modern times (the secularization process leading up to the French Revolution), and modernity (starting with the Enlightenment). As mentioned by Mathias Albert and Tobias Werron in the introduction to this book, 'structural' Eurocentrism is indeed a fundamental problem in global history. This is especially true for periodization issues. Ideas for overcoming Eurocentrism, 'provincializing Europe' (Chakrabarty, 2000: 3) and 'decolonizing comparative studies' (Mignolo, 2013: 101) are important steps – especially with respect to our analytical concepts including concepts of historical change and periods. However, the problem with periodization is not only the false universalization of European historical experiences. A closer look reveals that whatever periodization a historian may propose, it is always based on *comparative practices*. The aim of the present chapter is to outline the productive power of comparing with regard to the division of history into epochs and to also consider how comparative practices in historical studies ought to look in order to meet the requirements of a periodization of global history.

The chapter therefore first presents an introduction to the challenges and shortcomings of conventional concepts of epochs. Going beyond postcolonial criticism, it argues that Eurocentrism is only a symptom of an even more fundamental challenge. In order to better understand the core challenge of periodization, the second part of the chapter goes back to the founding fathers of European historiography when the periodization of history became a key issue in history writing. Since the heyday of Eurocentrism in nineteenth-century historicism, epoch making has always been based on comparing different velocities and drivers of change. Eurocentrism, so the argument goes, is caused not only by universalized time concepts but also by justifications of periodization based on comparison. Finally, the chapter discusses different practices of comparing when it comes to periodization issues in current global histories.

Periodization in global history: challenges and shortcomings

History after Hobsbawm: Writing the Past for the Twenty-First Century is an anthology edited by John H. Arnold, Matthew Hilton and Jan Rüger and published by Oxford University Press in 2018 (Arnold et al, 2018). In their introduction, the editors elaborate on the role historians might seek in the present: that of helping twenty-first-century society to understand 'how we got there'. Edward Ross Dickinson presents his book on *The World in the Long Twentieth Century* in a similar fashion, yet even more resolutely: 'This book explains how we got here' (Dickinson, 2018: 8). What might sound like the natural concern of any historian turns out to be problematic, however: who are 'we' and where is 'there'? Both words, 'we' and 'there', are deictic: their meaning depends on the context. 'We', for instance, could address the readership or it could refer to the subject. In any case, whom does the pronoun 'we' include? The authors and their readers (that is a handful of academically trained historians in Europe and North America)? Or does it refer to the content of the book so that the 'we' are British society in *History after Hobsbawm*, and the US public in *The World in the Long 20th Century*? Or are 'we' humankind? Depending on whom 'we' includes and excludes, the answer to the question as to 'how we got here' will be completely different. This translates into the most fundamental challenge of history writing: whose history is being told? This challenge becomes even trickier if 'we' are writing global history. And it is trickier on both levels: that of the reader (history for whom?) and that of the subject (history of whom?).

The title *History after Hobsbawm* helps us to identify more challenges of writing global history. The title implies that in 2012, when Eric Hobsbawm died aged 95, we (the community of English-reading historians) not only lost a great scholar; with his death, a specific way of writing history also came to an end. Are 'we', the readers, experiencing a caesura, a caesura that might lead to a new historiographical period? Hobsbawm was an unorthodox Marxist with a clear concept of socioeconomic change. His famous 'triptych' on the 'short twentieth century' ended in 1970 when a 'Golden Age' reached its conclusion (Hobsbawm, 1994: 6). Hobsbawm's understanding of the 'Age of Extremes' as being driven by the antagonistic forces of capitalism and the global socialist challenge also marks an end 'to the beliefs and assumptions on which modern society had been founded since the Moderns won their famous battle against the Ancients in the early eighteenth century' (Hobsbawm, 1994: 11). Hobsbawm's observation that these assumptions had come to an end was broadly shared by other scholars. Anthropologists such as Eric Wolf and Johann Fabian showed that these assumptions had to do with how history has been conceived. Postcolonial theorists such as, most prominently, Dipesh Chakrabarty or postmodern thinkers such as Hayden White pointed out that time concepts and the concept of history itself were, more often than not, Eurocentric (Fabian, 1983; Chakrabarty, 2000) and relied on European-based narrative patterns (White, 1980: 14). On a global level, the histories excluded those who had already been silenced in national history writing (Spivak, 1994).

Postcolonial criticism of epoch concepts

During the last 25 years, first the spatial and then the temporal turn provoked a new approach to history (Dorsch, 2013). As a result, global history based on global connections and entanglements, or – as Sunjay Subrahmanyam would have it – a 'connected' but not necessarily common or shared history, had to include the voices of different actors from different world regions (Subrahmanyam, 1997). The existence of a general model for historical change – even if it were to allow for different paths into modernity, as Shmuel Eisenstadt (2000) argued – was questioned fundamentally. The outcome was a farewell to a conceptualization of historical change as a linear process (Subrahmanyam, 1997; Conrad and Randeria, 2002; Flüchter and Schöttli, 2015). As a consequence, historians such as Natalie Zemon Davis asked for multiple histories instead of an all-embracing concept of history in the singular (Davis, 2011). Hence one could argue that an epoch within historiography between the late eighteenth and the late twentieth century has come to an end. This historiographical epoch would have started with the enlightenment understanding of progressive development and the emergence of a concept of history in the singular (Koselleck, 2004: 33), and it would have come to an end with the dissolving of the idea of a progressive development in history, replacing it with a refragmentation of history into many histories.

A first glance at the history of academic historiography since 1800 supports this view. At the time, together with the concept of history in the singular, Eurocentric, bourgeois and also gendered time concepts were implemented in history writing (Smith, 1995; Epple and Schaser, 2009). The divide between so-called 'people with and without history', and also the division of labour between history and anthropology, then started to shape academia (Wolf, 1982; Ogle, 2015). With the help of 'progressive comparisons' (Steinmetz, 2015: 125), European scholars tried to prove that Western societies had reached a higher state of civilization than others. This is precisely what Dipesh Chakrabarty was describing when he introduced his 'not yet' formulation. Following nineteenth-century European or US scholars, some world regions – and, it could be added, all non-White people – were supposed to have 'not yet' attained the 'heights' of Western development (Chakrabarty, 2000: 7). Actually, the term 'development' has a history that can be traced back to Eurocentric eighteenth-century interpretations of human history as a story of progress. Since then, the term has become a global idea or even a global practice in the twentieth century (McVety, 2018: 23). If our aim is to overcome Eurocentrism, what would it mean in this case? Should we stop talking about different concepts of 'development'? Certainly not.

'Provincializing Europe' runs the risk of only showing that there are other provinces than Europe, that the world has many centres, and that developments within these centres could be compared. If we want a better understanding of how Eurocentrism works, we have to consider an aspect that has been overlooked so far: the distinguishing of different world regions as well as of different time periods and the idea of development rely on an everyday practice – the practice of comparing. Understanding this practice opens the door for an understanding of the condition of the possibility of Eurocentrism, and of other hidden elements concerning periodization. An in-depth analysis of comparative practices, however, reveals that comparing is not 'objective' in the sense that it puts into relation two pre-existing objects. Rather, it is a productive activity that creates the units to be compared in the first place. The eighteenth-century Eurocentric understanding of development was the outcome of both world–regional connections *and* comparisons carried out by enlightened European scholars at the time. Comparisons did not simply help to naturalize the differences between the West and the rest, they also brought into existence entities that could be compared as Europe and non-Europe, premodern and modern, civilized and uncivilized.

Why periodization is vulnerable – and unavoidable

All of this has a severe impact on our understanding of historical periods. If historical time is multilayered, if social changes happen simultaneously but point in different directions, and if they have different velocities, should we then still use the terms 'period' and 'epoch'? Though the possibility of periodization has been questioned by historians such as Frederik Cooper (2005), this questioning is now seen critically from a completely different angle: because global history and environmental threats came to the fore at the very same time, an interrelation between the two seems probable (Chakrabarty, 2000). This argument has heavily influenced a new paradigm of environmental history and the 'anthropocene studies group' – an interdisciplinary group of scientists and humanities scholars. They suggest that 'we' – that is, the human and nonhuman world – entered a new time period around 1800, and that 'we' might 'experience' (within the next 50 years or so) the end of this 'anthropocene' period. The time period thereafter would then be a post-human world (Dodd, 2017). The term 'social change' might not describe this correctly, because the 'social' is always connected to human interaction. The term 'historical change' comes with the same problem. Consequently, the anthropocene studies group works with caesurae when it comes to periodization (Mauelshagen, 2017). Replacing 'epochs' with presumably more descriptive caesurae, however, cannot solve the problem of periodization; it merely works around it.

A better understanding of how concepts of epoch work is required. Anyone who applies such a concept is claiming that there are criteria according to which a time span can be described as a cohesive period. Instead of merely pointing to a break, the epoch concept prescribes at least a minimum of inner consistency over the length of time in question. It becomes meaningful when it links up with some interpretation that goes beyond mere chronology. There are three possible ways of doing this: the weakest is to define an epoch as lying between two caesurae (as, for example, with the 'interwar period' or the 'Middle Ages'). An epoch concept is stronger when it invokes common features (for example 'feudalism'). However, the concept is at its strongest when it claims that a specific epoch is characterized by a general, comprehensive trend and can be conceived in terms of a process (for example, the 'age of industrialization').

These three examples show, nevertheless, how vulnerable epoch concepts are to criticism. The label 'the inter-war period' draws its clarity from historical *caesurae*. Its significance is easily questioned by a term that suggests a stronger cohesion. Charles de Gaulle, Winston Churchill and later the sociologist Raymond Aron, for instance, replaced the term 'the inter-war years' with 'the Second Thirty Years' War' expanding the period to include the two world wars (1914–45).[2] This new term referenced the seventeenth-century European war (1618–48) that had become synonymous with 30 years of uncontrollable violence. The fact that later politicians and historians took up the term again and applied it to the time between 1914 and

1945 shows how epoch concepts are constructed through comparisons with other epochs. Describing a specific time period as an epoch is always based on comparing.

It is the activity of comparing that brings about many specific difficulties, one of which is that comparisons highlight specific features and hide others. The term 'Second Thirty Years' War', for example, emphasizes the abyssal uncertainty of life, the unimaginable violence, the never-ending hardship and, last but not least, the apocalyptic destruction (Aron, 1951). However, the comparative term also hides the facts that there were voters who put the National Socialists in power, and that the genocide of Jews, Sinti and Roma and the extermination of dissenters had a clear strategic aim along with identifiable perpetrators who pursued it. The productive power of comparing, in this case, is the ability to conceal. That ability made the term 'Thirty Years' War' so attractive for national socialist propaganda as well in the later years of World War II. The term also erased from memory the Weimar Republic as a period of democracy in Germany (Kamber, 2004: 125). Comparisons are not innocent. Periodizations are not innocent either.

The concept of the 'Middle Ages' reveals even more difficulties in marking epochs. By indicating its position in the middle between two other epochs, it is marked as a somewhat deficient period between antiquity and modern times. Whereas the label 'Thirty Years' War' at first glance seemed to be neutral, pointing to analogies between two epochs, the original meaning of the term 'Middle Ages' shows that comparing is mostly accompanied by evaluation and is not a neutral activity. By talking about 'feudalism' instead, one underlines the similar economic and social structures existing in certain European regions during a specific period of time. This label brings the common features of an epoch to the fore. Initially, such a designation seems to reject comparisons and focus on incomparability. It seems to fulfil the historicist conception that 'every age is next to God' and is thereby unique (see von Ranke, 2010: 21). However, a closer look makes it clear that postulating incomparability and individuality (in this sense) does not work without engaging in some kind of comparative exercise.

The concept of the 'age of industrialization' points to further difficulties: Epoch concepts are often process concepts as well. 'Industrialization', 'secularization', 'modernization', as well as 'globalization' – all assert that history is a process moving in one direction that could be described as uniform. If it is assumed that every description of an epoch is based on some kind of inner coherence, this claim must be extended to cover developments. This shows that a very strong historical premise is inscribed in these concepts. A further difficulty can be seen with the term 'industrialization'. If a process is taken to be the fundamental characteristic of an epoch, then inclusions and exclusions are substantiated through temporal comparisons. Chris Lorenz (2017) has made the point that Western-type modernity and the invention of epochs hang together closely. And it was the historicist Johann Gustav Droysen who coined the term 'Hellenism' to underline his idea of history as a development of humankind to a higher moral level.

The argument has been mentioned already. The world was divided into regions that were considered to be spearheads of development and those that had 'not yet' been integrated into this process. Western-style nineteenth-century periodization, therefore, created forerunners, latecomers, resisters and deniers. This convincing postcolonial argument reached the mainstream of historical disciplines long ago. In line with this finding – though less emphasized or emphasized less frequently – temporal marking of this kind also applies to so-called 'hinterland regions' within the modern Western world. The characterization of specific groups as 'people without history' goes back to Marx and Engels. They were not referring to European colonies, but expressing 'the lack of sympathy with some national separatist movements in eastern Europe' (Wolf, 1997: x). Only a very few, carefully selected European zones belonged to what was taken to be the core of the 'modern Western world'. The construction of spatio-temporal orders within Europe has persisted in research on social history right up into the twenty-first century. Regions in the middle of Western Europe, such as the 'Bergisches Land' on the southern edge of the Ruhr area in Germany, were treated as having been forgotten by industrialization and the modern world. Only a shift away from the normatively charged process concept of 'industrialization' as the ideal-typical path to 'the' modern world can reveal that the Bergisches Land was a region already integrated into the colonial system in early modern times and until well into the twentieth century. It did not miss out on any progressive developments; its representatives cleverly exploited global economic structures, knowing full well how to use them to their advantage (see Epple, 2015).

Whereas the designation 'Middle Ages' served as a diachronic devaluation of an epoch of Western history, process concepts lead to synchronous hierarchizations within an epoch. They mostly consist of an evaluative idea of some idealized form of progress oriented towards European history. In other words, previous process concepts in history were always Eurocentric in their ideas of what constitutes a process; how, why and by whom it is initiated; which stages it passes through; and what positive and negative effects it has. Put briefly, the entire idea of historical change is formed against the background of a specific interpretation of European history. If we want to overcome Eurocentrism in epoch making, we have to realize that a specific time concept, concepts of historical change, periodizations issues and the inclusion and exclusion of counter-histories are all based on explicit or implicit comparisons. A closer look at the 'invention' of epoch making allows further insights into how periodization works.

Historicist concepts: Ranke and Droysen

Despite their undeniable Eurocentrism, it is worth taking a closer look at historicist concepts of history, historical change and human progress. The professionalization of history writing in the sense that 'history' became an academic discipline requiring specialized training with a clearly defined field of research and an elaborate methodology with source criticism at its centre emerged simultaneously in different regions of the world during the nineteenth century. University-based historiography more often than not went along with nation-building (Sachsenmaier, 2011: 25). Within that context, scholarship in the tradition of the German historicist Leopold von Ranke has been influential not only in European or Japanese history (O'Brien, 2018: xi) but also elsewhere in the world. This is not to say that Rankeanism was exported directly or that historicist concepts of history spread uniformly all over the world. However, it is interesting to note that a specific understanding of the relation between the nation as a 'part' and a general history in the singular as the 'whole' can be found in many different national historiographies at the time. In this vein, von Ranke's concept of the particular and the general became paradigmatic. What did that mean for historical change?

Leopold von Ranke was instrumental in establishing history as an academic discipline in Germany. One of his influential convictions was that every epoch was an individual unity with an individual value in its own right or, in his words, 'every epoch is immediate to God' (von Ranke, 2010). At the same time, and in a somewhat self-contradictory way, he also believed that the course of history (with history in the singular) was changing for the better. However, neither von Ranke nor other historicists assumed progress to be a linear process, even less so in global history. So, even though von Ranke always tried to refute the philosophy of history of his colleague Georg Wilhelm Friedrich Hegel at the Friedrich-Wilhelms University in Berlin, German historicists at the time were deeply influenced by Hegel's dialectical understanding of historical change.

Von Ranke's influential disciple Johann Gustav Droysen set the standards for history as an academic discipline in his seminal work outlining his principles of history (*Outline of History* [1864], Droysen, 1897). Droysen combined a dialectical understanding of historical developments with a constructivist approach to history writing. Historicists in some ways were constructivists *avant la lettre*. For Droysen, history writing was a productive process. In contrast to the radical constructivists of the late twentieth century, however, Droysen did not assume that historians 'made' history. Historians in his eyes only helped their readers to understand the course of history. He admitted that epochs – like the line of the equator – do not exist in an empirical sense (Droysen, 1972: 20). Epochs were not made by history but by historians: For him, epochs were 'perspectives that the thinking mind gives to the material for understanding it with more certainty' (Droysen, 1972: 20; translation AE). In his take, epochs and periodization were nothing but tools for making the purpose of history visible.

What was the 'purpose of history' in historicists' eyes? Following Droysen and other historians of the time, the purpose of man and humankind was to gain liberty. In their view, history had a telos. However, this did not imply that achieving this goal was seen as a linear path from the past to the future. The understanding of historical change in historicism was far more complicated (and elaborated). Whereas some enlightened philosophers in late eighteenth-century Europe might have thought of history as a linear story of progress from barbarism to civilization, a historicist understanding of history did not simply acknowledge countermovements or backlashes; countermovements and backlashes were the preconditions for any movement in the direction of the historical telos. Given that Droysen had studied with Hegel in Berlin, these opinions are hardly surprising. However, regardless of Hegel's influence, Droysen's major concern was to fight any lack of empiricism. Faced with Hegelian idealism as well as mere empirical positivism, Droysen tried to mediate between the two. This mediation is the key feature of his historical methodology. For him, professional history writing was not just based on source criticism, as von Ranke had requested. Professional history writing had to also include criticism of interpretation (Birtsch and Rüsen, 1972: 9). This is how periodization issues and comparing came into the picture.

Comparisons as the basis of periodization

Droysen mentions the 'comparative methodology' as only one methodology underlying others (*Outline of History*; Droysen, 1897: § Interpretation). For him, however, comparing is at the centre of periodization: in his view, any historian – and even more so if writing the history of humankind – has to measure the importance of a historical movement. In other words, the historian has to decide whether or not the historical movement in question is a step in the direction of greater liberty for humankind – assuming that increase in liberty is the telos of history. Weighing the importance of a specific historical movement with respect to progress in liberty relies on the practice of comparing. For Droysen, the telos of history was an indispensable tool that enabled professional historians to read and interpret sources in the right light. Only the 'telos' enabled historians to ask whether a historical movement was a step in the right or in the wrong direction. Having, so to speak, the 'big picture' in mind, the historian could come to terms with thousands of empirical facts that, without the 'big picture', might reveal nothing themselves about their significance. Comparing was the tool for making the significance of a specific historical period visible.

Obviously, Droysen had a point here. Of course, nowadays the idea of a telos has lost all of its persuasiveness. Droysen was an active Protestant (interpreting Catholicism as a countermovement), and his belief in God made it easy for him to focus on the telos and detect countermovements in history. Droysen was both a Christian and a Eurocentric historian.

Today, we need to ask whether there is a secular and non-Eurocentric 'way out', so to speak. If we look at the function that the assumption of a 'telos' has for history telling, Droysen's suggestions are not so far from current narrativist positions. It seems to be a mainstream perception in twenty-first-century academia that historians are telling stories when they seek to explain historical change. Their histories might be short stories covering events or longer stories dealing with comprehensive social transformations, but to tell them they have to assemble historical facts and identify the narration that explains why something happened earlier, and why something else happened later. In other words, the assembling of historical events, the design of the story, the emplotment – as Hayden White would have it (White, 2002: 191–210) – make history comprehensible.

Let me take this one step further: From Droysen, we can deduce that periodizations are abbreviated interpretations of historical movements with respect to a specific telos. He is very clear about the function of the telos for history writing: The telos shows the direction in which the river flows. The telos is the condition of possibility that enables the historian to distinguish between movement and standstill or countermovement. In other words, historians are in need of a 'telos', a telos compatible with the negation of the idealistic assumption of a general telos of history.

So far, we can note the following: periodization relies on comparing. Comparing requires a point of reference in relation to which developments can be weighed. We agree with the idea that history does not have a telos. Notwithstanding this, the presumed 'telos' of history has a structural function in history writing. Empirical facts and their descriptions do not themselves tell us anything about how they should be weighed in order to explain historical change. Hence historians, when writing about historical change, need something that fulfils the function that a presumed 'telos' of history had for history writing in nineteenth-century Europe. This is labelled the 'narrative objective' in contrast to an idealistic historical telos. In addition, we also have to consider the fact that historical change has to be conceptualized as multilayered and partly contradictory. Hence, historians have to distinguish between movements in different directions with different velocities and standstills. Different directions, different velocities, and different standstills are all relational terms. They can only be distinguished through comparisons with a narrative objective.

Comparisons, 'narrative objectives' and periodization in global history

Until the late twentieth century, periodizations in global history were almost always oriented towards a specific interpretation of European or Western history. Given that designations of epochs offer a condensed interpretation of historical periods of time, given that they are based on comparisons, and given that we want to overcome Eurocentric periodizations in global history, we must carefully select the comparative units with which we justify the periodization. Comparative units are like Droysen's metaphor of the equator: historians cannot find them in history. They can only justify them by means of the 'narrative objective' of their histories. It is the historian who creates a relation between different epochs, even more in cases where these do not follow each other directly, as in the example of the two 'Thirty Years' Wars' mentioned earlier. What are the units of comparison in current periodizations of global histories and what are their 'narrative objectives'?

It is interesting to note that periodization in history books is mostly multilayered, which is to say that different arguments for different divisions of specific periods show up in different contexts within one book: in the introduction and the concluding chapter, authors usually explain the pros and cons of their period of examination. Without using the terms 'periodization' or 'epoch', the justification of a period of examination is nothing other than a construction of a meaningful temporal unit. Additionally, in the more empirical chapters of their study, historians place the analysed events or structures within a specific epoch. In most cases, the reference to a certain epoch is not discussed in detail. But references, distinctions and thus comparisons to other units of examination or epochs are ubiquitous. When it comes to global history, the issue is usually addressed more explicitly because *global* periodization seems to be even more challenging.

Jürgen Osterhammel in his *Transformation of the World* dedicates one of three introductory chapters to the question 'Time: When Was the Nineteenth Century?' The answer is not, as one might expect, a clear-cut designation of an epoch, but a tentative approximation to dealing with the fragmented and multilayered nineteenth century. The fact that time orders, especially when it comes to epochs, are always relative to a specific culture, makes it very difficult to find justifiable periodizations. Osterhammel emphasizes that there is no analogy in other civilizations to the European sequence of antiquity, Middle Ages and modernity (Osterhammel, 2009: 93). Nevertheless, he finds arguments as to why one could argue that there might be a simultaneous beginning of early modern times between 1450 and 1600 in Eurasia and the Americas when trade boomed, new military technology was introduced, states were centralized and religions upheavals were common. Africa was different, though (Osterhammel, 2009: 101). Locating the beginning of what, with respect to European history, has been called 'modern times' seems to be even more difficult for Osterhammel. He enumerates different periodizations of different world regions or even countries that cannot be brought together under just one roof.

In other words, Osterhammel rejects the idea of a single 'narrative objective' that would make a *joint* periodization meaningful. Different 'narrative objectives' instead lie *within* the respective world region or country. Japan, for instance, experienced a good deal of societal movement, but no fundamental change until 1850; the Ottoman Empire experienced a century of reforms beginning in 1808 and lasting until 1908; for Africa, some historians have suggested allowing for a medieval-like period that only ended around 1800; and so forth. Having said this, Osterhammel also mentions tentative arguments as to why an epoch called 'Sattelzeit' (1770–1830), a term coined by Reinhart Koselleck, could, with good reasons, be applied globally: the reasons here range from the globalization of imperialism, via the emergence of new ideals of social inclusion, to a range of other social, economic and cultural factors. However, Osterhammel remains critical about periodization issues and always stresses the varying intensity of different developments.

Christopher Bayly, by contrast, employs a far stronger 'narrative objective' in the form of a quite literal increase in uniformization (which he distinguishes sharply from homogenization), illustrated by the uniform dressing of diplomats (Arab and African diplomats seem to be different here, however). Of course, Bayly is convinced that social and economic changes in the long nineteenth century were uneven and unsettling, and of course he emphasizes that political and ideological changes were 'catastrophic'. However, at the same time, he is also convinced that 'between about 1780 and 1914, increasing numbers of people decided that they were modern' (Bayly, 2004: 10). What is more, he also reveals to his readers political, social and economic trends characteristic of the period that went beyond a specific modern mindset. It is this narrative of convergence that is, on the one hand, a result of comparisons; on the other hand, the point of reference in relation to which the diversity of bodily practices in premodern times becomes evident.

In Bayly's 2018 book, *Remaking the Modern World 1900–2015*, the 'narrative objective' is weaker, but still strong enough to distinguish different global phases in the long twentieth century. An 'Idealistic Age' (1890–1914) was followed by the age of multinational rivalry and mass killing (1914–45), by a phase of forced stability (1945–79), and by a 'tipping point' between 1979 and 1991 that led into another phase that has continued until today and is characterized by fragmented wars. As in his earlier book, Bayly concludes that commerce, communication and warfare 'did indeed knit the world more closely together' (Bayly, 2018: 327). However, he also sees the reassertion of the power of the local, the regional and the national. Globalization for him is not a cumulative process. However, and in contrast to *Birth of the Modern World*, comparisons in this book have more to do with spatial differences than with globally distinct periods of time. This is because it is difficult for contemporary historians to compare their period of investigation with previous epochs – the reason for this being rather simple: contemporary history is not yet over, and this makes it difficult to define the unit of comparison.

Jane Burbank and Frederick Cooper are even more reluctant than Bayly when it comes to a narrative objective or to periodization. Their units of comparisons are spatially defined and do not help explain historical change. Their book on *Empires in World History: Power and the Politics of Difference* (Burbank and Cooper, 2010) focuses on what they call the 'political economy' of empires starting with ancient Rome and China. Of course, they do not deny a chronological order, but they do not derive a development out of it. In other words, the question 'how did we get there?' is not central. For them, different themes (such as the politics of difference, imperial intermediaries, imperial intersections and imperial imaginaries) are the guiding principles. As a consequence, periodization becomes less important. The historical order is transformed into a systematic order of different 'repertoires' of the political economy of empires. As periodizations are unavoidable in history books, Burbank and Cooper (2010: 17) identify 'key shifts in these repertoires'. With these shifts, they revise conventional chronologies by arguing, for instance, that European colonialism in the nineteenth century was, from a historical perspective, short-lived (Burbank and Cooper, 2010: 21). However, despite their reservations about process concepts, there is an undisputed, recurring theme throughout the book: transcontinental connections have continuously gained in importance. As a consequence, historical change enters as a hidden theme through the back door, and it may seem that a narrative objective is present after all.

This is different with the historians Pim de Zwart and Jan Luiten van Zanden and their book on *The Origins of Globalisation* (2018). They employ two different narrative objectives and explain them right at the beginning: they divide the process of globalization into 'soft globalization' that includes sustained global interaction, and 'hard globalization' that focuses on the integration of commodity markets. The former allows the period between 1500 and 1800 to be narrated as a time in which an integrated world economy was created by sustained cultural, political and economic interactions; for the latter globalization only started in the early nineteenth century. The two different narrative objectives thus transform into two different periodizations. Without using the terminology of this chapter, de Zwart and van Zanden illustrate how 'narrative objectives' shape the units of comparisons that allow for periodization.

Conclusion

This chapter has argued that periodization is a central, unavoidable and very complex task in history writing. It relies on temporal comparisons between different time periods. Historians, therefore, have to reflect on the productive power of comparisons. Temporal comparisons are only meaningful in respect to an objective. Only an objective makes it possible to see history as a process with a specific direction that also includes countermovements and standstills. However, understanding history as a *determined* teleological process is no longer convincing. It is the difficult task of historians to find convincing 'narrative objectives' to structure their story. The 'narrative objectives' set by historians are not simply products of their imagination. A 'narrative objective' must be convincing in the sense that it can be legitimized with historical evidence. Only then do comparisons between different time periods become meaningful and, once implemented, comparisons shape the way we think about different time periods.

Whatever the periodization looks like, comparing has a productive power. A good example is the Eurocentric periodization of history into antiquity, Medieval history, modern history and contemporary history. It has taken far too long to say farewell to these four epochs when it comes to global history. Once accepted as meaningful, comparisons have a sustained persuasiveness.

It is interesting to note that many global historians agree with an epoch being designated as the 'Making of the Global Economy' for the years between 1500 and 1800, and most would also accept the long nineteenth century as a meaningful unity to which World War I (1918) put an end. The unity of the contemporary period seems to be more controversial. This is because it is difficult to find a narrative objective that would make comparisons of the contemporary period with its predecessors meaningful. Good arguments can be brought forward that the end of the Cold War, the growing awareness of environmental issues, the end of decolonization, or the technological transformation and changes in communication that came along with the internet all mark global ruptures that could underpin such a narrative objective. However, what future historians will make of this past remains to be seen.

Notes

[1] This chapter was written within the framework of two interdisciplinary projects at Bielefeld University: The Research Training Group (RTG) 2225 'World Politics: The Emergence of Political Arenas and Modes of Observation in World Society'; and the Collaborative Research Center SFB 1288 'Practices of Comparing: Changing and Ordering the World', Germany, both funded by the German Research Foundation (DFG).

[2] The term 'Second Thirty Years' War' was introduced into long-lasting historiographical debates by the French sociologist Raymond Aron. The

German historian Hans-Ulrich Wehler took it up in his fourth volume *Deutsche Gesellschaftsgeschichte, 1914–1949* (Wehler, 2008). This provoked severe criticism. As Peter Kamber has argued, Raymond Aron himself put the comparisons between the two time periods into perspective and also mentioned the differences and the limit to the analogies between the two epochs (Kamber, 2004: 127).

4

Communication, Differentiation and the Evolution of World Society

Boris Holzer

Introduction

We tend to think that the history of world society begins in the nineteenth century, but in fact, a pattern of 'archaic globalization' based on the exchange of commodities and on intercultural contacts had already emerged long before (Bayly, 2004, 2005). Interconnectedness as we usually think of it, however, scarcely existed up until the mid-nineteenth century: the many white spots on the maps and the fragmentary character of knowledge of the world inspired Hobsbawm (2004: 59) to state that 'there was not, even in terms of geographical knowledge, one world'. The parameters of global connectedness changed dramatically during the nineteenth century, however, as railroad tracks and steamship routes allowed travelling within Europe and across the oceans with unprecedented speed and reliability, and the standardization of time made it possible to know not only *where* but also *when* a journey would end. Still, the development of a 'world society' was incremental and not without its hurdles: There were no airplanes and therefore long-distance journeys were time-consuming. Large parts of Africa, Asia and even America were still uncharted territory and difficult to reach at all. Telegraph cables connected the major European cities, the Americas and the colonial hubs in Asia, but the steep tariffs for sending messages limited the practical use of the telegraph to political and economic elites and prevented it from becoming a mass medium. The nation state and national collectives defined the new 'international' political stage, and diplomatic contacts and state visits flourished, yet large parts of the world were either under colonial rule or were governed by non-democratic regimes (if governed at all).

Despite those limitations, some features of contemporary world society were established or had at least begun to emerge by the end of the nineteenth century, most notably the interconnectedness through transport and communication networks, as well as the standardization and diffusion of political and other social institutions (Osterhammel, 2014). The global infrastructure for transport and communication improved by leaps and bounds: As early as 1872 it was possible to travel around the world in 80 days like Jules Verne's tourist pioneer Phileas Fogg, whereas in 1848, it would have taken a good 11 months. The rapid expansion of the transport infrastructure continued: 10,000 miles of railway lines in 1845 had already grown to 600,000 by 1920 (Lechner and Boli, 2005: 114–15).

The question of how significant those developments were echoes central topics of the debate about the origins of modernity. Did it start around that time, being basically a correlate of industrialization? Or had earlier political events, notably the French Revolution, already laid the groundwork? And were those actually the final outcomes of a societal transformation that had already begun with the European expansion and the revolution of its worldview in the fifteenth and sixteenth centuries?

From a sociological perspective, it is probably neither possible nor necessary to decide these questions.[1] The question of periodization is not as relevant as the question of how and why some basic structures of contemporary world society emerged at all. In that regard, the 'long' twentieth century – from the mid-to-late nineteenth century onwards – is of particular interest. Over a relatively short period of time, multiple transformations of the social world occurred that made global interconnectedness palpable and thereby popularized the *aspiration* for a global modernity. Even if we cannot observe a fundamental or sudden societal revolution during that period, the long-term transformation of which it forms an integral part is substantial enough to warrant closer inspection.

Contextualizing the long twentieth century requires a conceptual framework. To go beyond collecting and presenting evidence based on more or less spontaneous comparisons between 'now' and 'then', we need to consult a theory of society – not because it could give us an authoritative answer but because it allows us to formulate questions that point to pertinent events and developments. The choice of a systems perspective is usually controversial but in this case more than justified by the fact that communication is of primary interest in this period. Furthermore, the advantage of world society theory compared to, for instance, world systems or field theories[2] lies in the fact that it actually combines three distinct yet mutually complementary sets of theories: communication theory, differentiation theory and evolutionary theory. Its take on globalization therefore goes beyond identifying the modes of global transaction or tracing the dynamics of a particular sphere of action. It combines interests in the modes and possibilities of communicative relationships, in the specialization and differentiation of social action, and in the temporal unfolding and change of social structures.

This kind of theoretical design enables us to examine how the globalization of the nineteenth and twentieth centuries affected social contacts, societal groups and the form of social change itself. Regarding those three aspects, there is some continuity with previous and later forms of (proto-)globalization and there also is an instructive absence of certain features of contemporary globalization. The following sections are therefore structured along these three theoretical perspectives and seek to identify those events and developments that made a difference – regarding both previous and later manifestations of globalization.

From universal to instantaneous communication

Modern globalization cannot be understood merely in terms of material linkages and the mobilities of goods and people, insofar as communication technologies also played a pivotal role in the emergence and integration of world society. The emergence of new technologies of (tele-)communication rendered informational networks independent of physical transportation and thus added a decisive new dimension to globalization (Lübbe, 1996; Wenzlhuemer, 2010). In the 1870s telegraphic cables already connected Europe, South America, South Africa, Australia, India and China and thus gave rise to a rudimentary form of global connectedness (Wobring, 2005). New communication technologies played a pivotal role in globalizing economic, political and cultural relations (Osterhammel, 2009: 63–83). It is therefore hardly surprising that the roles of the telegraph, of news agencies and of print media have attracted a good deal of scholarly attention (Müller, 2016; Rantanen, 2009; Tworek, 2014, Chapter 11 in this volume; Winseck and Pike, 2007).

But how can we account for the impact that new communication technologies had on social change and on society as a whole? If we understand the long twentieth century primarily in terms of the emergence of new forms of mediated communication, a theory of society that focuses on communication should be able to offer some guidance. Yet telegraphy, being the major pertinent innovation of that period, does not fall squarely into either category of Luhmann's (1975b, 1997b) theory of communication, which distinguishes between distributive media (for example writing, printing, mass media) and 'symbolically generalized media' (money, power, truth, love). Although telegraphy allowed connections to be made across large distances almost instantaneously, it was in fact a point-to-point medium whose tariffs precluded the participation of larger parts of the population: 'The tentacles of global communications in the nineteenth and early twentieth centuries, the dense network of submarine and terrestrial telegraphs, were never a means of social or mass communication' (Müller, 2015: 441). However, telegraphy quickly became the backbone for the global operations of international news agencies that were thereby able to deliver news to audiences across the globe at unprecedented speed. The 'dematerialization' (Wenzlhuemer, 2010, 2013) of communication, although more or less limited to political and economic elites, thereby affected a broader audience as well.

The 'network compression' (Lübbe, 1996) effected by telegraphy was able to build on a previous step in the history of global communication: the *universalization* of communication. Throughout human history, the boundaries of societies had also been 'boundaries of the social world' (Luckmann, 1970). The boundaries drawn by communities of language and descent delimited potential partners for communication; people outside this perimeter were considered 'barbarians' and thus deemed unable to communicate. But even if other (potential) human beings beyond the boundaries of a particular society had to be acknowledged, that did not necessarily imply any interest in establishing social relationships with them. They could be and regularly were regarded as either too remote or too strange to warrant their inclusion within a shared horizon of the social world (Luhmann, 2017: 367–8). Against this backdrop, the European expansion of the fifteenth and sixteenth centuries, especially the discovery of the New World, marked a significant rupture by establishing a new, inclusive – and for the societies affected often overwhelming or even disastrous – pattern of social contact. The contact with and the integration of other societies was not avoided anymore but became a consciously pursued project. The question of the *moral* standing of other cultures was still a matter of dispute, as documented by the Valladolid debate (1550–51) about the rights of the colonized people in the New World (Hanke, 1974). Yet their *communicative* standing was firmly established – and exploited – by the conquerors, who used the knowledge about the indigenous worldviews in order to manipulate them to their own advantage (Todorov, 1985). Communication, *pace* Habermas, is not just a medium of understanding but also one of manipulation.

It is therefore no contradiction to note both that communication had become universalized and that it was not motivated by humanistic interest in other cultures but by the promise of economic gain, the pursuit of political expansion and missionary zeal. In order to achieve their goals, conquerors and colonizers had to rely on communication. Ever since the beginning of the European expansion, the history of world society has therefore also meant the expansion of communicative relationships. Those relationships were of course rarely genuine, sociable encounters, but already functionally specific in terms of political, economic, religious, or other criteria. The unity of world society as a system of communication must not be confused with normative integration or even solidarity.

At the beginning of the nineteenth century, the universalism of communication had already been firmly established but it still had little impact on everyday life. It did not imply that people were in touch across the globe. Besides the often specific and thus socially 'thin' nature of long-distance contacts, it was based on personal encounters and written communication. Newspapers and a 'mobile universe of books' (Osterhammel, 2016b: 816–18) provided an extensive web of communication. But worldwide interpersonal contacts would have been impossible from a technological point of view and meaningless from a sociocultural one. Yet knowledge about events and people abroad soon became so widely shared that it affected and altered the common-sense view of the world. The possibilities of telegraphic communication, actualized through news agencies since the 1870s, in particular enabled a new 'experience of simultaneity' across the globe (Conrad, 2016a: 460).

For the majority of the world's population, however, instantaneous communication was at best an imagination rather than an experience. Access to the 'Victorian internet' (Standage, 1998) was limited and expensive. Yet the attention attracted by the efforts to install a global network made sure that the possibilities of the new technology became part of the public imagination. The imagery of a global community of communication was further underpinned by a related development, which was stimulated by the demands of transport spanning different time zones: the standardization of time (Zerubavel, 1982). It must be regarded as one of the biggest interventions of society into what had hitherto appeared as a mere fact of nature. The thus established temporal frame of reference for all social action has, of course, become an indispensable backdrop of global connections – physical as well as communicative. But another aspect that deserves attention is the increasing specificity of the 'present'. Within only a couple of decades, a broad and diffuse understanding about what happened where, at roughly what time, gave way to a much narrower understanding of and interest in present events. That 'shrinking of the present' is, for instance, observable in the immediacy of news reports in Germany: While in 1856 only 11% of news was not older than one day, in the year 1906 that rate had risen to 95% (Osterhammel, 2009: 63–4).

The globalization of communication in the nineteenth century thus greatly enhanced the mutual awareness and perceived simultaneity of events around the world (Werron, 2016). Although that cannot account for the institutionalization of human rights much later, it already served as a backdrop for an emerging normative standard that everyone should not only be regarded as a potential partner for communication but also as a bearer of rights. Yet it still lacked, probably until well after 1945, a set of global media targeting a global mass audience in all parts of the world (Osterhammel, 2017: 34). We can thus discern more clearly how the new technologies of telecommunication laid the foundation for the more far-reaching transformation associated with radio and television. Their effects are in some ways already imminent in the uses of and even more so in the utopias about telegraphy. But those go beyond the societal consequences of telegraphy in at least two ways. First, they took the inclusion of a universal audience to another level by combining more efficient ways of broadcasting with audiovisual information rather than text. Second, they made it plausible to assume that everyone had the same knowledge about current events and thus created a much more immediate sense of a global social reality by way of an 'instantaneous integration' (*Sofort-Integration*) of world society (Luhmann, 1981: 318). In that regard, the telecommunication revolution of the nineteenth century prepared the ground for future developments that would then fully realize the potential of instantaneous communication.

Media of communication, universalism and differentiation

Why did the communication innovations of the nineteenth century succeed in a way that led to further improvements overcoming their previous shortcomings – especially regarding participation and reliability? Contemporary observers already expressed some doubts about the demand for the new technology, asking why people who are separated not only by spatial but also by cultural distances should be interested in communicating with one another at all (Müller, 2016). Strange as such reservations may seem from today's point of view, there had been little demand for such technologies for thousands of years. If a communication technology offers the potential to transcend limits of space and time, social structures must also give reasons to actually use it. Differentiation, particularly functional differentiation, does precisely that.

As noted previously, the expansion of social relationships has long since been associated with functionally specific communication, particularly with economic, political and religious forms of contact, exchange and domination. There are at least two different ways to theorize the link between functional differentiation and globalization. The first one highlights the 'specific universalism' of functionally specified communication, the second one, the increasing heterogeneity of functionally differentiated role structures. These two lines of argument are complementary but they may also be regarded as ways to address both the generic question of globalization and the changes that took place during the nineteenth century.

Although functional differentiation is closely intertwined with expansion, the shape and extent of globalization depends on the medium of communication. In terms of communication, the globalizing dynamics of functional subsystems rest with what has been dubbed 'specific universalism': within the specific demarcations of their functional domain, such subsystems adopt a universalistic perspective – that is, they observe anything and everything under the auspices of their 'code'. From the perspective of the economy, anything may be monetized, and from the perspective of the political system, anything may be turned into a matter of collective decision making. Generally speaking, expansion therefore is a correlate of the functional specialization of societal subsystems.

Major subsystems are associated with specific 'symbolically generalized media of communication' such as money, power, truth and love (Luhmann, 1975b). The fact that the economy, based on money, and science, based on truth, appear to be more effectively global in their operations has to do with the fact that their media revolve around the problem of transmitting and motivating certain kinds of experience, not of social action: The acceptance of truth or property claims merely requires adjusting one's expectations, whereas power is only effective to the extent that it motivates a particular course of action. Globalization in terms of extensive and intensive communicative relationships across distance therefore occurs most prominently in those fields that do not require collective coordination of action (Luhmann, 1975a: 55–8; 2017: 445).

Consider the case of modern science, whose mode of communication is fundamentally predicated upon the assumption that (scientific) truths are amenable to intersubjective validation and thus universal. Nothing could be farther removed from the scientific enterprise than Pascal's lament: 'Truth on this side of the Pyrenees, error on the other side' (Pascal, 1910: 104). In fact, Pascal made this remark in the context of his observations about the vicissitudes of standards of justice and thus referred to 'moral' truth, which obviously cannot lay claim to universal validity to the same extent as scientific truth. Although the universalism of scientific knowledge has been contested throughout history, the argument that truth and, in a similar vein, money foster globalizing perspectives in their respective domains is borne out by the high degree of transnationalization of both science and the economy in contemporary world society.

From the late eighteenth century onwards, a global political system has emerged, but it remains based on nation states. However, the paramount role of the nation state – that is, the 'primacy of segmentation in the system of world politics' (Albert, 2016: 150) – should not be misunderstood as an argument against globalization. In fact, the structural isomorphism of nation states, as well as the diffusion of nationalism(s), are consequences of globalization (Meyer et al, 1997; Stichweh, 2002; Werron, 2018, Chapter 9 in this volume). Yet the peculiar differentiation of the global political system into such units may have to do with peculiarities of power as a medium of communication: Power means to control someone else's actions through the threat of sanctions (Luhmann, 1979). It therefore presupposes a certain social proximity, for instance, to allow one to observe obedience or resistance. Although power may of course be used to establish hierarchies and chains of command, there are limits to the spatial expansion and social inclusiveness of such concatenations.

The analysis of the impact of symbolically generalized media yields some insights into the globalizing dynamics associated with modern society in general. It also helps us to understand why different social fields are more or less amenable to globalization. It does not, however, provide many clues as to specific historic developments, particularly concerning innovations of 'distributive' media of communication. In order to bring this aspect into relief, we need to consider how the differentiation of social structures impinges on the likelihood of long-distance contacts.

The argument that social differentiation entails the spatial expansion of relationships was originally put forward by Georg Simmel: differentiation means that formerly homogeneous social groups become more heterogeneous. New distinctions make people who used to be quite similar more and more different, and individualization is thus increased. The differentiation of social structures therefore 'loosens the bond to what is close by, weaving instead a new bond – real and ideal – to what is further away' (Simmel, 1958 [1908]: 530). In order to find a match for one's increasingly idiosyncratic combination of traits, the individual is driven to look for contacts beyond the social environment at hand.

This argument can be generalized beyond its focus on individuals and their group affiliations. Interests that motivate social contacts beyond 'what is close by' are related to subsystems of society that generate their own and very specific criteria of relevance. Science is a case in point, exhibiting both a long history of long-distance contacts and a more recent increase of differentiation through the establishments of new disciplines. Particularly in the late nineteenth and early twentieth centuries the globalization of science was driven by the increasing differentiation of the scientific field in specialized sub-disciplines, which lend new momentum to the institutionalization of communicative relationships beyond national borders (Stichweh, 2000, 2003). Echoing Simmel's argument, ethnologist Fredrik Barth describes the situation of the scientific specialist as follows: 'A scholar of Ugric languages wishing to discuss his latest paper on the structure of conditional clauses cannot go next door: like the lonely whales of Antarctica searching for a mate, he must seek a suitable partner for his task widely through the seas of society' (Barth, 1978: 168). The more specialized scientific interests become, the more likely that they require long-distance contacts between scientists. Among the structural consequences of the increasing internal differentiation of the system of science that became more and more salient after 1780 were the emergence of today's scientific disciplines, the coupling of research and higher education in universities and the increasingly specialized communication through journals (Stichweh, 2001).

Differentiation thus gives rise to new criteria of difference and similarity that stimulate long-distance communication to establish relationships with other like units. A slightly different manifestation of such a development has taken place in the political realm. The affinity between political regimes and communication technology is well established. Its most salient feature is how communication technology bolstered the *internal* integration of political units: Writing, in particular, offered entirely new opportunities for political integration and accordingly was a prerequisite for large empires (Innis, 1972). Later on, innovations such as telegraphy were employed as effective instruments of imperial control across distances (Wenzlhuemer, 2013: ch 4; Winseck and Pike, 2007). Telecommunication served to enhance the administrative power of colonial regimes but also gave their opponents a new instrument to gain and spread knowledge (Headrick, 2010). In modernity, both the 'imagination' of a national collective and the power structures of the territorial rule of nation states were bolstered by the immediacy of nationally focused channels of mass communication (Anderson, 1983; Deutsch, 1963). The expansion and the eventual climax of the global reach of colonial rule around 1900, as well as its decline and the concomitant rise of the nation state fall into a historic period marked by the increasing salience of technologies of long-distance communication (Go, 2011: ch 6; Wimmer and Feinstein, 2010; Wimmer and Min, 2006).

The internal communicative integration of political units is a prerequisite for their being distinguishable from other units. In addition, according to Simmel's argument, we should also be able to observe an increase of *external* relationships among the differentiated units. Around the mid-nineteenth century in particular there was an 'explosive acceleration' of social change in Europe, coupled with an 'unprecedented projection overseas' (Bright and Geyer, 2007: 69). The reasons for this are as manifold as the causes of capitalism. In addition to technologies such as the telegraph underpinning the new efforts to 'coordinate interactions *within* the world' (Geyer and Bright, 1995: 1047), the increasing competition among the emerging nation-cum-colonial states of Western Europe was the major driving force. The emerging differentiation of the world political system into discrete national units that basically share the same characteristics resulted in convergences not only of institutional structures but also of expansionary interests. Eventually, of course, it led to the breakdown of the colonial system and to the emergence of a great number of newly independent nation states after decolonization. These changes in the structure and scope of the nation state point to a profound transformation or 'update' of the Westphalian model (Maier, 2014).

The timing and the extent of that update is revealed by the structural analysis of international relations. In his analysis of alliance, trade and IGO networks between 1816 and 2001 (Maoz, 2010: ch 3) shows that the density of interstate relationships has increased, particularly with respect to the affiliation with intergovernmental organizations (IGOs). This development, which took off in the second half of the nineteenth century (see Koch, Chapter 6 in this volume), was given additional momentum by the founding of the League of Nations in 1922 and of the United Nations in 1947. From the perspective of differentiation theory, the IGO affiliation network is the organizational equivalent to long-distance contacts based on heterogeneity: nation states form relationships based either on the most general shared feature of being a member of the international system or on specific interests such as the coordination of transport and communication policies. Through the thus established interstate network, 88% of possible ties among states were already realized by the end of the nineteenth century (Beckfield, 2010: 1040).

These examples from the realms of science and politics reveal a peculiar structural pattern. The dynamics of the long twentieth century are characterized by processes of further and increased differentiation *within* subsystems of society. This stands in contrast to previous phases of globalization, notably the European expansion of the fifteenth and sixteenth centuries. This expansion and the new 'plus ultra' worldview underpinning it (Jochum, 2017) were already consequences of the shift towards functional differentiation and of the concomitant globalization of economic, political and religious networks of communication. Yet it seems that this early phase of globalization is best understood in terms of the 'specific universalism' of function systems (Luhmann, 1997b: 375) that transcends territorial boundaries and symbolic limitations and has thereby spurred efforts to eliminate any zones of ignorance and neglect, both socially and geographically ('*hic sunt leones*'). Empires are a case in point, insofar as they integrated economic, political and religious relationships across large distances but each of these spheres exhibited relatively low internal differentiation.

The specification of communication had long driven the expansion of its social and geographical reach, particularly in the cases of political power and economic transactions, but also of science and religion. From the mid-nineteenth century onwards, the increasing structural differentiation within established global fields gained greater prominence and provided new momentum to the globalization of (specific) social relationships. The emerging heterogeneity of social roles associated with differentiated domains dramatically increased the value of communication technologies capable of bridging spatial distances. It was thus a period of 'pluralizing' rather than 'concentrating' globalization – that is, a period of elaborating differences and distinctions within the subsystems of world society (see Osterhammel, 2016b: 815). This development was underpinned by a rapidly growing organizational field: Public administrations, central banks, universities and other organizations spread around the world, while genuinely global actors such as churches and intergovernmental organizations provided arenas for establishing and stabilizing relationships across distances.[3]

From the perspective of the theory of societal differentiation, the differentiation *within* globalizing subsystems of world society sets the long twentieth century apart from previous periods in which the establishment and expansion of global subsystems has played a more prominent role. Further and more comprehensive analyses of this aspect will need to address pertinent developments in other fields, such as the economy, law, education and the arts, in which we should be able to observe increasing international differentiation during that period of time as well.

From adaptation to fusion

In the course of the nineteenth century, the immediacy of telecommunication and the increasing interconnectedness through the communication media of subsystems has raised the integration of world society to a new level – not in terms of unified and homogenous social structures or a solidary world community, but rather in terms of a fusion of horizons of meaning. That development took place first in Europe, where the reckless imposition of European power onto the colonies was supported and indeed preceded by a worldview that fostered expansion and the inclusion of new perspectives (Jochum, 2017). The paramount importance of Europe's territorial-political and cultural expansion during that time is hard to deny, and it is not a matter of Eurocentrism to acknowledge the 'centrality' and even 'superiority' of Europe during that period of history (Osterhammel, 2014: xx). Although functional differentiation was not a European invention, its worldwide diffusion was greatly accelerated by both colonial politics and increasing communicative interconnectedness.

The expansion of functionally specific communication on the one hand and the immediacy of mass communication on the other contributed to first calling into question and eventually eroding societal boundaries that had hitherto been able to sustain a plurality of forms of differentiation among societies that seemed to be clearly distinguishable.[4] Depending on their degree of globalization, economic, political and other relationships grew more and more incongruent. It might still have been a reasonable belief at the beginning of the nineteenth century that the distance between China and Europe was big enough to warrant indifference, such that, when George Earl of Macartney, ambassador of George III, visited Emperor Qianlongin in the year 1793, the latter could still afford to blithely ignore the status of the British king and to show virtually no interest in economic exchange. But soon economic transactions as well as military clashes such as the Opium Wars made it impossible to ignore the world beyond the perceived borders of Chinese society.

In many cases colonial and imperialist power thus enforced the dismantling of walls and borders and the increasing entanglement of formerly isolated cultures and societies. However, in some cases, such as Siam, it also occurred without manifest violence or continued even after direct pressure had subsided. In any case, the expansionary thrust of the 'European' world society made it impossible to understand any country or region of the world in complete isolation from the rest of it. Even where substantial efforts were made to fend off foreign influence, such as Japan's *sakoku* ('closed country') policy, they were already based on a new understanding of one's position in the world and often faded away towards the end of the nineteenth century. As a result, a pattern of 'asymmetrical reference density' (Osterhammel, 2014: 911–14) prevailed: Major parts of the world were either forced or persuaded to observe closely the developments of Western Europe.

The broadening of the horizons of social meaning in all parts of the world had significant consequences, in phenomenological terms, for what is (somewhat ambitiously) called 'global consciousness' and, in structural terms, for social evolution. Before a 'world without others' (Tomlinson, 1994) became thinkable as yet another and more demanding phenomenology of the global, some kind of 'consciousness of the world as a whole' (Robertson, 1992) materialized in the less demanding form of the awareness of others within the same social world. Whether those others are perceived as strange, or as either superior or inferior, can only be established against the backdrop of a shared horizon of experience and action. Even substantial asymmetries do not deny but rather presuppose such a shared horizon. As the articulation of meaning includes differences and distinctions, a convergent horizon of meaning by no means implies a commonly shared worldview, but rather the awareness of other meaningful views of 'the' world.

As a structural correlate of the fusion of horizons of meaningful action into a singular global frame of reference, the single most important novelty in terms of societal evolution was the fact that boundaries that had hitherto separated one society from another became pluralized and therefore ceased to be meaningful as a distinction between a societal system and its environment:

> Neither archaic societies ... nor the non-European civilizations could regard the European bourgeois society and its colonial expansion as an environment which called for adaptation; for not only did they lack the capacity to adapt and to persist but also because that environment could not be kept at a distance, could not remain an environment because one wanted to be like it. (Luhmann, 2017: 729)

It could be added that even the desire *not* to be like them does not change the picture if, for instance, difference is pursued through emphasizing (and thus reinventing) a tradition, which hitherto had been taken for granted, with reference to something else. The less plausible it becomes to understand 'society' as a clearly demarcated unity that could refer selectively to its environment, the more salient become other, intrasocietal ways of establishing identity and difference, for example the less territorially bound and more fluid concept of 'culture' (Luhmann, 1995c).

When societies cease to be able to insulate themselves from communication that could previously be externalized, the only possible framework that could accommodate and encompass all social structures and all specialized fields of action – each drawing their own boundaries more or less independently of the political ones – is a single global social system. Evolution then cannot operate on and among different societies providing sources of variation anymore. Instead, evolution can only be the evolution of world society (Stichweh, 2007: 538). If multiple societies can no longer serve as the vehicles of evolutionary processes, neither further expansion nor the diffusion of innovations are available as problem-solving mechanisms; instead answers to problems of internal integration and of adaption to the only remaining environment, the physical one, must be produced within world society itself (Luhmann, 2017: 446).

The disappearance of individual units of evolutionary processes seems to be problematic because impasses and failures immediately concern the only social system there is. The developments discussed in the previous sections hint at how mechanisms of social evolution in world society are reinforced, particularly in terms of the variation of structures, one of the three mechanisms of evolution besides selection and stabilization (Luhmann, 1997b: ch 3).

First, due to the perceived simultaneity of events across the globe, it appears that more and more things happen at the same time. That increases the potential for evolution because the more things happen simultaneously, the less they can be planned and brought in line with prior expectations and planning (Luhmann, 1975d). Acceleration thus means more room for evolutionary variation.

Second, variation of social structures was also increased by a new tolerance, sometimes even a preference, for novelty. The topic is an old one from a European perspective – an appetite for novelty is certainly not exclusive to the long twentieth century. However, changes were quite suddenly adopted and sought after in many countries that had for a long time resisted change. In Japan and Thailand, for instance, the nineteenth century brought reforms that in those countries in particular cannot be explained by the exogenous influence of imperialism. Rather, those as well as other countries suddenly changed course and began to follow a path which made novelty desirable – rather than dangerous and reproachable (Luhmann, 1995b). That holds not just for the arts and for science but also for politics: the idea of a democratic opposition, a success story of the last 150 years, has turned the ability and indeed the obligation to say 'no' into a political institution – with profound consequences around the world.

If societal evolution into modernity began with the discoveries of undesired truths and unexpected continents shaking up the traditional worldview, it has since institutionalized an unprecedented tolerance for novelty. With negation being the basic operation of change and evolution in society, it therefore stands to reason that evolution has since then accelerated. However, the fact that there is no more sociality outside world society also means that evolution can no longer select from the models of a range of different societies. Luhmann argues that the reduction of a plurality to one single society as the arena and carrier of evolution is a risky development (Luhmann, 1972: 337; 2017: 295). That risk cannot be mitigated by the mere fact that variations are increasingly produced. But it finds a partial solution in the fact that variation is also contained by subsystems of society. In the area of knowledge in particular, the early nineteenth century marks the end of an encompassing evolution of ideas that could still be regarded as a single field and controlled by religious and moral considerations. That unitary model has since then largely been replaced by the evolution of separate knowledge domains: the trajectories of economic and political thought, of fads and fashion – in sports, in the arts, and in the mass media – are no longer coordinated by any central value or societal institution. Instead they are subject to dynamics internal to the respective subsystems and domains of knowledge, dynamics that show more and more consistency or at least interdependence across national boundaries.

Conclusion

A sociological perspective on the recent history of world society only begins with observing which kinds of social change occurred during a particular period of time. Not change as such, but – to borrow Huntington's (1971) formulation – the 'change to change' is pertinent. In other words, the sequence and timing of events and innovations is not as relevant as the question as to what extent they crystallize into new structures that alter the chances of future events.

Based on the angles provided by communication, differentiation and evolutionary theories, some general arguments can be derived from the historical observations of social change in the long twentieth century. The empirical evidence suggests that both the mutual differentiation (*Ausdifferenzierung*) of function systems and their internal structuration (*Binnendifferenzierung*) served as engines of globalization. It is worth separating these two aspects because central aspects of functional differentiation had evolved long before the modern forms of internal structuration of subsystems were realized. Internal differentiation was facilitated, maybe even driven by processes of 'network compression' that were enabled by the technologies of transport and communication of the late nineteenth century. The increased communicative connectedness provided by telecommunication and by differentiated role structures and knowledge domains also changed the parameters of societal evolution. In many respects, the early phases of the long twentieth century appear to have already foreshadowed the features and consequences of globalization that became more prominent later on. From the perspective of historical sociology, the novelties and the continuities of that long century are thus best addressed and explained as part of the somewhat longer history of modern world society.

Some of the most significant developments had their origins in the previous expansion of European society, particularly of political and economic spheres of influence and domination, or in technological innovations associated with industrialization. Notwithstanding the Eurocentrist bias of those developments, they ultimately resulted in a more polycentric world society in which centre/periphery relationships are far less uniform (for example, in science and religion), and which has institutionalized measures of (formal) equality within political units but also amongst them (for example, within the international system of nation states). A closer inspection of the empirical evidence is still called for, especially regarding the shape and impact of those developments in different world regions and across various social arenas. The dialogue between sociological and historical research thus needs to continue – and not in a manner in which the historians simply 'carry grist to the sociologists' mills' (Osterhammel, 2016a: 25). Occasionally they might also throw some sand in the wheels of the theoretical machinery. But more importantly, the historians' sand may give the sociological conceptual wheels more empirical traction.

Notes

[1] Regarding the problem of periodization in global history see Epple (Chapter 3 in this volume).

[2] See Go (Chapter 5 in this volume) for an elaboration and application of global field theory.

[3] A more comprehensive analysis would therefore take into account another form of differentiation: the differentiation of 'levels' of social systems from 'micro' to 'macro'. Luhmann (1975c) distinguishes between interaction, organization and society and argues that those three types of social systems become more detached in the course of societal evolution. Considering the extensive 'webbing' (Geyer and Bright, 1995: 1047) occurring during the second half of the nineteenth century, it may well be that not only the *idea* of 'networks' but also 'the network' as a type of social system had its historical roots here (see Holzer, 2011).

[4] The seeming self-sufficiency of some societies up until the nineteenth century obviously cannot mean communicative or material autonomy. Thus even though there are good reasons to avoid speaking of separate societies from a sociological perspective, prevailing self-descriptions in terms of social identities in a global environment still enjoyed some plausibility, particularly with respect to China.

5

Field Theory and Global Transformations in the Long Twentieth Century

Julian Go

Introduction

Pierre Bourdieu developed his theory of social fields through his analyses of religion, art and social class in European societies. But how might this theory address the larger theme of the present volume? In other words, how might Bourdieusian field theory account for the 'emergence and transformation' of international orders – as Albert and Werron (Chapter 1 in this volume) put it? And how might this field-theoretic account differ from other theoretical approaches? This chapter offers some preliminary thoughts on these questions by reference to three transformative processes (or macrohistorical turning points) during past two centuries that conventional historiographies recognize as crucial for the current political order: the expansion of colonial empires during the phase of 'high imperialism' (roughly late nineteenth to early twentieth century), the two world wars (1914–45) and the post-war end of formal colonial empires heralding the rise to dominance of the modern nation state (1946–present).

These three macrohistorical turning points might readily be narrated in terms of an array of other theoretical approaches. Of particular interest here might be differentiation and social evolution theory as discussed in other chapters of this volume (Holzer, Chapter 4; Stetter, Chapter 8). For instance, the first process under scrutiny – the period of 'high imperialism' starting in the nineteenth century – might be thought of as the creation of a system of 'stratified differentiation' (Albert et al, 2013a). Through the imperial expansion of Western states to encompass nearly the entire world, a stratified order of imperial states and their colonies was created. Similarly, the postwar end of empires and the creation of a global order of nation states in the twentieth century might be thought of as 'segmented differentiation': the hierarchical empires collapsed, yielding a system of nominally sovereign and equal nation states (Albert et al, 2013a; see also Luhmann, 1997a: 72). Or the process might be thought of as an intensified period of 'internal differentiation' by which new international organizations proliferated alongside nation states and the development of new 'practices, rules, and organizations' associated with new primary institutions (Stetter, Chapter 8 in this volume). Relatedly, drawing upon Holzer (Chapter 4 in this volume), the end of empires and the creation of the interstate order might be theorized as concomitant with the universalization of communication and thus the creation of a new global consensus around human rights and principles of national self-determination.

For this task, there is some guidance in existing scholarship but not much. Part of the problem is that Bourdieu's social theory is typically seen as a theory of social reproduction rather than transformation (Hilgers and Mangez, 2015: 11–2; Gorski, 2013). Furthermore, Bourdieu's field theory has been developed in relation to domestic-level processes, not international, transnational or global processes. IR scholars have indeed enlisted Bourdieu in their analyses and applied them to international issues, but they take from his larger theoretical conceptual apparatus only certain concepts, like *habitus* and *practice*, as a warrant for conducting micro-level ethnographic research in a discipline whose main concepts preclude such micro-level work (Adler-Nissen, 2012; Bigo, 2011). This is generative for IR research, but it leaves Bourdieu's field theory unattended. Only recently have some sociological works tried to apply Bourdieu's field theory to global processes.[1] Even then, Bourdieu's field theory has yet to be mobilized to apprehend macro-historical turning points such as the expansion or decline of empires. The goal of this chapter is to explore how Bourdieusian field theory might be deployed to make sense of global dynamics: in particular, the three transformations in global political order noted earlier: the rise of imperialism, world war and the decline of empires generating the proliferation of nation states. This, in turn, will help us better map the points of differentiation between field-theoretic approaches and other approaches discussed in this volume.

Field theory and the global political field

A field-theoretic account of global change requires, first and foremost, some notion of a 'field' that is global in scale. But for this, we must recognize that not all relations are 'fielded'. Fields only exist when social actors struggle or compete with each other over different forms of capital. If academics compete for status, there is an academic field. If religious leaders compete for followers, there is a religious field (see Bourdieu, 1991b). And so on. Without competition or struggle over capital, there are no fields. Fields, by definition, are spaces of struggle between actors over various species of capital. A field is 'a space of conflict and competition, the analogy here being with a battlefield, in which participants vie to establish monopoly over the species of capital effective in it' (Bourdieu and Wacquant, 1992: 17).[2]

To approach a field-theoretic account of global change, we must also recognize other key elements of Bourdieusian field theory. First, while fields are spaces of struggle, they are not anarchic. Fields consist of objective relations between actors (the field of positions) and the subjective and cultural forms of those relations. The cultural forms include the *illusio*: that is, the belief in the value of the game that is being played. They also include the 'rules of the game' to which actors (or 'players') adhere and which have been inculcated through socialization, thus embedded in actors' *habitus*. The rules might be taken for granted and therefore not questioned: part of the field's '*doxa*', or shared silent assumptions about what is acceptable in the struggle or not. Or those rules can be discursively elaborated and formally codified as law. Either way, actors struggle over capital but they do according to basic rules in the field. Fields thus have some basic order that transcends the sum of its parts. A field is a 'highly structured reality' in its own right (Bourdieu, 1989: 19).

Second, the types of capital over which actors struggle can be multitudinous. Economic capital is one form of capital at stake in many fields, but it is only one 'species of power' among other possible ones (Bourdieu and Wacquant, 1992: 97). Others might be 'cultural capital' or 'spiritual capital' in religious fields (Verter, 2003). The existence and values of these types of capital vary according to the field in question (there would not be 'spiritual capital' in the academic field) but, in any case, they can be just as important as 'material' capital like money, not least because they are potentially convertible to other forms of capital – cultural capital can help one accrue social capital, and so on (Desan, 2013). This means, relatedly, that fields are about *both* culture and meaning on the one hand as well as power and hierarchy on the other. Bourdieu does not oppose culture to power (Swartz, 1997). On the one hand, hierarchy and power are built into fields. The relative distribution of these types of capital defines the hierarchy of the field. Those who have the most capital in any given field are the dominant; those with little or none are the dominated. On the other hand, field hierarchies are sustained and reproduced through cultural processes – not least, legitimation. Bourdieu theorizes this as 'symbolic capital'. Those who are dominant in the field legitimate their monopoly over capital by adopting a particular 'stance' of worthiness. Symbolic capital is a type of prestige that accrues to the dominant and gives them the privilege of dominating (Bourdieu, 1977: 197). As Swartz (1997: 92) summarizes, Bourdieu insists that 'brute force or material possession are seldom sufficient for the effective exercise of power' and symbolic capital is often necessary 'for the effective exercise of political and economic power'.

How, then, might a global political field – or interstate field – be conceptualized? Briefly put, if we speak of such a global political field today, in the twenty-first century, we would say that this is a field of actors struggling with each other for various forms of capital. This field has its own 'rules' or terms of struggle ('norms'). The forms of capital at stake include economic capital (wealth), political capital (such as allies), cultural capital (recognition), symbolic capital (legitimacy) or what is elsewhere called 'security capital' (Go, 2008), that is geopolitical security. Other actors besides national states populate this field too, such as corporations, intergovernmental organizations (IGOs), international non-governmental organizations (INGOs), non-governmental organizations (NGOs), or even social movements and nationalist struggles. These become part of the global political field only if and when they end up conflicting with each other and national states over capital. Otherwise, they are better theorized in terms of the fields in which they typically operate and which might overlap with or intersect with the global political field but which are not necessarily the same – namely, a global economic field ('the world economy'), a transnational field of humanitarian organizations (Krause, 2014), and so on.[3] As we will see later, though, anticolonial nationalist movements do become important for understanding significant transformations in the global field of the twentieth century.

Two further related points warrant attention. First, the global interstate field is different from the national fields that Bourdieu tended to analyse in his own research. The main actors are not individuals but states and organizations. Some analyses could of course focus upon individuals – such as diplomats, state elites, managers, or whatever – but in this particular conceptualization of the global political field, at stake are states. It is an inter-*state* field. And, unlike more nationally based fields, there is no meta-capital or 'statist capital', because there is no world government that has come to monopolize the legitimate use of physical and symbolic capital.

The second crucial point is that this global interstate field is historically specific. That is, it is different from previous fields on the global stage. The current global political field of nation states used to be, until the mid-twentieth century, a field of empires: an inter-*imperial* field rather than an inter-*national* one. That inter-imperial field had different actors: not national states but empire states. It also had different norms or 'rules of the game'. Colonizing and ruling foreign societies was an accepted part of inter-imperial competition. It was part of the *doxa*: a taken-for-granted rule or 'norm'. Another part of that *doxa* was a set of racialized assumptions about who could or could not govern themselves: colonized peoples were assumed to be incapable and inferior in terms of their civilizational status (Jackson, 1993: 116–18). And while economic capital and security capital were at stake in this field of struggle among empires, so too was 'colony capital': having colonies brought prestige and wealth, and added security – and so was a highly valued convertible capital. Symbolic competition was also a part of this struggle. In the nineteenth and early twentieth centuries, Great Britain and the United States portrayed themselves as superior for their wealth, civilization and modernity, positioning themselves in direct opposition to the French, Spanish or Chinese (and vice versa). These mark attempts to accrue symbolic capital so as to legitimate imperial domination to weaker peoples, accruing their support, and thereby providing empires with political capital for their competition with each other (Table 5.1).

The contemporary field of national states is different. First, the main actors are not empires but national states. There are also additional international organizations like the United Nations, the International Monetary Fund, and the World Health Organization that play a role in the system as never before (though the degree to which these are the same political field as national states is an empirical question). Second, the rules of the game have changed: it is no longer acceptable to directly colonize other territories against their will. This even became institutionalized. In 1960, the United Nations adopted Resolution 1514, which declared colonialism a 'denial of human rights', contrary to the Charter of the UN and 'an impediment to the promotion of world peace and co-operation', They too use anticolonial rhetoric as a form of capital. Hence another difference in the present global-political

Table 5.1: Inter-imperial versus interstate global fields

Field	Dominant actors[a]	Rules of struggle	Capital
Inter-imperial (to mid-twentieth century)	Empire states	Colonization legitimate	Security capital Economic capital Political capital *Colony capital*
Interstate (mid-twentieth century to present)	National states	Colonization illegitimate	Security capital Economic capital Political capital *Pro-sovereignty capital*

(a) Other actors like trading companies or nationalist movements are also important possible players, but 'dominant actors' here refers to the main units that define the field, hence the units which other actors have to compete or contend with in their struggles.

field: there is no longer any 'colony capital'. If anything, a stance of anticolonialism, or rather a posture of supporting national sovereignty, is itself a form of capital (Go, 2008). During the Cold War, the US and USSR competed with each other to position themselves as more anticolonial and in support of national sovereignty. Today, anticolonialism has become a new discourse which pretenders to power – like India and China – try to deploy amidst their strategic positioning in the field (Miller, 2013).

The question of how this field transformed to the current field of nation states – with different actors and rules – is one question among other related ones that can also be fruitfully thought of in field-theoretic terms. And it raises the broader question: how might field theory account for transformation, if at all? Bourdieu never systematically sketched a clear theory of social change. But his various works do show that a field-theoretic account of social change is possible.[4] To be clear, such a theory would not be teleological. Keeping in line with Bourdieu's analytic sensitivity to contingency and relational dynamics, any Bourdieusian theory of change would avoid determinism, and rather specify mechanisms of change and outline possible directions or forms of change. First, in a Bourdieusian field-theoretic account, the main mechanism is struggle over capital. As actors strive to obtain more capital, the possibility for change is opened up. Second, these struggles can take different forms, and yield different types of change.

One is a 'succession' struggle: 'challengers' contend with dominant groups (or 'incumbents') to accumulate more capital and essentially seek to replace them (Swartz, 1997: 125, Bourdieu, 1992: 124). When that group is successful, there is a change in the field – new actors replace older ones as the dominant group – but the change is not structural. New groups enter a different position than before, but the overarching distribution of capital – the structure of the field – is not fundamentally altered.

The other form of struggle is a 'subversion' struggle: challengers compete with incumbents for capital but they do so in part by challenging the principles of the field that had been functioning to maintain the existing field hierarchy. They challenge which capital is valued, what constitutes symbolic capital, or even the very rules of the game (Bourdieu, 1992: 121). In various works, Bourdieu shows how this happens in fields like religion or art, when dominant actors' very 'monopoly over symbolic power' is often challenged by 'heretics' who propose 'heterodox' principles to undo the established 'orthodoxy' (Bourdieu, 1991b: 25; 1992: 72–7). By these subversion struggles not everything is challenged. Some elements of the *doxa* subtending oppositions in the field – which Bourdieu calls the '*illusio*' – do survive (Bourdieu, 1992: 227–8). But subversion struggles do much more than lead to the replacement of one group with another at the top. They can transform what should count as capital in the first place, overthrowing the very principles by which capital had been distributed in the field and hence the premise of the existing hierarchy. The 'principles of hierarchical differentiation' in the field are potentially overthrown, and in turn 'the very shape and divisions of the field become a central stake' (Bourdieu, 1992: 17–18, 127).

Global political transformations, 1800s–1960s

We can now conceptualize three transformations in the global order of the past centuries in field-theoretic terms: imperial expansion, war and the creation of an international order to replace the previous inter-imperial order.

Imperial expansion and war: struggles for succession

In the late nineteenth century, European and Asian powers embarked upon new territorial conquests. This has been known as the period of 'high imperialism'. In field-theoretic terms, this imperial expansion would be conceptualized as a process of field conquest or articulation. Imperialism took a number of different forms, from settlement to treaties of alliance and indirect rule. What was involved in some cases was a direct replacement of local fields (native societies) with settlers. This was a *conquest* mode of change by which local fields were erased. But in many other cases, imperial expansion involved *articulation*: colonial annexation followed by the tying of local political forms to the imperial states' control. 'Indirect rule', for example, did not involve replacing local political systems by the imperial power. It meant enlisting pre-established leaders (for example 'chiefs') as allies while keeping traditional forms of local society intact. Of course, this typically involved some changes in local society; and over time, especially as capitalist relations took over, native society did begin to slowly change (or 'develop', in the words of imperialists). But the point here is to avoid reducing imperialism and the incorporation of local societies into the world system as a simple process of erasure and takeover, as a diffusion of world society, or as differentiation. We must rather recognize that the non-Western peripheral societies that empire states seized in the nineteenth century also had local pre-existing fields – and sometimes trans-societal field relations – and that conquest and control was a complex process of articulating different fields together.[5]

More than just conceptualizing imperial expansion as a matter of field expansion or articulation, a field-theoretic approach pinpoints the determinants or causes of imperialism as matter of competition for capital. In all fields, actors struggle for capital – that is, position. They seek advantage and material or symbolic rewards. This struggle is what drives field dynamics, and it is this struggle that drove imperial expansion in the late nineteenth century. Here, more conventional accounts of imperial expansion offered in the rich historiography of empire are fitting: they show that Western and Asian powers sought out new territories for markets, raw materials, naval bases and prestige. A key example is the 'Scramble for Africa'. In field-theoretic terms, this inter-imperial competition that drove expansion would be conceptualized as a struggle for capital and its multiple forms (for example, economic capital, security capital, cultural capital, and so on). For instance, states sometimes colonized new territory not only for raw materials (economic capital) but also for status (symbolic capital). They also took new territory to prevent rivals from obtaining the capital offered by the territory: a relational struggle for strategic advantage.[6]

That imperialism was driven by the competition for capital is seen not only in existing historiographies. It is also seen in existing quantitative studies on the determinants of Western overseas imperialism over the past centuries. Using time-series data on rates of colonization and both national-level and global-level variables, Go (2011, 2014) and Edwards and Go (2019) find that the most important variable for explaining imperialism is hegemonic competition. Over the past three centuries, when the distribution of capital among the core states (the main actors in the field of power) was relatively equal (that is, a multipolar condition of fields), states were more likely to turn to imperial aggression overseas via colonization. When the distribution of capital was less equal (that is, when a single state dominated the field – a hegemon), colonization in the field was less likely. This is exactly how to account for the 'high imperialism' of the late nineteenth century: the global field was at its most competitive in terms of the distribution of capital. Alternatively, in the previous decades (the mid-nineteenth century), the global field was less competitive, and so rates of colonization were in fact much lower.[7]

In short, imperial expansion can be theorized as a struggle over capital, and hence, specifically, a struggle of *succession*. In the mid-nineteenth century, the British Empire was the dominant player in the global field, obtaining the greatest shares of economic capital and other forms. But rivals sought to obtain their own slice of the pie by taking colonies, in effect to replace Britain as the dominant player. Violent conflict between the dominant states, that is *world war*, can also be thought of in these terms. World war in a field-theoretic perspective would be a resort to violence as competition heightens to breaking point. This is most likely to happen when the distribution of capital in the field is more even (multipolarity). The Napoleonic Wars at the turn of the nineteenth century can be interpreted in this way. So can the wars of the early twentieth century. In the late nineteenth to early twentieth century, the multipolar distribution of capital first led to heightened competition for colony capital. But as colonies overseas were taken, leaving less open territory for core powers to colonize, they had to turn to territories already claimed or occupied by other states. This in turn generated war. DuBois (1915) long ago argued that this sort of competition drove World War I, and World War II can be seen similarly: Hitler, not able to take colonies abroad, sought them *within* Europe.

We can now summarize. Fields are sites of struggle for capital. In the late nineteenth century, as states competed for capital in struggles of succession, they first sought colonies – hence imperial expansion – and then violent war against each other. In turn, war 'reset' the field. World war ended up serving to redistribute capital, making the United States the winner of the struggle for succession. The field resorted to a unipolar/hegemonic state. To the victor went the capital.

Decolonization and struggles of subversion

The foregoing story upholds Bourdieu's principle that the main mechanism of field dynamics is struggle for capital. But another way in which fields might change is not just through struggles in the field of power – that is between core powers – but also struggles that involve weaker groups in the global field. This is how decolonization and hence the radical restructuring of the field into nation states happened. This change was different from the change resulting from world war. Whereas that change involved the replacement of one power with another in the global field, decolonization and the creation of an interstate order brought with it a change in the very structure and principles of the field: that is, entirely new 'rules of the game' whereby colonization was no longer legitimate, and states had to be organized as national, as opposed to colonial or imperial, states. This resulted from a subversion struggle that began in local colonial fields and then spread to the global level.

Colonialism itself generated the conditions for change. As noted, imperialism articulated local fields with the imperial field: local structures were harnessed for the political purposes of rule by the imperial state. Doing so involved incorporating local colonized peoples into the colonial state. By the early twentieth century, these local colonized political elites across different colonies and empires had begun to compete with state officials from the metropole for more control over government. Many of them had been educated in the colony or in the metropole as a result of colonial policies aimed at supplying the colonial state with native labour. They represented a rising middle class of westernized intellectuals, lawyers and bureaucrats who sought higher positions of power, more political representation and control over the state. This was a succession struggle occurring at the local level, intra-colonial fields. Within the colonies, colonized elites sought to obtain more capital from colonizers and ultimately replace them.

Yet as metropoles continually frustrated these movements, the anticolonial struggles for succession eventually became struggles of *subversion*. In this form of struggle, the dominated challenge the incumbents' position as they do in a succession struggle but they challenge them by questioning the very principles in the field that had been functioning to maintain the field hierarchy. As anticolonial nationalists sought independence, they likewise challenged the idea that non-white peoples were incapable of self-government. They challenged the racial *doxa* of the colonial era – that is, they challenged the 'rules of the game'. Of course, the *illusio* remained in these movements. Anticolonial nationalism assumed that there should be 'nations' that map onto state boundaries. But anticolonial nationalism nonetheless challenged the orthodoxy of the colonial and imperial fields and posited a radical heterodoxy – namely, that all peoples around the world,

Figure 5.1: Number of first anticolonial nationalist events in colonies, 1850–1990

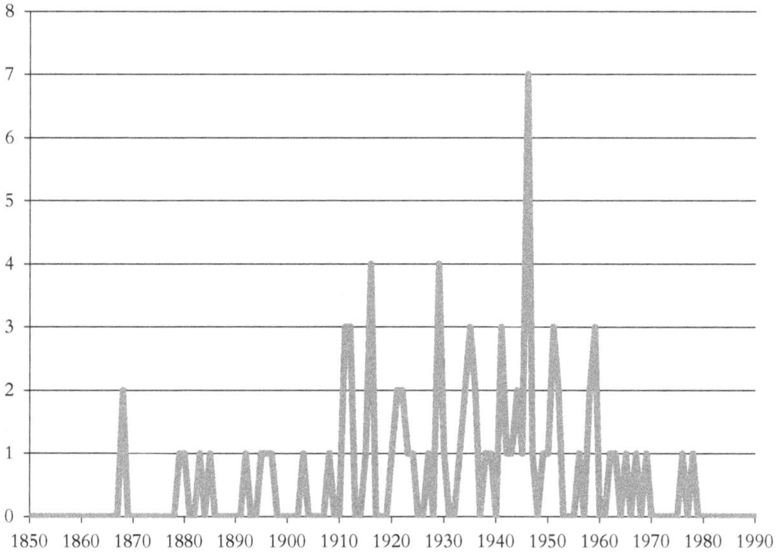

Note: This figure lists by year the number of first anticolonial events in the colonies of the formal colonial empires. The anticolonial nationalist 'event' refers to the establishment of a political party, organization or association that declares national independence as a goal; the beginning of a revolt, rebellion or political movement that declares national independence as a goal; or a declaration of independence or constitution establishing an independent national government.

Source: Go and Watson (2019)

regardless of race, were capable of nationhood, equal citizenship and self-government (Figure 5.1).[8]

Ultimately these movements were successful, partly because of the contingent relations between fields. The succession and subversion struggles began as struggles within the colonies, that is within local colonial fields. But *field homologies* or correspondences across colonies transformed these localized field struggles into trans-imperial international struggles occurring at the global scale, hence in the global political field. Despite their many differences, colonies around the world shared a structure of colonizer–colonized and metropole–colony, which is why definitionally they are 'colonies' in the first place (Osterhammel, 1999) – and which overlapped with a racialized binary of white/non-white. Colonized peoples around the world could thus find common cause. In fact, elites from different colonies came to acknowledge and recognize each other as part of the same movement and became emboldened by each other's experiences (Ballantyne and Burton, 2014: 170–81). They formed transnational alliances and forged connections with non-governmental organizations. The First Pan-African Congress in 1900, the Universal Races Congress of 1911, the First International Congress against Imperialism and Colonialism convened in Brussels in 1927, Bandung in 1955: at these and many other similar gatherings, anticolonialists consecrated their new heterodox ideologies and set the basis for a truly global movement. In 1945 Kwame Nkrumah wrote and issued a 'Declaration to the Colonial Peoples of the World' which was approved by a pan-African Congress held in Manchester in 1945. The Declaration set out the 'rights of all people to govern themselves' and affirmed 'the right of colonial peoples to control their own destiny'. It continued: 'All colonies must be free from foreign imperialist control, whether political or economic … we say to the peoples of the colonies that they must strive for these ends by all means at their disposal' (Boyce, 1999: 117). In these ways and others, anticolonial nationalists joined hands across local fields to challenge the racial orthodoxy. Along the way they, and their allies in the metropolitan fields, likewise articulated the idea of human rights and discursively tied them to the principles of national self-determination (Jensen, 2016).

As field homologies helped transform colonial struggles into a global movement, imperial powers felt new pressures. No longer just facing protests in one or another colony, they faced a global anticolonial movement that increasingly became an unprecedented threat. Furthermore, added to these pressures was inter-imperial competition. Besides their own colonial subfields, empires were also embedded in global imperial fields wherein they allied or competed with each other for economic, security and cultural capital (see Figure 5.2). But the increasingly global reach of anticolonialism added a new layer of complexity to the inter-imperial field: given that so many anticolonialists emerged, the core powers had to appeal to their interests in order to accrue political capital amidst their struggles against each other. While anticolonial nationalism for colonized and postcolonial leaders was a powerful force that could enable them to mobilize populations across religious, ethnic, gender and other lines, it also became a form of capital for imperial powers themselves. Symbolic competition among the great powers necessitated proving one's anticolonial credentials: states adopted anticolonial values as part of their effort to accumulate symbolic capital and convert it to political capital; that is, to legitimate their powerful position and win allies. Appealing to anticolonial nationalism was a new form of convertible

Figure 5.2: Imperial and colonial political fields

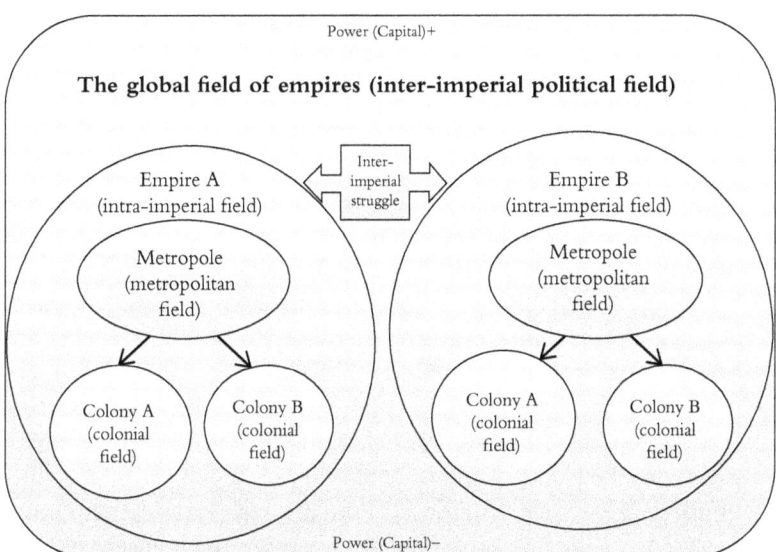

political capital: a way of winning support in wider fields of political struggle and thereby legitimating ones' position. As a result, colonialism became less an option than before. If anything, it became a liability.[9] The inter-imperial field thus became an entirely new field of nation states where colonization was no longer possible. The new 'rule' was that countries have to at least nominally respect the national sovereignty of all peoples regardless of race.

Field theory in comparison

Some of the differences between a field-theoretic approach and other possible theoretical approaches for theorizing global processes and transformations can now be briefly sketched:

- *Field theory emphasizes relationality.* Many theoretical approaches that might be enlisted for analysing global transformation are 'substantialist' in the sense that their conceptual objects are ontological entities – as in 'systems' – reducible to particular essences. World systems theory theorizes such a singular system with a singular essence (a global economic system of economic extraction from which all other patterns and relations derive). Meyer and colleagues' (1997) world society/neo-institutionalist theory posits a singular system too, though they see it as a 'society' of cultural scripts. Differentiation theory likewise posits a singular global system that is predicated upon communications and evolves – though in contingent and complex fashion – over time. Alternatively, Bourdieu's field theory is relational. 'Fields' are not like 'systems'. They are not essences. Rather, they are spaces wherein relations between groups play out; and those relations do not adduce to a singular 'system' following a singular principle by which it obtains its identity. Therefore, a field-theoretic approach to global relations and transformations would not think of 'the global' in terms of a singular system that does things – a system that differentiates, evolves or culturally shapes states. It would not begin with the notion of a singular system following a single logic or principle (of, say, economic exploitation, cultural mimicry or communication). It would rather look for multiple, intersecting and overlapping transnational fields (that is, relations of struggle), each with their own distinct distribution of capital, particular rules or norms of struggle, specific *doxa* and principles of hierarchization, and types of capital at stake.[10] It would treat the emergence, existence and substantive character of such fields as empirical questions; and it would think of them as social accomplishments rather than givens.[11]

- *Field theory and agency*. Relationalism is related to another issue: agency. In their introduction to this volume, Albert and Werron note that field-theoretic approaches direct attention to agency and practices. To be sure, Bourdieu's own studies of social fields in France place great emphasis upon the specific manoeuvres and strategies of 'players' in the field. This was seen in the analyses earlier: for instance, the transformation from empires to nation states was sparked by the political organizing and practices of anticolonial nationalists. This is one clear difference from world society/neo-institutionalist theories or differentiation theory, both of which focus upon world society and 'scripts' or 'systems' and narrate stories of global diffusion or differentiation which appear to occur behind the backs of actors.[12] But, to be clear, field theory's emphasis upon agency does not mean that field theory falls prey to reductionist theories like rational-choice theory or, its meso-level variant, realist IR theory. To the contrary, one of the implications of field theory's relationalism is that the 'actors' are always constituted by the wider field of relations of which they are a part. They do not come into the field with pre-formed identities and interests. To wit: the demands for national self-determination by anticolonial nationalists were a direct response to the colonialists' suppression of national self-determination, and still carried the colonialists' own political notions of nationhood (the *illusio* of the global political field). Similarly, metropolitan empires' interests in national self-determination for all peoples in the late twentieth century was a strategic response to the anticolonial nationalists' demands rather than an expression of the empires' presumably inherent political values (that is it was not due to 'American exceptionalism').

- *Field theory emphasizes conflicts over capital as the key principle of fields.* While there is no singular 'field' reducible to an essence, field theory does posit a specific mechanism that constitute and structure those relations: conflict over capital. By definition, fields only exist when there are these conflicts. This is one of the key points of difference between field theory and both world society theory and/or differentiation theory. Whereas the latter theories emerge from the Durkheimian–Parsonian sociological tradition rooted in late nineteenth-century theories of social evolution, Bourdieusian field theory is rooted in the conflict tradition extending back to Marx. The difference is crucial, for it means different concerns, categories and hence different conceptual tools. Differentiation theory focuses upon problems of social integration and order, and theorizes social relations as 'systems' (Albert et al, 2013a). It therefore highlights issues of values, norms and communications by which integration and order occur. Field theory, by contrast, focuses upon conflict and struggle over material or symbolic resources: not Durkheim but rather Marx, not Parsons but rather Coser, not Luhmann but rather Foucault. If 'system theory's master narrative is functional differentiation', as Holzer and colleagues (2015b: 6) aptly characterizes it, field theory's master narrative is conflict over capital.

- *Field theory and causal explanation.* Differentiation theory in the tradition of Luhmann tends towards descriptions of processes as they unfold over time rather than causal explanations. At most, as Thomas (2013) points out, differentiation theory tends towards functionalist explanations. By contrast, Bourdieu's field theory follows the critical-realist tradition of causal explanation by highlighting causal mechanisms that are typically taken by positivist approaches as invisible and hence, presumably, non-existent (Steinmetz 1998, 2007). The causal mechanism is not unlike the causal mechanism specified in the Marxist tradition: social groups struggling against each other for capital. This emphasis upon causal mechanisms not only distinguishes a field-theoretic approach from differentiation theory (or related social-evolutionary theory), but also from world society/neo-institutionalist theory that does not often specify causal mechanisms and rather describes global processes of diffusion.

None of this is to say that a field-theoretic approach is somehow preferable or superior to other approaches. It is merely to point out what a field-theoretic approach captures that other approaches might not. The blind spots of field theory as an analytic for understanding global transformation can also be elaborated. For instance, when we scale up Bourdieu's theory to the global level where the main actors are states rather than individuals, how can we conceptualize something like *habitus*? Or, to take another issue: Bourdieu's field theory of change is not deterministic or predictive. It does not predict whether succession struggles or subversion struggles will be successful. One might contend that this failure discounts Bourdieu's field theory as a *theory* of change in the first place. Still, if the point of *theory* is not to predict but to help us conceptualize and see that which we might not otherwise see, then a Bourdieusian field theory remains a theory at least in this limited sense; and it remains a theory that can help us see that changes in fields do not happen behind actors' backs – as some other theories might imply – but rather due to agents jostling and struggling for a variety of things, whether it be privileges, position, power, or – in the case of anticolonial nationalists – basic human dignity.

Notes

1. See Go (2008), Krause (2014), the essays in Go and Krause (2016), and Bernhard and Schmidt-Wellenburg (2020).
2. Werron (2015a, 2015b) usefully distinguishes between conflict and 'competition', stressing, among other things, that the latter entails a third party. Bourdieu's definition of fields does not involve as fine a distinction. Actors might conflict for capital or compete for it; either case would constitute the basis of a field. This chapter uses the terms 'competition', 'conflict' and 'struggle' more or less interchangeably.
3. For examples of religious actors in a transnational field, see Petzke (2016) and for insurgencies see Bultmann (2014).
4. A field theoretic account of social change should be differentiated from a practice-theoretic account of change. The latter has to do with how social actors might change their habitus, and it typically occurs as social actors confront new fields that first yield a 'hysterisis' of the habitus and then compels actors to possibly reflect upon and change their habitus. The former, however, is not about how individual habituses might change but how macro-level transformations – that is changes in fields – might occur.
5. This is akin to what Marx referred to as the *formal* subsumption of labour: as it expands, capital first enlists labour as it finds it before transforming it into abstract labour. Relatedly, it is akin to the 'articulation of the modes of production' in the early development of global capitalism: the tying of pre-existing forms of labour to capitalist markets. Such articulations entailed processes that at times required violence and coercion. But they also sometimes entailed slower processes of change.
6. Note that this theory of imperial expansion differs significantly from theories that emphasize the imperial states' internal needs: that is, theories that claim that

imperialism results from elites seeking to distract populations or from domestic financiers seeking outlets for capital. A field-theoretic account instead emphasizes international relations in the global field.

7. This heightened competition gets at a key variable in fields: the relative distribution of capital (Krause, 2016).

8. A time-series database on each country's first anticolonial nationalist event shows something of the growth of these movements. After the initial revolts of the Latin American republics, anticolonial nationalism erupted around the world beginning after World War II (see Figure 5.1).

9. This process, which was drawn-out and complex, is described elsewhere (Go, 2008).

10. And again, while fields are constituted by a particular logic (a logic of struggle over capital), they are not reducible to an essence; indeed, highlighting Bourdieu's relational principles (as opposed to 'substantive' theories that posit a single essence), Bourdieu at times intimates that fields do not even really exist: they are at most a heuristic for capturing certain social logics.

11. See Go and Lawson (2017b) for a discussion of how relationalism undergirds recent work in IR and historical sociology.

12. And of course one of the points of world society/neo-institutionalist theories is to claim that rational individual 'actors' are a construction of world culture; hence the agent is actually 'culture'.

6

Organization(s) of the World

Martin Koch

Introduction

In his classical text on international organization, *Swords to Ploughshares*, Inis Claude (1959: 43) stated:

> It is useful to consider the nineteenth century as the era of *preparation for* international organization, and, for this purpose, to treat 1815, the year of the Congress of Vienna, and 1914, the year of the outbreak of World War I, as its chronological boundaries. Starting thus, we establish the years which have passed since the momentous events of 1914 as the era of *establishment of* international organization, which, in these terms, comes to be regarded as a phenomenon of the twentieth century.

According to this quote, the nineteenth century was a period of war and anarchy among states and state-like entities that led to World War I. It was a period of preparation because the idea of international organization was not yet born, but rather emerged from the destructive consequences of that war. In this narrative, the foundation of the League of Nations is the starting point for the period in which the idea of organizing the international sphere was born and international organizations were established. In the second half of the twentieth century, and in particular after the end of the Cold War, international organizations emerged as 'pieces of global governance' (Karns and Mingst, 2010: 5–8) that were active in almost all policy fields. In organizing these policy fields, international organizations took over more and more extensive duties and responsibilities for their member states. However, their function was not limited to facilitating cooperation between member states. Quite the contrary; international organizations provided an action frame that served as a reference point for both states and non-state organizations.

Even though this is a very short and simplified description of the history of international organization(s), it is nevertheless widely shared by scholars in International Relations (IR). They see the twentieth century as the period of international organization and the foundation of international institutions of various kinds, most notably international organizations, that are evolving as actors in world politics in the twenty-first century.

This chapter takes a closer look at the emergence of the idea of international organization. It reflects on the actual concept of organization, which saw the light of day in the nineteenth century, and regards organization and the founding of (international) organizations as key features of global social change (see Albert and Werron, Chapter 1 in this volume). It argues that the perception of some kind of organization for the world accompanied the foundation of states from its very beginning. The emergence of states is not a precondition for international organization(s): rather, states and international organization are co-constitutive. Thus the period between the Congress of Vienna and World War I was not the period of '*preparation for* international organisation' (Claude, 1959: 43), it should rather be seen as the founding period of world organization, the phase when the idea of organizing and organizations as such emerged in almost all fields of society, or the phase in which world society turned into a world organization society. This chapter aims to make three interrelated points: (1) the idea of organizing, that is establishing order, was deeply rooted in debates among legal scholars in the nineteenth century; (2) in that period, the idea of world organization was not limited to a world of states, but contained a more comprehensive and encompassing understanding of the world; (3) organizing the world took place in different forms that are still relevant today or have been reinvigorated in recent years.

This chapter is neither a conceptual history of international organization nor a thorough analysis of debates among legal scholars in the nineteenth century. In line with the general goal of this volume it is a modest attempt to trace the idea of organizing the world and to provide a heuristic model for understanding different forms of organizing. Interestingly enough, these different forms were not merely characteristic of a short episode in the nineteenth century, only then to disappear in the twentieth. The opposite is the case. It is the Cold War that is the outlier period here, while four distinct forms of organizing the world that emerged in the nineteenth century still have a substantial impact on world politics today. To think of organizing only with reference to international organizations is therefore a rather restricted version of the conceptual richness that emerged during the nineteenth and the early twentieth centuries. The present chapter focuses on the terms 'world' and 'organization' and intends to show how different forms of organizing the world that developed in the nineteenth century still shape world politics today.

The following section begins with a discussion of the foundation of international organizations in IR and suggests that the concepts of organization and world, as set forth in nineteenth-century writings on international law, are worth a closer look. Each of the terms encompasses two different meanings: 'organization' can be regarded as the process of generating order or as the institutionalization of order; 'world' can mean either the totality of states or a community of *and* beyond states. Using these different meanings, four types of world organization are distinguished and explained – international law, international conferences, international organizations, and a world state/world statehood – and it is shown how these types are still relevant today.

Organization and world in the foundation of international organizations

Books on international organizations (such as Rittberger et al, 2011; Davies and Woodward, 2014; Archer, 2015) usually start with a rather short historical section. They consider the term 'international organization', which was invented by James Lorimer, a Scottish legal scholar (Lorimer, 1884), name a few international organizations that were founded in the second half of the nineteenth century, for example the Central Commission for Navigation on the Rhine (CCNR), the International Telegraph Union (ITU) or the Universal Postal Union (UPU), before turning to the end of World War I and the foundation of the League of Nations and the International Labour Organization (ILO) in 1919. The latter two are prominent examples for the interwar period that paved the way for the second half of the twentieth century when most international organizations, in particular the UN system, emerged. Accordingly, the nineteenth century was a period of interstate wars and anarchy among states as there was no such thing as an international organization. Lorimer shares this perception and states that 'there is no international organisation which overrides the judgement of the individual State, each State must be the judge in its own case' (Lorimer, 1884: 128) so that '[i]nternational organisation has thus no substantive value' (Lorimer, 1884: 190).

The two meanings of the term international organization mentioned earlier characterize debates in IR. First and predominantly, it is a process of coordination among states represented, for example, by international conferences, treaties, diplomatic relations and so forth. It describes how states coordinate their actions to deal with a problem in a certain policy field affecting their relations with each other. International organization, therefore, is an expression of the free will of states to act in a coherent manner to solve a common problem but, as such, it has 'no substantive value' for states. It is merely a process of problem-solving and 'not an end in itself' (Lorimer, 1884: 190). But Lorimer noticed the peril in an institutionalization of these agreements, that is, the fear of international organizations (usually used in the plural form) emerging. While international organizations are regarded as an embodiment of processes of organizing – corporate bodies, public international unions and the like are 'significant expressions of, and contributors to, the process of international organization' (Claude, 1959: 5) – Lorimer is deeply sceptical about such an embodiment as states are the ultimate actors that cannot and must not be overruled by international organizations.

Although this general storyline is widely accepted and shared, it neglects the debates that preceded the development of international organizations in the nineteenth century and their impact on world politics. Before dealing with these debates and the views expressed in them, it is perhaps worth wondering why questions concerning how to organize relations among states arose in the nineteenth century. Political scientists, historians and international legal scholars agree almost in unison that certain conditions have to be met before international organization is possible and likely: (1) states have to exist and function as political units; (2) there has to be a substantial intensity of contact between the states; (3) there also has to be an awareness of common problems that emerge from states' coexistence; and (4) need for a rule-based mode that helps regulate the relations among states has to be recognized (Claude, 1959: 17; see also Potter, 1945; Osterhammel, 2009: 580–602; Schermers and Blokker, 2011). The Congress of Vienna in 1815 marks the point in time when these conditions were met and 'emperors and statesmen began to think and to talk of "some form of international organization" instead of war and offensive alliances as a practical method of constructing international society' (Woolf, 1916: 23). International legal scholars at that time asked how order between the political units could be created. Even though questions about how to create a social order – such as the *polis* in ancient Greece – are much older, the conditions mentioned earlier only occurred after the establishment of territorial states in Europe and the intensification of contacts between them. However, Law (1994: 7), referring to Marx, Braudel, Foucault, Elias and Latour, notes that the phase between 1400 and 1800 was a crucial precondition for this development as a series of changes took place in Europe (the invention of printing, the Reformation, early capitalism, early modern states, the discovery of the Americas, colonialization and so forth) that led to a reorganization of modernity. Organizing and ordering social life in all fields of society became central ideas in that phase, and the international political field was no exception.

While legal order among citizens is established by a state, legal order among states needs to be created by states (Lorimer, 1883), otherwise states would remain in a state of nature in which their relations are characterized by mutual arbitrariness (Hegel, 1821: 340). The creation of order among states seemed all too natural if states did not want to suffer the consequences of an existence in an anarchic environment 'where every man is enemy to every man' and life is 'solitary, poor, nasty, brutish, and short' (Hobbes, 1651: 78). According to Bluntschli (1873: 7–12), the pursuit of order is a natural law for both men and states. Even though states strive for order, a global legislative body is missing; therefore international legal scholars were sceptical about an organization of the world (Bluntschli, 1866: 8; Lorimer, 1884: 128). This debate on how to order relations constituted the pivotal problem of international law in the nineteenth century. Can there be international order among states even if there is no legislative body? What would such an organization of the world look like? These questions entail two dimensions that need further elaboration. First, the meaning of organization needs to be explained and how organization and order are interrelated; second, it has to be elucidated who or what is to be organized when the world is in question?

Organization and organizations

The term 'organization' stems from the Greek *organon*, which means tool or instrument. It was used in late medieval French (*organiser*) and refers to the development or coordination of parts of a body to carry out vital functions (Walter-Busch, 1996: 7). According to a German dictionary of 1799, organization is the process of arranging a country in a French way, 'the old government will be abolished and a new government consisting of professors, lawyers, doctors and clerics who were already in cahoots with the French will be installed' (*Wörterbuch der französischen Revolutionssprache*, 1799: 19). Even though this explanation is exaggerated, it demonstrates that organizing is understood as a process of creating order in a specific way. This idea of organization as creating order among states gained widespread acceptance over time. Order does not necessarily imply an international or a supranational body, it could be any form of coordination among political units or a framework for action as a reference point for political units to distinguish between acceptable and unacceptable conduct (Trueblood, 1899; Schücking, 1908). The concept of organizing and ordering is sometimes superseded by the notion of governance as 'the sum of the many ways individuals and institutions, public and private, manage their common affairs' (Commission for Global Governance, 1995: 2). It emphasizes the non-hierarchical steering of an organization or a state and implies that even non-members such as civil society groups can participate in governance processes. While governance highlights the involvement of various groups to deal with a common problem, organizing means the generation of (legal) order. However, this does not imply a single, pure order. It is rather a heterogeneous, plural and incomplete process of social ordering that sometimes generates formal organizations (Law, 1994: 2).

Kennedy (1987: 848) emphasizes that institutionalization practices are generally taken to mark a move 'from chaos to order'. The foundation of an international regime and international institutions is seen as a sign of maturity in a state system. Organizing is part of this narrative of progressive movement. It describes the taming of violence and war. While war is associated with chaos, peace emerges from the organization of the international system, 'the institutionalisation of international life can seem the very essence of peace' (Kennedy, 1987: 859). Therefore, organizing, the creation of order and organizations is a necessary step for states if they want to overcome anarchy, chaos and the state of nature.

But what exactly are organizing and order among states? To arrive at a more elaborated understanding, a little support from the sociology of organization is useful. Ahrne and Brunsson (2011) study organization, that is the process of organizing, outside of formal organizations. They face a problem similar to the one faced by legal scholars in the nineteenth century, and study whether organization can be observed in an unordered, anarchical environment and, if so, what kind of organization. They define organization as 'a decided order in which people use elements that are constitutive of formal organisations' (Ahrne and Brunsson, 2011: 86) – elements, that is, such as membership, hierarchy, rules, monitoring and sanctions. In their definition, Ahrne and Brunsson highlight the concept of a *decided* order. Order is not a natural given – even if it is in the nature of men (Bluntschli, 1873: 6) – it is something that is deliberately decided upon. Decisions about how to organize relations are 'statements representing conscious choices about the way people [or political units] should act or the distinction and classification they should make' (Ahrne and Brunsson, 2011: 86).

States or political units that wish to organize do not always actually have the opportunity or the political will to build a formal organization; they may, however, be willing to partially organize their relations and use one or a few organizational elements (Ahrne and Brunsson, 2011: 87). States and political units can decide to organize on the basis of membership – for example, by granting each other a status of recognition which they do not accord to others, as was the case in the Concert of Europe and the Quadruple Alliance. They can decide on hierarchies in the way they organize. A hierarchy does not have to have one state on top, superior to the others. Hierarchies are already in place if certain rights and obligations are granted to selected members. A state could, for example, have the right to set the agenda for a meeting, chair a meeting or shape a debate if it has a specific right to speak. Consider Prussia's role in the nineteenth-century customs union of German states, the *Zollverein* (1834–71; see Mattli, 1999). Rules are another way of organizing relations. They can apply to the group that voluntarily drew them up, but can also be imposed on other states and political units, even if they did not play a part in creating them, with respect, for example, to standards of communication. If a state decides not to use the standard, it will risk being excluded from communication beyond its own borders (see Tworek, Chapter 11 in this volume). In some cases, the rules of an international organization – for example the CCNR – can have an impact on other states that want to establish a similar kind of order based on similar rules, for example, when regulating navigation on rivers. Monitoring is another key element in organization. States routinely observe one another, as in the case of military attachés in diplomatic affairs who have been observing the military capabilities of other states since the mid-nineteenth century (O'Connor Witter, 2005). Finally, a group of states can decide to impose sanctions against another state to condemn a certain behaviour or action of the state. The formation of an alliance against a state can be conceived of as a sanction if the allied states – even if they are not attacked – decide to pool their military strength against the offender (White, 1995).

Besides different elements of partial organization, the process of organizing can lead to a community among units with a common identity (Böckenförde and Dorn-Van Rossum, 1978: 620). Thus, the term organization describes both the process of organizing and an institution that may emerge from this process or that has been founded for the purpose of organizing (Kennedy, 1987). This organization embodies the political order among units – be they individuals (as in the organization of a state) or states (as in the organization of the world) (Grimm and Grimm, 1854: vol 13, column 1339).

The idea of organizing the world is closely linked to the idea of peaceful coexistence among states. Organization is thus the counter-concept to anarchy, a state of permanent threat and uncertainty (Lasson, 1871: 36). To guarantee peaceful interrelations between states both organization (along the lines of common rules) and organizations (that manage and monitor peaceful relations) are required. According to Trueblood (1899: 146), international organizations are a pivotal condition for a truly human society in which goods do not lead to battles of distribution among states. Goods should rather be administered and distributed for the wealth of men, and organizations that establish a general political order for the world would be the precursors of a world state. They would not only symbolize an authority above states, but even more, such organizations could have the potential to finally unite all states, tie them together and thereby overcome conflict and war (Trueblood, 1899).[1] No less important a reason for a world state is the removal of friction and the danger of war by the creation of a feeling of unity in a common organization.

> One can easily imagine what the history of the United States would have been if they had become simply States without any common governmental tie. If the union of local governments in a national organization has done so much to remove friction and causes of war in the United States, in Great Britain, in France, in Italy, in Germany, what might not be expected in this regard from a union including them all? (Trueblood, 1899: 126)

In this quote, Trueblood expresses the deeply rooted idealistic hope of a world state in a *Leviathan* sense. Member states could renounce their right to declare wars because this world state would guarantee every state's existence. Here, the world state appears not as a threat to national sovereignty, as an oppressor, or as a limitation of states' capabilities (see Lorimer 1884), but as an organization serving a higher good, the eradication of war by enforcing order among states (see Claude, 1959: 371).

World and state

In addition to the concept of organization, international legal scholars in the nineteenth century discussed what it takes to be organized. Interestingly enough, the notion of the international was significantly less well established at that time than in the following centuries.[2] International legal scholars rather asked how to organize the *world*, although their world was quite a Eurocentric one. Even though territories and countries outside Europe were known, ideas about the world were primarily focused on Europe and the Western world (Hobson, 2012). The notion of the world had basically two meanings. On the one hand, it referred to the sum of all states. This meaning emphasizes the differentiation of the world in units, that is, states, with no authority above them. The state is the highest representation of morality and the absolute power that stands vis-à-vis other representations of morality (Hegel, 1821: 337). Even though states interact, there is no orderly relation among them as each state has to keep in mind the arbitrariness of others (Hegel, 1821: 339), and states exist in a state of nature (Lasson, 1871: 35). There is always a war of all against all. Even if this war is not violent, it persists as a war of guile and malice. So there cannot be a guaranteed legislative order among states, and without any guarantees there is no law (Lasson, 1871: 35–6). Order among states needs to be generated as it does not naturally evolve. Accordingly, intensified relations among states triggered by commerce and people travelling can lead to linkages between countries being consolidated. International law is then responsible for delivering the rules that create a frame for states' interaction – even though there is no guarantee that states will not cross the boundaries when following their particular interests (Bluntschli, 1873: 33; Lorimer, 1884: 214).

On the other hand, the concept of world implies a *community* among states. Despite the 'precarious character' (Lasson, 1871: 48) of international law, relations among states are not characterized by enduring conflicts and wars but by economic and cultural exchange. In this regard, international law has fewer legal functions as it does not have the power to enforce law. It rather has a socializing function establishing rules of prudence not legal imperatives ('Klugheitsregeln nicht Rechtsgebote') (Lasson, 1871: 49) for states. This reading of international law was underpinned by economic relations, trade and commerce in the nineteenth century that led to interactions and relations between states such as trade rules (see Stafford, Chapter 12 in this volume) or rules for navigation on seas and rivers. The first international organization, the CCNR (1815), emerged at the interface between trade, transport and international politics. It established common rules for river navigation and a homogenization of tariffs among the customs posts on the Rhine (Central Commission for Navigation on the Rhine, 1966; Weber, 1983: 19–24). Its primary function was, and still is, to promote and maintain the freedom of navigation and the equality of treatment of all states. Even though it took some effort to establish the CCNR,[3] its merits were soon recognized. In this case, the member states decided on rules to order an ostensibly 'apolitical' field. Navigation on the Rhine was not seen as touching the very existence or survival of a state but rather as something that could benefit all riparian states by facilitating and smoothing international trade. This argument was the cornerstone for the establishment of further international organizations, such as the Commissions for Navigation on the Elbe (1821), Weser (1823), Maas (1830) and Danube (1856). Even river navigation outside of Europe was organized in a similar way with the foundation of the Commission for Navigation on the Congo River (1885) (Weber, 1983: 21–4; Herren, 2009: 15–25). Other organizations of that period produced standards for telegraphic communication and the postal system such as the International Telegraph Union (1865) and the Universal Postal Union (1874). The primary aim in establishing these organizations was to set a common frame for communication in order to facilitate trade across countries (see Tworek, Chapter 11, and Stafford, Chapter 12 in this volume). This was the mainspring of international cooperation and led to the establishment of common rules as rules of prudence. Von Liszt (1898: 1) argues that goods do not belong to a state but are the property of mankind. Therefore, trade in goods has to be organized not solely in one state but across the community of states for the wealth of mankind. While the latter is the overall goal, the state is the political instrument that has the means to achieve this goal.

In the second half of the nineteenth century, the perception of the world as a community of states (von Liszt, 1898: 85; Schücking, 1908: 120) or as a social organization among states gained more acceptance (Trueblood, 1899: 90). This type of organization was characterized by consent-based rules of international law (Bluntschli, 1873: 59), such as the formal equality of all states as members of the international community and the recognition of certain principles, for example, those of sovereignty, non-intervention and non-aggression (von Liszt, 1898: 83–8). However, one has to bear in mind that, although international legal scholars perceived the world as a community of states, they did not have the geographical world in mind. The world was limited to the so-called 'civilised world' (Liszt, 1898: 17), 'civilised states' (Bluntschli, 1873: 1) or just 'civilisation' (Lorimer, 1884: 1). Being civilized was a characteristic reserved for European states, Russia and North America, while other regions such as Asia, Africa, Latin America and Oceania were simply ignored. They were rather seen as uncivilized spaces.

Additionally, for some legal scholars the world as a community of states implied a social unity, characterized either as a community with a supranational status vis-à-vis states (Fried, 1908: 15) or even as world society (Schücking, 1908: 120). The latter concept of the world implies that the state is merely an intermediary step to a society of human beings that will emerge out of the dense net of intertwining relations among men in areas such as trade, transport, communication and labour (Trueblood, 1899: 90).

> The abundance of close relations and joint activities permanently established among states in recent decades is most impressive to the careful observer. The older treatises gave most attention to the state of war; in the future the relations of peace will occupy three fourths of the space and attention. The law of war will sink to the relative unimportance which criminal procedure holds in municipal law systems. This vision of world-wide cooperation is indeed inspiring and grateful. Its beauty and strength rest on the fact that millions are working together quietly, in the pursuit of their various living interests, toward the organization of world unity. It is not a thing imposed from above by force, or dictated only by a higher rationalism, but it is the almost instinctive work of active men building wider and wider spheres of affiliation. (Reinsch, 1911: 11)

According to Reinsch, the state is not dispensable but it is less important. As people are the driving forces working towards the organization of world unity, '[i]nternational cooperation has become an absolute necessity to states' (Reinsch, 1911: 10). The only thing missing is a supranational political organization, such as a world state, resting upon world unity.[4] Here, the world is perceived as a community of humankind with overarching global interests. These interests are expressed in the foundation of non-state organizations aiming at organizing the world in various fields that turned it into a world organization society.[5] Examples of this development are the Association for Labour Legislation (1900), the World's Alliance of Young Men's Christian Associations (1855), the International Committee of the Red Cross (1863) and the International Olympic Committee (IOC, 1894). The latter is an interesting example: Pierre de Coubertin,[6] founder of the IOC, followed the archaeological excavation of Olympia in the 1880s and soon afterwards developed the idea of organizing an event on the model of the ancient Olympic Games in order to overcome national egoisms and raise international understanding across countries and cultures.[7] The first Olympic Games of modern times took place in 1896 in Athens. When other organizations such as the League of Nations wanted a special relationship with the IOC, or even considered placing the IOC under their auspices, the Committee made it very clear that it was the sole authority empowered to organize the Games (Mason et al, 2006: 53; Nelson and Cottrell, 2015: 7–8) and that the members acknowledged the position of the IOC by accepting its principles (Müller, 2000: 209). Looking back at the history of the IOC, it developed from a non-governmental organization to a 'world government' (Peacock, 2010: 41) capable of forcing cities to obey to the philosophy of the Olympic Games.

Types of organizing the world

The earlier discussion on the meanings of both organization and world has had two preliminary results. First, organization can be seen either as a process of generating order among units that have only some of the elements of an organization (membership, hierarchy, rules, monitoring, sanctions) or as an institution that embodies that order and is characterized by all the elements of a formal organization. Second, the world can either be seen as the sum of states that are connected via transport and trade – this perception emphasizes the role of states as sole units and powers – or, alternatively, as a community of and beyond states. Even though the world is internally differentiated into states, the driving forces of the community are rather non-state entities such as groups, associations and organizations that increasingly evolved during the nineteenth century. These entities interact and develop overlapping interests beyond the state that lead to global forms of cooperation.

In the following part, four different types of world organization will be introduced that display the different semantics of organization

Table 6.1: Typology of world organization

	Organization semantics		
World semantics		Organizing (process)	Organizations (institution)
	Sum of states (international)	(1) International law	(3) International organizations
	Community	(2) International conferences	(4) World state/ statehood

and world: international law, international conferences, international organizations and a world state/statehood. Additionally, it will contain a brief exposition of how the four types are still relevant today (Table 6.1).

International law

International law is a means of creating order among states. It comprises international treaties and agreements among sovereign states as a decided order establishing a frame of reference for action, even though it does not contain a constraining law (*ius cogens*). Stafford (Chapter 12 in this volume) shows how world trade was legally organized in the nineteenth century by rules, norms, principles and the foundation of international organizations aiming at the ideal conception of free trade. Simultaneously, international law has a socialization function as a 'gentle civilizer' (Koskenniemi, 2001). However, as Anghie (2004) noted, international law and the principle of sovereignty had a communizing impact only in and for European states (Stetter, Chapter 8 in this volume). In other parts of the world, the principle of sovereignty was rather part of the 'civilising mission' (Anghie, 2004: 114). Thus, the world was not made up of equals, but was differentiated between sovereign and non-sovereign entities, intra- and extra-European political spaces (Stafford, Chapter 12 in this volume). '[T]he sovereign state can do as it wishes with regard to the non-sovereign entity which lacks the legal personality to assert any legal opposition' (Anghie, 2004: 34). This binary differentiation conforms to the differentiation between a civilized and a non-civilized world. Even discussions about an international government to establish rules for peaceful relations among states followed this narrative (Hobson, 1915: 15). The universalization of international law had the effect 'of suppressing and subordinating other histories of international law and the peoples to whom it has applied' (Anghie, 2004: 5). International law is often a result of international conferences and the basis for the foundation of international organizations (see later).

While in the nineteenth century some international legal scholars were rather sceptical whether and how international law could help to organize relations among states in the absence of a world legislator and with no supreme referee or mediator above states (Hegel, 1821: 339; Bluntschli, 1873: 7), international law gained in importance in the twentieth century. Even without the power of law enforcement international law includes those rules of prudence that contribute to global socialization. The International Criminal Court (ICC) is an example insofar as it has the jurisdiction to prosecute international crimes of genocide, crimes against humanity and war crimes. However, it is still debated how efficient the ICC can be if states like the US refuse to cooperate or, in the case of Russia, withdraw their signature from the statute. Others criticize the selection and prosecution bias of the ICC, alleging that it does not investigate crimes committed by richer or more powerful countries, for example crimes allegedly committed by Israel in the course of Operation Cast Lead 2008/9 (Dugard, 2013).

International conferences

International conferences are a form of organizing the world where states and non-state groups, organizations and individuals deal with a common issue. These conferences and congresses took place with increasing frequency in the nineteenth century and had – at least in the self-perception of participants – less of a political than a technical character since they were supposed to find technical solutions and rules to level the playing fields in transport, trade, communication, war and peace and so forth (Gruber, 1919: 168). As a consequence of these conferences, common standards and regulation were agreed (see, for example, the river conferences). International conferences were not seen as secret meetings but rather as open to the world community. In this regard the Russian ambassador Muraviev proposed in 1898 that the Hague Peace Conferences aiming at arms limitations agreements and procedures for peaceful arbitration should be public and non-state actors should be able to observe the negotiations (Steller, 2011: 241). In connection with these conferences a global public sphere emerged that followed the conferences and their results.

International conferences have continued to play an important role in world politics up to the present day. They are not merely world events for political representatives but a forum for various organizations, interest groups and individuals, as instanced by the World Economic Forum, the World Social Forum or the Munich Security Conference. In becoming quite open, conferences have lost their technical character. One could even argue that international conferences offer a forum where interests can be pursued on a global level by those who find it difficult to work their way through national politics and international organizations. Besides the conferences already mentioned, regular international summits of a new kind have also been occurring that are less open to the public and at the same time highly political, namely meetings of the Group of Seven (G7) or Group of Twenty (G20). Even though these groups share many similarities with international organizations they consistently refuse to organize themselves like formal organizations. They prefer to remain as groups showing almost all elements of formal organizations: members (regular participants), hierarchies (for example the Troika preparing the agenda), rules (communiqués have binding effects both within and beyond the G7 and G20 countries), monitoring (observing the results of previous summits) and sanctioning (for example the exclusion of Russia from the G8 after the annexation of Crimea).

International organizations

International organizations – such as administrative unions – are an institutionalized form of organizing the world. Instead of arriving at agreements between states (and non-state organizations) in international conferences, international organizations were founded to put rules, procedures and agreements into practice (Gruber, 1919: 238). Fried (1908: 21) stated that besides national administrations, international administration emerged as clear proof of an integration of the international organism. He regarded the world – particularly world trade and world politics – as differentiated into functional areas, in which administrations sometimes even show supranational characteristics. However, international organizations do not act in their own right. They are rather seen as functional and apolitical means to facilitate interactions between states. Following the example of international administrations, more and more international organizations were founded in the second half of the nineteenth century (Murphy, 1994).[8] This development led to a vision and the anticipation that the foundation of a single world (meta-)organization capable of organizing all other international organizations and states would be the logical final step: 'national law, the increasing international cooperation through diplomacy, conferences, commissions and arbitral boards, all foreshadow a complete political unity of the world, a great international world state' (Trueblood, 1899: 125).

Although the idea of a world organization has not yet been realized, international organizations are a success story as far as ordering relations among states goes. More than 300 international organizations exist today, covering almost all fields of world politics. Once a new political field is demarcated, the foundation of an international organization follows soon afterwards – as, for example, in the case of renewable energies and the International Renewable Energy Agency (IRINA) founded in 2009. Once in existence, international organizations rarely die. They do so, however, if world political turning points occur, such as the end of the Cold War that led to the dissolution of some international organizations such as the Warsaw Treaty Organization. International organizations were regarded as functional instruments in the nineteenth century (Fried, 1908), an idea that was taken up again after World War II (Mitrany, 1948), and have continued to evolve as actors in world politics until today. Emphasizing their neutrality and the dedication to their mission (Barnett and Finnemore, 2004) helps international organizations to act as norm entrepreneurs, as mediators or brokers between states, and as third-party observers of international agreements (for the latter see Müller, Chapter 13 in this volume).

World state/statehood

Finally, the semantics of world organization is linked to the normative idea of world statehood or even a world state. Ideas of a supranational order refer to Kant's (1984) concept of perpetual peace. Kant, however, argued that states would not accept a supranational institution. It is more likely that states will band together in a *foedus pacificum* (Kant, 1984: 16). The idea of *foedus pacificum* was later revised by Woolf (1916) and Hobson (1915) and led to the establishment of the League of Nations (Wilson, 1919). The foundation of a world state was still the final aim, but in the early twentieth century it seemed a vision that could not yet be achieved. As Bluntschli (1863: 43) noted, the world state is an ideal of progressive mankind. Even though a world state can only be accomplished in the coming centuries, there is the deep desire for an organized community among all civilized peoples (Bluntschli, 1863: 43).

These different types of world organization diminished in the inter-war period and almost vanished after World War II. Although international law, international conferences and international organizations still existed and increased in scope and number, they were not regarded as part of the world organizational narrative in all its nineteenth-century conceptual richness. After the end of the Cold War the idea of a world state/statehood gained some relevance again. In particular, global governance research and the impact of international organizations on world politics raised hopes that – if not a world state – forms of world statehood would soon become apparent. However, recent political developments in North America and Russia have scaled down expectations, and even Wendt's claim that a world state is inevitable (Wendt, 2003) and will be realized within 150 years seems far too optimistic.

Conclusion

This chapter started with a quote by Claude describing the nineteenth century as a period of preparation, before international organization was able to flourish in the twentieth century. Even though this interpretation is widely shared in IR, it is misleading. The nineteenth century should rather be regarded as a period of foundation and a conceptual richness of ideas on how to organize the world.

The chapter has sought to make three points. First, the idea of organization is deeply rooted in debates among international legal scholars during the nineteenth century. Organization as a concept is not limited to formal international organizations but describes the process of generating a decided order among political units which might encompass different elements (members, hierarchy, rules, monitoring, sanctions). Second, the idea of organization was not limited to the world of states. Even though the nineteenth century is known for the birth of international organizations, it is more adequately described as the period of organizing the world so that it could become not merely the sum of states but also a community of states driven by non-state organizations, trade organizations and other interest groups. Third, organizing the world brought into being different forms that still survive (international law, international conferences and international organizations) or have been lately rediscovered (a world state/statehood). These forms express different ideas of organization as a decided order and of the world that needs to be organized. Semantic distinctions with respect to the world diminished in the twentieth century; emphasis was given to the international. The nineteenth century, however, was less state-centric. Some international legal scholars regarded the state only as an intermediary step on the way to a world state constituted as an organized community of all peoples aiming to finally overcome war. Paraphrasing Bartelson (2010), the world was organized globally well before it became organized internationally.

Notes

1. The discussion on the role of international organizations as a precursor of a world state was revisited about 100 years later by Alexander Wendt in his article 'Why a World State Is Inevitable' (Wendt, 2003).
2. For a more detailed analysis on the semantics of international and world politics see Albert (2016) and Bartelson (2010).
3. It took the member states 17 years until 1832 to negotiate as they had to clarify the exact interpretation of all legal clauses.
4. However Reinsch (1911: 10) was rather pessimistic concerning the establishment of a world state.
5. For a detailed analysis of the history of non-governmental organizations and transnational civil society see T. Davies (2014).
6. Born in 1863, Coubertin was shaped by France's defeat in the Franco-Prussian war 1870/71. He had the idea that French men could become physically stronger by the means of sport and sporting competition.
7. This overall idea is best expressed in Coubertin's conviction that the important thing in life is not the triumph but the struggle, the essential thing is not to have conquered but to have fought well (Müller, 2000).
8. Between 1864 and 1914 30 international organizations were founded in different policy fields (Murphy, 1994).

7

Particularly Universal Encounters: Ethnographic Explorations into a Laboratory of World Society

Teresa Koloma Beck

Introduction

This chapter explores the relevance of experimental action and experiences in the dynamics of global social change. It does so by looking at a type of experimental setting that is of major relevance in world politics: international military and humanitarian interventions in armed conflicts. Launched in perceived emergency situations, such interventions try to create large-scale political, societal and economic change under conditions of conflict, violence and insecurity. At stake in such constellations is more than the society that is being intervened upon. It is global order itself. Societies subject to intervention are 'laboratories of world society'. In them an abstract and global epistemic, normative and political order comes to be enacted, stabilized, and made negotiable in human interaction, which makes them productive fields for the study of social change in world society. This chapter will pursue that idea here, looking at the intervention in Afghanistan (2001) and basing the argument on ethnographic fieldwork carried out in and around Kabul in 2015. The chapter speaks to theoretical debates on change in world society as well as to discussions about the role and potential of ethnographic research in studying global orders and relations.

Experiments inside and outside of research settings are attracting increasing attention in the social sciences. Driven in part by the mainstreaming of science and technology studies, in part by an ever more acute awareness of hitherto unknown global problems, experimental forms of action have once more become a relevant topic within the social sciences as well as among policy makers (see, for example, Stiegler and Werner, 2016; Bogusz, 2018; Engels et al, 2019). The notion of the 'laboratory' – or, more frequently, the 'lab' – has gained prominence not only in technology-driven fields of policy making, but basically everywhere where actors try to signal that they are working on issues relating to the 'grand societal challenges' of our time.[1] Though in many instances the notion of the 'lab' might be no more than a fashionable cue for innovative thought, it is also of conceptual relevance when thinking about change in contemporary societies. Traditionally, the laboratory used to be a place where knowledge was generated through the manipulation of things and processes in a controlled environment. In 1989, however, Wolfgang Krohn and Johannes Weyer, both sociologists of science and technology, were already pointing out that in contemporary societies experimental forms of knowledge production tend to transcend the walls of the laboratory (Krohn and Weyer, 1989, 1994). They argued that recent technological and political developments had created challenges that could only be dealt with by testing preliminary ideas and hypothetical knowledge in real-world contexts. As spaces conceived as transitory sites for the production of change proliferate, society itself becomes a laboratory.

International interventions are a case in point. They are not just sites in which an order is enforced, but experimental settings in which the knowledge to deal with previously unfaced challenges is produced in action. Analytically emphasizing this aspect points to the role of interventions in the transformation of global political and social orders.

This chapter sketches the potential of such an approach based on the author's own ethnographic research into the intervention in Afghanistan. For reasons of clarity, the analysis focuses on one field of interventionist politics that has attracted particular attention and controversy: policies to empower women. The aim, however, is not only to reconstruct empirical dynamics. The ethnographic approach highlights the fact that research on world orders is not external to its object of study. It is situated and entangled in particular ways and needs to account for this situatedness in its methods and theory. From such a perspective, 'women in Afghanistan' is not just a domestic policy issue, but a discursive site in which the role of womanhood and gender in world order is staged and (re)negotiated.

The next section describes how politics and policies regarding women in Afghanistan became a subject relevant to the study. The third section outlines the conceptual framework, reconstructing international interventions as laboratories of world society, while the fourth sketches specific empirical dynamics, drawing on ethnographic research in Kabul. The fifth and final section summarizes the main insights.

Entering the field

When my research interest shifted to the intervention in Afghanistan, women's issues were not the centre of attention. Based on previous work on life in warscapes, I was interested in the socio-spatial organization of everyday life and the social production of security. To facilitate research in Kabul, I cooperated with an Afghan civil society organization that had for many years been engaged in grass-roots peacebuilding initiatives throughout the country. The organization employed me part-time as an 'international advisor' appointed to a particular project. Instead of paying me a salary, they supported my research logistically, paying for my flight, providing office space, mobility and, most importantly, security. Although this arrangement was made out of purely pragmatic considerations, sharing the everyday life of Afghan colleagues turned out to be a productive starting point for my enquiries into everyday life in Kabul.

Although women's rights and empowerment were not the focus of the study, this entry into the field brought me into close contact with a particular group of well-educated urban women to whom the question of women's empowerment and women's rights was of personal as well as of professional concern. They were professionals working for Afghan civil society organizations, journalists working for independent news media, academics or students. They belonged to the cultural elite of the country, but not to its political or economic one. Unsurprisingly, many were still young, in their twenties and thirties, yet in different life situations: some still living at home, others married with children. Some of the older ones had seen the reforms introduced by Soviet rule in the 1980s. Quite a few had lived abroad for extended periods of time, mostly in neighbouring countries where their families had been in exile, but two had been abroad on their own, studying or receiving professional training. Powerful local traditions of female homosociability facilitated ethnographic engagement with these women in the field, and in these exchanges, their struggles for rights and empowerment were a recurring and unavoidable topic.

Most interestingly, however, 'women in Afghanistan' had become an issue in this research long before I entered the country. The topic was brought up continually by people with whom I engaged while preparing for my stay intellectually and pragmatically. Driving these conversations was not an empirical interest in the place, but some kind of concern for me 'as a woman' going to 'such a place'. Whether I would be wearing a headscarf was a question posed frequently, sometimes with curiosity, sometimes as an open challenge. And my affirmative answer was not always received with comprehension. Even before leaving for Afghanistan, I felt I was being forced into a battle over the female condition, in which historically recent West European experiences and aspirations were promoted as a global norm. Ethnographically, the situation of women in Afghanistan did not present itself as a domestic issue, but as a global concern, raising questions about the universality of supposedly universal norms and the right to enforce them.

How is it possible, in research and academic writing, to do justice to this entanglement? A starting point would be to acknowledge that 'women in Afghanistan' is a research subject that cannot be addressed without also considering those who, from the outside, take such a vivid interest in their fate. 'Women in Afghanistan' are part of a transnational social imaginary. Their situation and their struggles bind attention and fuel emotions not only inside the country, but also among observers and publics outside of it, most importantly in the so-called West. This persistent interest is explained less by the situation itself – there are other places in the world where life for women is similarly difficult – as by the symbolic position the country has occupied in the social imaginary of world society since 2001, when a US-led military and humanitarian intervention started out with the aim to transform the Afghan state and society. From the beginning, the 'liberation of the women of Afghanistan' was one of the most fervently advertised goals of this project. Not only women's rights organizations but also the media and celebrities from the world of entertainment launched campaigns to draw attention to the conditions in which the female population of a far-away Central Asian country was living. Afghan women and their fate featured in news media as well as in society and people's magazines like *Glamour* and *Vogue* and on *The Oprah Winfrey Show*. Even small, local women's organizations put the issue on their agenda and were eager to host events or expositions featuring Afghan women. The latter's struggles for their rights and empowerment came to be inscribed into a transnational social imaginary shared by observers and activists around the globe, including within Afghanistan itself. It is an imaginary which merges supposedly universal ideals of gender equality and women's emancipation with a narrative of interventions as measures by which the powerful in the world come to rescue and restore 'normality' in places wrecked by natural or manmade disasters. This social imaginary is more than an epistemic frame by which 'people in the West' make sense of life in a place far away from their own reality. It is an ontological machine, which, conditioning engagements and interactions, brings into being the world it describes (Law and Urry, 2004; see also Aradau and Huysmans, 2013). Therefore, engaging as a scholar, activist or politician from 'the West' with the situation of women in Afghanistan is never only about 'them', but always also about 'us', who belong to the power centres of an asymmetrically structured world society. The following section proposes the concept of the laboratory as a framework for researching such global entanglements created by humanitarian interventions and other forms of universalist politics.

Humanitarian interventions as laboratories of world society

Drawing on insights from world polity and world society research, humanitarian interventions like the one in Afghanistan can be described as empirical constellations marked by encounters between particular localized contexts with so-called rationalized 'Others' (Meyer, 1994) or universalized third parties (Werron, 2012b), that is, with actors who present themselves as representatives of humanity and as agents of universalized norms such as human rights, peace and democracy. World society and world polity research has shown that actors of this type have been growing in numbers and influence since the late nineteenth century (see also Chapters 6, 13 and 14 in this volume). In a world political system which, for centuries, had been structured by competition and conflict between the interests of nation states, their rise introduced a new, rival paradigm: global governance based on universal values. Humanitarian interventions are the most pointed expression of this new paradigm as they claim to protect and defend – in situations of urgency – the most basic of all universal values: the integrity and dignity of human life. In the following a conceptual framework will be sketched which is intended to highlight the relevance of interventions and structurally similar contexts in the dynamics of social change in world society.

Humanitarian interventions in world politics

Interventions are multi-sited social phenomena. They connect the local contexts that are intervened upon to the power centres of world politics, and through them to other local contexts in the world. They also link these places to a potentially vast variety of publics, in which, drawn by the 'spectacle of suffering' (Boltanski, 1999, 2007), institutional actors as well as ordinary people take an interest in the fate of men and women in faraway places. In this sense, humanitarian interventions are truly global political projects. However, they are based on a starkly asymmetric representation of world society. They describe a world divided into well-functioning, 'modern' or 'civilized' regions on the one hand and 'problem zones' on the other (Calhoun, 2004). And there are few social contexts in which the distinction between 'the West and the rest' (Hall, 1992) would be more pronounced than in this context (Nayak and Selbin, 2010). The perspective of the power centres of world society is presented as a neutral view from the nowhere of normality, whereas what is observed appears as a deviation. Narratives about the need to 'restore normality' discursively transform highly contentious political interventions into seemingly neutral acts of assistance (Calhoun, 2004: 379; see also Calhoun, 2010).

Global publics are a constitutive element in these dynamics. Understood as an emanation of the very humanity in whose name interventions take place, these publics are needed to affirm the importance of the undertaking and legitimize its pursuit. Through the relay of global publics, interventions enact a global political topography of 'here' and 'there', which connects and divides at the same time. They normalize pity as a form of distanced engagement with the suffering of strangers in faraway places (Boltanski, 1999, 2007; Calhoun 2004; 2010: 51). And they enact an iconography that underscores the otherness and anonymity of the people there (Calhoun, 2010: 31–3). In so doing, however, they (re)produce the idea that the suffering of even distant 'fellow humans' matters. In this way they contribute to the (re)production of conditions in which affective and very personal experiences of global sociability can emerge.

Empirical constellations like this play an important role in the constitution of world society. They are sites at which a global structure or system becomes a subject of observation, experience and struggle. Here, the universal finds itself confronted with its other – not in abstract discursive exchanges, but in tangible encounters of embodied actors.

Researching interventions as laboratories of world society

This chapter proposes to conceptualize such empirical constellations as laboratories of world society, emphasizing that they are sites at which knowledge of the potentials, limits and challenges of globalized social orders and relations is tested and produced. They emerge wherever modernist universalist projects are put into practice 'on the ground' and then come to be confronted with an Other that cannot be absorbed or co-opted. Such constellations have been described not only in the literature on interventions, but also in research on environmental and nature protection projects among indigenous populations (Verran, 2002) or in studies on the fate of people convicted for 'crimes against humanity' by international criminal courts (Devresse and Scalia, 2016).[2] In all these contexts universalist engagement seems to be confronted with something outside universality, with a particularist Other that stubbornly and at times violently resists the appeal of universalist projects. As a consequence, the distinction between 'internationals' and 'locals', and between 'the universal' and 'the particular', comes to pervade these social contexts. It is produced and reproduced in everyday interactions, in institutional as well as in organizational arrangements. In short, it becomes constitutive of the organization of social life.

The notion of the 'laboratory' draws attention to the fact that these empirical contexts are marked by the proliferation of experimental practices. They are concrete places in the world, populated by embodied actors, in which rationalized Others try to figure out how to deal with the 'grand challenges of our time'. In doing so, they enact a real-world laboratory in the sense expounded by Krohn and Weyer: theoretical assumptions are put into practice under close supervision, attempts are made to control boundary conditions, effects are observed and analysed meticulously by specialized actors, and adjustments are made so as to optimize results. A major twist in Krohn and Weyer's conception is their structural definition of the laboratory setting. What defines the laboratory are the features of the 'experimental situation' just described. The latter are not necessarily brought about by the deliberate action of one actor. More frequently, such real-world laboratories emerge as an effect of the interconnected practices of various actors (Krohn and Weyer, 1989: 356–9; 1994: 175–6).

Humanitarian interventions in armed conflicts can be conceived as places of condensed experimental action of this kind. They are marked by a particularly intentional and activist relation to change. The need to effectuate it – in institutions, in organizations, in relations, in people – structures these places in discourse and practice. Rationalized Others who act in the name of world peace, universal sciences or just humanity set out to transform a society in an accelerated way. But in doing so all actors, international and domestic, operate under conditions of risk and insecurity. Practices successful in one conflict setting are – at best – rough indicators of how to approach another. The only way to generate the knowledge needed to solve the problems at hand is to test how ideas work out in practice.

Krohn and Weyer (1989: 349–52; 1994: 173–4) point out that such settings raise important questions of legitimacy and accountability. Is it justified to deliberately interfere with the life and wellbeing of people without being certain of the outcome? Because of this, experimental practices are only rarely identified as such. Instead, the experimental actions necessary to gain much-needed knowledge are presented as the application of an already consolidated expertise (Krohn and Weyer 1989: 349; 1994: 173). Therefore, humanitarian interventions and other real-world laboratories are places of tension, of conflict, sometimes even of struggle as actors are faced with the need to simultaneously deal with accelerated processes of knowledge production and learning as well as with their social costs. They are places in which the universalist norms and asymmetries that structure world society find particularly strong expression. But they are also places in which these very norms and asymmetries are continuously challenged and renegotiated in the encounter of embodied actors. Exploring these empirical contexts is instructive in understanding how global orders are enacted, appropriated and transformed in dynamics of interaction and processes of organization. It means investigating global social ordering and transformation at the frontiers of modernist universality, where structures and dynamics are not consolidated and normalized, but unstable and contested and therefore particularly accessible to analysis.

Such research, however, is faced with a crucial problem: the question of its own analytical situatedness. Julian Go has pointed out that any research into the 'global condition' risks becoming trapped in narratives of modernity, empire and civilization (Go, 2016: 1–17). When one is researching the empirical constellations in question, this problem is particularly pronounced, because in the struggles at the epistemological and political frontiers of universality, the researcher is always already situated. Even if fiercely critical of universalist politics or practices, she is herself an agent of a modernist project, of an order of knowledge which is closely related to the order of power in world society. Under such conditions, the ideal of a 'neutral' analytical vantage point is an obvious illusion. Yet how can the analysis then proceed? Is it possible in these particular constellations to develop research that does not simply feed into narratives of empire and modernity?

In sociology the typical reflex to this kind of question is a call for critique and better theory. The positionality of the research perspective needs to be exposed and a more appropriate theoretical framework constructed. The following analysis can be read as an attempt to address this problem from a different angle: to escape the shadow of empire not by working on theory, but on methods of social inquiry.[3] It draws on Donna Haraway's work on situated knowledge (Haraway, 1988), in which she elaborates that the positionality of research is neither a trap nor a flaw, but constitutive to analytical vision. Haraway proposes to deliberately and strategically use 'positioning' in processes of research and analysis so as to deal with the blind spots and limitations imposed on the sciences by their patriarchal, colonial or imperial legacies. The following considerations on empowerment politics for women in the laboratory of the intervention in Afghanistan is inspired by this approach.

Women in Afghanistan as a global cause

Afghanistan had been a battleground for modernization and a 'laboratory for experiments with "modernization theory"' (Manchanda, 2017: 180; see also Cullather, 2002) throughout the second half of the twentieth century. The status of women in Afghan society had always been an important site of this struggle. Women's issues had been politicized in projects of political and social reform under the progressive government of Amānullāh Khān (1919–29) as well as under Soviet occupation (1978–92) and Taliban rule (1996–2001). When the US-led Operation Enduring Freedom, in autumn 2001, declared the 'liberation' of Afghan women a primary objective, it could mobilize already well-established discursive and iconographic tropes. In a radio address to the nation in November 2001, the American First Lady Laura Bush proudly stated: 'Because of our recent military gains in much of Afghanistan women are no longer imprisoned in their homes. They can listen to music and teach their daughters without fear of punishment. The fight against terrorism is also a fight for the rights and dignity of women' (The American Presidency Project, 2001). And despite fierce criticism that such statements exploited popular feminism to justify a war (Abu-Lughod, 2002; Eisenstein, 2002; Hirschkind and Mahmood, 2002), 'women in Afghanistan' continues to be a key topic not only for national, international and non-governmental actors engaged in the intervention project, but also in media, art and research. In my own work, the many questions I have received regarding my experiences 'as a woman' in Afghanistan testify to the exceptional status of the topic. It came up not only in conversations with people from 'the West', but also with Afghans, it was raised by women as well as by men, by colleagues from within academia as well as by people outside of it.

This importance attached to women's issues in the Afghan intervention context is only in part explained by the actual situation of women in the country. Female members of the population face hardships in other places in the world that receive much less political and popular attention. Women's rights, protection and empowerment are relevant, because they appear to epitomize the universalist pretension of the intervention project. Being linked to physical reproduction, gendered social and societal structures are to be found everywhere, and the idea that social peace depends, among other things, on a balanced relationship between women and men appears across cultures. Concerns for gender equality, gender justice or women's empowerment are as ubiquitous as masculine domination. As the topic speaks to the experiences, sensibilities and emotions of people worldwide, it can very credibly be framed as a truly universal concern and is, hence, particularly suited to underscoring the legitimacy of universalist politics.

In the history of global governance, gender equality is, therefore, among the oldest and most differentiated of global norms. It figured in the UN Charter from the first draft of the document,[4] and a specific body to deal with it, the Commission on the Status of Women within the United Nations Economic and Social Council, was created as early as 1946. Whereas, initially, the Council's work focused on improving the legal status of women worldwide, the 1970s saw an increasing depoliticization, as rights-based approaches gradually came to be displaced by humanitarian understandings of women's issues (Olcott, 2017: 19–52). This reinterpretation further underscored the 'universal' and 'politically neutral' nature of the topic and made it a perfect fit for the framework of interventionist politics emerging after the end of the Cold War. In the context of the intervention, policies relating to women's rights, protection and empowerment are particularly suited to bolster the legitimacy of the intervention project. Moreover, they are a policy field in which the transformative pretensions of the intervention project can be most comprehensibly staged. The reason is that politics relating to women's issues is intended to produce change in literally all spheres of society: not only in political institutions, but also in organizations, families, social relations, the conventions of interaction and sociability in the broadest sense and – fundamentally and most importantly – within the subjects themselves. Looking at the intervention in Afghanistan, Lina Abirafeh (2009: 2) points out that 'Women in Afghanistan are used as the barometer for aid agencies to measure social change'. In the same vein, Ben Walter (2017: 2) argues that the veiled Afghan woman is at the centre of the political iconography of the intervention: she 'existed in Western imaginations as a subject in transition from the personification of a barbaric and backward time to that of a modern liberated citizen of a democratic Western-liberated Afghanistan'. The social change achieved regarding the status of women in Afghan society is, consequently, used as an indicator of, or even as a stand-in for, social change at large.

Resonating with experiences across national and cultural contexts worldwide, women's rights, protection and empowerment are a field of policy making that lends particular credibility to the universalist pretensions of global governance. It produces a semblance of unity among heterogeneous actors gathered around a shared concern, and creates a stage for interventionist social change. Policies around 'women's issues', therefore, play an important role in the universalist politics of global governance and are particularly suited to bolster the legitimacy of the intervention.

On the level of practice, however, this unity quickly disintegrates. What on an abstract discursive level appears as a universal concern explodes into a multitude of – not infrequently incommensurable – problems and claims formed in the horizon of particular collective and individual histories and experiences. This kind of disintegration happens wherever universal norms come to be discussed and negotiated in greater detail. The intervention setting is, however, particular inasmuch as it systematically forces people with different and opposing experiences and perspectives – 'rationalized Others' and the 'local population' – into situations of interaction. And as the gender difference tends to bear somehow on all interactions and relations, women's issues and gender equality norms are negotiated not only in women's empowerment programmes and similar contexts, but wherever women and men find themselves confronted with an interpretation of the allegedly global norm different from their own.

Intervention projects systematically deploy embodied actors with their life histories and experiences as 'representatives of humanity' into a 'local' context. They therefore systematically produce conflictive encounters between 'the universal' and 'the particular' in lifeworld contexts. As a consequence, intervention settings become real-life laboratories in which a global order is enacted, appropriated and transformed in dynamics of interaction and processes of organization.

The reminder of this section presents some empirical material from the research in Kabul to illustrate these dynamics.

Afghans striving for women's rights and empowerment

The urban, well-educated women I met during my research in Kabul contextualized their individual lives as being part of a broader struggle towards greater liberty, recognition and influence for the women of Afghanistan. Z is a typical example: a young lawyer who worked with a civil society organization, representing in the legal system women who suffered domestic violence and abuse. We met during a day-long workshop and she was passionate about her profession. As an adolescent she had successfully struggled against being married to a cousin. Her grandfather had made this arrangement when she was still a child, and she had opposed it, insisting on her right to self-determination. She knew all too well the relations of force unfolding within families, but she had also had the experience of confronting them and prevailing. Working in one of the southern provinces, she explained how difficult it was to treat cases of domestic abuse, because the women concerned did not want to subject themselves and their families to the public exposure of a court. The civil society organization she was working with offered mediation as an alternative approach, in which the perpetrator made a commitment to change and the organization accompanied the family concerned for at least one year. In her professionalism and passion she seemed to represent the unchained, emancipated Afghan woman that women's rights activists in the West had been dreaming about since the fall of the Taliban – but for one tiny detail: a face veil was attached to her beige-coloured headscarf. The light tissue moved gently with her breath and speech. She struggled to eat the cookies offered during coffee breaks. And at lunchtime she sat with me in a corner, released one side of the veil, holding the loose end so as to shield her face from the room and using the free hand to put tiny bits of food into her mouth.

Showing a passionate commitment to women's emancipation, while at the same time wearing what is perceived by many as the very symbol of women's repression, Z did not conform to the social imaginary of 'women in Afghanistan' which dominates coverage in the 'West'. Yet she is typical of the group of urban, well-educated women whom I met during research, in at least four regards. First, as is clear from the impetus of her speech, she has a definite sense of participating in a struggle which transcends her personal life story and is political in nature. Second, as her trajectory shows, engaging in this struggle touches her personal as well as her professional life. Third, as indicated by her wearing the face veil, participating in this struggle does not mean detachment from her context of origin. And fourth, as the account of her work suggested, there seemed to be an understanding that improving the situation of women in Afghanistan was impossible by working with women alone, but necessitated working on gender relations.

To the Afghan women I met in the field, participating in the struggle for women's empowerment was not chiefly about public acts of heroism, at least not in the sense that prevails in media coverage that reaches us 'here'. The urban centres of Afghanistan have assuredly seen audacious individual and collective activism – as well as violent resistance to it.[5] But, similar to the early phases of women's emancipation in the so-called West, most of the struggle for gender equality and women's rights takes place in everyday life, with the workplace and the family as its most important arenas. These are the places in which women's empowerment and recognition are negotiated and achieved, but also questioned and put at risk.

Whereas in rural areas traditionalist demands that women stay in the house continued to be highly influential, the female professionals I met during my research belonged by definition to a more liberal urban elite. Nonetheless, their professional life was marked by tensions between modernity and tradition, which had to be negotiated continuously. Western media coverage of Afghan women fighting their way into traditionally male professions, for example the police or the army, simply describe the most spectacular aspect of this problem. Cultural norms weigh heavily in less contested workplaces as well, for example norms which limit heterosocial interactions to people belonging to the same household, and oblige the women to preserve their individual and family honour by guarding against violations of their dignity (see Anderson, 1982). The women in my field, who, contrary to traditionalist claims, participated in professional and hence public life, seemed to be under particular pressure to prove that they were both capable professionals and honourable women. They were careful in choosing their workplaces. A, a woman in her thirties who worked for a civil society organization, explained to me how, after a number of unpleasant experiences in previous jobs, she had immediately trusted her current employer because the elderly project manager who had conducted her job interview had not looked at her once, but had sat with his eyes fixed on the papers on the table in front of him.[6] To avoid the tensions and risks related to heterosocial interactions, many female professionals ended up working on women-related issues or, more generally, in fields and on topics which brought them into contact mostly with other women. Many then made it their cause to promote ideas of women's empowerment among them. However, for all my informants, this professional engagement was rooted in strong personal experiences. These had created – as in Z's successful refusal to marry or A's persistent quest for a decent work environment – a sense that greater liberty and self-determination were not only deserved but also possible. Having lived abroad or having experienced a different social context played a recurrent role in these narratives. A, for example, had lived from puberty to early adulthood in Pakistan, to which her family had been exiled; others had spent time in Iran for the same reason or had received scholarships to study abroad.

As hinted in A's narrative, however, the workplace was not only an arena in which ideals of women's emancipation, empowerment and recognition were realized, but also one in which women were exposed and at risk. The household, to which traditionalists wanted to confine them, was not only a place of domination and control, but also a place of protection. Without that, they always risked being perceived as easy prey. In the workplace, their subjective and objective safety depended, according to all accounts, on the willingness of older men in higher positions to enforce a respectful organizational culture and, most importantly, not to engage in predatory behaviour themselves.

Embracing emancipatory ideals, the women I met nonetheless stayed connected to their social context of origin and made efforts to conform – like Z wearing the face veil – to more traditional expectations. This should, however, not be mistaken for half-heartedness or betrayal; it is part of the logic of a society in which no one can survive alone, where men and women alike gain resources and meaning only within the framework of a family and a household. This is more than a cultural imperative. Although it is true that cultural traditions in the region conceive of human existence as social existence and have no concept of individual life outside of relationships of responsibility and respect (see Anderson, 1982), it is the war which gives these cultural rules a pragmatic urgency. In a situation of persistent internal armed conflict and economic instability, family and similarly close networks are essential in providing social security. Therefore, the women I met, committed as they were to their cause, modulated the verbal and bodily expressions of this commitment according to the situational context (see also Billaud, 2013). Unlike the women's movement in Europe in the 1970s, which happened at the height of the European welfare state, Afghans – whether women or men – cannot radically turn against the interests and/or values of their families, because the latter provide the only social security network there is. 'Youth compromises because of the insecurity of the future ... As we are not certain how things will turn out, we make our little compromises.'[7] These words of a male youth activist are even truer for the women who are the focus of this chapter.

Recognizing the social importance and practical indispensability of family ties has an important implication for the question in hand. It suggests that the emancipatory life stories of my female informants would have been impossible without the support of, or at least some kind of license from, their male relations. Accordingly, these biographical narratives were populated by fathers, brothers, uncles and husbands, who had encouraged and protected them and of whom they spoke with great reverence. L, who worked as a high-ranking officer in one of the national ministries, for example, told how her brothers had urged her to fight for this position. When applying, she had passed the admission test as the best of the four applicants; nonetheless, the minister wanted to give the job to one of the male candidates. L's brothers persuaded and motivated her not to give in easily.[8] On the other hand, women working in responsible positions could tell stories of promising female colleagues whose professional careers had come to a sudden end with their marriage.[9]

Against this background the widespread sense that the improvement of the situation of women would not be achieved by focusing on women alone, but depended on a reconfiguration of gender relations, comes as no surprise. In the urban, educated milieu I was studying, younger people, among themselves, were usually open and relaxed in heterosocial interactions – provided they trusted each other and considered themselves to be in a safe environment. Interactions were animated, at times even flirtatious. In a focus group discussion with a gender-mixed group of young political activists, participants expressed how much they enjoyed and longed for this kind of carefree exchange among women and men, occasions for which were few and far between.[10] How peculiar these interactions were in the overall context became clear when suddenly an elder appeared on the scene. Immediately, people fell silent, laughter subsided, gazes went to the floor and the women fingered their headscarves, pulling them tight. Interestingly, what is perceived in the 'West' as a struggle between men and women, inside the country appeared, at least to some extent, as a struggle between generations. And whereas the notion of a 'women's movement' was not very prominent among the women I engaged with, the idea of belonging to a 'youth movement'[11] had much more resonance.

Besides these four aspects, which resonated in the encounter with Z, the lawyer from Afghanistan's south, field research revealed one more important detail: the situation of women and the struggle for improvement is a major concern not for women alone, but also for men. The most important reason is that a central aspect in the traditional ordering of gender relations is that men are responsible for the women of their household. This sense of responsibility not only produces practices of surveillance and control, which are emphasized in discussions in the 'West', but also practices of care. During research I met a number of men belonging to the same milieu of young, urban, well-educated and globally open Afghans, who were continuously worried about the security of their wives or sisters, whose more independent lifestyles they supported. Because of these anxieties they at times felt pushed towards decisions that appeared paradoxical not only to outside observers but also to themselves. P, for example, who was responsible for four sisters and supported them in their studies, told me that he urged the girls to wear face veils on their way to the university. Politically, he was not supportive of the veil, but he was afraid that his sisters might become victims of one of the acid attacks that had been repeatedly perpetrated on loosely veiled female students in the university district of the city.[12]

While the global imaginary of women in Afghanistan tells a straightforward tale about a battle of the sexes, about male domination and the repression of women, ethnographic encounters in the milieu I studied showed a much more complex constellation. But how does what has been described in this section relate to the intervention project explored before?

Encounters: women's rights and empowerment in the practice of intervention

At first glance, it might seem that in their idiosyncratic, culturally rooted logic these struggles of Afghan women (and men) in the ordinary run of everyday life are somewhat disconnected or 'decoupled' (see, for example, Meyer, 2000) from the grand scheme of humanitarian politics. But this is not the case. Not only because, as explained previously, policies around women play a key role in the interventionist project of social engineering and are, therefore, evoked and mobilized continuously, but also because, for the women in question, the intervention warrants the legitimacy of their claims. In a constellation of simultaneous but conflicting normative orders, it provides the normative framework in which their position is recognized, promoted and defended. Therefore, when women talked publicly or in formal settings about their struggles for greater liberties and recognition, they would frequently evoke two publics at once: the audience to which their activities and initiatives were directed, and the global public that represented 'humanity' and lent legitimacy to their speech. In this sense, the intervention appeared not only as an important, but as an essential ally in the struggles for emancipation.

Yet this resonance in discourse did not necessarily translate into harmonious partnerships. Instead, cooperation was frequently marked by tensions and ambiguities. The latter were fuelled, on the one hand, by differing and conflicting ideas about womanhood, women's emancipation and empowerment and, on the other hand, by the perception that in their daily practices, the foreign professionals of the intervention not infrequently acted contrary to the ideals of gender equality and women's empowerment that they ostensibly promoted.

Although the women in my field of research were outspoken advocates of women's emancipation and empowerment, the concerns and ideas they associated with these terms were not the same as those of the foreign interveners. The preceding section already mentioned that they tended to discuss these issues in the context of generational and household relations. Although they clearly identified traditional structures and practices in families and society at large as the major source of the lack of freedom for women, there was no sense of a general opposition between emancipation and family, emancipation and motherhood or emancipation and religion. In conversations about how Afghan society would have to change in order to afford greater personal liberty for women, the examples and models most frequently brought up were not Germany, Great Britain or Canada, but Iran and Pakistan. Such views, of course, were at odds not only with the discourses of the intervention, but also with the ideals and self-perception of its 'Western' personnel.[13] Due to the inescapably intimate dimension of all gender politics this constellation was, hence, more than a difference of opinion. It was a confrontation between conflicting images of what it meant to be an emancipated woman that took place in everyday interactions. There was, among the female professionals of the intervention, a tendency to parade, in offices and meeting places, attributes of 'Western' femininity. Especially women working in the power centres of the intervention, that is, for UN organizations or for government agencies related to major International Security Assistance Force (ISAF) contributors, made a point of not adapting their attire and appearance to the cultural context they were working in. Staying true to what they considered to be expressions of emancipation, refusing to accept the rules imposed on women regarding appearance and behaviour in Afghan society, was not just routinized action, but understood as a contribution to the emancipation and empowerment of Afghan women. Yet among the Afghan women in my field, the short sleeves and plunging necklines, the make-up and the shed headscarves were not perceived as a political statement supporting their struggles, but as disrespect towards the life they were living.

Clothing and attire were not the only issues in which practices that were deemed to be particularly emancipatory by the interventionists were perceived by Afghans in exactly the opposite way. Some studies point out that the emphasis on women alone did not resonate well with larger parts of the population, including women themselves. Lina Abirafeh (2009: 55–7) reports widespread anger about the treatment of men in international gender equality programmes. Ashraf Zahedi (2011) problematizes the misrepresentation of the role of men in Afghan society in international women's empowerment programmes and stresses the importance of the cooperation of Afghan men and women in working on gender equality. Maliha Chishti and Cheshmak Farhoumand-Sims (2011) denounce the selectivity of global feminists in Afghanistan working with a small group of urban activists with whom they could easily connect and agree while neglecting the vast majority of women in the country.

Yet, as explained previously, tensions between interveners and Afghans around women-related issues resulted not only from these cultural struggles in everyday life. They were also driven by dissonances between the ideals promoted in the discourses of interventionist politics and some of the actual practices of humanitarian organizations. The problem here was not half-hearted commitment; women's empowerment was doubtlessly not only high on the international agenda, but also personally important to many of the female intervention staff. The problem was that ideals of gender equality were frequently at odds with other organizational goals and necessities in a social context organized around strong patriarchal principles. The authority of men in Afghan society, for example, created a tendency within foreign and international humanitarian organizations to favour men and not women as responsible contact persons when cooperating with Afghan organizations. The need for counterparts who could reliably speak on behalf of the organization trumped ideals of gender equality.

Even worse than these tensions between operational objectives were instances where the organizations that were part of the universalist intervention project failed to protect the basic rights of their female staff. As explained earlier, sexual harassment at the workplace was an issue many of my female Afghan interlocutors were worried about. Twice, however, I was told about situations in which an Afghan woman had been molested by a higher-ranking Afghan man within an international humanitarian organization. In both cases the women had reported the incident to a 'Western' superior, but to no avail.[14] On a very personal level, experiences like this put into question the truthfulness of intervention politics.

In relations between Afghan women and the protagonists of the intervention, therefore, alliance in discourse coexisted with practices of distinction and conflictive interactions. On a normative level these interactions revealed the particularity of the universalism promoted by the intervention. As emancipated Afghan women did not easily buy into the role model of 'Western' womanhood, this role model was itself put into question – and intervention staff who identified with it felt compelled to defend it. Differing norms and ideas about female selfhood and the place of women in society were performed and confronted in situations of interaction between real women, pushed to defend not abstract norms but their way of life and being. In a cultural context already marked by hypersensitivity regarding gender difference, humanitarian engagement further politicized the category of gender and hence amplified its importance – not only for Afghans, but also for the interventionists themselves, who, in response to the importance attributed to gender difference in the Afghan context, came to be faced with particular scrutiny regarding gender equality within their own organizations.[15]

The ethnographic perspective reveals how in the laboratory of the intervention, the distinction between 'the universal' and 'the particular', between 'agents of humanity' and 'local population' is enacted and deconstructed at the same time. The distinction asymmetrically preconfigures lifeworld encounters, not only between Afghans and 'internationals', but also within these respective groups. But people then confront one another as embodied actors who carry with them personal experiences and collective histories. When gender equality or women's empowerment are evoked under such conditions, what appear as abstract universal principles at the level of policy making are transformed into often very personal concerns.

Conclusion

As embodied actors in their day-to-day lives come to be invested in the enactment of, and struggle over, allegedly universal ideals of gender equality, the intervention becomes a real-world laboratory for exploring the challenges and limitations of global forms of sociality. Therefore, interventions like the one in Afghanistan are relevant not only to people in the respective country and the professionals of humanitarian politics. They are sites in which the order of world society is (re)configured in experimental action. Abstract universalized epistemic, normative and political orders collapse into concrete situations and places and condition existences within them. Under such conditions, interactions take place not as encounters between people from different (parochial) contexts, such as, for example, between 'Americans' and 'Afghans'. They take the form of encounters between 'the universal' and 'the particular', between 'the global' and 'the local'. Yet, at the same time, they challenge and subvert exactly these distinctions as embodied actors in lifeworld interactions cannot strip themselves of their experiences and their personal and collective histories.

This chapter has attempted to show why politics and policies around 'women's issues' are particularly likely to create these kinds of entanglement. They rely on an intuitively credible illusion of universality. They therefore underscore the universalist pretensions of interventionist politics and make it easy to connect affectively to the otherwise anonymous and distant suffering that legitimizes humanitarian politics. Women's rights, protection and empowerment are a policy field in which social change can be most comprehensively staged. Its role in interventionist politics, however, points to the importance of gendered social relations in world order more generally.

Notes

[1] Beyond the fields obviously driven by technology, organizations with 'lab' in their title work on issues ranging from peace, democracy and justice to city planning and business design and to education and family counselling.

[2] The idea of 'laboratories of world society' as a specific type of empirical context emerged in discussions with the sociologist Tanja Bogusz who did embedded ethnographic research with an expedition on maritime biodiversity to Papua New Guinea (Bogusz, 2018: 372–405). Although at first glance situated in an entirely different empirical context, her observations regarding the particularities of interactions between 'Western' scientists and 'local' populations resonated with my analyses from Afghanistan.

[3] For an insightful discussion about the importance of methods of inquiry in developing a sociology for a globalized world, see Law and Urry (2004).

[4] The second paragraph of the UN Charter's preamble evokes the body's determination 'to regain faith in fundamental human rights, in the dignity and worth of the human person, *in the equal rights of men and women* and of nations large and small' (my emphasis).

5   Shortly before my arrival in Kabul, for example, the student Farkhunda Malikzada had been beaten to death by an angry crowd in Kabul. Violence was incited by the allegation that she had burned the Quran, which later turned out to be untrue. Videos of the killing were spread widely on social media. In the early weeks of the research, the shock of this event was very much present in interviews and conversations relating to women's politics and empowerment.
6   Fieldnotes, 5 May 2015.
7   'Debating the future of Afghanistan', discussion at Humboldt University Berlin, 12 May 2014.
8   Interview, 21 April 2015.
9   It is important to note that it is not necessarily the husband who is opposed. Quite frequently, more complex family dynamics revolving around powerful elders are at work.
10 Focus group discussion, 25 April 2015.
11 In Afghanistan, the term 'youth' encompasses anyone who is no longer an adolescent but not yet an elder.
12 Interview, 17 May 2015.
13 It needs to be emphasized that a significant number of the people working for humanitarian organizations in Kabul came from non-OECD countries. Only rarely, however, did they work in higher-ranking positions. Their influence on organizational policies accordingly remained limited. During my stay, I shared a house with a humanitarian professional from South East Asia and another from sub-Saharan Africa. Both frequently complained about what they perceived as a racist system.
14 Fieldnotes, 10 April 2015.
15 A telling example is an article by Kailah M. Karl published in the *American Intelligence Journal* (Karl, 2012), that argues for the necessity of women in Psychological Operations (PSYOP) in Afghanistan. The author, a staff sergeant (SSG) with the US army, had herself been deployed to the province of Paktika. And she does not disguise the fact that her proposals are based on the frustration experienced in her own work.

8

From the First Sino-Roman War (That Never Happened) to Modern International-cum-Imperial Relations: Observing International Politics from an Evolution Theory Perspective

Stephan Stetter

Introduction

What in the world happened so that over the course of human history not only did institutionalized cross-border relations between polities become common practice, but in global modernity a thing called the 'international political system' was eventually established – a system of global reach, that is to say, within which struggles over collectively binding decisions are played out? This is a system with a remarkable internal complexity that includes a myriad of actors, rules, traditions and mythologies, many of which date back to premodern times. It is also a system in which the specific type of hierarchical (imperial and colonial) relationship that dominated international politics when it took its modern shape during the nineteenth century has continued to play the same prominent role up until the present. Drawing from historically oriented scholarship in international relations (IR) and global historical sociology – while being theoretically anchored in the world society approaches of modern systems theory – this chapter studies some central dynamics that have shaped the evolution of international politics and its imperial underpinnings. This approach allows for a better understanding of what happened after the modern international political system became firmly established as a distinct and recognizable social field rather than one based on conventional IR theories. However, this system and its field-specific power constellations are anything but static. They were the result of social evolution and have been subject to ongoing transformations ever since. Accounting for these changes from a theoretical perspective and showing how they are linked to the field-specific power relationships being played out in this system is the main conceptual concern of this chapter.

Change and transformation is understood here as a process of social evolution. According to Luhmannian systems theory (Luhmann, 1995a, 2012/13; Andersen, 2003), social evolution is triggered by communicative variations in a given social field. While such fields are integrated in larger contexts such as world society as a whole, systems theory also stresses the relative autonomy of evolution in a given social field or system. International politics, it is argued in what follows, is such a field. Starting out from the aforementioned observation that the modern international political system stabilized as a social form in the course of the nineteenth century, the chapter then proceeds to argue that an increasing external and internal differentiation of this system is, from a theoretical vantage point, a core feature of its ongoing evolution. Differentiation has two dimensions here. External differentiation is understood as a growing autonomy of the field-specific dynamics within this system vis-à-vis other systems and fields such as national or regional political systems, the economy, or the systems that underlie law, religion and the like (think here of the actors, practices and institutions that make up this specific system, but not others – foreign ministries, diplomats, humanitarian interventions, UN peace-building and so on). Internal differentiation, on the other hand, refers to an increasing complexity of field-specific institutions, forms of actorhood and struggles (practices) over positions within this field (for example, the seemingly ever growing number of actors that claim a stake in political struggles within this system).

With this delineation of the system's external/internal differentiation as its starting point, this chapter then also takes a closer look at the field-specific power relations in play within the system. Drawing on the sociology of empire (Go, 2011; Steinmetz, 2013, 2014), it is argued here that the broader social conditions to which the external/ international differentiation of world politics relates are, in particular, the underlying imperial or (post)colonial fundamentals of social ordering in the international system and world society as a whole – without resorting to simplistic notions of a binary division in world politics between a powerful West, on the one hand, and a marginalized global South, on the other. In other words, the study of the 'formal' features of international politics as a field, characterized by external and internal differentiation, has to be complemented by an analysis of the concrete historical settings and contexts in relation to which this field emerged in the first place and has been evolving ever since. Addressing these imperial and (post)colonial underpinnings not only highlights the specific historical circumstances in which the modern international system took its present shape, it also allows the (complex) forms of path dependency that define power relationships in international politics today to be reconstructed in all their complexities.

The next section introduces the core concepts of communication, differentiation and evolutionary change. The third section introduces evolutionary perspectives on the emergence of international politics in general and the modern international political system in particular, paying special attention to the notion of external/internal differentiation. Some of the complexities of these imperial underpinnings are then discussed in the final section with a view to contextualizing the specific forms of power relationship that shape international politics' neverending transformations in global modernity.

Communications, differentiation and evolution

Communications are at the heart of society, generally speaking, and of (international) politics as a distinct social sphere (Albert et al, 2008). Moreover, communications – in particular the communication of contestations, understood in evolutionary terms as discursive 'variations' – are the central trigger for change in (international) politics and world society at large (Luhmann, 2012/13; Stetter, 2014). This kind of perspective based on communication theory advances a radically constructivist understanding of society that brings another angle to how we study communications, in addition, that is, to material understandings that highlight the linkage between communications and technology (see Tworek, Chapter 11 in this volume). Thus, the effects of communications exchanged between Alter and Ego cannot be controlled by these or other actors. In fact, the very notion of actorhood is part of social construction (Meyer and Jepperson, 2000). This double contingency of communications – Ego and Alter remain 'black boxes' for each other and for others – is the starting point for the emergence of social orders as discursive forms that aim to reduce complexity and generate societal expectations by ensuring that temporarily stable structures – understood as communication complexes – are socially upheld. This requires, from a theoretical angle, the availability in discourse of mechanisms that ensure the otherwise unlikely acceptance of communications within any system.

Social complexity then sets in whenever communications are 'clustered' in relation to specific social contexts. Such contexts might gain relative autonomy from each other – that is, they become distinct social fields held together by a field-specific 'anchoring' of communications that shapes that specific field and not others. For example, politics as a social field is shaped by the 'anchoring' function of power as a symbolically generated medium of communication (see Holzer, Chapter 4 in this volume). The anchoring in relation to 'power' ensures that communications are observed with respect to how they relate to defining or contesting specific political projects and how they shape struggles over the institutions, rules and norms that should collectively govern such polities. The social evolution of politics as a field then draws from the basic binary set-up of communications, namely the distinction between yes-communications (accepting a given power-based demand) or no-communications (contesting power-based demands). This binary structure allows us to study how communicative clusters or fields emerge, consolidate and change, both for society as a whole and for specific systems or fields (Spruyt, 1994a; Modelski, 1996).

The contingency prevalent in social encounters – meaning that it cannot be determined ex ante whether the path of 'yes' or that of 'no' communications will prevail – sets in motion evolutionary dynamics that occur at faster or slower paces. Formally speaking, social evolution can be understood as the sequencing of variations, selections and restabilizations of communications. Variations and social change are socially possible because communication offers allow for two principal responses. The first is acceptance – and often a given social context and its established hierarchies are conducive to acceptance. Drawing on Max Weber's notion of *Herrschaft* (political rule), the power of charisma, tradition or social conventions often renders the acceptance of communication offers likely (Schlichte, 2015). Other factors conducive to acceptance are a limited spatial reach for communications, which puts Alter and Ego in a state of permanent interaction, or simply the fact that not disagreeing is often less cumbersome that contesting. Variations, by contrast, set in when contestations are uttered, that is when a communication offer encounters a 'no' of whatever kind – in which case the emergence of conflicts becomes more likely (Messmer,

2003, 2007). Selections take place if such variations are repeatedly picked up in societal discourse. Selections take different forms, and range from rapid changes (that is revolutions) to more subtle ways of remembering possible variations that may even survive or be revived in societal discourse – for example, the way the idea of ancient Greek democracy was revived in modern European philosophy and politics. Finally, restabilizations are about the 'sorting' (Vrba and Gould, 1986) of communications into relatively stable expectations about what constitutes 'normal' social reality. Such restabilizations are sometimes underpinned by coercive means. Yet they are also accompanied by more subtle notions of legitimacy and normality, as when a given social order, stratification or functional differentiation among them begins to be taken for granted.

That is why the most general form of restabilization, at a society-wide level, is referred to in modern systems theory as differentiation (Luhmann, 2012/13; Albert et al, 2013a; Kleinschmidt, 2018). This is based on the notion in modern systems theory that, in contrast to Parsonian sociology or normative theories such as those of Habermas, society is integrated by diversity, heterogeneity and conflict. Moreover, the concept of differentiation brings in a historical perspective, too. Thus – using very broad brushstrokes here (for more see Luhmann, 2012/13) – over the course of history human societies were defined by a limited number of basic forms of differentiation and their evolution. The most basic form can be termed segmentary differentiation. Historically, this form characterizes in particular pre-Neolithic hunter-gatherer societies, which exhibited – to the best of our contemporary knowledge – little differentiation into social roles and hierarchies within and were also characterized by little intervention into other bands' affairs (see later). Due to their small size and practical barriers to uttering variations – transgressors could simply be expelled, having little chance of surviving alone in a largely 'uncivilized' nature – such segmentary societies were, from a historical perspective, very stable. Change was slow, and for most of their history humans as a species have lived in such segmentary societies – that is, in similar units with little internal role differentiation and a limited amount of institutionalized interaction with each other.

The Neolithic revolution – and in particular the combined effect of the technological innovation of agriculture at given locales and the emergence of territorially fixed sacred places – dramatically changed societal differentiation. This process resulted in the emergence of villages, of larger village complexes understood as chiefdoms, and later on of cities, as new social forms of organizing polities. A widened pool of communications – resulting inter alia from the growing size of communities – confronted societies with novel forms of differentiation that over time became dominant social structures. Thus, within village complexes and cities, hierarchies and role differentiation played an increasingly prominent role. Chiefdoms consolidated, which, over time, restabilized society by differentiating it along the binary distinction between a 'leadership' apt for religious and political office (and warfare), and a separate stratum of society that, generally speaking, served this ruling class.

This form of stratificatory differentiation was then mirrored, on a cross-border level, by the emergence of centre–periphery differentiations that distinguished dominant political-religious (city) empires, on the one hand, from suzerain polities, on the other. For (city) empires – such as Egypt, Mesopotamia or China – technological change epitomized by the invention of script was central, for it triggered the emergence of a bureaucratic class at the domestic level, while allowing for the formalizing of external relations, including the proliferation of an empire-wide lingua franca. Yet the invention of script was also a risk, for it widened the pool of communications in society, thereby rendering no-communications more likely, at least amongst those able to read and write. In order to control for these effects, recourse to religiously grounded founding myths – in particular the practice of ascribing godlike status to rulers, was the means by which to contain internal and external challenges to stratified rule. Seen from this perspective, it is hardly surprising that the massive widening of the pool of communications in early modernity, which set in with the technological invention of the printing press and other distributive media (see Holzer, Chapter 4 in this volume), not only posed an immense challenge to stratified rule but also triggered an increasing complexity of 'code-related' communications that over time fostered the autonomy and selfish reproduction of distinct social fields anchored by symbolically generated media of communication, such as power (politics), money (economy), truth (science), love (intimate relations) and others. It is this process – a growing autonomy of code-related forms of differentiation – that is referred to in modern systems theory as functional differentiation.

International politics: internal and external differentiation

As discussed in detail elsewhere (Luhmann, 2000; Stetter, 2008), politics – a social practice existing in all forms of differentiation highlighted in the previous section – has become a distinct and self-reproducing social system in modern social orders. When talking about functional differentiation with respect to politics as a distinct social system, the focus is on the social struggles, anchored in relation to the symbolically generated medium of 'power', that define the (legitimate) field positions of actors and the norms, practices and collectively binding decisions that govern different collectivities and polities, including a global political system defined as a 'field of actors struggling with each other for various forms of capital', as highlighted by Julian Go in Chapter 5 of this volume. As long as communications in this context are primarily seen as being about 'power', as an empty signifier that 'anchors' communications, rather than about the social reproduction of a given stratified class, it is possible to talk of the restabilization of a functionally differentiated system of politics. Other forms of differentiation do not disappear. The function system of politics integrates other forms of differentiation such as segmentation, stratification (for example, permanent hierarchies of distinct groups of people in a given polity) and centre–periphery relations. The totality of communications anchored in such power-related struggles define the (ever changing) discursive borders of the political system in society, while technological changes such as the global expansion of means of transport and communications have led not only to the emergence of a political system of planetary scope, but also contributed to a widening of the pool of possible yes- and no-communications. In a nutshell, this is what Mathias Albert and Tobias Werron refer to in the introductory chapter when arguing that world society can be conceived as 'a single social system that is internally differentiated into many social systems and their subsystems'.

It is within this function system of politics that an *international* political system emerged as one of its subsystems. It is in relation to the restabilization of this international political system that one can speak of its external differentiation. Thus, as for example both Albert (2016) and Barry Buzan and George Lawson (2015) have highlighted, international politics restabilized as a subsystem or social field in the course of the nineteenth century. This was the time when permanent forms of interlinked communications regarding 'international power' became institutionalized at planetary scales, inter alia through technological innovations such as the telegraph. Moreover, on an ideational and practice-related level, this period witnessed the emergence of socially shared and institutionally anchored notions of 'international' actorhood and 'international' political practice, in particular the guiding principles for legitimizing (and contesting) political rule such as the ideas of the 'balance of power', 'international law' and 'imperial stewardship'. Finally, this period was also characterized by the emergence and mushrooming of international organizations and transnational political entanglements in the form of non-governmental organizations (NGOs), for instance the antislavery and anticolonial movements, that 'invented' the international as a realm of action. As a result of these evolutionary changes, over time second-order observations of an international political system 'really' being out there shaped political discourses at the local, national, regional and global level. In other words, the notion of international politics as a distinct subsystem or field of politics, was selected and restabilized. As the global historian Jürgen Osterhammel (2009: 566; my translation) observed, 'the nineteenth century was the epoch in which international relations, as we know it, was born'. The external differentiation of international politics, understood as an increasing differentiation of this specific system/field from its social environment – such as other subsystems of politics at national or regional levels and other social systems such as the economy, law or religion – set in.

Internal differentiation then relates developments within a field. What is of relevance here in particular are the increase in internal complexity, epitomized inter alia by an ever growing number of relevant actors, as well as the increase in prevalent – and often contradictory – norms as well as arenas of political struggle at international scales. Variations play a particularly prominent role here. Thus, contestations of established international hierarchies allowed marginalized or less powerful actors – such as small states or colonized people – to contest the legitimacy of the international order. Such contestations/variations continually trigger new selections. If selections are repeatedly referred to in political discourse they lead to restabilizations within the subsystem of international politics – in other words, incremental rather than revolutionary adaptations of this system. The emergence of the global human rights regime between the 1850s and 1950s/60s, the consolidation of regional political subsystems, the 'legalization' of world politics, but also the securitization of North–South relations in the contemporary era can be read as results of selections of this kind that attest to a growing internal differentiation and build-up of complexity in international politics (Abbott et al, 2000; Reus-Smit, 2001; Buzan and Wæver, 2004; Bilgin, 2012). The variety of actors and the existence of many different arenas of practice within this internally highly complex and evolving field ultimately facilitate the communication of contestations. Thus, while entrenched power differentials endure, for instance between superpowers and other states or between the global North and the global South, the diversity of arenas in which international politics are played out ensures that struggles over field positions and legitimate courses of action are hard to contain. If NGOs or relatively weak states fail to convince superpowers, they shift arenas of action in order to pursue their objectives. This, for example, happened with the successful institutionalization of the International Criminal Court (Deitelhoff, 2009). In other words, the internal differentiation of international politics provides an immense amount of possibilities for contestations and denigrations of existing social structures, which allows international politics as a system to experiment with all sorts of selections to restabilize its changing, yet path-dependent, institutional shape.

This kind of evolutionary perspective on international politics closely resonates with historically oriented research in IR on the *longue durée* of international systems (Buzan and Little, 2000). Thus, the idea of the 'international' is not something that emerged in a moment of quasi-divine creation or something that can clearly be associated with concrete benchmark dates or time periods, in the way that, most commonly in IR, the Peace of Westphalia is held to mark a benchmark date. To be sure, to speak of international politics as a global affair requires some form of at least potentially realizable interconnectivity between people and places all over the world. Moreover, it also requires some form of shared sense that the world is a (social) whole – second-order observations, that is to say, that ensure that the 'international' is not just practised but also figures as a social form that is believed to be 'real' and out there. From that perspective, the global outreach by Europeans from the late fifteenth century gradually restabilized international politics as a global system locked in to a Western-centred hierarchy (see the following section). Yet other 'international' systems in all but name and at smaller, (inter-)regional scales had already existed for millennia. And it is from these multiple vantage points and beginnings that the modern international political system emerged and has been evolving ever since.

This is not the place to recount the history of politics as a form of organizing human social life (see again Buzan and Little, 2000). Suffice it to say here – picking up on what has already been referred to – that hunter-gatherer bands, in particular after the emergence of language (often estimated to have taken place around 70,000 BCE), engaged in institutionalized forms of cross-border relations, mainly to exchange food, luxury goods and mating partners, but also in order to engage in shared religious rituals that reflected a shared form of identity and destiny. Trade, elite relations and rituals all attest to early forms of diplomacy – core practices in international politics even today – and invite us to reflect on how contemporary diplomacy has deep roots in human history (Stetter, 2016). It was then, however, the systematic monopolization of political power in chiefdoms, and in particular in city states and early empires such as Egypt, Mesopotamia and China, and later on in Byzantium, the Holy Roman Empire, the Abasside Caliphate and other places, which transformed these already existing forms of 'international' relations into something political, namely a social realm in which power-related hierarchies between a centre and a periphery (and internally between a ruling political-cum-religious elite and the rest) became established. Within such transboundary realms, rules governing asymmetric cross-border relations were negotiated, maintained, defended and legitimized. This was facilitated by the emergence of script, which set in motion processes of bureaucratization and militarization. With knowledge and military might centralized, hierarchies between centres and peripheries played a particularly prominent role in ancient civilizations, for example in the eastern Mediterranean in which small kingdoms became diplomatic Others within a stratified system dominated by one or more regional powers. Thus, small polities, such as the Phoenicians or Israelites, were part of a regional system in which Egypt and Babylonia acted as hegemons. This period also witnessed the emergence of a legal stabilization of these premodern 'international' systems through forms of arbitration and a gradual emergence of the idea of sovereignty, as in the international relations between Greek city states (Reus-Smit, 1997). But none of these instances of international relations *avant la lettre* was yet global in scope. The absence of relations between regional hegemons of their time, such as the Roman and Chinese empires, is a case in point. Both 'superpowers' somehow knew of each other's existence, exchanged some luxury goods – via intermediaries such as the Parthians – but actually had almost no direct contact with one another, except for some very limited exchanges via messengers who visited the other realm but without establishing any permanent institutional superstructure: a first Sino-Roman war therefore never happened. Even the Mongol Empire of the thirteenth century, the empire with the greatest territorial extent that had ever existed up to then, may have stretched over huge swathes of territory in Eurasia, but was in no way global in scope. What this short reflection on the 'deep' history of international relations shows is that some of the core institutional foundations of international politics as we know them today, which shape the external and internal differentiation of modern international politics – primary institutions (Buzan, 2004) such as great power prerogatives, war, diplomacy, trade, elite interaction, the balance of power (for example, between Christianity and Islam in the context of the crusades and their aftermath), legal arbitration/international law, sovereignty and others – have deep roots in history and have evolved over centuries, if not millennia. Thus, modern diplomatic practice is, for example, deeply rooted in imaginaries of sublime diplomatic grandeur perfected by the Byzantine Empire (Neumann, 2005).

Notwithstanding the deep roots of many international practices in human history, there is still ample reason to focus on the nineteenth century as the formative epoch for the 'international' as we know it today. The English School's notion of the primary institutions of international society is a good starting point here. While many of these primary institutions have, as just highlighted, a long history, they nevertheless evolved into *global* institutions only during the nineteenth century. Remember, primary institutions are understood in the English School as broader systems of meaning that operate in a given social realm and, in the terminology of communication theory, 'anchor' communications within this realm. If primary institutions – such as war, sovereignty, balance of power, human rights, colonialism, international law and so on – are considered by a sufficient number of actors to be part of the 'international', then they engender a range of legitimized forms of actorhood and practices, but also open up political space for contestations. They allow the international political system to be distinguished from its social environment, because these primary institutions shape field-specific struggles in this realm and not in others (say intimate relationships or symphonic orchestras). They reinforce the relative autonomy, or external differentiation, of international politics as a distinct subsystem. Moreover, primary institutions contribute to an increasing internal differentiation of international politics by providing multiple access points for a wide variety of actors to demand their 'legitimate' share in international arenas, to get their voices heard, and to challenge entrenched power relationships, for example, through human rights advocacy, anticolonial resistance and other means.

Imperial-cum-international relations: reflections on power and opposition in modern world politics

Notwithstanding the fundamental shift to functional differentiation, the modern international system is not devoid of entrenched hierarchies; quite the contrary (Mattern and Zarakol, 2016). One should not, therefore, misunderstand the notion of a growing external and internal differentiation of international politics as an argument in favour of an ever growing autonomy and polycentrism that is rendering power politics and hierarchies increasingly obsolete. In fact, hierarchies are central to modern international relations. They are visible at local and regional levels, for example, in the shape of entrenched hierarchies between families, ruling regimes, governing parties, dominant ethnonational-religious groups or powerful interstate alliances vis-à-vis their competitors in many parts of the world (for the Middle East see Stetter, 2008). Yet from a global perspective, it has been the imperial and colonial condition, out of which the modern international system has developed since the nineteenth century, that has had a particularly long-lasting and globally encompassing effect in shaping international hierarchies, including those at local and regional levels. As highlighted previously, hierarchies in the form of imperial underpinnings were part of international relations in premodern eras, too. However, what is noteworthy about the modern order is that while such imperial hierarchies were formative for international politics prior to World War II, and have shaped postcolonial identities and practices ever since, they are largely absent from IR's core ways of theorizing. This can only come as a great surprise to an observer with even the most rudimentary empirical knowledge of international relations post-World War II.

After the demise of the British Empire, the United States and, until the 1990s, the Soviet Union competed for global imperial predominance, ironically both under the pretext of being anti-imperialist. Instead of an end of history, the 'West' as a larger conglomerate is today arguably at the heart of norms and practices of military intervention, peace-building, human rights, democracy promotion, free trade and many other realms of action that shape 'empire' (Hardt and Negri, 2000) as a decentralized entity in contemporary global modernity that provides the broader social context within which many of the political struggles, and also the civil and interstate wars of our era unfold – as do the global imperial ambitions of actors as diverse as the US, the EU, China, Russia and others. Yet rather than silencing opposition, as one would envisage in a stratified society, such modern-day hierarchies open up ever new spaces for contestation and denigration – both in the West and the global South – directed against such things as 'neoliberalism', 'globalism', 'Western culture' or 'Western hypocrisy'. These contestations often take the form of 'postcolonial anxiety' in the sense that concrete historical experiences with Euro-American imperialism during the nineteenth and twentieth centuries underpin, and render plausible, suspicions of the West throughout the global South – while this same 'postcolonial anxiety' (O'Riley, 2007) also shapes the continuity of Orientalist stereotypes, nationalist populism and the politics of fear in the West. This only underlines, following what Albert and Werron argue in the introductory chapter, the fact that social fields engender 'practices and agency' including the constant struggles within the field of international politics that securitize, defend, challenge, maintain or redefine such imperial and (post)colonial hierarchies.

Against this empirical background, it is quite astonishing how the imperial and (post)colonial underpinnings of international politics, independently of how important they might be considered in concrete settings, have traditionally been covered in IR – or rather how they have not been covered at all. So, looking at international politics from a historical angle and thus highlighting the way that this social field is embedded in a millennia-old tradition of imperial hierarchies and other practices enacting the 'international' stands in marked contrast to how theorizing in this discipline developed in its 'first hundred years' (Dunne et al, 2013). So, notwithstanding some noticeable exceptions, IR can be understood as a largely 'ahistorical' science with a strong inclination for abstract theorizing that remains silent about the entrenched hierarchies in international politics (Buzan and Little, 2001). This lack of historical and sociological depth has led some observers to argue that there is a fundamental crisis in IR theory, a shocking diagnosis for a discipline that takes great pride in its theory-based identity (Dunne et al, 2013). Thus, the claim that the discipline suffers from historical amnesia and that this translates into theoretical numbness holds particularly true when one looks at the so-called core IR theories, those theories that have shaped the discipline's major debates and self-perceptions since the 1920s (Lapid, 1989). As Hobson (2012) has shown, these theories omit the imperial and (post)colonial past and present of international relations, thereby presenting a theoretical picture of world politics that is deeply embedded in Eurocentrism and therefore exhibits serious theoretical and empirical flaws. Thus, somewhat ironically, canonical IR theories – such as liberalism, realism, social constructivism or global governance – are strongly shaped by history, in the sense that what is at the core of these theories are time-bound extrapolations from the specific historical era in which the theories emerged and, moreover, in a second step these temporally situated experiences were transformed into allegedly timeless, abstract 'laws'.

In other words, core IR theories tend to deduce general laws from the specific historical context during which they emerged, while at the same time invisibilizing this temporal embedding. Liberalism evolved from post-World War I utopias of self-determination and democracy (and alleged Western civilizational supremacy). Neorealism, while claiming to have 'discovered' timeless laws of international politics, to a large degree generalized from the specific historical constellation of bipolarity during the Cold War (and legitimized US hegemony). Governance theories celebrate mainly post-World War II international organizations and multilateral treaties (and thereby cherish alleged Western rationality and the rule of international organizations), whereas social constructivism is heavily focused on those norms, practices and identities that rose to prominence on the world stage after the alleged 'end of history', for instance, liberal democracy, market liberalism and human rights (thereby legitimizing inter alia 'progressive' non-state actors). What unites these core IR theories, in spite of their different ontological and epistemological claims, is not only the invisibilization of their respective historical origins, but also their joint rootedness in a Eurocentric way of observing the 'international' that has imperial hierarchies as its blind spot. Of course, one should not equate these theories with the entire universe of theorizing in IR. There are many other schools and theories at the core and at the many fringes of the discipline – such as post-structuralism, securitization theories, world society theories, postcolonialist, neo-Marxist approaches, and many others, including historical-sociological schools of IR such as the English School – that have contributed during the last decades to a renewed interest in history and have uncovered the relevance of the imperial and (post)colonial underpinnings of international politics on many scales.

Drawing on these diverse literatures, two aspects of how, in global modernity, imperial-cum-international relations emerged as a distinct social field are of particular importance. These are the contingency of this process, on the one hand, and its concrete manifestations in primary institutions, on the other. As far as contingency is concerned, European expansion and subjugation of most parts of the planet in early modernity should be understood as a non-linear pathway. Other polities – particularly Chinese and Arab, but also steppe people like the Mongols (Neumann and Wigen, 2018) – possessed similar political, military, cultural, technological and economic means to Europeans. Yet, for a bundle of reasons, these other polities did not become the main drivers of the planetary expansion that took shape from the late fifteenth century on. As another word of caution, one also needs to be aware that this European global outreach did not immediately lead to the emergence of a thick political system at global scales. For example, the peace treaties of Osnabrück and Münster of 1648 are a good example of the fact that international relations were still mainly regional in scope. With regard to IR theories' Eurocentric myopia, it is quite telling that the discipline has, until today, generalized from this European system and the notion of '1648' when dealing with global international relations. This not only downplays the relevance of other forms of organizing interregional political relations in global modernity – for example, hierarchical relations within the Ottoman Empire – it is also blind to how these evolving ways of organizing relations between European polities were not considered relevant for extra-European international relations, as is evident from how non-European polities and people were treated by European powers in international conferences from Vienna 1815, to Berlin 1878 and 1884/85, and on to the post-World War I peace conferences in Sèvres and elsewhere.

From an institutional perspective, the imperial underpinnings of contemporary international relations then relate in particular to two dimensions. First, Europeans increased their grip on other world regions, and the new international system became planetary in scope, culminating in the subjugation in the course of the nineteenth century of erstwhile relatively autonomous regional systems such as the Ottoman Empire and China, the latter losing its status as one of the wealthiest and most powerful empires within a few decades between 1800 and the Opium Wars. Only a few non-European polities – Japan, Siam, Ethiopia, and to some extent the Ottoman Empire, for example – were able to fend off European imperial outreach while at the same time struggling to become accepted players in an international system increasingly shaped by racist underpinnings that legitimized European imperial rule and rendered self-determination by non-Europeans a complex political struggle. Second, what emerged was a global political system governed by a number of central overarching institutional principles, or primary institutions, that inherently related to imperialism. These were, in particular (see also Osterhammel, 2009), the notions of a standard of civilization, and a balance of power between or governance by the Great Powers (see also Buzan, 2004; Albert, 2016). The global international system that emerged in the nineteenth century was backed up by permanent forms of international political organization that had the governance of global affairs as their objective and which drew from these two principles. This did not end with the *fin de siècle* but shaped the twentieth-century global political order as well, for example in the context of the Mandate System of the League of Nations after World War I or the institutionalization of veto power to mainly Euro-American powers in the UN Security Council after World War II. That is the background against which various literatures, from Buzan's (2014) reflections on how the standard of civilization shapes political practices in the contemporary international order to critical peace-building literature and postcolonialism, underline in great detail how such imperial underpinnings, rather than being a relic of the past, need to be considered a building block of the contemporary international order. These underpinnings shape this field's structures, imaginaries and practices on many levels. Major evolutionary changes, such as the emergence of a codified global human rights regime, the delegitimization of racism at the UN level, decolonization and many others then highlight how these imperial underpinnings, rather than cementing power distributions, form the background foil for a variety of political struggles. These in turn engender not only contestations against real or perceived forms of imperialism, but also manifold instances of selection and restabilization within this evolving system. To stress this point, the evolution theory perspective suggested here strongly implies that the imperial and increasingly racist underpinnings of global political order have been transformed in the course of the last two decades. The notion of systemic transformations advanced by Julian Go in Chapter 5 of this volume (distinguishing between imperial expansion, war and international order) is one way of studying how variations, selections and restabilizations interrelate – and how legacies from the imperial beginnings of this system shape, in complex and sometimes paradoxical ways, the struggles over capital and legitimacy in this field.

Conclusion

Highlighting the imperial and (post)colonial underpinnings of international politics in global modernity is, seen from the evolutionary perspective unfolded in this chapter, an argument in favour of understanding first and foremost the complexity of this social field and how political struggles are organized within it. Talking about modern imperial-cum-international relations, in other words, is not supposed to be an intellectual shortcut enabling the world to be neatly divided into a (bad) West and a (marginalized) Global South. It is rather an argument in favour of systematically bringing historical and sociological depth to the study of this social field. A focus on history is required since the formative period of our contemporary order is the nineteenth century, and the path-dependencies related to the specific forms of actorhood and institutional parameters were established in this period and have transformed themselves in complex ways ever since. And sociology is required because, rather than silencing opposition, hierarchies in a modern social order shaped by functional differentiation are not a mechanism to minimize the likelihood of contestations, new selections and systemic restabilizations. They are rather a recipe for engendering ever more dynamic, yet often contradictory, critical assaults on and objections to these very enduring, yet evolving hierarchies.

9

Nationalism as a Global Institution: A Historical-Sociological View

Tobias Werron

Introduction

Nationalism just does not seem to want to disappear. On this account alone, it represents a major challenge for theories of global change. As globalization scholars, we constantly set ourselves to discover global connections and global structures where long-standing traditions in our disciplines primarily see national histories, national phenomena or national problems. But while going beyond methodological nationalism is certainly the right thing to do, it can easily distract one from the fact that the history of nationalism, too, is a globalization story: the story of a model of collective identity and state organization that has spread globally and transformed international politics profoundly in the past two centuries (Mann, 1997; Wimmer and Feinstein, 2010). The neglect of this story is one of the reasons for the recurring surprise at the alleged 'resilience' or 'resurgence' of nationalism in the last roughly 40 years.

At the peak of the enthusiasm for globalization in the mid-1990s and early 2000s, there was a lot of talk about the 'end of nationalism' and the 'end of the nation state'. Back then, in the not so distant past, many globalization theorists assumed that the time had come for a 'flat world' and a truly 'cosmopolitan age'. Nationalism and the nation state were considered too small for the big problems, too big for the small problems and thus bound to be replaced by global or more local forms of identity formation and political organization as a consequence of increasing globalization (see, for example, Friedman, 2005; Ohmae, 1995). By contrast, the last few years have seen a growing discourse about a 'new nationalism', which can refer to phenomena as diverse as the nationalist rhetoric and politics of authoritarian governments (for example, China, Russia, Turkey, Hungary), independence movements (for example, in Catalonia and Scotland), the rise of nationalist parties in Europe (for example, the Front Nationale in France and Alternative für Deutschland (AfD) in Germany), or the increasing popularity of protectionist economic policies (for example with the Trump administration in the US).

Was nationalism dying in the 1990s while it is now 'new' and 'resurgent'? The contrast between these two debates is even more striking considering that it is not the first debate of its kind. Around 1980 lots of articles and books appeared that talked about the 'resurgence of nationalism' or about a 'new economic nationalism', often producing arguments that could be copy-pasted without much change into the current debate. And 40 years ago too, the new nationalism was often described as a counter-reaction to globalization, except that globalization was not yet a fashionable term, and terms such as 'world-wide integration' or 'internationalization' were used instead (see, for example, Hieronymi, 1980; Mayall, 1984).

If there is any logic to these debates, it is the logic of repetition: after each globalization debate there is another nationalism debate, followed by another globalization debate and so on. After some decades of experience with such debates, then, we might conclude that it is time for a fresh look at the relationship between nationalism and globalization that might help prevent us from being surprised by the resilience of nationalism over and over again. Such an approach could start with two general insights.

First, theories of global social change should go beyond mere critique of methodological nationalism by making nationalism a central topic of globalization research (Pryke, 2009). The standard critique of methodological nationalism rests on the insight that there is nothing natural about nationalism and the modern nation state (Wimmer and Glick Schiller, 2002; Chernilo, 2006a). Going beyond this critique, globalization theorists should be able to account for the possibility that particularism, too, can be enabled and reproduced by globalization processes (see, for example, Robertson, 1995). Modern nationalism is a prime example of this logic, and it has arguably been entangled with globalization dynamics right from its beginnings in the late eighteenth to early nineteenth century. Any attempt to explain the resilience of today's nationalism, therefore, should be based on an understanding of the long-term historical relations between nationalism and globalization.

Second, studying this historical relationship will encourage us to overcome an epistemic flaw in thinking about nationalism in much of the social science literature, and particularly in sociological theory: the tendency to see nationalism primarily as a conspicuous and aggressive political ideology (see, for example, Heywood, 2017). Sociological theorists have often combined this view with a depiction of nationalism as a simplistic worldview favoured by people who have trouble dealing with the complexities of modernity (Giddens, 1985; Stichweh, 2000). Associated with this view is a notion of the modern nation state that, if taken to the extreme, excludes nationalism from the very object of analysis. Anthony Giddens, for instance, in his *The Nation-state and Violence*, draws a clear line between the 'power container' of the nation state, on the one hand, which he sees as a perfectly modern institution, and nationalism, on the other hand, which leads him to the surprising conclusion, for a sociologist, that nationalism is 'in substantial part a psychological phenomenon', which becomes important only when the 'sense of ontological security is put in jeopardy by the disruption of routines' (Giddens, 1985: 218). For Giddens, then, modernity has brought us the nation state but has no inherent need for nationalism – as if the nation state was possible without nationalism. Such views are partly responsible for the neglect of nationalism in sociological theory, dating back to the classics (Smith, 1983), and live on in the tendency of globalization scholars to think of globalization and nationalism in terms of a zero-sum relationship, where more globalization means less nationalism (and vice versa).

To rethink the relationship between nationalism and globalization, we should conceive of the former not just as an ideology but as a global institution: a largely taken-for-granted feature of the modern world that is woven into the very fabric of global modernity. Such a conception can build on ideas that have gained prominence in the literature on nationalism of recent years but have not yet been systematically combined with historical globalization studies. This strand of the nationalism literature argues that nationalism can operate not just in 'hot' ideological ways but also in inconspicuous, 'banal' ones (Billig, 1995; Brubaker, 1996; Hutchinson, 2006; Fox, 2017). Nationalism can appear, for instance, in the form of everyday national references in the media, in institutionalized dimensions of global systems such as sports or the arts, as the taken-for-granted addressee of global models of development, or as a mode of argumentation that introduces implicit notions of scarcity into political discourse and thus helps reproduce the very idea of conflicting 'national interests'.

This chapter aims to show how the inconspicuous side of modern nationalism is connected to globalization processes and how, on this basis, it has helped turn nationalism into a global institution. The main aim is to try to specify the ways in which the inconspicuous reproduction of modern nationalism has been intertwined with globalization processes since the mid-to-late nineteenth century. The first section starts with conceptual remarks that introduce my understanding of modern nationalism, defining it as modern discourse for legitimizing statehood on a global scale. On this basis, a distinction is developed between four modes of reproduction of modern nationalism: two conspicuous mechanisms, which are called here 'identity nationalism' and 'conflict nationalism', and two inconspicuous ones, which are called 'institutionalized nationalism' and 'scarcity nationalism'. The following section connects these conceptual insights to the historical and sociological literature on globalization. It starts with a brief analysis of changes in the infrastructure of global communication since the mid-nineteenth century (see also Tworek, Chapter 11 in this volume), and goes on to show that the inconspicuous mechanisms for the reproduction of nationalism are connected to globalization dynamics in multiple ways. This section distinguishes a number of 'globalized' types of institutionalized nationalism and scarcity nationalism, putting particular emphasis on the latter: a nationalist discourse based on the idea that the world is a place with scarce – as opposed to abundant – resources. The conclusion argues that the difficulty of understanding nationalism as a global institution is indicative of more general questions that pose a major challenge to the analysis of global social change.

Conceptual remarks: modern nationalism

Analysing nationalism as a global institution requires a concept of nationalism that captures both its ideological and banal-institutional elements. For this purpose, a working definition is suggested, inspired by constructivist contributions to the nationalism literature, particularly from Craig Calhoun (1997) and Umut Özkirimli (2010). Combining their insights, I understand modern nationalism as a discourse that incorporates three elements:

- the construction of collective identities (cultural element);
- the legitimization of political claims made by these identities (popular sovereignty = political element);

- the idea of a world order divided into nations or nation states (universal or global element).

Seeing nationalism as a legitimizing discourse consisting of these three elements has the advantage of capturing both its ideological and its institutional dimension. A discourse can be the outcome of an aggressive struggle between conflicting ideological positions, but also of routinized ways of writing, speaking and interacting, and both forms contribute to making nationalism a global institution.

Moreover, distinguishing between the cultural, political and global elements of this discourse draws attention to the relationship between them. While the relation between the first two has been intensively discussed in the literature on nationalism for quite some time and was famously captured in Ernest Gellner's (1983) metaphorical description of modern nationalism as aiming at a 'marriage' between nation and state, culture and politics, the relationship of the first two with the global element has attracted less attention. This is unfortunate because it is the third element that best explains why nationalism, irrespective of differences of opinion between 'modernists' and 'anti-modernists' in the nationalism literature (Smith, 1998; Gorski, 2000), should indeed be considered a modern institution. By establishing the principle of national legitimacy as a universal model, nationalism has transformed European 'international society' in two ways: it has helped to expand the outer limits of the state system 'to a point where they are coextensive with those of the globe', and it has encouraged the 'penetration of central government activity', both internally by expanding state power and responsibility and externally by increasing the range and density of international relations (Mayall, 1990: 33–4). Focusing on the global element of the modern nationalist discourse thus calls attention to the historical process in which nationalism, over the past 200 years or so, has helped transform the early modern state system into the global nation state system.

This view emphasizes the modernity of nationalism and the nation state system without denying continuities with the early modern system. Core institutions of the latter such as sovereignty, diplomacy and international law are just as characteristic of today's global nation state system. However, it was nationalism that first introduced a source of legitimacy with universal, and thus potentially global, scope, attracting all kinds of social groups looking to legitimize their respective state-building projects in an increasingly globalized environment. It was the rise of the nationalist worldview, with its peculiar combination of particularistic and universalistic elements, which made the globalization of the European state system possible, including, most notably, the expansion enabled by the resistance of anticolonial movements outside of Europe. And in that regard, nationalism is undeniably modern.

Conspicuous and inconspicuous mechanisms of reproduction

This conceptualization also affects what we might find interesting about the history of modern nationalism. The nationalism literature has a number of favourite topics that have been studied over and over again. Many of them relate to the aforementioned assumption of a 'marriage' between nation and state, which suggests focusing on how this marriage has been arranged in particular cases and protected against dissolution or divorce. This implies two logical possibilities. How have existing states created and 'married' their respective nations, and how have nations created and 'married' their respective states? The interest in these questions is reflected by the fact that studies of nationalism have been working with typologies based on the distinctions nation versus state or cultural versus political element since at least the mid-twentieth century. Examples range from early distinctions between 'ethnic' and 'civic' nationalism (Kohn, 1950) to more recent ones like 'cultural-ethnic' versus 'official' (Anderson, 2006) or 'state-led' versus 'counter-state' nationalism' (Tilly, 1994). Other questions which have occupied the nationalism literature in recent years are: what roles did elites play in the making of national collective identities, and how were national collective identities and their political claims popularized and turned into mass phenomena (Hroch, 2005; Wimmer, 2002, 2013, 2018)? How can we explain the global diffusion of nationalism (Wimmer and Feinstein, 2010)? What was the role of anticolonial nationalism in this process (Go and Watson, 2019)?

These are important questions, of course. However, they do not exhaust what globalization scholars could find interesting about nationalism. Given the understanding of nationalism suggested previously, one of the questions they do not address is the making and stability of nationalism as a global institution. What are the sources of the legitimizing power of nationalism – as a global discourse – in a world already more or less completely divided into nation states? Asking this question draws attention to the insight that nationalism legitimizes not just individual nation states, but also the world order that undergirds the relationships between all nation states. Nationalism is the discourse that holds the nation state system together.

What, then, are the main mechanisms of reproduction of this discourse? Based on an inductive analysis of both the nationalism and globalization literature, I suggest distinguishing the four mechanisms of reproduction I have already mentioned. Two of them are conspicuous – identity nationalism and conflict nationalism – two less conspicuous – institutionalized nationalism and scarcity nationalism:

- Identity nationalism is based on open, often aggressive construction of national collective identities and their political ambitions, particularly by means of narration (construction of national histories) and symbolization (national flags, monuments, anthems, and so on). Identity nationalism revolves around questions like 'What is German?', 'What is English?', seeking answers in the re-description of historical experiences, cultural characteristics, religious belongings, and so on. Most research on nationalism has focused on this kind of reproduction, finding that 'nations' are highly artificial products of nationalism that share a limited symbolic and narrative repertoire (for an overview of recurring characteristics see Calhoun, 1997: 4–5; Edensor, 2002). In other words, all nationalisms resemble each other in how they claim their own singularity.
- Conflict nationalism legitimizes national collective identities and their political ambitions via demarcation from other national collective identities, particularly in 'hot' situations of conflict. Many contributions to the nationalism literature have focused on this mode of reproduction, showing how the legitimacy and popularity of nationalist identity claims are helped by the opportunity for distinction provided by conflict situations from low-intensity political disputes to wars (see, for example, Hutchinson, 2004, 2017; Wimmer, 2013). Equally, the ability of nationalists to jump on opportunities and use conflict situations to promote their cause has proved to be a vital source of legitimacy and success for modern nationalism.

Identity and conflict nationalism work together in constructing and defending the political claims of national collective identities. Another shared characteristic is that they are hard to overlook because both operate openly, visibly, often aggressively. For this reason, they cannot explain how nationalism has turned into a seemingly natural, taken-for-granted institution. For this purpose, we first have to acknowledge that, sociologically speaking, taken-for-grantedness should not be taken for granted. The appearance of naturalness is the outcome of constant work and social construction. It is at this point that nationalism's two other mechanisms of reproduction prove to be important:

- Institutionalized nationalism aims to capture the everyday use of national identity markers, particularly in the national media and in the global field or global systems. Examples are the use of words like 'we' and 'they' in news or sports coverage, the taken-for-granted display of national maps in weather reports and likewise the everyday reference to national statistics in scientific research ('methodological nationalism').
- Scarcity nationalism, on the other hand, draws attention to the impact of the idea that the world is stocked with scarce resources that each nation can only acquire at the expense of other nations. Assumptions of scarcity are sometimes openly theorized, as in some versions of 'economic nationalism'. More often than not, however, they are implicitly introduced into the political discourse, partaking in nationalist sense-making in rather inconspicuous ways.

While identity and conflict nationalism are involved in the open and aggressive production of national collective identities in and beyond situations of conflict, institutionalized and scarcity nationalism specialize in the implicit maintenance of national collective identities and their political ambitions. In a sense, they operate by making themselves disappear. It is no surprise, then, that they have been less frequently discussed in the literature. They are, however, particularly important when it comes to explaining the historical transformation of nationalism into a global institution.

Globalized reproduction: the transformation of nationalism into a global institution

Modern nationalism emerged around 1800. Most scholars locate its beginnings in revolutionary France, some in the anticolonial Americas (for the latter view, see Anderson, 2006).[1] Irrespective of such differences, we can safely say that, in the early-to-mid-nineteenth century, two basic models for the construction of national identities and their political ambitions were ready for 'pirating' (Anderson, 2006): a primarily political model aimed at legitimizing and stabilizing a given state structure ('official nationalism', 'state-led nationalism'), and a primarily cultural model that usually aimed at the founding and legitimizing of new states ('ethno-cultural nationalism', 'counter-state nationalism'). While French and Spanish nationalism are examples of the first type, most nationalist movements are examples of the second – or, possibly, of further types, such as 'irredentist nationalism' (in the case of Germany and Italy) or postcolonial nationalism. The early formation of these models required the aggressive construction of new collective identities and intense political struggle and thus was likely to have been dominated by the 'hot' mechanisms of reproduction, identity nationalism and conflict nationalism. Moreover, conflict nationalism seems to have played a major role in the transformation of both models into a universal 'nation form' (Goswami, 2002), namely, a *global* model ready for worldwide adoption. This transformation took place in what might be called a 'co-colonial' constellation from the late nineteenth to the early twentieth century, when nationalism, as a legitimizing political discourse, was used on both sides of the colonial divide, juxtaposing the 'expansionist nationalism' of the Western imperial powers with the 'defensive nationalism' of anticolonial resistance (for these two terms see Osterhammel, 2009: 904).

The transformation of nationalism into a global model under postcolonial circumstances draws attention to globalization processes that started between the mid-nineteenth and the early twentieth century and changed the environment in which nationalism could operate. It is therefore useful to take a brief look at these processes before returning to the history of nationalism.

First and foremost, this included changes in the infrastructures of global communication that reflected a number of interrelated developments (Werron, 2019, 2020a). First, changes in the technological infrastructure, including the introduction of new telecommunication technologies (telegraph, telephone, wireless), which for the first time in history effectively decoupled the speed of communication from the speed of transportation of people and goods (Wenzlhuemer, 2007). Second, changes in the symbolic infrastructure, that is, of categories of time and space, which led to the invention of a 'world time' and worldwide time zones that allowed for the temporal comparison of events within and across time zones (for the long-term institutionalization of this spatiotemporal vocabulary see Ogle, 2015). And third, changes in the sociocultural infrastructure of communication, which included the formation of a 'global media system' based on a global oligopoly of new agencies (Winseck and Pike, 2007; Müller and Tworek, 2015). The latter implied the rise of our current concept of 'news' and of a professional journalism that continually reports and comments on news around the world, addressing mostly national audiences. All of these developments, amplified by further telecommunication technologies, from the wireless telegraph to radio and television to digital technologies, are still relevant today. This suggests that they indeed mark the beginning of an era of globalization – the 'long twentieth century' (Dickinson, 2018) – that began in the mid-nineteenth century and is still going on today.

The rise of an infrastructure for global communication also affected the reproduction of nationalism. As we have already seen in our discussion of the co-colonial modelling of nationalism in the late nineteenth to early twentieth century, it made it easier for nationalists to observe each other simultaneously in a global media environment, amplifying and accelerating their tendency to imitate each other's templates for identity construction (identity nationalism) while also intensifying conflicts and mutual demarcation on a global scale (conflict nationalism) (regarding Britain and India, see Headrick, 2010). Moreover, it also affected the inconspicuous modes of reproduction, which helped turn nationalism into a seemingly natural feature of the modern world.

Institutionalized nationalism

According to Benedict Anderson's influential definition, nations are imagined identities that emerged as products of the 'print capitalism' of the eighteenth and nineteenth centuries, conceived in newspapers and other print outlets and integrated into the political conversation until they were taken for granted. It can therefore be argued that nationalism was institutionalized right from the start. This is one of the reasons why Anderson rejected the description of nationalism as just a political ideology, arguing that it 'would make things easier if one treated it as if it belonged with "kinship" and "religion", rather than with "liberalism" or "fascism"' (Anderson, 2006: 5).

Institutionalization via the media has been an integral part of modern nationalism since its beginnings. Likewise, the relationship between nationalism and globalization was institutionalized by the global media system from the latter's establishment in the mid-nineteenth century (telegraph network, news agencies, professional journalism). This led to the emergence of a number of new types of institutionalized nationalism. By treating the whole world as a constant source of 'news' and selling that news to national media, the global media system helped create what might be called perspectival nationalism. The term highlights the idea that the institutionalization of national news coverage should not be equated with a focus on national topics, actors or events. Rather, national media include 'foreign news' by reporting on the world from a national perspective. The global institutionalization of nationalism is affected by this in two seemingly contradictory but in fact complementary ways. On the one hand, national news coverage provincializes the world by experiencing everything from a national perspective. In this spirit, the headline of a Scottish newspaper reporting on the sinking of the *Titanic* read 'Aberdeen man lost at sea' (Luhmann, 1996: 60). On the other hand, the global media system connects the national perspective to the world by providing a standardized political vocabulary that can see and compare 'political leaders', 'presidents', 'nationalist agitators' and so on all over the globe (this is what Benedict Anderson [1998: 33] calls 'seriality'). The world, then, is described from a national perspective and for a national audience, but in a more or less globalized language of news. We are all still taking part in this logic today, whether we read the *New York Times, Guardian, Frankfurter Allgemeine Zeitung* or *Neue Zürcher Zeitung* and whether we buy print editions of the papers or read them online.

There are two further variants of institutionalized nationalism that can be analysed as products of globalization processes. The global institutionalization of the nation state is the product particularly of the rise of international organizations from the mid-nineteenth century. As the term 'international' indicates, these organizations incorporate the division of the world into nation states into their very structure (for the broader world-political context which cannot be discussed here, see Go, 2008; Buzan and Lawson, 2015; Albert, 2016). And the larger the number of international organizations, the more natural the idea of a world exclusively consisting of nations (and their respective states) may come to appear. International organizations and other global observers, from political journalists to social scientists, also contribute to the naturalization of the nation state system by addressing nation states as the primary actors responsible for the progress of humanity (Meyer et al, 1997). On this basis, a particular kind of nationalism, namely a liberal, friendly and cooperative kind, has been quietly built into global models of development, helping transform the division of the world into nation states into a quasi-natural part of the modern worldview. And again, both of these processes really took off in the mid-to-late nineteenth century.

The last type of institutionalized nationalism mentioned here might be called the global 'banalization' of national differences. It is connected to the formation of global fields or systems beyond the political sphere: fields such as science, the arts or sport. On the surface, these 'cultural fields' operate based on universal criteria of scientific, artistic or athletic excellence. They have learned, however, to integrate national symbols and differences in their everyday operations and to use them to attract public attention.

The emergence of modern sport since the mid-nineteenth century, for instance, has led to the establishment of globally standardized rules enforced by international associations as well as of global criteria for athletic excellence promoted by sport journalists all over the world. However, it is precisely these standardized rules and global criteria that also allow for the global comparison of national achievements and identification with national teams. In this way, national differences have become an integral part of the everyday logic of global sports (Werron, 2010, 2015a). The same kind of logic applies to the arts and sciences (Nobel prizes, university rankings and the like), producing an 'expressive isomorphism' that combines universally homogenous criteria for the evaluation of performances with the constant definition of national differences (Regev, 2011). The 'methodological nationalism' in the (social) sciences, which takes the 'national society' for granted as a reference point and data source (Wimmer and Glick Schiller, 2002) partakes in this logic, too. In all of these cases, the national is institutionalized globally in 'banal' ways.

Scarcity nationalism

Scarcity nationalism, in the definition here, conceives of the world as a place provided with scarce goods that nations can only acquire at the expense of other nations (for a more detailed version of the following argument see Werron, 2018, 2020b). The concept of scarcity nationalism offers a new sociological and historical perspective on variants of nationalism, some of which are usually discussed under the title 'economic nationalism' (Helleiner and Pickel, 2005). 'Scarcity nationalism', however, draws attention to all kinds of scarcities, not just economic ones, and thus helps to identify a general mechanism that can also work with non-economic goods, such as legitimacy or prestige. The following remarks focus on economic variants of scarcity nationalism which are still prominent today and work in rather 'banal' ways. A full account of the history of scarcity nationalism would have to include further variants, particularly aggressive political ones revolving around scarcities of territory and natural resources. The latter played essential roles, for instance, in modern ideologies discussed by John M. Hobson as 'racist imperialism' and 'Eurocentric imperialism' (see Hobson 2012: 106–30; 150–82).[2]

The historical formation of scarcity nationalism is particularly interesting as it takes place in an era, modernity, that has given rise to ideas of 'growth', 'productivity' and 'progress', ideas that form the basis of the modern belief that the number and quality of goods of all kinds can be increased without limits and that international competition and conflict can be mitigated by division of labour, growth and international cooperation (see, for example, Wright, 2001; Cohn, 2016). These beliefs are also at the core of the modern liberal 'world culture' or, as Immanuel Wallerstein (2011) would put it, the 'centrist liberalist' worldview shared by international organizations and similar global actors. In this worldview, there are no inescapable scarcities. We might therefore suspect that the formation and enduring influence of scarcity nationalism has to do with its willingness to imagine scarcities in a world where the dominant liberal worldview is increasingly unwilling to do the same.

At first glance, scarcity nationalism resembles mercantilism, the leading economic theory between the sixteenth and the eighteenth centuries. In early modern times, economic growth was not yet imaginable in any systematic terms. Accordingly, mercantilism tended to conceive of international trade as a zero-sum game, where one state's trade advantages of necessity implied disadvantages for its trade partners.[3] Scarcity was central to this thinking. Modern scarcity nationalism, however, is different from mercantilism in that it operates in an environment where growth is increasingly imagined as a realistic possibility. The challenge for scarcity nationalism in this environment is to make scarcities *appear* natural and self-evident anyway.

To do this, scarcity nationalism can rely on a basic fact: the land surface of the earth is limited. In a world divided into nation states, it seems obvious that nation states can expand their territory only at the expense of other nation states. This is mostly taken for granted and thus is rarely discussed. Land surface area, however, is just one of many reference points for notions of scarcity. Based on the core ideas of scarcity nationalism – the division of the world into nation states, the earth's limited land surface – almost any good can be framed and perceived as scarce, whether natural resources, money, people, sales opportunities, or even attention, legitimacy or prestige. Against this background, four kinds of scarcity nationalism can be distinguished that have emerged since the mid-nineteenth century, shaped by the infrastructures for global communication outlined previously (always bearing its mercantilist predecessors in mind).

First, there is the type of scarcity nationalism that developed in the context of the rise of classical political economy (the French physiocrats, Adam Smith, David Ricardo and the like). Among the lasting contributions of classical political economy is a new kind of thinking about economic scarcity on the one hand and growth, or wealth, on the other: 'free competition', it argues, creates a situation where producers and sellers compete for the favour and money of consumers, leading to increasing productivity that can create wealth for the whole of 'society' (or, as Adam Smith put it, for 'the public'). In other words, the competitors in the market have to suffer from a specific kind of scarcity, a scarcity of consumers (or their money), to create an abundance of goods for all; scarcity at the level of market competition leads to the growth and progress of society as a whole (on the historical development of this discourse see Werron, 2015b).[4] Starting with David Hume ('Of the Jealousy of Trade', 1742) and Adam Smith (*The Wealth of Nations*, 1776), this kind of thinking was often combined with a preference for free trade as the policy considered to be the best fit with a free market economy (for these and other examples see Burckhardt, 1992; Irwin, 1996). It was probably best captured in David Ricardo's theory of 'comparative advantage' (set out in *On the Principles of Political Economy and Taxation*, 1817), which holds that free trade is always advantageous for all trade partners. Even if a country might be able to produce all kinds of goods more efficiently than its trade partners, it benefits from free trade because free trade allows it to concentrate on the production of those goods that it can produce most efficiently (for example, linen), allowing other countries to concentrate on other goods (for example, wine). In many ways, this still seems to be the mainstream view of neoclassical economy on international trade (for a sophisticated updated version see Irwin, 2009).[5]

This standard view on free trade was, and still is, the perfect adversary for scarcity nationalists. In the mid-nineteenth century, the German economist and politician Friedrich List was the most influential proponent of the nationalist opposition. In his *Das nationale System der politischen Oekonomie* (The National System of Political Economy, 1841), List described the British proponents of free trade as 'bottomless cosmopolitans' who had developed a type of economic reasoning that was too abstract and overlooked the importance of differences in *national* development. Free trade, he argued, is only advantageous for trade partners insofar as they share a similar stage of *internal* economic development.[6] The basic assumption of scarcity underlying this argument is that producers in underdeveloped countries first need a national market to develop the skills (product qualities, efficiency of production) needed to survive in a global market economy. This requires national markets to be protected from foreign competition. According to List, it is precisely the ability and willingness to protect national markets that distinguishes an actually developing *Volkswirtschaft* from the free-trading 'national economies' imagined by the British 'bottomless cosmopolitans'.

Given the central role of the development element of the argument, this variant of scarcity nationalism can be called developmental nationalism. Its global spread from the nineteenth to the twenty-first century cannot be discussed here in detail (for examples from the nineteenth century, see Bayly, 2004: 300–2). For our argument, suffice it to say that the core elements of this view were firmly in place in the mid-to-late nineteenth century, helping protectionist trade policies around the world to emerge, including in the United States, where 'Listian nationalists' largely succeeded in defeating the 'Cobdenite cosmopolitans' (Palen, 2016). And though proponents of free trade in the US and elsewhere were able to strike back in the years after World War II, the overall patterns of the debate do not seem to have changed much since the nineteenth century (for a more recent version, see Chang, 2002). Development nationalism still shares the core idea of liberal economic theory that in the long run all countries will and should be able to grow together in an integrated global economy. And, just as in liberal theory, consumers and their money are imagined as scarce goods that countries and their respective producers compete for. Developmental nationalism, however, does *not* buy into the logic of the 'comparative advantage' and the unlimited advantages of free trade.

With this story in mind, it is also easier to understand other types of scarcity nationalism that developed in the nineteenth and twentieth centuries. Some of these were based on more radical ideas of national autarky and self-sufficiency, often arguing against the mainstream liberal worldview with its emphasis on the protection of the interests of consumers. Here, thinking in terms of scarcity often manifests itself in quite aggressive ideological terms. An important example is the kind of 'national protectionism' (Rosanvallon, 2013) that was championed by leading politicians and in specialized publications during the French Third Republic (1870–1940). The main characteristic of this type of scarcity nationalism is that it emphasizes the interests of producers and workers, rather than consumers, and focuses on political, rather than economic arguments, sometimes accepting economic disadvantages for the purpose of political mobilization. Such views have sometimes been called 'neo-mercantilistic' (Cohn, 2016: 16), though this is questionable given that they have at least two characteristics that distinguish them from their early modern predecessors. First, they aim at producing *national* legitimacy; second, they share the modern dynamic notions of scarcity and growth, only with a more nationalistic twist.

A recent example is the economic nationalism propagated by the US administration of President Donald Trump. It resembles the rhetoric of Friedrich List and the developmental nationalists in many ways. The 'bottomless cosmopolitans' of List are replaced by 'the globalists'; the German *Zollunion* (customs union) is replaced by a variety of protectionist policies (tariffs, renegotiation of trade agreements, cancellation of multilateral agreements). Basic notions of scarcity are similar too, defined in terms of consumers and their money, rather than natural resources and products, as is the ultimate goal of national growth through success on global markets. What seems to be missing, though, is the long-term optimism shared by Friedrich List and his fellow developmental nationalists. Protectionism here is not a means of achieving an advanced stage of development with the final goal of free trade for all. It is rather a means of preserving your own advanced development *against* other countries, including developing ones. This seems to imply a somewhat tragic worldview, where the intensity of the struggle of all nations for their share of the global economy is not weakened by growth and increasing wealth – if anything, it is intensified by the global expansion of the ideal of economic growth and the ensuing entitlement of all nations to participate in it. Tragic nationalism, then, seems to be an appropriate name for this version of scarcity nationalism.

Beyond developmental and tragic nationalism, two further globalized forms of scarcity nationalism deserve mention. First, there is the nationalism of competitiveness, the product of a more recent liberal discourse, presumably starting in the 1970s, which assumes that all transnational corporations, under the pressure of fierce competition on global markets, are forced to constantly search worldwide for the best and cheapest production sites. In this view, nations are imagined as being in constant competition for the production capacities (and taxes) of those corporations. To appear as attractive as possible to corporations, they have to constantly improve not only their political institutions, economic infrastructure and tax systems, but also cultural characteristics such as their work ethic and informal social networks. In this worldview, therefore, the world consists of 'competition states' (Cerny, 1997) which are more or less 'competitive' (Porter, 1990) and together build the 'new systems competition' (Sinn, 2003).

Again, the commonalities with and differences from other types of scarcity nationalism are instructive. The nationalism of competitiveness shares with the types outlined earlier the modern assumption of scarcity, that is, the idea that consumers and their money are inescapably scarce. With development nationalism it shares a belief in the long-term advantages of free trade, leading to prosperity and constant growth. With tragic nationalism it shares the belief that growth does not mitigate the intensity of (international) competition. At the same time, it disagrees with both of these in that it sees the short- and long-term solution not in some kind of protectionism but in the continual modernization of political and sociocultural institutions. It aims, in other words, at transforming global market pressure into constant pressure for political modernization.

There is a final version of scarcity nationalism that is historically linked to the nationalism of competitiveness. We might call it 'We are already here' nationalism. Its basic assumption is that the wealth of a nation is the result of the hard work of its members and/or inhabitants. It therefore conceives of the wealth of a nation as a scarce good that should only be consumed by its members. What makes this kind of nationalism particularly interesting is that, although extremely exclusionary, it can still work without any obvious element of ethnocultural nationalism (for a particularly pure version of this argument see Coulter, 2015). All it says is: If you weren't here before, and thus didn't contribute to our wealth, you are not welcome now. It is perfectly inclusionary with regard to the present and radically exclusionary with regard to the future. As such, it is a perfect weapon against any kind of migration, as well as a perfect rhetorical cover for any kind of racism or xenophobia. In so doing, it transforms assumptions of scarcity into radical political conservatism.

Conclusion: analysing nationalism as a case of global social change

This chapter has tried to show how an analysis of 'banal' forms of nationalism can be combined with insights from the globalization literature to gain a new understanding of the resilience of modern nationalism. It has argued that nationalism is a modern political discourse that is reproduced in both 'hot' (conspicuous) and 'banal' (inconspicuous) ways, and that since the mid-nineteenth century its more inconspicuous mechanisms of reproduction – institutionalized and scarcity nationalism – have been differentiated into further types that exemplify the various ways in which nationalism has been built into the very fabric of global modernity. The inconspicuous modes of reproduction discussed here mostly operate in everyday and implicit ways that can easily be overlooked and, if overlooked, make it difficult to fully appreciate nationalism's power and resilience. If we wish to avoid being surprised by nationalism over and over again, we should study the history of these inconspicuous types of global nationalism in more detail.

This chapter has tried to give a preliminary sketch of this story. Against the background of a rising infrastructure of global communication since the mid-to-late nineteenth century, it has identified a number of rarely discussed variants of nationalism. The types of institutionalized nationalism mentioned were perspectival nationalism (seeing the world through the lenses of national media); the global institutionalization of the nation state, particularly in and by international organizations; and global 'banalization' of national differences, particularly in cultural global fields like sport, the arts and science. It then identified and discussed four types of scarcity nationalism: development nationalism – seeing all nations as competitors for a global audience of market consumers, combined with the idea that a certain level of development of national markets is needed for them to be able to participate in the international competition (Friedrich List and his followers); tragic nationalism – seeing all nations as competitors for a global audience of market consumers, combined with the idea that the intensity of the struggle is not diminished by the possibility of growth; nationalism of competitiveness – seeing all nations as competitors for the favour of companies/corporations that are attracted by low taxes and functioning political institutions; and 'we are already here' nationalism – seeing wealth as a scarce good created by those who are already domiciled in a territory and barred to everyone else.

This list is not meant to be exhaustive, of course, and the types mentioned could be studied in much more detail, looking, for instance, at the interplay between conspicuous and inconspicuous mechanisms or their impact on the current 'new nationalism' (for a preliminary take see Werron, 2018). What this analysis already suggests, though, is that the resilience of nationalism is based on largely inconspicuous modes of reproduction that have differentiated into various types in the past 150 years or so, shaped by changes in the infrastructure of global communication and global structures since the mid-to-late nineteenth century. It thus might be useful to think about the nationalism–globalization relationship in terms of a long twentieth century that starts in the mid-nineteenth century and is still going on today (Dickinson, 2018; on periodization see Epple, Chapter 3 in this volume).

What can we learn from this perspective for the analysis of global social change? On the theoretical level, the history of scarcity nationalism might turn out to be particularly important, because it gives insight into how nationalism has managed to incorporate modern notions of growth by combining them with notions of scarcity. This has helped nationalism to combine an optimistic global outlook with taken-for-granted assumptions about 'national interests', 'national competition' and 'national development'. This kind of adaptive inventiveness has helped transform it into the resilient legitimizing discourse it is today. It did so particularly from the mid-to-late nineteenth century, when an emerging infrastructure of global communication allowed nationalists to connect their reasoning to the world in new and more effective ways. In other words, nationalism *stabilized* itself by connecting to processes of global change. The globalization of nationalism, rather than simply a story of change, is a story of increasing, and increasingly inconspicuous, continuity and stability; if anything, it is a story of stability caused by change.

This implies that focusing on global change, important as it is, runs the danger of overestimating change at the expense of continuity and stability. Studying global change, we should always keep in mind that belief in change is integral to modern ideologies of progress and rationalization. This also tends to affect our thinking as historians and social scientists: We study change partly because we, as moderns, expect change. The difficulty of making sense of the resilience of nationalism is an example of how this habit, if not countered by interest in stability, can diminish our ability to understand important global phenomena.

This analysis, then, suggests two general lessons for scholars of global social change. First, an empirical and historical lesson: if nationalism is any indication, global institutionalization has been closely connected to the emergence and expansion of a global media system since the mid-to-late nineteenth century (as outlined by Tworek, Chapter 11 in this volume), which has provided the infrastructure for a global vocabulary that has shaped social structures worldwide in often inconspicuous ways. If we wish to make sense of such phenomena, then we should see the history of global media not just as one globalization story among others but as the one that all scholars of global social change should take into account. And second, a methodological message: when setting out to study global social change, we should always remind ourselves to think of the possibility of mechanisms of global institutionalization, namely, modes of social reproduction that in themselves may change all the time but whose primary effect is continuity, stability and persistence rather than change.

Notes

1. For a nuanced take on the relationship between the French Revolution and nationalism, see Hont (2005: 448): 'A comparison of pre-nineteenth century and post-French Revolution notions of nationalism suggests that the French Revolution

was an anti-nationalist revolt that failed.' This remark reflects the insight that, during revolutionary times, 'nationalism' was largely used as derogatory word, suggesting that the revolution was shaped by an increasingly nationalist environment, rather than being nationalist in and of itself.

2   Many thanks to Stefano Guzzini for pointing out to me the historical significance of such connections between scarcity nationalism and aggressive-fascist types of nationalism.

3   Jean-Baptiste Colbert, minister of finance under Louis XIV of France, saw trade as 'un combat perpetual en paix et en guerre entre les nations de l'Europe, à qui en emportera la meilleure partie' (a perpetual struggle in peace and war between the nations of Europe as to which would take away the best portion) (Silberner, 1939: 35).

4   We should be careful, however, to avoid attributing all elements of liberal 'political economy' to Adam Smith. For a nuanced recent reading of Smith see Hearn (2018), who shows that market competition was not as central to Smith's reasoning as is often claimed today, and that Smith was rather sceptical of the kind of thinking associated with the term 'political economy' in his time. Smith's emphasis rather was on the benefits of division of labour and the dangers of interstate competition, making him an early proponent of free trade.

5   How this theoretical stance affected actual trade politics is, of course, a different question altogether. For a sceptical view see Osterhammel (2018); for a detailed analysis of the relationship between free trade ideology and US trade policy see Irwin (2017). The similarly complicated relationship between 'Free Trade' as a sweeping political ideology and free trade as an economic theory and political practice is discussed by Trentmann (2008).

6   List explained the nationalist background of his own position as follows: 'The main characteristic of my system is ... nationality. It is based on the nature of nationality as a link between individuality and mankind' (List, 1922: LIX [1841]; my translation). On the historical context of List's writing see Hewitson (2010: 253–7).

10

States and Markets: A Global Historical Sociology of Capitalist Governance

George Lawson

Introduction: politics and economics

Until the nineteenth century, politics and economics were not discrete fields. In Europe during the early modern period, power and profit formed a single logic: property and title went hand in hand with administrative offices; warfare was conducted by 'privateers' as well as 'crown' forces; and sovereignty was closely bound up with commerce. Power and profit only became formally demarcated during the course of the nineteenth century. During this period, 'economic' interactions were increasingly carried out through 'faceless' transactions via the 'symbolic token' of 'generalized money' (Simmel, 1978: 332–3). Under these conditions, every product was exchangeable, including labour. Hence, for the first time, 'free labour' could be sold (as wages) according to market logics. The bracketing of a 'private' sphere of market exchange had the simultaneous effect of generating a 'public' sphere of political regulation. The economy became the realm of civil society mediated by logics of market exchange ('the self-regulating market' organized through 'the invisible hand'), while politics became the realm of the state governed by the national interest (*'raison d'état'*).

The decoupling of politics and economics was as much ideal as it was real. It was ideal in that states and markets remained tightly intertwined: just as the market required the state to recognize private property and provide a legal apparatus that could sustain accumulation and enforce contracts, so the state required the revenues that accrued from property, accumulation and contracts. But it was also real inasmuch as market logics were given a degree of autonomy, both semantically and legally. The separation of states and markets that, from a contemporary viewpoint, appears natural can be traced to practices that emerged during the nineteenth century (Giddens, 1985: 135–6; Rosenberg, 1994: 126). Any discussion of the relationship between states and markets is putting back together what was once an organic whole.

This chapter examines the relationship between states and markets over the last century and a half, since the emergence of the first stage of globalization. Its goal is to demonstrate the extensive entanglements through which logics of rule and gain have been sustained. In keeping with the remit of this volume, it shows that these entanglements are not random, but structured. They are also laden with power asymmetries. In this way, the chapter both builds upon and extends insights from global history into international relations (IR) and historical sociology. It borrows a key concept from global history, entanglements, but shows how entanglements are patterned through power relations. On their own, claims about entanglements tell us relatively little. But when seen as the building blocks of structural formations that serve as vectors of historical development, then entanglements become an analytical rather than a descriptive device. The result is both a differentiation between, and a sequencing of, state–market complexes. In this respect, there have been four main phases in the modern relationship between states and markets: the first, running from the third quarter of the nineteenth century to World War I, was marked by high flows of capital and finance; the second, during the inter-war years, was marked by capital controls and, as a result, a reduction in global transactions; the third, from 1945 to 1973, saw a gradual relaxation of capital controls and the partial recovery of financial and capital flows; the fourth, from the early 1970s until the present day, has been one of relatively unconstrained controls and, therefore, high capital mobility (Eichengreen, 1996: 3).

States and markets

Before outlining the chapter's main narrative, it is worth clarifying two background issues. First, this is a story painted in broad brushstrokes rather than pointillist techniques – it is more Rothko than Seurat. It accepts many of the points made by contributors to this volume, most emphatically Angelika Epple (Chapter 3), which point to the importance of recognizing multiple temporalities and perspectives and thereby constructing historical narratives that pluralize time and place. I have contributed to this task elsewhere (for example Lawson et al, 2010). But on this occasion, the chronology is organized largely around 'leading-edge' examples of the state–market nexus. This is, as Epple points out, not a neutral strategy. In fact, it is one that provides a particular interpretation of the ways in which entanglements of rule and gain have been structured. This chapter makes no claim to have provided a settled story and still less one that has universal application. The chapter's organization represents a strategic decision about how best to provide a global historical sociology of the relationship between states and markets.

This leads to the second issue. The use of the term 'global' in this chapter does not signify an ontological space with a logic of its own – there are relatively few sites of social action that are constituted at the planetary scale. Rather, 'global' is used as an encompassing term intended to capture the multiple entanglements between states and markets. Concretely, these entanglements are enacted through people, materials, polities, institutions, technologies, discourses and so on – what we might collectively term transboundary encounters. But rather than tie analysis to a particular scale of analysis or mode of entanglement, the term 'global' is used as a means of capturing the many sites through which states and markets intersect. In this sense, the promise of a global historical sociology of states and markets lies in two dynamics (Go and Lawson, 2017a): first, the transboundary dynamics that enable the emergence, reproduction and breakdown of patterns of entanglements; and second, the historical emergence, reproduction and breakdown of structured entanglements between states and markets.

Globalization Mark 1

Globalization and the capitalist crisis were born together, in the last quarter of the nineteenth century. The deepening of transnational trading circuits, enabled by the commercialization of agriculture, the two industrial revolutions, imperial expansion and deepening communication networks, meant that far-off places became intimately connected. In 1889, the British bank Barings, one of the largest investment houses in the world, failed to sell a large issue of Argentinian bonds. When, the following year, the Argentinian government defaulted, Barings' holdings became worthless. The subsequent 'panic' meant that capital flows to Argentina all but ceased for five years. Such crises were regular features of the first stage of globalization.

Even more destructive was the world's first global-scale depression, which took place between 1873 and 1896. The depression had three major impacts on economies around the world. First, it induced deflationary pressures that pushed the prices of commodities down to, and sometimes below, the cost of production – between 1871 and 1895, the price of grain fell by a third, the price of textiles by 40%, and the price of sugar, tea and coffee by nearly 50% (Schwartz, 2000: 140). Second, as prices fell, there was a decline in metropolitan demands for 'peripheral' products.[1] The results of such a drop-off were extreme, leading to widespread poverty and, on some occasions, famines. Third, depression was met by capital flight from peripheral polities, a process that, again, prompted major turmoil. The depression of 1873–96 was the precursor to twentieth century industrial and trade cycles, just as the Barings crisis portended later financial panics. Both illustrated the ways in which the global expansion of capitalism could result in dramatic price fluctuations and commodity speculations, with cascading effects for economies and polities around the world.

During this period, there were two main modes of state–market interaction. A minority of states, led by Britain and the United States, were self-declared liberal capitalist states. Liberal capitalist states sought to provide the maximum possible space for the 'self-regulating' market, for example through accepting the strictures of a 'neutral' mechanism such as the gold standard. A majority of polities combined liberal economies with political illiberalism. This liberal–illiberal combination was in keeping with prevailing views that capitalism did not easily align with democracy. For many of both its detractors and advocates, capitalism prompted tendencies towards oligopoly (Mann, 2013: 132–3). Most industrializing states (gradually) extended the franchise to (some) propertied men. But any further extensions were circumscribed by concerns that the working class would limit private property and favour radical redistribution. More often than not, industrialization took place under the guise of interventionist, often authoritarian states. Exemplifying this trend were Japan and Germany, the original 'developmental states' (Blyth, 2013: 134).

Beyond Japan and Germany's rapid state-led development, the most striking feature of the late nineteenth-century global economy was the rise of the United States. The ascent of the US was rapid: its share of global production climbed from 23% in 1870 to 30% in 1900 and 36% in 1913 (Panitch and Gindin, 2012: 28). US growth was predicated on the emergence of a new type of firm that took over the whole productive process, from the supply of raw materials to manufacturing, wholesale, research and development, and retailing. Housing the entire productive process within single firms prompted gains in economies of scale that, in turn, prompted advances in productivity: from 1870 to 1913, US productivity went from being 14% lower to 20% higher than Britain's (Panitch and Gindin, 2012: 28). Also crucial to this advance was the introduction of the moving assembly line, which helped to reduce the cost of labour, shorten production time and, as a result, lower prices. The consequence of these innovations was the arrival of mega-firms: by the end of the nineteenth century, the largest company in the world was US Steel, which produced 40% of the world's supply (Topik and Wells, 2012: 615–16). In 1904, 318 American companies produced 40% of US manufacturing output. One of the biggest companies of them all, Ford, employed 120,000 workers on a 2,000 acre site in Illinois, while sourcing its own wood and rubber directly from plantations it owned in Latin America.

The emergence of giant transnational corporations like Ford was a significant step in the development of modern capitalism. In Britain, the Companies Act of 1862 was a turning point, reducing the costs of forming a company, removing the need to receive legislative approval for one, and limiting the liability of shareholders. Comparable acts were signed in France (*Loi Sur les Sociétés Commerciales*) in 1867 and Germany (*Aktienrechtsnovelle*) in 1870. From this point on, there was a major increase in portfolio investment as companies pooled investments into high-interest, often long-distance, infrastructural and public works projects. Transnational companies invested in mining, plantations, railways and ports, often with the backing of states, which supported firms through a range of practices, such as the subsidies provided by the British government to shipping companies for the carriage of mail. The rise of such companies went hand in hand with the growing power of these states. Markets and states were deeply entangled.

Globalization in retreat

World War I brought the first era of global capitalism to an end, opening a period of economic nationalism and regionalism. During the inter-war years, core states split into three main blocs: the US and the Americas, which retained the gold standard; the UK-backed sterling area, which moved towards a system of imperial preferences; and a Central European zone, centred around Germany, which operated tight currency controls. Japan and France ran smaller blocs in East Asia and the Francophone sphere respectively. To some extent, these zones marked a perpetuation of pre-World War I trends. Even during the high-water mark of the first global era, one third of Britain's trade took place within its empire (Frieden, 2006: 47). During the 1930s, fascism, socialism and various forms of populism sought to embed productive activities within authoritarian political orders. The result was a tightening of the relationship between states and markets. The pre-war Polish state, for example, produced 100% of the country's munitions and armaments, 80% of its chemicals, 50% of its metals, and 90% of its air and road transportation (Schwartz, 2000: 249–50). Such figures were not uncommon.

The political and economic fragmentation of the inter-war years was deeply constituted, particularly after the Great Depression, which saw international trade drop by two thirds. This drop-off hurt both core and peripheral states alike. In the core, there was a major retraction in economic output, as well as wide-ranging bank failures, foreclosures and a surge in unemployment. In the periphery, there was a collapse in commodity prices and a near collapse in exports as core states raised tariffs and devalued their currencies. The geopolitical consequences of the Great Depression led to 'economic warfare' as rival visions of political economy competed through trade wars, competitive devaluations, debt repayments and exchange controls. By 1936, all Eastern, Southern and Central European states were authoritarian. Increasingly, it was liberal ideas of political economy that were marginal. The result was a disembedding of many of the logics that marked the first phase of globalization and a re-embedding of rule and gain around national and imperial polity forms. While the former weakened one type of entanglement between economic and political forces, the latter served to tighten the relationship between states and markets.

The golden age

After 1945, there was a concerted effort to move away from the protectionism of the inter-war years. Most core states adopted a Keynesian approach, using state stimulation to produce mild inflation that was, in turn, linked to stable rates of growth. Keynesian ideas also lay at the heart of a host of new international financial institutions (IFIs), most notably the Bretton Woods Institutions: the International Monetary Fund, which was intended to act as a global lender of last resort, and the World Bank, which was to provide loans and investment. Although the agreement to create a permanent International Trade Organization was not enacted, states did establish a General Agreement on Tariffs and Trade (GATT), which began the process of reducing tariffs. GATT (later the World Trade Organization) did its job, albeit in fits and starts. Via a number of multilateral trade rounds, states reduced tariffs on manufacturing products from an average of 40% in the 1940s to an average of 5% by the end of the century.

For a generation after World War II, the turn to Keynesian stimulus and management helped to reinvigorate both growth and trade. This was the 'golden age' of 'embedded liberalism' (Ruggie, 1982). Between 1950 and 1973, per capita GDP around the world rose by an average of 3% per year (equivalent to a doubling every 25 years), while trade increased by 8% per year (Maddison, 2001: 24). At the heart of the 'embedded liberal' order was the United States. The war had devastated European states, both winners and losers alike: by the end of the war, German GDP had returned to its 1890 level, while living standards in Britain had fallen by a third (Frieden, 2006: 261). In 1946–47, an estimated 100 million Europeans lived on rations of just 1,500 calories per day. The United States, by contrast, had seen its economy grow substantially during the war. In the five years after World War II, this boom continued, fuelled by a 60% rise in personal consumption (Panitch and Gindin, 2012: 83). The US used its wealth to provide aid (including the Marshall Plan) and foreign direct investment (FDI) to Europe, and encouraged the development of the European Coal and Steel Community (1951) and the Treaty of Rome (1957). It also provided substantial aid and investment to Japan. This turn towards Europe and Japan formed part of a reorientation away from investment in peripheral states towards investment in core states: in the quarter century after World War II, the US invested three times as much in Europe and Japan as it did in Latin America (Frieden, 2006: 293). High value-added industries, such as cars, oil and chemicals, became deeply embedded features of trade and investment between industrialized states. During the 1960s, FDI increased by twice the level of global GDP, while international trade grew 40% faster than global GDP (Panitch and Gindin, 2012: 114).

If Keynesianism endorsed an activist state in terms of developing and managing markets in the core, states in the periphery went even further in establishing a leading role for the state in development projects. Such projects split into two basic models: 'import substitution industrialization' (ISI) and 'export-led industrialization'. Most peripheral states, including India and virtually every Latin American state, followed a strategy of ISI. In contrast to the majority, the 'Asian Tigers' (South Korea, Taiwan, Hong Kong and Singapore) followed 'export-led industrialization'. On the one hand, this meant adopting many of the same state-led strategies found in ISI countries: protecting manufacturers, undervaluing currencies (and thereby distorting prices), and subsidizing nascent industries through tax breaks and cheap credit. State institutions, such as Economic Planning Boards and State Development Banks, ensured that the interests of state and capital were mutually aligned. On the other hand, the state-led development of the Asian Tigers was oriented towards exports. In the case of South Korea, foreign investment, mainly from the US and Japan, acted as the impetus for the state to subsidize a move into low-quality, low-price goods (particularly consumer nondurables such as cheap clothes and plastic toys), which were mostly overlooked by industrialized economies. Once this bridgehead had been established, profits were reinvested in capital equipment and advanced technologies, which were directed towards new export products, most notably consumer durables (such as household goods), heavy industry and, later, electronics. Crucially, and unlike ISI states, capital was only allocated to firms that met export targets. This made competition tough.

Export-led industrialization proved to be as successful for the Asian Tigers as it had been for Japan. Enabled both by astute state-led policies and by extensive aid and investment from foreign backers, the Asian Tigers tripled their GDP per capita in a little over two decades – by 1988, they accounted for 8.1% of world trade, almost double the share held by the whole of Latin America (Frieden, 2006: 317). In South Korea, exports increased at an average rate of 8% per year between 1962 and 1989; per capita income rose by a factor of 52 during the same period (Zeiler, 2014: 312). The success of the Asian Tigers' 'strategic development' influenced Chinese leaders to 'open up' through a combination of export-led industrialization and 'labour-intensive development' in the late 1970s. China also followed the Asian Tigers in using authoritarian governance to maintain a system of low wages, while keeping both labour organizations and dissent in check. If embedded liberalism marked the first structural entanglement of the post-war era, embedded authoritarianism marked its second pattern. Both, again, demonstrated the closeness of the relationship between states and markets.

Neoliberalism

The golden age of global capitalism was based on a close relationship between states and markets. As with the inter-war years, crisis forced a shift in this relationship. The crisis of the early 1970s arose because of three main dynamics: first, a fiscal crisis in a number of Western states prompted by high inflation (partly brought about by the fourfold increase in oil prices by the Organization of the Petroleum Exporting Countries (OPEC) in the aftermath of the Yom Kippur

War) and increasing international competition (not least from the Asian Tigers); second, the collapse of the Bretton Woods system of semi-fixed exchange rates due to contradictions between the needs of the international monetary system and domestic politics, particularly in the US; and third, the emergence of deregulated Euromarkets that acted as slush funds for speculations again the dollar. During the 1970s, the United States experienced its first trade deficit since the late nineteenth century as investment flowed overseas, both to Europe and the Asian Tigers. Industrial output in core states fell by 10% in 1974, while the same year saw the inflation rate in the ten largest non-communist countries average 13% (Zeiler, 2014: 285). Over the decade as a whole, around two thirds of the world's states grew more slowly than they had during the 1960s. In a number of core polities, some business elites began to favour an alternative to Keynesianism – neoliberalism.

The contrast between neoliberalism and Keynesianism was striking. Keynesianism favoured capital controls and fixed exchange rates, and its stated objectives were full employment and stable growth, guaranteed by an interventionist state. Neoliberalism saw deregulated markets rather than interventionist states as the basic source of a vibrant economy. Neoliberals argued that governments distorted the market by seeking short-term fixes to market disequilibrium (such as printing money). In contrast, neoliberals assumed that capital flowed naturally to the most productive sectors of the economy. As such, they favoured deregulation so that market forces could stimulate entrepreneurial activities. The primary policy emphasis for neoliberals was the control of inflation that, it was assumed, would stabilize prices and avoid wage–price spirals that, in turn, led to unsustainable levels of public spending. For neoliberals, lower taxes allowed individuals greater freedom, while also translating into higher levels of both consumer spending and private sector investment. Neoliberals were relatively sanguine about the impact on state finances of this move – a rolling back of the public sector in order to stimulate entrepreneurial activities was a central component of the neoliberal framework. As one of the architects of neoliberalism put it, the heart of capitalism was 'the separation of economic power from political power' (Friedman, 1962: 9).

Although early experiments in neoliberalism took place in Chile under the Pinochet regime, it was only with the elections of Margaret Thatcher in Britain and Ronald Reagan in the US that neoliberalism became instituted in core states. Thatcher and Reagan were the vanguard of a broader neoliberal movement made up of state elites, entrepreneurial networks, think tanks, financial journalists, academics and IFI officials (Stedman Jones, 2012: 134–5). This vanguard exported neoliberal policies – competitive exchange rates, control of the money supply, inflation targets, the reduction of capital and currency controls, lower rates of taxation and so on – around the world. Structural adjustment programmes, liberalization and floating currencies became conditions of international investment and, more importantly, marks of 'good' conduct. The Washington Consensus provided a list of ten 'must do' policies, an 'instruction sheet' of neoliberal 'fundamentals' that diffused widely. This diffusion took place despite periodic crises, including the Latin American sovereign debt crisis of the early 1980s, the Nordic banking crash of the early 1990s, the 1997 financial crisis in emerging markets, and the bursting of the dot-com bubble at the turn of the century. By 2000, virtually all Organisation for Economic Co-operation and Development (OECD) states had abandoned capital controls. States, regional organizations and international organizations had all become carriers of neoliberal orthodoxy.

In many ways, neoliberalism represented the repurposing of dynamics begun in the first era of globalization. As with the last quarter of the nineteenth century, a lack of capital controls fostered the rise of financialization. Financialization was less about the dominance of the financial sector than it was about the dominance of financial activities (Krippner, 2011: 2). This period saw financial services become far more profitable than productive activities. In 2009, oil futures trading was worth ten times the value of physical oil production and consumption, while foreign exchange trading ran at 73 times the value of global trade (Mulgan, 2013: 19). Major manufacturers, such as Ford, began to generate more profits through financial instruments, such as the financing of loans to buy cars, than from selling cars. In a return to the portfolio investments pioneered by British companies in the late nineteenth century, late twentieth-century firms became bundles of assets through which investors sought to collect interest, dividends and capital gains rather than generate profits through productive growth. This shift was enabled by 'neoliberal statecraft', which opened up the regulatory environment in global finance, spawning the emergence of a shadow economy of off-balance-sheet derivatives (Krippner, 2011: 149). In 2010, the value of contracts taken out on these derivatives amounted to $700 trillion, a sum that equated to the world's total GDP over the preceding two decades (Duncan, 2012: 30). As these innovations spread around the financial system, banks raised leverage to unprecedented levels – in 2011, the operational leverage of Deutsche Bank was 40:1 and its asset footprint was worth 800% of German GDP (Blyth, 2013: 83).

In this way, financialization, dependent on the accumulation and recycling of debt in the form of derivatives, and increasingly reliant on short-term trades between interlocking institutions, ran well ahead of productive capital, producing a chronically leveraged – and, therefore, highly volatile – system. This volatility was laid bare by the volume of financial panics that took place in peripheral and semi-peripheral states during the 1990s. In part, these crises emerged from the mobility of capital that arose after the lifting of capital controls. During the decade as a whole, $1.3 trillion of private sector capital was invested in developing states (compared to $170 billion during the 1980s). These were often speculative investments that departed soon after arriving. In 1996, the inflow of private capital to Thailand amounted to 9.3% of GDP. The following year, as the Asian financial crisis picked up pace, this capital headed for the exit – the outflow of private capital from Thailand in 1997 was worth 10.9% of GDP (Panitch and Gindin, 2012: 255). Such crises were the forerunners to the global financial crisis of 2008. Although the causes of the global crisis had less to do with capital mobility than with the systemic risk prompted by financial interdependence and an overreliance on property markets, their basic package of excessive leverage and debt was common to many previous crises. The scale of the crash was, however, more severe than almost all of its predecessors. Between 2008 and 2011, OECD countries lost an average of 8% of their GDPs (Blyth, 2013: 45–6).

Neoliberalism is, therefore, the most recent act in a longer-term dynamic fuelled by the relationship between states and markets. The period since the last quarter of the nineteenth century has seen a number of ebbs and flows in this relationship. During the first era of globalization, liberal capitalist states forged transnational entities and extended both investment and trade, while illiberal capitalist states initiated state-led development programmes. During the inter-war years, capitalism retreated behind national and regional blocs, before being marked by 'embedded liberalism' in the core and a strategy of either ISI or export-led development in the periphery. More recently, neoliberalism promised a return to differentiation in the form of the liberal concept of the autonomous, self-regulating market. Yet, as the previous discussion makes clear, neoliberalism spread through a global political apparatus made up of IFIs, states, lobbying groups and more. This most recent stage of global capitalism provides further support for the claim made by Fernand Braudel (1977: 64) that: 'capitalism only triumphs when it becomes identified with the state'.

States and markets in the contemporary world

In the contemporary world, debate about the relationship between states and markets revolves around the competition between different modes of capitalist governance (Buzan and Lawson, 2014b). Following the market reforms in China in the late 1970s and the collapse of state socialism in Eastern and Central Europe between 1989 and 1991, capitalism has become pre-eminent. Almost every state organizes its economy through capitalist logics and takes part in global regimes around trade, production and finance. China became a member of the WTO in 2001; Russia became a member in 2012. Rather than 'capitalism or not', the question in the contemporary world revolves about how to embed capitalism politically, with the main divide being between liberal and authoritarian modes of governance.

Although the universalization of capitalism has narrowed the global ideological bandwidth, the relationship between states and markets is quite diverse. This goes well beyond the standard 'varieties of capitalism' distinction between 'liberal market economies' and 'coordinated market economies' (Hall and Soskice, 2001). This typology has two faults. First, it is formed almost exclusively from the experience of Western states. Second, the main point of differentiation does not include sufficient attention to the governance structures within which markets are embedded. Globalizing the analysis helps to address the first lacuna. The second can be overcome by stressing the ways in which markets are embedded politically. The result is not just two types of democratic capitalism (liberal and social democratic), but also two forms of authoritarian capitalism (competitive authoritarian and state bureaucratic).

These four modes of capitalist governance are oversimplifications intended to tease out differences for the purposes of analytical clarity and empirical comparison. They are best understood as occupying points on a continuum, one end of which is defined by the complete separation of economics and politics, the other by their complete union. Since no known forms of capitalism meet either extreme condition, the four forms of capitalist governance do not reach either end of the spectrum. Liberal capitalism seeks to maximize economic autonomy, combine this with democratic governance and minimize the role of the state. Social democratic capitalism seeks to balance the market, the state and democracy. Competitive authoritarian capitalism favours state control over the market and constrains democratic governance. State bureaucratic capitalism attempts a complex, fluid mix of state ownership and market relations, while rejecting democratic governance outright.

There are two caveats to note about how these four modes of capitalist governance relate to the actual experience of states. First, most states are hybrids, containing features drawn from more than one category. Contemporary Russia, for example, is a mixture of state bureaucratic and competitive authoritarian capitalism. Most countries in Central America, and some in South America, combine competitive authoritarianism with aspects of market democracy. Somewhat counterintuitively, the outlier to the post-2008 austerity regime favoured by both liberal democratic and social democratic states is the United States, which pursued a policy of fiscal stimulus intended to break the liquidity trap and boost aggregate demand long after other democratic capitalist states wound down such programmes. These hybrid forms of capitalist governance muddy distinctions both within and between democratic and authoritarian groupings. Second, states often shift between categories over time. Chile under the Pinochet regime was a mixture of state bureaucratic and competitive authoritarian capitalism; since the ending of military rule, it has instituted capitalism along a mix of liberal democratic and social democratic lines. This is far from being the only example of such movement in capitalist governance over time: change is the norm rather than the exception.

With these caveats in mind, individual states can be placed loosely within this typology. The US, the UK and other Anglophone countries best represent liberal democratic capitalism; states in much of continental Europe, South America, India, Japan and South Korea exemplify social democratic capitalism; Russia, a number of states in the Middle East, sub-Saharan Africa, Central America and South East Asia characterize competitive authoritarian capitalism; China, Vietnam, most of the Gulf monarchies, including Saudi Arabia, and some Central Asian states are the main bastions of state bureaucratic capitalism. As things stand, the trajectory of many states in the world is away from liberal democratic capitalism towards the other three forms of capitalist governance. This includes core liberal democratic capitalist states, many of which are facing a concerted populist challenge, often oriented around protectionist policies that seek to disembed their polities from regional and global IFIs, or at least weaken ties between them. At the same time, some authoritarian states are becoming increasingly personalistic, relying on an unstable mixture of despotic power and patronage. Russia under Putin, China under Xi and Turkey under Erdogan all display these characteristics. To some extent, the rhetorical and substantive nationalization of economic competences and the weakening of transnational alliances resembles dynamics last seen during the inter-war years.

The difference between contemporary world politics and the interwar years is that, despite the turn towards authoritarian populism, capitalism is a near-universal feature of contemporary world politics. At the same time, because of the way capitalism turbocharges profit, it is virtually a necessary condition for great power standing. If there was one overriding lesson from the Cold War, it was that non-capitalist economies could not compete with market economies over the long run, particularly when economies became more oriented around information and services. Yet, because capitalism fosters permanent change, it is always attended by trade-offs in terms of growth, inequality, efficiency and stability. Capitalism is legitimated by generating wealth in the form of growth and profits. But this wealth is unevenly distributed, something accentuated by the tendency of the rate of return on capital (particularly inherited wealth) to exceed growth in either income or output over the long term (Piketty, 2014), a dynamic intensified by the hyper-mobile worlds of finance and technology, which are difficult to regulate and tax (Milanovic, 2016).

The result is the fostering of extreme inequality. With extraordinary profits available from the money magic that sustains financialization, a caste of super-rich individuals has effectively sealed themselves off from the rest of the world. The world's richest 8% earn half of the world's income, the richest 1% own more than half its wealth, and the world's 1,000 or so billionaires hold twice as much wealth as the entire continent of Africa (Bregman, 2017: 217). At the same time, the poorest two thirds of the world's population owns just over 4% of its wealth and nearly 650 million people around the world are undernourished (Bull, 2013: 15; Therborn, 2012: 14). Most people outside the super-rich are worse off than they were 10 or 20 years ago: 80% of American households, 90% of Italian households and 70% of British households saw their incomes either stagnate or decline between 2009 and 2016 (Muñiz, 2017: 12). Since 2008, Britain has experienced its longest period of decline in real incomes since consistent records began at the end of the Napoleonic Wars (Lanchester, 2018: 5). If we think of the world as an apartment block, over the past generation the penthouses at the top have got larger, the apartments in the middle have been squeezed, the basement has been flooded, and the elevator between floors has become broken (Subramanian and Kessler, 2013: 21).

All forms of capitalist governance are, therefore, compelled to maintain growth as a means of mediating the politics of inequality. If growth slows or reverses, and inequality remains, there is the risk of an ugly and potentially violent politics of redistribution coming to the surface. This is true across the spectrum: China is as politically addicted to growth as the US. And it is exactly what is currently taking place around the world. Sluggish growth in many core states has allied to a shift in post-industrial economies, which has seen the emergence of ever more flexible (and therefore insecure) labour markets alongside increasing automation and the loss of a range of social protections. This is an environment in which many people feel abandoned and even more feel powerless. Over the past generation, manufacturing jobs have retracted throughout the West, in part because of China's hyperventilated development, in part because of offshoring and the development of global value chains, and in part because of a profound digital disruption. A slide first presented at an IBM event in 2015, and that subsequently went viral, summarizes this digital disruption crisply: the world's largest taxi company owns no taxis (Uber); its largest accommodation provider owns no real estate (Airbnb); the world's largest global phone companies own no infrastructure (Skype, WeChat); the world's most valuable retailer has no inventory (Alibaba); the most popular media owner creates no content (Facebook); the fastest growing banks have no actual money (SocietyOne); the world's largest movie house owns no cinemas (Netflix); the largest software vendors don't write the apps (Apple and Google). In this context, populist anger is hardly a surprise. It is fuelled, at least in part, by mega-corporations that produce little of substance, employ few people and pay little tax. And it is helping to reshape the basis of the relationship between states and markets.

It is not the case, therefore, that diverse entanglements of states and markets will converge around a single model of democratic capitalism. That assumption rests on the argument that only democracy can contain the social forces unleashed by capitalism, provide capitalism with political and social legitimacy, and foster the high levels of creativity and innovation that underpin growth. But state-led capitalism has its own advantages, not least in its ability to concentrate capital in strategic sectors and distort competition through subsidies and currency manipulation. This suggests that the contemporary world will be home to a range of forms of capitalist governance. Both democratic and authoritarian modes of capitalist governance face major challenges, most notably how to sustain growth while keeping inequality and environmental damage in check. The narrower ideological bandwidth of the contemporary world does not, therefore, lead axiomatically to stable international order. The competition between varieties of capitalist governance will be with us for some time to come.

Conclusion: varieties of capitalist governance

Over the past 150 years, states and markets have been mutually constituted. The notion of 'private' market exchange as autonomous from 'public' governance has been challenged both by specific practices, such as state-led development, and a deeper-lying interdependence, which has its roots in modernity itself. Any view that sharply differentiates states and markets rests on a sleight of hand in which markets are seen as natural forces rather than policy practices and as realms of depoliticized technical expertise rather than sites of political contestation. This occludes the ways in which the 'free market' itself is a political condition, an ideal that can be extended or reversed. Since the late nineteenth century, one of the main tasks of states has been to establish regulatory orders that enable capitalist accumulation on the one hand and protect citizens from the dislocations arising from this accumulation on the other. This has produced considerable varieties in forms of capitalist governance, which remains central to contemporary world politics. The relationship between states and markets has taken many turns. And it takes place on multiple scales of world politics. But it is central to the emergence and evolution of contemporary international order.

Beyond this particular narrative, this chapter has illustrated the wider benefits that arise from a cross-fertilization of global history, historical sociology and IR, which supports a global historical sociology of states and markets. In this approach, the global is a panoramic, encompassing category, allowing the analyst to examine developments beyond the experiences of particular peoples, states, institutions and regions. It is a perspective that is useful for highlighting patterns and sequences, linking descriptive work on entanglements with analytical enquiry into the shape and direction of these interactions. It is less good at providing a granular analysis of events, processes and mechanisms. For this, the reader should turn to the chapter by James Stafford (Chapter 12). Nor has it questioned the standard temporality of this relationship, seeing it largely through the lens of leading-edge developments. In this sense, the chapter serves simultaneously as a complement and, to some extent, contrast to Chapter 3 by Angelika Epple. Most notably, the chapter provides an opening for further study of the embedding and disembedding logics that lie at the heart of the relationship between states and markets in modern world politics.

Note

1. 'Core' and 'periphery' are used in this chapter in an analytical rather than explanatory sense, that is, as a means of indicating the positions of polities within the 'core–periphery order' ushered in by global modernity (see Buzan and Lawson, 2015: 17).

11

The Impact of Communications in Global History

Heidi Tworek

Introduction

Every global history at least pays lip service to communications and transportation revolutions. Jürgen Osterhammel noted in his magisterial work of nineteenth-century global history that telegraphy and railways represented a 'fundamental break' with the past (Osterhammel, 2009: 126). These types of claims raise many questions (on periodizing, see Epple, Chapter 3 in this volume). What type of break – political, economic, cultural, technological, social? How do we measure a 'before' and 'after'? What may have stayed the same? Why do historians claim these effects for telegraphy, but not other communications technologies like wireless?

Histories of the world economy similarly recognize the importance of communications. Steven Topik and Allan Wells described telegraphy as one of the 'sinews of the world economy' in their contribution on global commodity chains to *A World Connecting*, a volume on various aspects of world history from 1870 to 1945 that totals over 1,000 pages and is one of six similarly sized books discussing world history from antiquity to the present (Topik and Wells, 2014: 113). Global commodity chains in staples like wheat and stimulants like tobacco could only travel along sinews that emerged in the nineteenth century to tie together the world economy. Topik and Wells singled out legal frameworks, monetary standards, energy sources, and various forms of transportation and communication infrastructure (shipping, railroads, canals, telegraphy) as the key sinews.

Perhaps unwittingly, Topik and Wells used one of the key metaphors of the nineteenth-century global telegraphic system. This portrayed the world as a body with telegraphic nerves wired around it (Otis, 2001). The muscular metaphor of sinews similarly depicts the world as a singular corporeal entity to be controlled and tamed. It implies that global historians often take the 'taming' as a precondition for globalization, though that 'taming' frequently resulted in violence against colonial populations. Communications systems are not just preconditions for globalization; they are an integral strand of institutionalizing flows across borders and controlling them. They created and were created by the increasing integration of nineteenth-century international society. They often deepened international connections that had already existed, rather than remaking time and space anew. At the same time, communications (or the two-way exchange of information) could become part of battles to remake the hierarchy of international relations, whether by Germans during the first half of the twentieth century or Third World nations pushing for a New World Information and Communication Order (NWICO) in the 1970s. One way to unpick this Gordian knot is to think through concretely the many impacts of communications on the world economy, politics and social change. Metaphorical comparisons for communications are legion. But the impacts of communications were not uniform nor were they predetermined.

Historians of the world economy, and global historians in general, are well aware of the importance of communications infrastructure and content firms. Like sociologists (see Holzer, Chapter 4 in this volume), historians have also seen communications as a key driver of global social change. Yet they often produce sweeping statements about how communications created change. In other words, assessments often do not consider what impacts communications companies and technologies actually exerted. Impacts need not mean rupture. As Mathias Albert and Tobias Werron point out in the introduction to this volume, 'stability, persistence, or continuity are just as much in need of explanation as are change, transformation, or discontinuity'. Communications' contribution to global social change was uneven and difficult to measure. By showing different forms of historical impact, this chapter argues against broad and sweeping statements about global effects of communications. Sometimes, the spread of communications infrastructure did not change underlying political and economic conditions, but reinforced and perpetuated them.

Infrastructures are 'big, durable, well-functioning systems and services, from railroads and highways to telephone, electric power, and the Internet' (Edwards et al, 2009: 365). Scholars of interwar Europe (Badenoch and Fickers, 2010; Schipper and Schot, 2011) have explored how infrastructure networks like motorways or electricity created transnational connections long before political or economic integration. A term mainly imported by engineers into English from French in the early twentieth century, 'infrastructure' became common bureaucratic currency during discussions over development in the post-war era, particularly from the 1960s. It became 'world-making', or a word to describe the physical instantiation of Western military and economic visions around the world (Carse, 2017: 31).

Communications infrastructures, whether telegraphy, post or TV, have often developed in parallel with content firms to deliver information over those infrastructures. Jürgen Habermas' historical work on communications is best known for how he traced the waxing and waning of a 'public sphere' (*Öffentlichkeit*). Habermas also observed, though, that 'technological developments in the means of transmission of news' enabled and accelerated what he called 'the organizational unification and economic interlocking of the press' (Habermas, 1989: 187). In other words, Habermas argued that the nineteenth-century spread of telegraphy fostered the growth of large media companies that monopolized the public sphere. Yet technology's impact is more complex and more multidirectional, sometimes helping dispossessed voices to be heard in ways that the technology's innovators did not anticipate.

Understanding the impact of communications can also help the interdisciplinary thrust of this book to integrate sociology with history and International Relations. A global history of how communications affected populations around the world shows why communications played a key role in differentiation, for example. Communications did not cause colonialism, but it helped to entrench imperial rule for decades before anticolonial activists used some Western communications systems in their favour. The historical record, then, is not simple. There is no straightforward causal relationship between communications and social, economic and political change. Rather, there are multiple, overlapping impacts that can function differently in different times and places. This point can provide a basis for assessing our contemporary situation, where American-owned social media companies appeared to be drivers of democratic social change during the Arab Spring of 2011, but now seem to foster conspiracy-theory-driven violence and the rise of strongman leaders around the world. A tool that seemed wired for democracy became a weapon of would-be authoritarians. If we wish to consider communications seriously as a driver of social change, we need a clear historical assessment of how communications technologies, infrastructures and firms did and did not affect societies, politics and economics around the world.

The body of this chapter will present nine different forms of impact, subdivided into four clusters of cultural, economic, political and environmental impacts. This is not just for the sake of producing a checklist. Rather, it is meant to illustrate the myriad uneven global effects of communications over time and space, while tracing out some concrete examples of the interaction between communications and broader societal change.

Cultural effects

The most commonly asserted impact for communications is cultural. This is often misunderstood. Every communications technology is praised for shrinking time and space (that phrase occurs in both Zeiler (2013) on the post-1945 period with TV and Topik and Wells (2014) on telegraphy). Historians of telegraphy (John, 2010: 2) have long since discredited the assertion by Standage (1998) that telegraphy was the 'Victorian internet', yet the book continues to resurface like a zombie, even cited in very recent histories of the world economy like Topik and Wells (2014). If we think of the internet as a mass communication medium, the telegraph was not such a medium. Letters were the main way that most people communicated across distance. The post, not telegraphy, was the real Victorian internet (John and Tworek, 2019; Shulman, 2015).

Historians of communication have instead shown that the cultural impact of telegraphy often lay in *representations* of how time and space had changed (Wenzlhuemer, 2007, 2010), rather than ordinary people's experience of that technology. This was particularly true for submarine cables that were used by a tiny fraction of the population. Only around 90 firms consistently used the transatlantic submarine cable system in the late nineteenth century. Governments used cross-border cables to govern, particularly the British over their empire. Finally, most people, even in the West, experienced international telegraphy indirectly through reading press reports and journalism that was supplied through telegraph (Müller, 2016). As one cable reformer, MP Henniker Heaton, put it around the turn of the twentieth century, submarine telegraphy was 'beyond the means of 99 percent of the population' (Müller, 2015).

In the United States, even domestic telegraphy only became a mass medium after reforms in 1910.

Much scholarship has analysed how the rise of journalism in the nineteenth century created new sources of information for increasingly urbanized populations in Europe and North America. The effects of journalism on most citizens are more difficult to trace than elite beliefs about those effects. Elites often feared the 'mass hysteria' or mass persuasion that newspapers or radio could exert (Campbell, 2010; Sumpter, 2006; Wardhaugh, 2013); they also frequently assumed that published opinion mirrored public opinion. By the inter-war period, sociologists like the American Robert Park or the German Ferdinand Tönnies pushed back against these simplistic assumptions. Even as communications scholarship grew increasingly sophisticated, it remains important to point out that journalism was just one form of reporting the news that arose in a particular context (Tworek and Hamilton, 2017), that readers interpreted news in many ways, and that the cultural effects of journalism remain multifarious. The focus on journalism also unintentionally perpetuates a Western-centric model of information-gathering (Zhao, 2012: 144).

Contemporary analysts similarly tend to attribute positive and negative cultural impacts to social media. These assessments may be warranted, but they are often made with little scholarly analysis. Facebook and WhatsApp have certainly contributed to increased violence in India because fake rumours spread more swiftly. Facebook messages amplified and accelerated the horrifically violent ethnic cleansing of the Rohingya from Myanmar, as an independent report on the human rights impact of Facebook in Myanmar (commissioned by Facebook) confirmed (BSR, 2018). Yet genocides and ethnic cleansing occurred long before Facebook. The Rwandan genocide in 1994 was spurred by radio broadcasts. Social media may have altered the dynamics of communications, but history cautions against overblown assertions of unprecedented cultural effects.

Economic effects

Current analysis of internet firms similarly overstates the novelty of the economic effects of large communications firms. In fact, telecommunications firms played a particularly strong role in fostering a world economy, a term that had very German and Austrian roots (Slobodian, 2015). There are four interrelated economic and financial impacts.

First, communications companies were some of the first multinational enterprises (MNEs) and offered a model for how MNEs operated and were structured. One leading business historian has noted that 'multinational strategies had always featured in the telecommunications industry' (Jones, 2005: 105). Companies like the Swedish firm Ericsson manufactured in Russia and created sales subsidiaries in China and Mexico in the 1890s. Some scholars have depicted telegraph companies as the quintessential MNEs of the modern period. This is a 'controversial point', with others pointing to medieval banking in Italy or the Dutch East India Company (Topik and Wells, 2014: 281, note 74). Still, telegraph, railroad and steamship enterprises inaugurated 'the modern era of multinational corporations' because 'international cartels, consortia, joint investments from different countries, and mixed public and private investments capitalized and coordinated these singularly far-flung enormous enterprises' (Topik and Wells, 2014: 85). Yet many global historians, like Osterhammel, spend little or no space discussing the multinational firms that made global telegraphy possible. Osterhammel only mentions the Eastern Telegraph Company once and does not delve into how it was one of multiple companies in the Eastern and Associated Telegraph Company conglomerate (Osterhammel, 2009: 1027).

Business history provides a way to trace communications firms across time and space, taking the firm as the unit of analysis rather than a territory. Submarine cable companies in particular became 'a vital cornerstone in the rise of Western managerial capitalism' (Müller and Tworek, 2015: 264). Firms like the Eastern and Associated Telegraph Company (the major submarine telegraph company) were among the first to separate capital investment from managers and control. While older family firms had grown by reinvesting profits, cable companies expanded by attracting capital from investment banks and using firm structures like the joint-stock company. These structures and financing methods were not wholly new: they had been used for other infrastructures like railways and steamships. But cable companies made them multinational. These new methods enabled submarine cable companies to become some of the largest multinational enterprises in the world and created precedents for how other MNEs could dominate other sectors. Submarine telegraph firms based themselves in London, because the city offered the easiest access to capital, engineers and technical know-how. London became entrenched as a 'global city' (Sassen, 2001) partly because cable companies paved the way for other MNEs to base themselves there.

Second, communication companies enabled other companies to expand abroad. In the post-1945 period, telex and transatlantic telephone connections made it easier for US headquarters to communicate with subsidiaries. The number of transatlantic telephone calls rose from 250,000 in 1957 to over 4.3 million merely four years later (Zeiler, 2013: 266). The structure of communication networks could significantly affect where MNEs operated, for instance due to better communication links between the US and Latin America than, say, the US and East Asia in the late nineteenth century.

This begs the important question of whether communications infrastructure amplified existing trading networks or helped to create them. In the late nineteenth century, the American James Scrymser believed that laying cable connections between North and South America would improve trade and investment between the two continents. Government officials similarly saw value in the initiative, as it would help them to temper the strength of British investment and trade in the region. Cables laid by Scrymser's Central and South American Telegraph Company created closer ties to the United States, while the Bureau of American Republics provided commercial information about investment opportunities in Latin America (Ahvenainen and Britton, 2004; Britton, 2013). American capital flows to Latin America increased fivefold from 1897 to 1914, although British investment was still greater (Taylor, 2003). Still, new cable connections could not create trade *ab novo* just because government officials subsidized cables. Communication networks generally intensified connections between already connected places. The Pacific cables laid around 1900 made losses and did not create the demand that cable boosters anticipated (Müller and Tworek, 2015). Other companies and investments did not develop between Canada and Australasia simply because a cable now connected Vancouver and Brisbane. Communications could help the spread of other MNEs, but communications alone did not make firms go global.

The third impact of communications is more specifically the strand of financial globalization. Arguably, communications had intertwined with international finance for centuries before telegraphy. One example is the role of ships that often conveyed financial news. Only with the rise of stock markets and public credit did old communications routes become intertwined with profit-seeking based on international affairs. The eighteenth century saw the advent of speculation in news as a key concept tying together diplomacy, international finance and the burgeoning press. Speculation was 'not just a gamble on the future;

it was also a means of viewing events from afar' (Slauter, 2009: 767). Merchants, commercial agents and investors in financial markets became hungrier for foreign news that arrived through correspondence carried on ships and from interviews with ships' captains. The four- to six-week delay of waiting for ships to cross the Atlantic enabled speculation over events that could prove highly profitable. Speculation thus became 'a central organizing principle of political news in the revolutionary Atlantic World' (Slauter, 2009: 792). The boom and bust of financial markets, symbolized by the infamous Dutch tulipmania of the 1630s (Goldgar, 2007), could happen before new communications technologies emerged.

The advent of steamships in the 1840s considerably accelerated the exchange of news across the Atlantic (Kaukiainen, 2001). If we put submarine telegraphy into this longer trajectory, it appears as less of a break than a continuation of an older quest to send information more swiftly across seas. Still, submarine telegraphy reconfigured parts of the stock market by enabling news, stock prices and orders to move faster across oceans than goods or people. Telegraphy became 'the adhesive of the global market' (Topik and Wells, 2014: 85). The futures market expanded exponentially to trade on the time difference between purchase and arrival of goods. Futures markets had existed before telegraphy, however, with a key example being the Japanese rice market. What had changed was the scale of trading, the potential profits, and the emergence of Chicago as a key location for communications in the first age of globalization (Engel, 2015). Similarly, lower communication costs in the post-World War II period enabled the swifter spread of financial systems like credit cards. Computers became increasingly central. IT exports from the US rose from 4.9% of GDP in the mid-1980s to 8.2% in 1998 (Zeiler, 2013: 320).

It swiftly became clear, however, that communications might have deleterious consequences on financial markets by fostering panic as swiftly as cables fostered integration. Negative consequences appeared soon after the first successful transatlantic submarine cable in 1866. The speculation of the eighteenth century became the 'transatlantic speculations' that led to the panics of 1873 (Davies, 2018). Many believed that telegraphy exacerbated the financial crisis of 1873 by supplying information on American railroads to Europe far faster (Davies, 2016). During later crises like German hyperinflation in the early 1920s, one state official thought that banks receiving information over wireless worsened the crisis through excessive trading (Tworek, 2019).

Analysts today similarly worry about 'flash crashes' because algorithms now govern much stock market trading. These algorithms produce high-frequency trading, meaning automated buying and selling of stocks at hyperfast speeds to take advantage of milliseconds to reap profits. Trading occurs so fast that massive sell-offs can happen within seconds, if certain conditions arise. This happened during the flash crash of 6 May 2010, an event that raised fears amongst traders that high-frequency trading could spur death spirals in stock prices. These fears of technology are remarkably reminiscent (Borch, 2016) of the concerns provoked by previous communications technologies like telegraphy and wireless. Communications technologies may accelerate financial globalization or enable new forms of speculation, but they may have played less of a causal role than it seems at first. The impact of communications in this area may be more of degree than of kind.

The fourth impact is a more direct relationship between communications companies and stock markets. Communications MNEs have mattered for stock markets since the creation of joint-stock cable companies, but increasingly so since the 1980s. Stockholders in cable companies and other infrastructure firms like shipping included not just the rich, but also smaller middle-class investors. Some women too gained a modicum of financial freedom through investment in sailing companies until the 1880s (Doe, 2010) and then cable companies. Women who never used submarine cables themselves could still receive income from the profits of those firms (Müller, 2016).

Since the 1980s, though, the deregulation of communications created a massive upsurge in communications MNEs' place in stock markets. Historians have emphasized the 1970s as the decade when the world experienced 'the shock of the global' (Ferguson et al, 2010). For communications, the 1980s were more crucial, particularly for the US where the Reagan administration broke up Bell systems and brought an anti-trust case against IBM. On 1 January 1984, the *New York Times* called the break-up of Bell 'a new era for American telecommunications and for American business' (Pollack, 1984). As the article noted, it also helped to inaugurate a new global era of telecommunications, as newly privatized telecommunications companies (telcos) expanded across borders. By 2001, three telcos (Vodafone, Deutsche Telecom, Telefonica) were among the top 15 non-financial multinational firms.

Mobile telephony offered new opportunities for firms ranging from Nokia to Blackberry, which for a time put Finland and Canada on the map as hosting headquarters of major mobile phone companies. IBM's resolution of the anti-trust case brought by the Reagan administration birthed the personal computer by combining IBM hardware, Intel processors and the Microsoft operating system. This was a model others could copy and which produced ever more affordable PCs for personal as well as business use. Apple's second rise under Steve Jobs from the mid-2000s rested fundamentally on personal devices like the iPod for music and particularly the iPhone from 2007 onwards.

American-owned communications and media platforms have become increasingly central to stock market performances. In May 2018, the FAANG (Facebook Apple Amazon Netflix Google) companies represented 11% of the standard index of the top 500 companies in the US, the S&P 500, more than double the percentage of 2013, just five years before (Molla, 2018). These companies' dominance has many causes, but a key factor was the continuing trend of deregulation. Under the Democratic administration of Bill Clinton, the Communications Decency Act (CDA) of 1996 contained a critical section (section 230) that removed liability from any company hosting content online that was uploaded by others. Section 230 enabled Facebook, Twitter, Google and others to expand rapidly because they bore no legal responsibility for content on their sites. Google, for example, was not liable for the content of any link that its search engines suggested. This dramatically reduced costs, enabling near exponential user growth. The trend of communications companies' importance for stock markets continues to accelerate as Chinese internet companies like Baidu, Alibaba and Baidu-spinoff iQiyi (the Chinese Netflix) have IPOs (Initial Public Offerings).

Political effects

As Lawson's chapter in this volume points out, states and markets have retained 'extensive entanglements' (Chapter 10). Many political and economic effects of communications were intertwined, though they are separated here for analytical clarity. While the economic and financial impacts of communications are wide-ranging, scholars have also claimed numerous political effects for communications at different geographical scales.

The first political impact was within national and colonial territories. Historian Charles S. Maier has examined the overlap and development of what he called 'identity space' and 'decision space'. Identity space was the area to which people felt they belonged, like a town, a region or a nation state. Decision space is the area over which a political entity has jurisdiction. Starting in the 1860s and up to the 1960s, nation states became citizens' main self-described identity and their main jurisdiction in many parts of the world, whether Italy, Japan or the United States in the 1860s or, later, decolonized territories ineluctably taking the form of nation states in the 1950s and 1960s. This development was tied to the creation of national infrastructures, like railways and telegraphy. Maier also noted 'a third spatial domain that has never been bordered so rigidly, indeed that challenges the territorial limits that prevail at any moment – what might be called the *communication space* in which ideas and cultural goods are exchanged' (Maier, 2016: 301, note 8, emphasis in original). But this definition appears in an endnote; communication space and its effects remain implicit.

Sometimes, communication space could reinforce the decision and identity spaces of the nation state. The British government, for example, nationalized landline telegraphy by buying all the British landline cables through the Telegraph Purchase Bill in 1868. Landline cables were cheap and affordable for most Britons. On the other hand, communications could cement imperial control or semi-colonial control. The British colony of India could be ruled more directly once submarine and landline routes linked South Asia to the United Kingdom. Railways and telegraph lines in India were laid for the convenience of British imperial officials, not Indian subjects (Mann, 2017). 'Telegraphic imperialism' (Choudhury, 2010) could consolidate imperial rule, including by creating more comprehensive surveillance systems.

Surveillance could intertwine with the militarization of communications infrastructure, particularly during wartime, or in authoritarian regimes to ensure compliance with the dominant political system. For decades in the post-war era, the Central Intelligence Agency (CIA) and West German intelligence services co-owned Crypto AG, a company that supplied encryption devices to 120 countries. Only in 2020 was it publicly uncovered that the American and West German intelligence services had used that ownership to enable easy decryption of communications (Borger, 2020). Often, innovations in communication emerged from cooperation between companies and militaries, or companies were allowed to pursue commercial exploitation of military innovations, like the long-run history of the Defense Advanced Research Projects Agency (DARPA) and the internet. In turn, the success of communication companies could spur greater investment in military R&D.

Still, anticolonial leaders could use communications to challenge imperial rule. While living in South Africa, Mohandas Gandhi founded his own newspaper that fought back against what he decried as Western norms of swift news spread by telegraphy. He promoted instead slow reading and contemplation as a form of resistance to British imperialism (Hofmeyr, 2013). A few decades later, landline telegraphy became a 'double-edged sword' used by Indian nationalists to coordinate and protest the colonial system (Headrick, 2010). Communication space challenged the given limits of identity space and decision space at the same time as it reinforced the power of states to communicate in the first place.

At the same time as communication space was critical for shaping nation states and empires, it could also promote the institutionalization and standardization of world society – a second form of political impact (see also Chapter 14, by Daniel Speich Chassé, on statistics as another form of standardization). This standardization almost simultaneously occurred through both private cartels and international organizations. The first successful transatlantic submarine cable was laid by a private company in 1866; in 1865 the first major international organization, the International Telegraph Union, was founded. These developments laid the groundwork for a telegraph age dominated by Anglo-American multinationals. This decade also saw the first informal workings of the news agency cartel, creating cooperation between news providers as well as infrastructure companies.

From the start, telegraphy seemed to require international coordination for technical standards. The International Telegraph Union (ITU) emerged in 1865 when Switzerland brokered between two competing systems in Europe to suggest coordinated standards and a bureau to regulate them headquartered in Berne (Balbi et al, 2014). It is no coincidence that two of the first major international organizations – the ITU (1865) and the Universal Postal Union (UPU, 1874) – both addressed communications. The very first international organization was created in the aftermath of the Napoleonic wars, the Central Commission for the Navigation of the Rhine. It was concerned with transportation on the Rhine and communicating standards to enable smooth sailing (Spaulding, 2018). Organizations like the ITU and UPU standardized technical aspects of communication, but not the content transmitted (Tworek and Müller, 2015). Standard-setting could also be deeply political. The United States sought to define standards for satellite communication in the 1950s and 1960s to prevent any Soviet attempts to build a global system and include Third World countries in a Soviet orbit (Slotten, 2015).

Although standardization through international organizations often seemed the route to upload influence from a nation state to the international level, influence could flow in the opposite direction. Parcel post in the United States is a clear example. In 1880, some member states of the UPU devised a convention to exchange parcels across borders. At that time, the US only had private express firms that delivered packages. Thirty years later, however, the US Postal Service introduced a parcel post system designed directly to comply with the UPU convention. The service became a huge success from the start. Six months after its introduction in January 1913, around 300 million packages had been delivered and many private express companies were near collapse or had gone out of business (Laborie, 2015). The international could shape national standards and business.

Governments were not the only actors that influenced standardization. Communications MNEs did as well. Almost from the start, submarine cable companies sent representatives to attend ITU meetings and influenced decisions, even if they did not have an official vote. Communications companies promoted standardization and influenced international coordination – that is, had international policy impact. More broadly, cable companies helped to set precedents for how companies might be included in international organizations and influence technical standards in particular. They influenced, for example, how many characters were counted for a word and which entities determined rates, enabling them to keep prices high and the volume of transatlantic telegrams low (Müller, 2015). The US and Canada would harken back to submarine cable companies' role in the International Telegraph Union when they campaigned for companies to be included in meetings of the new International Telecommunication Union, created in 1932 to combine international regulation of radio and telegraphy (Tworek, 2020).

A third political impact was how communications could offer a route to influence the international order. That influence might be to stabilize the current international order or to upend it. While the previous impact examined how communications fostered technical standardization, this impact considers how elites tried to use communications for political or economic ends. Communications tools, technologies and firms could be used in multiple ways depending on larger political, economic and cultural contexts. The British and Germans provide contrasting examples. The British saw technologies like cables as 'instruments to stabilize an international *status quo* favorable to their nation while Germans viewed products of engineering as tools to transform the international environment that stifled their political ambitions' (Rieger, 2005: 18). Around 1900, the British subsidized a cable between Vancouver and Australia to complete an All-Red Route around the world. The British and their imperial officials could now send cables around the world that only touched on British soil. This development was meant to stabilize British imperial rule.

Meanwhile, the Germans wanted to duplicate cables to avoid using cables that those governments believed were controlled by the British. The Germans started to subsidize research and development in new technologies like wireless to bypass cable systems. Many cable companies relied upon state subsidies for communication companies to compete with other nations, as international tensions grew. In the first half of the twentieth century, Germans tried to use new wireless technology and news agencies to bypass what they saw as a Franco-British-dominated global information environment. Germans came to see communications and media as a vital way to influence global geopolitics, economics and cultural attitudes towards Germany. While Germans did not fully succeed, they did cause consternation amongst many other nations when German (and later Nazi) news was printed around the world (Tworek, 2019).

Like Germany, Japan saw communications and communications infrastructure as part of the accoutrements for an imperial and international power. The Japanese cooperated with the Danish to lay telegraph lines. They invested in wireless technology (Yang, 2010). From the 1930s, the Japanese vision of a Great East Asia Co-Prosperity Sphere (Yellen, 2019) included sovereign telegraph, wireless and radio communications to enable the Japanese to run their hierarchical empire.

In the second half of the twentieth century, arguments about communications dovetailed with postcolonial and Third World nations' critiques of an international order that seemed skewed against them. Inspired by United Nations Educational, Scientific and Cultural Organization (UNESCO) research (Brendebach, 2018), Latin American and Third World nations started to argue for a New World Information and Communication Order (NWICO) in the 1970s (Freije, 2019). These nations decried the hegemony of Western news providers, particularly Western news agencies, around the world. At the same time, they pushed for a New International Economic Order (NIEO) that would similarly overturn Western hegemony. While neither the NWICO nor the NIEO substantively changed the structure of international communications, the NWICO debates show how central communications were to Third World visions for a different international society.

The twenty-first century too has seen communications become a fundamental part of international politics. Though the effects on American votes remain disputed, Russian funding for the Internet Research Agency to create fake accounts for 'real Americans' on

Twitter has become a key staple of international policy debates. China's Central Television (CCTV) and news agency Xinhua, Qatari-funded Al Jazeera and RT (Russia Today) are all recent examples of state-supported news organizations that implicitly and explicitly portray certain pictures of the world.

Environmental effects

Finally, there were environmental impacts, though these were mostly felt in colonies and the global South. Submarine telegraph cables required insulation to protect them from the ocean. After initial experimentation, rubber was found to be the most durable insulator. In the nineteenth century, rubber came mainly from gutta percha. The gutta percha required for telegraph cables was taken from rubber trees in Malaysia and South East Asia, devastating forests there (Tully, 2009). This material provision reproduced and reinforced imperial hierarchies. Submarine cables benefited imperial elites; they consolidated the dominance of Western MNEs and imperial governments. At the time, cables were often seen as dematerializing information; even later historians have often adopted this vocabulary. Yet the sourcing for cables was very much material and had highly detrimental material effects for colonized peoples in South East Asia, who lost forests that had helped to sustain them for centuries. Although much work remains to be done on the environmental impacts of communications, telegraphy is one example of the hidden outsourcing of supply chains and the global hierarchies of production.

The impact of sourcing has continued up to today: some of the tin in iPhones is probably mined by children on Indonesia's Bangka Island (Merchant, 2017a). Other rare earths in iPhones came from exploitative labour practices and mining in Latin America (Merchant, 2017b). Disposal has a similar global distribution. Over the past few decades, electronic goods like TVs and so on are increasingly dumped in developing countries, and Africa in particular. The networks of production and disposal reproduce older colonial hierarchies in ways that those celebrating communications' emancipatory qualities generally do not recognize.

Conclusion

Law and Urry (2004) have urged social scientists to take on questions of complexity and understand that cause and effect are not simple. This dictum is most often egregiously violated for communications, with little understanding of how tenuous some of those claims really are. Generations of scholarship have worked to understand communications effects; these contradict the often sweeping assertions about how communications created change in the past. Impacts are not unidirectional. Communications did not cause everything that scholars have claimed for it, but rather forms part of a complex interaction with other political, economic, social, technological and cultural factors.

A significant body of literature on communications in global history means that any scholar can incorporate communications into work on global social change. Historians of the world have seen communications as more global than most other industries. Yet they have often made overly broad generalizations about impacts like how communications technologies transformed time and space. Communications companies have, though, had myriad impacts on finance, politics, environment and culture. Like any multinational enterprise, communications firms had positive and negative effects on different parts of the world. The most positive impacts often appeared in the North Atlantic, the most negative in colonies and the global South. Impacts were uneven and sometimes unexpected.

When we start to think about communications networks as constructing 'the global', we can see how 'the global' is uneven and exclusionary, how it privileged certain types of connections over others, and how it is politically, economically and technologically determined by imperial and Western norms. We also see the importance of denaturalizing infrastructures and of sceptically analysing claims that communications could produce such sweeping effects.

Scholars can do more than simply incorporate communications into their work: they can think more carefully about where, when, how and why communications affected the economy, politics, environment and culture. They can think more carefully about who benefited from denser communications connections and who was disadvantaged even further. Here, sociological theories may prove most useful to aid global historians to conceptualize broad change across time and space as well as consider how apparently dramatic changes like submarine telegraphy may mask the stability of political and economic hierarchies. Most importantly, communications historians will have succeeded when scholars move beyond platitudes about how another communications technology shrank the world.

12

The 'Long Twentieth Century' and the Making of World Trade Law

James Stafford

Introduction

Since the 1990s, the concept of 'globalization' – usually understood as the increasing economic, social and cultural integration of world regions – has become a leitmotif for popular and scholarly narratives of global social change in modernity (Eckel, 2018). The history of global economic integration is commonly narrated as forming two great 'waves' in the later nineteenth and later twentieth centuries, interspersed by an era of 'deglobalization' characterized by two world wars and the formation of autarchic economic 'blocs' (Chase-Dunn et al, 2000; Bordo et al, 2003). Theorists working in a Marxian world-systems tradition have similarly associated two eras of stable capitalist globalization with the presence of strong economic and military hegemons: the British Empire in the nineteenth century and the United States in the twentieth (Arrighi, 1994).[1]

This model of globalization as a homogeneous absolute – something that is either present or absent, rising or falling – obscures more than it reveals. As Stefan Link has argued, arguments that claim similarities between a 'first' and 'second' era of globalization – and thereby imply that our present 'deglobalization' will terminate in a bloody conflagration on the scale of World War II – understate the extent to which 'different periods of globalization have relied on distinctive political and institutional architectures'. What is required is a more granular account of the 'politics of globalization' – one capable of appreciating the variety of 'structured engagement' between polities of all kinds and 'foreign trade and capital' (Link, 2018: 347).

States and markets, George Lawson tells us in the present volume, have been mutually constituted. The broadening and deepening of global economic integration has been enabled by state action, just as states have been empowered – and constrained – by the expansion of markets to a global scale. Drawing on Chapter 5 by Julian Go, we might further observe that the structure of the global political field was transformed by decolonization after the mid-twentieth century. The 'reglobalization' of the world economy after 1945 occurred in connection with the elaboration of an international, as opposed to an inter-imperial, understanding of a legitimate global order. Taking the mutual constitution of states and markets seriously must mean, therefore, that we examine the interactions between the basic structures of the international system and those of the global economy.

This chapter builds on these insights by offering a new narrative of the emergence of a global 'system' of trade law since the mid-nineteenth century. It argues that, while the extent, depth and nature of global economic integration may have dramatically varied over this period, we can identify a continuous attempt to establish and elaborate systems of inter-polity law designed to regulate economic exchanges on a global scale. This, it is suggested, should be seen as a central feature of global social change in the 'long twentieth century'. Rather than a period of US hegemony in the capitalist world system (Arrighi, 1994), this 'long twentieth century' should be understood as the elaboration of global communicative infrastructures (Dickinson, 2018; Werron, Chapter 9 in this volume). The telegraph, the radio, the news agency and international organizations all survived, and in some cases thrived, during the inter-war collapse of global economic integration (Tworek, Chapter 11 in this volume). A similar logic of continuous elaboration can be identified, it is suggested, in the field of world trade law, which has provided a different kind of infrastructure for the world economy in its various phases of integration and fragmentation.

The rise of world trade law enabled, and was encouraged by, the expansion and growing status of a transnational body of trade diplomats, consuls, economists and economic lawyers, who were significant actors, alongside multinational firms and leading capitalist states, in the fashioning of a global political economy. Projects of international economic law were often associated with liberal ideals of 'free trade', but they were pliable instruments, which could also support regionalist or protectionist ambitions. The development of 'fundamental institutions' (Reus-Smit, 1999) of global economic order – commercial treaty systems, consular jurisdiction and international organizations – should be analysed as part of 'world politics' as well as the 'world economy' (Albert, 2016).

This chapter starts from a key insight from the Bielefeld approach to world society, which has it that the expansion of global consciousness and communication need not produce a teleological drive towards social integration (Luhmann, 1997a). A 'deglobalized' world economy, with dramatically reduced cross-border or interregional flows of goods, people and capital, can readily coexist with a global political and media system. We need not, therefore, expect the development and expansion of institutions and expert communities associated with international economic law to be perfectly synchronous with the 'real' or 'underlying' integration of the world economy, or the continuance of a successful drive for market expansion and capital accumulation by hegemonic capitalist powers.

A second theoretical impulse comes from Chris Reus-Smit's (1999) concept of 'fundamental institutions' and 'regimes' of international order. This is a useful framework for historians, because it encourages us to develop an expanded sense of international 'political' history as encompassing broader patterns of ideological and institutional development. From this perspective, the differing institutional forms that world trade politics have taken – bilateral and multilateral treaties, interstate diplomacy and global arbitration – can be related to broader 'visions of global order' (Bell, 2007) that are political in character, but nonetheless have significant economic features.

It is important to draw this distinction at the outset, because the history of world trade law is usually narrated as a subsidiary question for histories of the world economy. It is considered from the standpoint of one of two problematics: that of the geopolitical power of hegemonic centres of capital accumulation; or of the ability of a community of sovereign states to 'cooperate' to ensure 'free trade'. The first section of this chapter makes a case for a different approach, emphasizing the need to write the history of world trade law into the broader history of international law and international political thought. From this perspective, it is argued, two key conceptual transformations are vital. The first concerns the structure of the international system itself, and the legitimacy of empires and nation states within it. The second concerns the meaning of 'free trade', which was changed from a pre-political state of 'natural liberty', requiring non-intervention from public authorities, to a set of codified legal rights, enshrined in interstate treaties. These two transformations together make it possible to think of a world trade 'system' as it exists today, based on legal arbitration between a global community of notionally sovereign states.

The subsequent two sections focus in more detail on the legal institutions and expert communities associated with world trade law since the mid-nineteenth century. They consider successively the political and legal structure of nineteenth- and twentieth-century trade law, and the normative conceptions of the relationship between sovereignty and commerce that underpinned them. In the nineteenth century, a regime of reciprocity and bilateralism overlapped with a commitment to the multilateral, collaborative regulation (and exploitation) of relationships in the non-European world. In this bifurcated order, inter-European trade treaties were negotiated by professional diplomats, while consuls gained far-reaching rights of jurisdiction and protection over European and non-European subjects in South America, the Ottoman Empire and East Asia.

Following the breakdown of the European 'Most Favoured Nation' regime during World War I, an emergent cadre of legal and economic experts linked to the institutions of the League of Nations developed the model of a global, multilateral system. This was partially realized in the General Agreement on Tariffs and Trade (GATT), and remodelled through the application of neoliberal and functionalist theories of global governance in the making of the World Trade Organization (WTO). The 'legalization' of the GATT regime after 1994 (Abbot et al, 2000) entailed a further change in the balance of power between diplomats and international lawyers in the framing of world trade law, as the latter came to assume an increasingly important role within the arbitration structures of the new WTO.

Hegemony and cooperation

The global trade regime after 1945 is a favourite case study for a vast set of debates in international relations and international political economy. These revolve around the question of whether the raw power of the United States, or the system of multilateral institutions that it has sponsored since 1945, are the determining factor in the continuing existence of a functioning global political economy (Saull, 2017).

The concept of hegemony has produced a striking narrative of the history of the global trading system that makes it subordinate to a broader narrative of the indispensable agency and/or functional necessity of powerful states – first Britain, latterly the US – committed to the stabilization of global capitalism. The economic historian Charles

Kindleberger, a State Department official who played a key role in designing and administering the Marshall Plan, wrote a history of US protectionism in the Great Depression as a warning of the dangers of the US shrinking from 'leadership' in world trade following the related debacles of Vietnam and the breakdown of the Bretton Woods system (Kindleberger, 1975). Hegemony appears as a function of enlightened self-interest: the US provided free trade and financial stability as a 'public good' to all other states in the capitalist world.

For Kindleberger, the Depression was an intermezzo between two upward cycles of integration and prosperity in the world economy. The first, in the mid-to-late nineteenth century, had been guaranteed by 'free trade Britain' through its abandonment of the Navigation Acts (restricting ports to native shipping) and the Corn Laws (protecting domestic agriculture). Britain exercised the crucial 'leadership' that led the surrounding states to also lower their own tariffs in the course of the 1850s and 1860s. The argument is admirably crisp: 'Manchester and the English political economists persuaded Britain which persuaded Europe, by precept and example' (Kindleberger, 1975: 51). It is repeated and expanded, with strikingly little revision, by Jürgen Osterhammel in his landmark global history of the nineteenth century (Osterhammel, 2014: 455). Where Kindleberger, in terms suggestive of his biographical relationship with Keynesian international macroeconomics, focused on the role of hegemons as recyclers of trade surpluses and providers of financial stability, Osterhammel's description of Britain as a source of specifically *legal* norms – non-discrimination via the 'most favoured nation' clause – suggests a contrasting, ordoliberal sensibility. As a recent essay in praise of *Freihandel* – 'free trade' – set out, it is only the *combination* of hegemonic agency and binding rules that can uphold the benign liberal order identified with both the nineteenth century and the post-Cold War era (Osterhammel, 2018).

In nineteenth-century historiography, a research paradigm centred on the ideological identification of the British Empire with 'free trade' and the rise of global capitalism has extended deep into the fields of national political, social and cultural history (Trentmann, 2008; Todd, 2015; Palen, 2016). There is certainly ample evidence that the inhabitants of the nineteenth century felt and experienced their world to be dominated by a 'free trade' that was largely a British invention. This has not deterred economists and political scientists from developing a rival research programme in the history of nineteenth-century commercial liberalism, centred not on the hegemonic agency of Britain and its empire but the political-economic determinants of 'cooperation' among members of the European state system.

Just as hegemonic and institutionalist agendas were fashioned in response to the crisis and redefinition of US power in the 1970s and 1980s, so the expanded interest in the internal, or 'bottom-up', dynamics of nineteenth-century bilateralism has been driven by the alleged 'failure' of the WTO in the wake of the Doha Round and the development of narratives of contemporary world politics, centred on the emergence of 'multipolarity' following another round of US imperial overreach in Afghanistan and Iraq. This research agenda has usefully complicated the Kindleberger–Osterhammel hegemony narrative by highlighting Britain's relative *lack* of importance in the framing and maintenance of the nineteenth-century trade regime, at least within Europe itself.

Traditional diplomatic histories of late nineteenth-century British policy had already highlighted that, far from being the champion of free trade treaties, Britain was quick to withdraw from them and return to a stance of unilateral free trade (Marsh, 1999). Here, too, the temptations of presentism were hard to resist: one British historian of Germany, writing in the wake of the British government's struggle to secure passage of the Maastricht Treaty through parliament, waspishly argued that Britain's persistent aversion to European treaty politics amounted to a kind of 'British *Sonderweg*' (Davis, 1997). As the authors of a recent survey of the Marxian hegemony literature on nineteenth-century Britain noted, 'Britain ... was able to shape the world economy without making or enforcing rules within the core areas' (Lacher and Germann, 2012: 119).

Abandoning hegemony, however, comes with its own downsides. By reconceiving the nineteenth-century trade regime as a set of cooperation problems between self-evident, equal – and rational – political units, political scientists such as Robert Pahre (2007) and Bryan Coutain (2009) leave themselves open to justified criticism on the grounds of Euro- and state-centrism. This vision of international society is itself a historical product of the era that research on 'free trade' and cooperation seeks to analyse. Europeans have persistently convinced themselves that their societies and institutions constitute the world, or the 'civilized' part of it, and that non-European peoples and territories exist 'outside' of it, in a state of natural 'freedom' or 'barbarism'. Europeans' insistence on market access and security of property led them to engage in the violent reordering of the varied and sophisticated political and economic cultures of Africa, Asia, Australia and the Americas. Sovereign entities on the fringes of the 'civilized' world, such as the Ottoman Empire, China, Japan, the independent states of South America, and at times even Russia, were treated as liminal cases, not fully deserving of the reciprocity and inclusion offered to core European states (Lorca, 2015).

One of the first tasks for a history of world trade law that locates it in broader frameworks of global social change, then, is to consider far more systematically the persistence of empire and hierarchy within global political economy: rendering this, rather than the necessity or otherwise of hegemony and cooperation in guaranteeing 'waves' of globalization, a central subject of research. A second is to consider the conceptual transformation of the idea of 'free trade' itself. For much of the eighteenth and nineteenth centuries, free trade ideology rested on the idea that a pre-political state of 'natural liberty' could be recreated through the removal of restrictions on trade. After the mid-nineteenth century, the creation and reproduction of this space of 'natural liberty' began to be systematically attempted through the instantiation of positive legal norms that were binding on the sovereign, 'civilized' states of Europe. Once this process was set in motion, however, the structures of international trade law began to take on a life of their own – one that could accommodate a range of economic visions beyond the British liberal ideal of 'free trade'.

Bilateralism, non-discrimination and bifurcation: the nineteenth-century order

The mid-nineteenth century is classically regarded as a period of 'liberal' hegemony and the widespread diffusion of 'free trade' ideas in Europe. It was also, however, the period in which a 'positivist' account of 'international law' – as a necessarily codified, legible set of principles, binding on all 'civilized' countries rose to prominence in Europe's empire states (Koskenniemi, 2001, 2008). The close relationship between these two developments can be perceived in a series of concrete legal and institutional innovations that took root in the middle decades of the nineteenth century. Foremost among these was the norm of non-discrimination in both intra- and extra-European trade. This overturned early modern practices of using discriminatory clauses in commercial treaties to manage an intra- and extra-European 'balance of power' (Alexandrowicz, 1957; Alimento and Stapelbroek, 2018).

At the mid-century high noon of 'liberal internationalism' (Bell and Sylvest, 2006), the 'Cobden–Chevalier' treaty network inaugurated by Britain and France bound together 13 European states and empires via nearly 60 bilateral treaties (Lampe, 2009, 2011). These produced a low and uniform 'conventional' tariff on key industrial and agricultural goods traded across Europe, through the operation of interlocking 'Unconditional Most Favoured Nation' clauses (Pahre, 2007: 283–95). Using commercial treaties in this manner was a significant conceptual innovation. In the decades after the Napoleonic Wars, arguments for free trade had been derived from 'natural', not 'international', law, relying on pre- or extra-political models of 'commercial sociability' (Hopkins, 2015).

From the 1850s, however, economic liberalism was aligned with legal positivism by a disparate coalition of journalists, manufacturers, diplomats and international lawyers, all of whom came to see the value of the 'commercial treaties' as instruments of economic integration (Howe, 1997: 70–108). The increasing codification of trading freedoms through interlocking treaties had the effect of placing treaty law at the centre of a new institutional model for 'free trade'. In a memorandum authored after successfully completing negotiations for the British–Austrian Treaty of 1865, the British negotiator Louis Mallet argued for a new understanding of tariffs as forms of 'international taxation ... a proper subject of international regulation' (Mallet, 1891: 92).

The basic functioning of the most favoured nation system can be illustrated by a simplified account of the relationship between Britain, France, the German Zollverein and Belgium following the surge of commercial diplomacy in the early 1860s. Each state was connected to the other by a bilateral agreement covering tariffs and shipping rights relevant to the state with which it was concluded. The inclusion of most favoured nation clauses in each individual treaty had the effect of linking them together, meaning that as the network expanded in geographical scope it also expanded its coverage of commodities and economic activities. If a new trade concession was granted to the most recent state to join the network, then it was generalized 'backwards' to every other state that participated. By the same token, if a provision was to be renegotiated, or the network abandoned altogether, then the costs of departure were multiplied by the sheer number of goods and states involved in the system (Coutain, 2009).

This encouraged convergence in tariff levels, and led to the term 'conventional tariff' to describe tariffs set through the operation of interlocking most favoured nation clauses. 'Autonomous' or 'general' tariffs were applied by key states, such as France and at times Germany, on goods and states that were not participants in the system, thereby retaining the political benefits both of selective trade protection and of bargaining power in future negotiations. Britain, with its baseline, unilateral commitment to low or zero tariffs, had little to bargain with when treaties came up for revision or renewal (Marsh, 1999).

The counterpart to 'liberal internationalism' within Europe was inter-imperial collaboration in the sphere of 'informal' and 'commercial' empire. In the 1820s, the British and French disavowed any attempt to secure exclusive commercial advantages in the newly independent states of South America (Bethell, 1987: 212), breaking with the precedents set by previous European treaty practice in South Asia (Alexandrowicz, 1957). In Japan and China, meanwhile, the one-sided application of 'most favoured nation' clauses was used to enable a united front among the European powers from the 1850s, restricting the ability of both Asian empires to gain leverage over European colonizers by discriminating among them (Auslin, 2006; Martinez-Robles, 2015). The principle of 'extraterritorial' jurisdiction in the Ottoman Empire, China and Japan was collectively maintained by Britain, France and the United States, although competition for territorial and merchant concessions steadily increased into the 1890s and 1900s (Kayaoğlu, 2010; Cassel, 2012). Across the varied landscapes of 'informal' or 'commercial' imperialism, new conceptions of law were used to open new markets to European goods and capital, while producing mechanisms to contain or eliminate the potential for inter-imperial conflict. Consuls, who had long exercised representative and judicial functions in communities of foreign merchants in port cities around Europe, increasingly assumed extensive powers of arbitration and 'protection' over both European and local subjects (Case, 2018).

The most spectacular example of this collaborative form of legal, commercial imperialism was enacted, however, in Africa. The Final Act of the Berlin conference of 1884–85 aligned legal internationalism, 'free trade' and imperialism in a complex multilateral agreement that might best be understood as an extraordinary kind of 'commercial treaty' (Geiss, 1988: 264). In both the ambition of its attempt to use an international legal instrument to contain inter-imperial friction, and the extent of its exclusion of indigenous populations from legal consideration, the Berlin Act went a step further than the 'unequal treaties' imposed on extra-European states that were still notionally sovereign. Rather than the small enclaves of the Asian 'Treaty Ports', it created a vast zone of 'equal treatment' in the Congo Basin – one that was quickly eaten up by European corporate concessions, as the resultant Congo Free State scrambled to address the gaping revenue shortages left by the Act's tariff and franchising regime (de Courcel, 1988: 259–60).

For much of the nineteenth century, the British Empire constituted a state system of its own: a distinct 'nested hierarchy', existing alongside, and within, the 'international society' constituted by the European powers (Benton and Ford, 2016). Canadian and Australian turns to protection, in partial response and emulation to that of the United States, were a significant embarrassment to 'free trade' Britain in the later decades of the nineteenth century (Howe, 2007; Bairoch and Burke, 1989). In combination with the relative marginalization of Britain within European commercial treaty negotiations after 1875 (Davis, 1997; Marsh, 1999), this failure to impose 'free trade' even on formal dependencies suggests the need for a more variegated and nuanced impression of nineteenth-century British 'hegemony'. At least for those 'civilized' states with the institutional capacity and cultural capital to resist British imperialism, trade policy could act as an effective counterweight to Britain's overwhelming dominance of finance and shipping.

Many histories of nineteenth-century Europe still maintain that, following the financial crisis of 1873, the continent turned back towards economic protectionism (Bairoch and Burke, 1989, Evans, 2016). On this basis, they conclude that the treaty system of the 1860s was an ephemeral phenomenon, with little real importance in the evolution of the European economy (Osterhammel, 2018). Yet it created a framework for the international coordination of commercial policy that outlived the mid-century high-water mark of European free trade. Despite the strength of protectionist feeling in the French Third Republic, it maintained its commitment to a form of the European treaty system after defeat in the Franco-Prussian War of 1870–71 (Oncken, 1891). After 1892, the German Empire took the lead in fashioning a new round of treaties, aimed not at the undifferentiated freedom of trade, but the gradual expansion of markets for its growing industries (Torp, 2014). The principles of reciprocity and non-discrimination among the 'civilized' nations of Europe were maintained even in an environment of rising tariffs. It was only with the outbreak of World War I that the system can truly be said to have broken down.

Elsewhere in this volume, Martin Koch proposes 'two semantics of the world', the 'international' and the 'global', as coming into being in the course of the nineteenth century (Chapter 6). Nineteenth-century trade politics can be seen as 'international', because it relied on bilateral treaties that were often time-limited and subjected to periodic denunciation and renewal. Compared to other areas of nineteenth-century economic life, the extent to which they were subject to formal international organization was strikingly limited. Commercial treaties did not follow the pattern laid down, for example, by postal treaties, in which a collection of early and mid-century bilateral agreements was transformed into a multilateral regime associated with an international organization, in this instance, the Universal Postal Union founded in 1874 (Murphy, 1994). The most that was achieved was the Brussels Tariff Union (1890), an international institution for disseminating information concerning participating states' overall tariff levels. The national tariff, vital to the revenue interests of most of Europe's states, remained too important an instrument to abandon to a broader range of multilateral institutions (Milward, 1982).

Globalism, hierarchy and arbitration

The inter-war decades present a moment of counterpoint in the history of this 'international' political economy. During and after World War I, the organizational forms of international collaboration were significantly extended, but global trade and investment flows all but disappeared. In recent decades, a wave of revisionist scholarship has recovered the significance of inter-war internationalism, looking past simple narratives of failure to examine the nature and legacies of the institutions, proposals and intellectual networks that were constructed in the orbit of the League of Nations (Pedersen, 2007; Clavin and Sluga, 2017). War itself was a significant spur to international economic cooperation, with inter-allied agreements to supply grain and raw materials setting precedents for economic cooperation among members of the League of Nations (Trachtenberg, 1977). The collapse of nineteenth-century globalization heightened, rather than diminished, interest in the dynamics of the 'world economy' and the possibilities for managing them.

Daniel Speich Chassé observes in this volume that the UN today 'rules the world', despite its lack of coercive authority, through the production of information and norms (Chapter 14). In the inter-war period, the League of Nations fulfilled a comparable function in still more challenging circumstances. The Economic and Financial Section of the League, alongside private market institutions such as the International Chamber of Commerce and the Bank of International Settlements, sustained and expanded arenas in which world trade could be studied and discussed; even as depression and looming war stymied concrete efforts towards the reduction of tariffs and trade discrimination (Clavin, 2013, Decorzant, 2011).

By examining the precedents set by the commercial treaties of the nineteenth century, lawyers and economists at the League and the Hague Academy of International Law reimagined the most favoured nation clause. Instead of being tied to individual bilateral treaties, this was understood as a general binding principle of 'non-discrimination', which was to form the heart of a revived liberal trading system. At the World Economic Conference of 1927, a surprisingly broad range of delegates concluded that a multilateral trade agreement, with the 'unconditional' most favoured nation clause at its heart, offered the best hope of stabilizing the world economy (Clavin, 2013: 43–7). Nineteenth-century legal internationalism was thereby recast and regenerated on a multilateral basis. The norm of 'non-discrimination' subsequently formed the core of the General Agreement on Tariffs and Trade; enshrined in Articles I and III, but initially confined to a far smaller range of states than had been present at the 1927 conference (GATT, 1986).

The juridical counterpart to the famous 'embedded liberalism' of the post-war capitalist world lay in what Andrew Lang terms 'purposive law'. Until the formation of the World Trade Organization, the resolution of trade disputes between signatories of the GATT was subject to a process of 'positive consensus'. Independent expert panels assumed a growing role, but this remained advisory. The ultimate power of decision rested with signatory states and their professional diplomats; the resolution of disputes relied on their capacity to autonomously achieve consensus (Lang, 2014).

World trade was thus understood as a set of political relationships that were consciously designed and maintained through a continuous process of diplomacy. The goal of the system was not, or not solely, to do with achieving ever greater levels of trade 'liberalization'. Down to the 1970s, multilateralism was presented as an end in itself: the goal was not 'free trade', but the containment of potential trade conflicts between national welfare states. The elimination of the geopolitically motivated systems of trade discrimination that had disfigured the inter-war system, rather than the relentless dismantling of trade barriers, provided the core justification for the system. As in the nineteenth century, there was little interest in constitutionalizing trade politics or securing its autonomy from other spheres. A high degree of cultural and normative consensus enabled cooperation to persist in the absence of strong legal sanctions: the autonomy and policy space accorded to national economies was consequently assured, in theory if not always in practice (Ruggie, 1982).

Both the inter-war and post-war orders rested on culturally homogenous cliques of experts. These constituted a closed and partial system for those on the outside: the GATT was subject to criticism from coalitions of 'new states' from the 1960s onwards (Ogle, 2014). In arguing for a 'New International Economic Order', 'Third World' groupings employed the UN as a rival forum to the GATT. They sought to radically reconceive notions of sovereign equality and self-determination, creating a secure basis for postcolonial independence through a codification of economic, social and resource rights (Getachew, 2019). Critically – and in common with contemporary arguments for the reconciliation of 'trade and human rights' – this agenda involved a demand to significantly revise the international norm of non-discrimination. A right to development implied preferential treatment for the global South from its former colonizers, as well as an expansion of carefully structured preferential agreements and customs unions among 'developing' countries and with the socialist states of the 'Second World'.

The 1960s and 1970s witnessed challenges from those that were largely excluded from these practices: women and ethnic minorities, rank-and-file trade unionists, consumer groups at the domestic level; 'Third World' governments at the international. Interlinked attempts to democratize both national and international society generated additional forms of complexity that these loosely codified, hierarchical modes of consensus governance proved unable to contain. The result, in both national and international political economy, was a flight from political entanglement: what W. Davies (2014: 12) terms the 'disenchantment of politics by economics'. Within the GATT regime, this manifested itself as a retreat into an increasingly technical, formalized and economistic conception of world trade law, informed by hitherto dissident neoliberal and functionalist theories of 'global governance'.

Both the nineteenth- and mid-twentieth-century trade regimes rested on a broader political imaginary that can be understood as 'internationalist'. While the 'world economy' existed as an analytical proposition, trade governance was managed collaboratively by sovereign states. As recent works by Or Rosenboim (2017) and Quinn Slobodian (2018) have demonstrated, however, mid-century internationalism was accompanied by an important critical undercurrent of more ambitious federal, functionalist and 'ordo-globalist' thinking. After 1945, transnational communities of lawyers, sociologists and economists observed that a world of territorially segmented nation states, beholden to national electorates, had failed to secure free trade between the wars. They would continue to fail unless they were supplanted by more comprehensive and binding institutions to secure market transactions against political 'interference'. Rosenboim and especially Slobodian's work suggests that, while 'neoliberalism' was certainly an ideology of class revanchism (Jackson, 2011), it was also a novel, complex (and rather strange) set of responses to the tensions inherent in using national democracies to organize a global economy.

Neoliberalism left vital traces in the institutional architecture of the reformed GATT–WTO system and an expanding web of bilateral investment treaties. These have increasingly acted to generalize norms of capital mobility and investment protection adopted by members of the OECD (Abdelal, 2009). The ambition of the organization was heightened by its expanded scope: unlike any previous treaty system, the WTO can claim to be truly 'global', incorporating 164 member states as of 2016 (WTO, 2018). The 'Geneva school' reformers of the 1970s and 1980s revived and expanded post-war multilateralism, coupling it with a more extensive and coherent framework of 'constitutionalized' economic law (Slobodian, 2018: 218–62). They demanded a far stricter and more expansive interpretation of the norm of non-discrimination enshrined in Articles I and III of the GATT, determining whether policy measures constituted discrimination not on the basis of their intention but on their potential to 'distort' markets for goods and services (Lang, 2014: 254–7).

The WTO and its dispute resolution mechanisms were thereby reimagined as a means for creating perfect competition among a global community of producers and consumers. Mere political consensus would be replaced by a higher logic of legal decision that would promote 'global public goods' that transcended mere 'international' politics. In the words of Ernst-Ulrich Petersmann (1988: 57):

> If governments and those engaged in international trade do not remain convinced that observance of the rules promotes their national and individual self-interests, the rules may cease to be respected. And if the rules are not set in a framework of an effective 'legal system' of mutual 'checks and balances', ensuring that the public good of legal certainty and undistorted international competition is not unduly sacrificed to short-term exigencies and special interests, the rules may prove incapable of playing their crucial role. International legal disciplines designed to constrain the abuse of discretionary powers in trade and monetary policy cannot remain effective if their interpretation and observance are considered to lie within the discretion of the governments whose powers the rules were designed to constrain.

This more expansive conception of the purpose of global trade governance – as an engine of market competition, rather than a forum for international conciliation – was complemented by significant reforms to the process of dispute resolution. The original GATT principle of 'positive consensus' ensured that political decision making was not overdetermined by forms of legal and economic expertise. The specialist 'panel reports' commissioned to examine treaty violations and the extent of legitimate countermeasures could only be adopted unanimously, that is, with the assent of the parties directly affected. Diplomats, not economists or lawyers, remained in charge. The Uruguay Round inverted this relationship; the principle of negative consensus entails that notionally advisory discussions of dispute are adopted as binding unless all member states – including the beneficiaries of the decision – agree to reject it (Howse, 2016: 13–26).

This principle represents a sophisticated, but fundamentally altered, compromise between the principles of sovereignty and globalism: decisions of the appellate body remain de jure advisory, but are de facto automatically binding. While, after the year 2000, the substantive jurisprudence of the appellate body has increasingly resiled from the neoliberal economic agenda promoted in Uruguay (Lang, 2014: 313–53; Howse, 2016: 30–6), its reach and autonomy in the early decades of the twenty-first century remained undiminished.

Conclusion

To date, research agendas in history, social theory and international relations have mostly been concerned with 'globalization': the coalitions, ideologies and regimes of accumulation driving greater or lesser degrees of global economic integration. This chapter, by contrast, has argued that a set of norms and institutions, addressing themselves to an idea of the economy, but existing mainly within the social system of world politics, can be seen to constitute a separate field of inquiry. The legal modes and frameworks governing interstate commerce are every bit as politically charged and contestable as the content of economic policy itself. Moreover, they are analytically and normatively separable from this content: international commercial cooperation was, and remains, possible in the absence of a substantive commitment to a policy of global market integration.

The historical relationship between 'international law' and 'free trade', while driven by a kind of ideological affinity, has never been politically straightforward. Even today, not all 'trade agreements' are 'free trade agreements'; customs unions and regional trade pacts can create boundaries and exclusions for polities outside of their reach (Viner, 1950). 'Free traders' have often been sovereigntists and unilateralists, while 'protectionists' have been deeply committed to transnational projects of economic governance. This was the case in the last decades of the nineteenth century, when Germany, France and Italy were more active fashioners of inter-European commercial treaties than 'free trade' Britain. Indeed, current perspectives on the reform of the WTO focus precisely on the separation and re-synthesis of these two dimensions (Rodrik, 2018), proposing that the structure and institution of the WTO be preserved, but its substantive jurisprudence shifted in the direction of minimizing trade conflicts, rather than maximizing global economic integration.

This recharacterization of the history of world trade law has significant implications for the question of periodization. The rise of commercial treaties from the mid-nineteenth century, and their extensive deployment to codify and protect rights of trade and capital throughout the world economy in both the nineteenth and twentieth centuries, points to a novel and intensive entanglement between two new concepts, that of 'international law' and the 'world economy', that were not present to the same extent before this point. Both were products of the middle decades of the nineteenth century, when a treaty-making 'revolution' (Keene, 2012) coupled with a brief but meaningful turn to 'free trade' among the major European powers to lock in a passing affinity between the cooperative regulation of the European economy and European politics.

Over the course of the 'long twentieth century' that separated the Cobden–Chevalier treaty from the foundation of WTO, the evolving legal and organizational structures of intra- and extra-European trade generated an increased role and status for new agents of transnational economic interaction: from specialized trade diplomats and consuls to legal experts with juridical roles inside treaty organizations. The role and visibility of these agents endured, and expanded, in line with the increasing organization of international economic life through international bodies and conferences: a process that intensified, instead of diminishing, through the breakdown of the nineteenth-century world economy in the middle decades of the twentieth century. It is not only the forward march of 'globalization', but its crises and uncertainties, that have provided vital spurs to the making of world trade law. The relationship between politics, law and economics in the history of global social change is one of counterpoint, not harmony.

Note

[1] This chapter was written within the framework of the Research Training Group (RTG) 2225 'World Politics: The Emergence of Political Arenas and Modes of Observation in World Society' at Bielefeld University.

13

Third-Party Actors, Transparency and Global Military Affairs

Thomas Müller

Introduction

This chapter explores the limits of a process of global social change that can be labelled the institutionalization of world society. Since the second half of the nineteenth century, transnational and international organizations have collected, produced and published comparative data on a variety of aspects of world politics (see Ward, 2004; Speich Chassé, 2016; and Daniel Speich Chassé, Chapter 14 in this volume). This process has created a complex global system of ongoing quantified observation and evaluation of patterns, trends and problems in world politics and also in other parts of world society. In this system, transnational and international organizations mostly act as third parties that track and assess the competition among states over goods such as security, wealth, prestige and legitimacy. They stand outside the competition, but, by reporting on how states fare in it, they nevertheless – at least potentially – influence how the competition is perceived and hence how it plays out (see Werron, 2012b, 2015a).[1]

The chapter traces the emergence and effects of such third-party actors in the field of global military affairs. It makes two arguments, one about the scope and one about the impact of the institutionalization of world society. First, global military affairs are no exception to the rise of third-party actors over the last century and a half. The literature on security politics generally focuses on the practices and institutions through which states assess the military competition in world politics.[2] It neglects the third-party actors that likewise produce data on the patterns of expenditures, capabilities and trade in global military affairs. The group of third-party actors notably includes the United Nations (UN), the International Institute for Strategic Studies (IISS) and Stockholm International Peace Research Institute (SIPRI). Second, while the emergence of this group of third-party actors has fundamentally changed the system of observation and comparison in global military affairs, it has (so far) not changed the underlying dynamics of military competition. Global military affairs thus show that, as the introduction to this volume highlights, it is important to think about both change and continuity in narratives of global social change (see Albert and Werron in their introduction to this volume).

The chapter is structured in the following way. The next section discusses the potential effects of third-party actors on competitive dynamics in world politics. The crucial question is whether states and other relevant constituencies regard the third-party actors as experts and authorities that provide relevant and reliable knowledge. The third section distinguishes four phases in the emergence and evolution of third-party actors in global military affairs since the late nineteenth century. Due to the reluctance of states to submit information on their armed forces to international organizations, this evolution gave rise to a constellation in which the IISS and SIPRI – rather than international organizations – are the key nodes in the circulation of comparative knowledge on global military affairs. The subsequent section discusses the impact of the third-party actors, who raised the level of transparency by providing a new level of aggregate accounts. The new level of transparency did not, however, resolve the problem of uncertainty, with states generally not regarding these accounts as adequate substitutes for their own data-gathering. The third-party actors nevertheless changed the dynamics of public and political debate, since they were considered to be authoritative providers of data, which forced states to reckon with the accounts that they published. The conclusion reflects on the implications for research on global social change.

Uncertainty, transparency and third-party actors

The promotion of transparency in global military affairs is an important goal of third-party actors such as the UN, the IISS and SIPRI. Global military affairs can be defined as those aspects of world politics that relate to the development and deployment of armed forces in both peacetime and wartime. Like other dimensions of world politics, global military affairs feature a complex mix of cooperation, competition and conflict. States engage in arms races with one another, go to war against each other, form military alliances and cooperatively or coercively seek to control the distribution, trade or use of weapons and weapons systems through arms control agreements. Military affairs acquired a global dimension through European colonialism from the sixteenth century onward (for a critical discussion see Sharman, 2018). This is not to say that all aspects of global military affairs are global in scope, but that they take place against the background of a globalized system of practices, templates and norms regarding the development and deployment of armed forces (see also Farrell, 2005).

Transparency has been conceptualized in varied ways, ranging from the disclosure of information via the openness of practices and knowledge to the accountability of political institutions vis-à-vis the public (see Krause Hansen et al, 2015: 118–19; McCarthy and Fluck, 2017). To make something more transparent means to make it more visible and to increase the amount of information that is available on it (see also Lord, 2006: 5). In military affairs, states generally seek to strike a balance between openness and secrecy. States reveal information about their own armed forces as part of democratic procedures (for example, the disclosure and public justification of defence budgets) as well as in order to impress their rivals (for example, as part of deterrence practices or politics of prestige). At the same time, states also employ various practices of classification and concealment to prevent their rivals from acquiring information that would compromise the effectiveness of their own armed forces while striving to collect as much and as precise information as possible about the armed forces of their rivals (see Bousquet, 2018; Green and Long, 2020).

In security studies, the lack of sufficient transparency about intentions and capabilities is considered to be a key cause of conflicts. States can misinterpret and miscalculate the distribution of military capabilities if they have only incomplete information about it. Moreover, if one side has more information than the other, this information asymmetry can lead to different interpretations of the same distribution of capabilities. Such information problems are emphasized by rational 'bargaining' theories of war (see Fearon, 1995: 391–3). 'Security dilemma' approaches, in turn, stress that uncertainties about each other's intentions and capabilities can cause states that are status quo-oriented to end up in a destabilizing arms race anyway. These dynamics arise when states have incomplete or ambivalent information about the rationales that lead other states to increase their military capabilities and consequently mistake each other's defensive moves for aggressive intentions (see Jervis, 1978; Booth and Wheeler, 2008; and Glaser, 2010).

These approaches treat the promotion of transparency as a matter of the interaction between states that compete against each other. 'Bargaining' approaches posit that states are not always interested in more transparency and sometimes 'withhold or misrepresent' (Fearon, 1995: 395) information that they have about the distribution of capabilities in order to maximize their bargaining outcomes. Increases in transparency result, in this perspective, from sustained interaction in the form of negotiations or wars that gradually reveal the actual differentials in relative power. For 'security dilemma' approaches, by contrast, uncertainties about intentions and capabilities can be reduced and even resolved through credible signals by means of which states assure one another of their defensive, peaceful intentions. To be credible, such signals usually have to involve changes in military capability, for instance through unilateral arms reductions or agreement to verifiable arms control measures (see Glaser, 2010: 63–72, 94–101; Booth and Wheeler, 2008: 168–9). To put it differently: for 'security dilemma' approaches, it is not an increase in information per se, but an increase in information that is deemed by the states involved to reliably indicate benign motives that lessens the uncertainty and hence the potentially destabilizing dynamics of competition among states.

These approaches provide important insights into the conditions under which transparency can tame military competition in world politics. By looking only at the states that compete against each other, they neglect the role of third-party actors. Third-party actors are actors that are not directly engaged in a given military competition. Such actors may be neutral states, transnational non-governmental organizations (NGOs) or international organizations. While the institutionalization of world society has permeated other policy fields to a stronger degree,[3] it has also occurred in security politics.

Third-party actors contribute to the promotion of transparency in global military affairs in two ways:

- Some act as intermediaries who facilitate the exchange of information among states. In some cases, a third-party actor publishes the data provided by the various participating states. The UN, for instance, issues annual reports on the military expenditures data reported by its members (see UN, 2019). In other cases, a third-party actor organizes a data exchange without the data being disclosed to non-participating states or the public. An example of this is the 'Global

Exchange of Military Information' managed by the Organization for Security and Cooperation in Europe (see OSCE, 1994, 2011).
- Others construct, compile and publish their own datasets. The IISS and SIPRI are examples. While often drawing on information published in government reports and newspaper articles, the datasets nevertheless increase the level of transparency by providing *aggregate* data on, and accounts of patterns and developments in, global military affairs that are otherwise not publicly available. The qualification 'publicly available' is important insofar as it is likely that some states, because of their superior intelligence-gathering capabilities, possess more detailed data on at least some aspects of these patterns and developments. In this sense, the datasets make global military affairs more transparent for the public, but not necessarily for the governments of all states.

The institutionalization of world society has created a system of transnational and international organizations that produce and publish quantitative knowledge on the various problems dealt with in world politics. One way to approach this system is to read its history as the emergence, expansion and sophistication of international statistics (as Daniel Speich Chassé does in Chapter 14 in this volume). Another (complementary) way is to read it as the emergence of third-party observers that increase the 'pressure of comparison' (Kelley and Simmons, 2019: 491) in world politics by making the performances of states more transparent and by publishing evaluations of these performances. The literature on indicators and rankings develops such a perspective (Werron, 2012b; Broome and Quirk, 2015; Kelley and Simmons, 2019). For this literature, the rise of third-party observers has amplified the competition among states over 'soft goods' such as prestige, reputation and legitimacy.

While soft goods certainly matter in global military affairs, military competition is foremost about 'hard goods': about capabilities that enable states – or other actors – to wage war against each other. How does that change the effects of transparency generated by third-party actors? What remains the same is the basic condition required for third-party actors to have any effect: they need to be regarded as experts that produce relevant and reliable knowledge. This condition is stressed by the realist and rationalist approaches that dominate security studies and that highlight the 'high information threshold' (Rathbun, 2007: 538) that third-party actors have to exceed in order to (re)shape how states perceive each other's intentions and capabilities. It is likewise stressed by the constructivist approaches that dominate the literature on indicators and rankings and that emphasize expertise and authority as the forms of power through which third-party actors shape the competition among states (see Broome and Quirk, 2015: 826; Kelley and Simmons, 2019: 496–8). What is different is both the nature of the competition and the objective of most of the third-party actors as the latter generally seek to foster an atmosphere of transparency that tames – rather than exacerbates – the military competition in world politics.

An evolution in four phases

Information about armed forces has been and is published by a variety of third-party actors ranging from commercial publishers through scholars and research institutes to international organizations.[4] The aim of this section is to chart the gradual emergence of the present-day constellation of third-party actors that (a) regularly publish data on the worldwide patterns of military forces and the arms trade and (b) are central to the public dissemination of comparative knowledge about these patterns. The scope of the following brief history is therefore comparatively narrow. It neither seeks to identify the first third-party actor that published worldwide data on armed forces or the arms trade[5] nor to cover all the third-party actors that published such data. It moreover brackets efforts by states to publish such data[6] as well as third-party actors such as the OSCE that organize exchanges of information about armed forces without publicly disclosing the data.

The present-day constellation of key third-party actors emerged in four phases. In the first phase, from the 1880s to the 1900s, several commercial publishers started to regularly publish compilations on the navies of the world. In 1886, for instance, the British parliamentarian Lord Brassey first published his *Naval Annual* that commented on current developments in the naval policies of Great Britain and other powers and included statistics on naval forces (see Ranft, 1986: xvi–xviii). Initially, the *Naval Annual* only compared the relative sizes of the British, French and Russian navies. Starting in 1897, it widened the comparative horizon to include 'the Navies of all the principal Naval Powers' in the world (Brassey, 1986 [1897]: 30). In the same year, Fred Jane, a British artist who painted pictures of warships, first published his *All the World's Fighting Ships* that included statistics on the world's navies as well as silhouettes of the major warships of the time. He also developed a naval wargame for military and civilian players (Brooks, 1997: 7). Similar books were published in other countries too.[7] These books, which drew on publicly available sources, were designed as reference works for the broader public on the then ongoing naval arms race among several great powers.

The second phase, the 1920s, saw the development of statistical yearbooks by the League of Nations' Disarmament Section. The *Armaments Yearbook*, which was published from 1924 to 1940 in 15 editions, marked the first attempt by an international organization to comprehensively collect and publish data on military capabilities and expenditures in the world (see Goldblat, 2002: 21–2; Lincove, 2018b). Established to prevent another world war, the League of Nations promoted disarmament. Article 8 of its founding Covenant tasked the Council of the League of Nations with developing plans for the reduction of national levels of armaments. In the same article, the members of the League committed themselves to 'interchange full and frank information as to the scale of their armaments, their military, naval and air programmes and the condition of such of their industries as are adaptable to warlike purposes' (League of Nations, 1920: 5). The League's Disarmament Section accordingly proposed a mandatory mechanism for this information exchange, which was, however, opposed by France and other states. As a French diplomat insisted, 'disarmament questions must not be dealt with outside governments' (quoted by Webster, 2005: 501). The Disarmament Section consequently compiled the data for the *Yearbook* from publicly available sources. The first *Yearbook* covered the armaments, defence budgets and military-industrial production of 37 states. Over the years, the number of states included grew to over 60. The Disarmament Section additionally published a statistical yearbook on the global arms trade from 1926 to 1938.

After World War II, the United Nations did not continue the League's practice of publishing yearbooks on military expenditures and capabilities. Instead, two research institutes were founded in the late 1950s and late 1960s that began to publish such information annually (third phase). The IISS was established in London in 1958 to promote the study, debate and exchange of information on the impact of 'modern and nuclear weapons and methods of warfare' on 'the problems of strategy, defence, disarmament and international relations' (ISS, 1958: 1).[8] To provide a 'firmer basis' for public debates (ISS, 1959: 1), the institute has published *The Military Balance* annually since 1959. *The Military Balance* initially focused on the East–West balance. Its coverage was then gradually expanded to cover all states with armed forces in the world. It provides data on the size of the armed forces, the armaments, as well as the military budgets and expenditures of these states.

SIPRI, in turn, has published an annual *Yearbook* since 1969. The first *Yearbook* described its purpose as to 'fill a gap' (SIPRI, 1969: 5). As the UN did not publish a yearbook on questions of armaments and disarmament, no 'authoritative international source' existed that provided information on 'recent trends in world military expenditures, the state of the technological arms race, and the success or failure of recent attempts at arms limitation or disarmament' (SIPRI, 1969: 5). SIPRI's *Yearbooks* notably provide statistical data on worldwide military expenditures and arms transfers as well as on the international arms industry. Since the mid-1980s, the Natural Resources Defense Council and later the Federation of American Scientists (FAS) have published data on the arsenals of nuclear powers (see Norris and Kristensen, 2015) and also contribute the chapter on the world's nuclear forces to the *SIPRI Yearbooks*.

The *fourth phase* then saw the establishment of transparency measures at the UN level. In 1980, the General Assembly adopted a voluntary reporting mechanism for military expenditure data, arguing that 'greater openness in military matters' constitutes 'an important first step in the move towards agreed and balanced reductions in military expenditures' (UN General Assembly, 1980). The reported data have been published annually by the UN General Secretary since 1981. In 1991 the UN General Assembly, furthermore, established a 'Register on Conventional Arms' to which states, again on a voluntary basis, can report data on their arms transfers and, if they are willing to do so, also background data on their level of armaments. The UN likewise annually publishes a report on data received from UN members (see Goldblat, 2002: 246–8). Both reporting mechanisms, though, suffer from 'low participation levels'. For instance, an average of 40% of UN members submitted data on their military expenditures over the period 2002–08 and the participation rate afterwards fell to around 25% for the period 2012–16 (see Tian and Wezeman, 2017).

The four phases cumulatively gave rise to a small group of key third-party actors that produce and publish data on the worldwide patterns in armaments and arms trade. During the Cold War, *Jane's Fighting Ships*, the IISS's *Military Balance* and SIPRI's *Yearbooks* were among 'the best known' and most widely used 'annual reference sources on military affairs' (Albrecht et al, 1980: 8). *Jane's*, the IISS and SIPRI are arguably still key nodes in the global circulation of aggregated data and accounts of the worldwide patterns in armaments and the arms trade alongside the US *World Military Expenditures and Arms Transfers* reports, the Federation of American Scientists' publications on nuclear arsenals and the UN's incomplete datasets on military expenditures and conventional weapons.[9]

The constellation of third-party actors in global military affairs differs markedly from that in global economic affairs and development politics. In the latter two policy fields, international organizations such as the UN, the IMF and the World Bank play key roles in the aggregation and circulation of comparative knowledge (see Ward, 2004: 63–139, Mügge, 2016, Speich Chassé, 2016 and Speich Chassé, Chapter 14 in this volume). In global military affairs, by contrast, the reluctance of states to accept mandatory reporting mechanisms prevented the League of Nations – and effectively later also the UN – from establishing similar systems for the standardization, reporting and aggregation of comparative data on military expenditures and capabilities. The reluctance to disclose such information also explains the only semi-transparent nature of the OSCE's mechanism of information exchange. As a consequence, two think tanks – the IISS and SIPRI – publish more comprehensive data and are more relevant nodes in the public circulation of data on military expenditures and capabilities, the arms trade and the global arms industry.

Besides the reluctance of states to report to international organizations, there are three other factors that have enabled and shaped the evolution of the constellation of third-party actors. The first of these, an enabling factor, is that the transparency generated by the third-party actors would not be possible without a pre-existing basic level of transparency about the armed forces, arms trade and arms industry that they report on. As mentioned, most third-party actors build their datasets from publicly available sources. They raise the level of transparency, but they can do so only because states – to varying degrees – practise some level of openness about their armed forces. The second, both an enabling and an amplifying factor, is the international communication networks (see also Heidi Tworek, Chapter 11 in this volume). Newspapers, specialized journals and in the last two decades also the internet are important sources for third-party actors besides government reports. The media and the internet are, moreover, important channels for third-party actors to distribute their data and interpretations to a broader public audience beyond the immediate readership of their printed annual data publications. The third factor is the demand for transparency and data generated by arms races and arms control efforts. All of the third-party actors mentioned began to publish their data in the context of ongoing arms races (for example, Jane's, the IISS and SIPRI) and/or efforts to curb and control arms dynamics and races (for example, the League of Nations, SIPRI, the UN's reporting mechanisms).

A limited but discernible impact

The last century and a half thus saw the emergence of a group of third-party actors that added a new level of observation and comparison to global military affairs. This section discusses whether and how the latter were affected by this change in the constellation of actors. What the new level of transparency did *not* achieve was to prevent new arms races and wars. The impact was in this sense not transformative enough to end the dynamics of military competition. Such a benchmark, however, overlooks the fact that the third-party actors have usually had a more modest objective and have framed the promotion of transparency as no more than a first step towards a better governance of global military affairs.

The changing constellation of actors nevertheless had a discernible impact on those affairs. Their data was regarded as relevant and reliable by some, though not all, constituencies of actors. The following discussion maps three dimensions of this differentiated impact. The third-party actors made overall patterns and developments in global military affairs more visible (first subsection). States, though, did not regard the new data as a substitute for their own data (second subsection). Nevertheless, the third-party actors changed the dynamics of public and political debates (third subsection).

More visible overall patterns and developments

States sometimes publish comparisons of their own armed forces with those of rivals. This happened both before and after the gradual emergence of the group of third-party actors. But states generally do not regularly publish data series on the volume of worldwide military expenditures, the worldwide arms trade or the nuclear stockpiles of the world's nuclear powers.[10] Third-party actors, on the other hand, such as the IISS, SIPRI and the FAS do regularly produce knowledge about such overall patterns and developments in global military affairs. By doing so, they make it possible to describe and debate them in ways that were previously not possible.

This knowledge helps the third-party actors as well as others to better substantiate their arguments about problematic patterns and developments in this field. The League's *Yearbooks*, for instance, 'made it possible to bring the problem of armaments within the reach of the general public for the first time', as one arms control scholar noted (Goldblat, 2002: 22). Similarly, while the UN's own reporting mechanism provides only an incomplete description of the worldwide volume of military expenditures, the UN can draw on the more comprehensive accounts compiled by other third-party actors. UN publications on disarmament accordingly use SIPRI data to describe trends in the global arms trade and global military expenditure (UN, 2018: 47).

Moreover, by regularly updating and republishing their data series, third-party actors make visible both continuities and changes in the patterns over time. They thus effectively establish and institutionalize an ongoing monitoring of the evolution of global military affairs. Besides trend analyses in their publications, third-party actors such as the IISS and SIPRI also contribute to this monitoring practice through launching new editions of their annual flagship publications with press conferences at which they highlight continuities and changes that they deem to be important.

Data not used as bases for arms control agreements

States regard the data published by the third-party actors as useful for some purposes. During the Cold War, for instance, both East and West relied on IISS data to make arguments about the military balance between NATO and the Warsaw Pact without divulging their own (classified) data. To give two examples: in 1972, NATO issued a report on *Allied Defense in the Seventies* that dedicated a whole chapter to the East–West balance. NATO used IISS data to protect its own internal intelligence data (see NATO, 1972a: 20; and 1972b). In the 1980s, the Soviet Union published a booklet series entitled *Whence the Threat to Peace* that discussed the East–West balance and that similarly relied on IISS data as one of its sources (see, for instance, USSR Ministry of Defence, 1982: 4).

Crucially, however, states have so far not regarded the data published by the third-party actors as credible and reliable enough to serve as a basis for arms control agreements. The question of data was notably a recurring matter of dispute in Cold War conventional and nuclear arms control negotiations. In the second half of the 1970s, West and East sought to resolve their dispute over the state of the conventional balance in Europe in the Mutual and Balanced Force Reductions negotiations through the exchange of data on the numbers of their troops. As the West did not accept the data submitted by the East as accurate, the data exchanges did not end the dispute (see Goldblat, 2002: 220–2). Beginning with the SALT II Treaty between the US and the Soviet Union in 1979, the arms control treaties, on Western insistence, incorporated procedures for both data exchanges and the verification of the treaty implementation. A coupling of data exchanges with verification measures underpinned the Intermediate-Range Nuclear Forces (INF) Treaty of 1987, the Treaty on Conventional Forces in Europe (CFE) of 1990 and the Strategic Arms Reduction Treaty (START) agreement on strategic nuclear forces concluded in 1991 (see Abbott, 1993: 36–7, 40–1). Transparency measures were in this sense crucial to the arms control agreements, but they did not involve third-party actors.

One exception is the International Atomic Energy Agency (IAEA). The IAEA is integral to the verification procedures of the nuclear non-proliferation regime based on the Non-Proliferation Treaty of 1968 (see Sossai, 2013: 406–7; Carnegie and Carson, 2019). Its data is widely accepted as reliable information on whether or not states comply with the regime, though the cases of Iraq and Iran show that states do not always concur with the IAEA's assessments. The IAEA is purposely designed to offer what other third-party actors such as the IISS and SIPRI cannot: data backed by intrusive verification measures (for example sensors, on-site cameras and on-site inspections). The advantage of tasking a third-party actor to perform these verification measures is that states do not have to grant each other mutual inspection rights. The IAEA, though, is a special case of a third-party actor producing data on global military affairs: its objective is not to gather information about the size of arsenals or the volume of trade – as the IISS and SIPRI seek to do – but to check that *no* nuclear arsenal exists and *no* trade in nuclear weapons (technologies) takes place.

A new competition over public opinion

Third-party actors changed the patterns of expertise in global military affairs. As governments generally only partially disclose information about their armed forces, they enjoy an information advantage vis-à-vis their public and other actors. By publishing aggregate accounts that synthesize different government reports and combine them with other sources, third-party actors create an alternative source of information and lessen the information asymmetries. What is more, third-party actors such as the IISS and SIPRI have developed a reputation over time as objective, authoritative providers and interpreters of data on military capabilities and expenditures (see Albrecht et al, 1980: 49, 68). This ascription of expertise and authority empowers them to influence public debates on global military affairs.

This makes it more difficult for states to convince national and transnational publics of their interpretations of the state of global military affairs. To use another example from the Cold War: the

East–West military balance was portrayed by the IISS most of the time in line with Western interpretations (see Lunn, 1989: 60). Sometimes, however, there were dissonances which, for instance, posed a problem for NATO when it sought to counter Soviet booklets with its own booklets in the early 1980s. The problem was, as the British defence minister put it, that 'seemingly neutral publications such as those of the IISS enjoyed a greater credibility' with the public (German Foreign Office, 2012 [1981]: 1618; my translation). In a similar vein, a journalist from *The Economist* explained to NATO staff that he relied on IISS instead of NATO figures because the former were 'more objective' (NATO, 1982).

The advent of third-party actors that were considered authoritative providers of data added a new dynamic to public debates. Governments were now in competition with the third-party actors over whose interpretation resonated most with the public.[11] To put it differently, while governments usually still prefer their own data to those of third-party actors, they have nevertheless – because of the third-party actors' influence on public opinion – to react to and engage with the latter's data and interpretations. At a minimum, this creates pressure on states to justify why their numbers differ from those of the third-party actors. The German government, for instance, in its arms export control report, explicitly highlights the differences between SIPRI's methodology and its own for determining the volume of arms exports (see Bundesministerium für Wirtschaft und Energie, 2019: 33).

Conclusion

This chapter has discussed a change in the constellation of actors in global military affairs: the emergence of a group of third-party actors that publish worldwide data on key patterns in this policy field. This change formed part of a broader process in which the importance of international organizations and NGOs in world politics has grown. As in other policy fields, this process was instrumental in the emergence of aggregate, quantitative descriptions of the overall patterns of expenditures, capabilities and trade in global military affairs.

The limited impact of third-party actors in global military affairs underscores the fact that the institutionalization of world society – while a fundamental change in itself – did not fundamentally change the dynamics of competition in some fields. In global military affairs, third-party actors created novel overall accounts of the competition for hard goods that made it possible for states and other actors to observe, problematize and debate this competition in new and more substantive ways. Yet, as states continued to prefer their own data over those of third-party actors for military planning and arms control, the new level of transparency generated by the third-party actors did not fundamentally alter the dynamics of military competition in global military affairs.

At the same time, the history of third-party actors in global military affairs testifies to the interplay between parallel processes of global social change. Notably, the third-party actors greatly benefited from the expansion of global communication networks. These networks enabled them not only to gather publicly available information but also to distribute their data via print media and today the internet to an audience that is much broader than the readership of their annually printed data compilations. Besides, demands for more transparency were not limited to the global military field. Rather, they were part of the more general rise of democratic models of government and governance in world politics. These two processes – the expansion of communication networks and the spread of democratic modes of politics – created conditions that were conducive to both the emergence of third-party actors and their indirect impact on the global military field via their influence on public opinion.

Notes

1. I would like to thank the participants at the workshops in Osterhofen in June 2018 and Bielefeld in March 2019 for their valuable and constructive feedback. I am also grateful to the Deutsche Forschungsgemeinschaft for funding the research on which this chapter draws and which forms part of project A01 'Comparing Forces and the Forces of Comparison' within the SFB 1288 'Practices of Comparing' at Bielefeld University.
2. On the history of military-related information-gathering and intelligence, see O'Connor Witter (2005), Warner (2014) and Bousquet (2018). The literature on how states compare their capabilities often treats the process as a background theme and focuses more on the elusive accuracy of the assessments rather than the evolution of the practices employed to produce them. See, for instance, Murray and Millett (1992), Wohlforth (1993), Glaser (2010: 194–200) and Hironaka (2017).
3. For a history of the organizing of world politics via international organizations see Chapter 6 by Martin Koch in this volume.
4. Albeit now dated, the research guide published by Albrecht and colleagues (1980) remains the most comprehensive overview of the range of actors publishing information on armed forces and the arms trade. For a recent overview of transnational and international organizations publishing such data, see Lincove (2018a).
5. Brassey's and Jane's were not the first to publish such data. *Löbell's Jahresberichte* published information about the armed forces of many states from the mid 1870s (see Lincove, 2018b: 15). Likewise, the *Almanach de Gotha* already included select data on the naval forces of European and non-European powers before the 1880s.

6. The US Arms Control and Disarmament Agency and later the US State Department have published data on 'World Military Expenditures and Arms Transfers' (WMEAT) since the mid-1960s. The reports can be found online at https://2009–2017.state.gov/t/avc/rls/rpt/wmeat/index.htm
7. The first edition of the French series *Flottes de combat* was published in 1897 and first edition of what would later become known as *Weyers Flottentaschenbuch* was published in 1900.
8. The IISS was founded as the 'Institute for Strategic Studies' and added the 'International' to its name in 1971. During the Cold War, though, its membership was Western rather than global.
9. The UN's (2019) website on military expenditures implicitly acknowledges the relevance of the IISS and SIPRI by providing direct links. The website additionally links to Transparency International.
10. The already mentioned US *World Military Expenditures and Arms Transfers* series is currently the only exception.
11. For the competition over authority in world politics, see generally Sending (2015).

14

Technical Internationalism and Global Social Change: A Critical Look at the Historiography of the United Nations

Daniel Speich Chassé

Introduction

Historians who account for global social change stand in a somewhat peculiar tradition that approaches the past of international organizations through national lenses. There is a predominant narrative that goes back to Immanuel Kant's short essay on 'Perpetual Peace' (Kant, 1977), and by and large the lead question in historiographical scholarship is: to what extent was Kant's vision realized in global politics? This chapter, by contrast, ventures into the technical basis of global sociability from a historical perspective. Such a view renders the nation an effect of global communication rather than an agent. The argument is that global numerical statistics on territories, populations and economic potentials over the past centuries have created a vast political space in which the nation features as a result, not as a prime mover. Numbers rule the world in manifold comparative frameworks by setting norms and designing communicative devices such as balance sheets for companies and states and comparative sets of statistics on territory, population and economic potential.

The topic covered in the following pages is the history of the United Nations (UN). Mainstream historiography treats UN history as a grand international power contest. Political historians are relatively well informed about past debates in the UN Security Council in which powerful nation states have articulated their interests more or less successfully. But beyond this assumedly political realm their accounts tend to fray. Historiography on the technical history of the UN as represented by the Economic and Social Council (ECOSOC) and its specialized bodies remains rather sketchy. The chapter tentatively suggests the notion of technical internationalism as a general framework for the analysis of these governing organs. Scholarship in the sociology of world society and international relations theory has produced ample evidence of the fact that global social change was never primarily powered by national interest nor – as it were – by great individuals. Structural processes of a more anonymous nature loom large. They constitute a global communicative convergence concerning the aims of social change and were agents of change in their own right.

Thanks to international organizations, geodetic information about the planet can be taken for granted and it is easy to tell the time anywhere according to a coherent system. It is roughly known how many people live in the world and how the population is distributed across the continents. There is no doubt as to which countries are relatively poor and which are relatively wealthy in terms of seemingly hard facts. But it is less well known who produced this knowledge historically and who keeps it plausible now it is at our fingertips. It is necessary to demonstrate the agency behind these anonymous processes. Individual European scholars began to gather statistical facts about the planet during the seventeenth and eighteenth centuries and perfected their work in the subsequent periods. They established universal frameworks for administering space, time and economies and thus created a necessary condition for the expansion of capitalism. Empires, multinational enterprises (MNEs), missionary societies and non-governmental organizations (NGOs) also engaged in the data-finding venture to some degree. However, the most important agent in statistically standardizing political communication over the nineteenth, twentieth and twenty-first centuries was the nation state. The social power of this collective imagination can probably not be understood without a close look at the comparative work of numbers. National governments created statistics on their territory, population and economic potential and used statistical data in order to observe other comparable political bodies. In order to do so they required shared norms and standard procedures, and this requirement made international cooperation a necessity.

Of course, long before the founding moment of the UN (at the end of World War II), the more or less systematic gathering of facts and information had become instrumental in the execution of political power. There is a long but thorny history of relations between knowledge and power. What statistical bodies do is often considered to be a mere 'technical' rather than a 'political' practice. However, upon closer inspection this kind of dichotomy between the technical and the political seems to be too simple. Monitoring global change through numbers is not an innocent venture but full of politics. For example, the popularization of national income accounts through the abstraction of a Gross Domestic Product (GDP) is probably one of the most important historical achievements of the UN system. But, as this success is mainly a technical one, it has so far not been adequately appreciated by historians of international politics.

Most of the special organizations within the UN system were created during the epoch of imperial decline post-1945 and can be related to the emergence of a global political imagination of a 'family of nations' according to the Westphalian model. Looking at the history of technical expertise mainly in the field of international economic development, the question is what the establishment of comparative statistical apparatuses through these organizations might tell us in retrospect. The first section briefly sketches existing narratives of the UN system and points to specific shortcomings. These findings are then, in the second section, measured against an approach based on technocratic internationalism or a 'technical' history of international organizations. The third section discusses the history of macroeconomic knowledge production as an example of the interrelation between global statistics and global governance. The fourth then focuses on the political problem of the administration of global difference through the technical bodies in the UN system, while the fifth suggests a larger temporal framework for the study of global statistics. The general idea is to deepen understanding of the history of international organizations, the historical scholarship on which is separated from the theoretical debates in sociology and political science by a surprisingly large distance.

Questioning histories of the UN

Until recently, historians seldom dealt with international organizations and, when they did, they approached them from the standpoint of national historiography via questions concerning the shape of relations between sovereign states. One example of such a narrative is Paul Kennedy's account of the 'parliament of man' (Kennedy, 2007). The book starts with Kant.[1] It sets out from the enlightened idea that humankind is able to govern its collective life reasonably and takes as a normative basis the national body politic organized in the form of a republic. According to a realist approach to the study of international relations, humanity as a whole is imagined as a finite number of such sovereign states that interact with each other as if they were single human beings conscious of what does them good. They are conceived as person-like agents who follow their individual interests mainly at the cost of others. To such a view, war between sovereigns appears as a naturally given condition that needs regulation.

To Kant and his many followers the global political realm appeared as an anarchical sphere of unfettered (national) egoism. They posited that the only possible way of organizing the world rationally was to institute a world parliament that could legitimize some kind of a world government through the consequent application of a rule of law. The Concert of Europe that was defined at the Vienna Congress in 1815, shortly after Kant died, is a first example of such a potentially global construction. It was followed by the rise of an international humanitarian movement that was given a strong impetus by the individual members of the Calvinist elite in Geneva who were responsible for the creation of the International Committee of the Red Cross (Finnemore, 1996). The subsequent accords on martial law that gave rise to international humanitarian law have been analysed by Martti Koskenniemi (2001) as a 'gentle civilizer of nations' that temporarily brought some civility into the anarchy of world politics.

For Paul Kennedy, the founding of the UN in 1945 appears as a major civilizational achievement that followed immediately, and necessarily, on the hitherto unseen level of brutality and violence among sovereign states during World War II. While the founding of the UN in San Francisco in 1945 was indeed an attempt at creating something like perpetual peace on earth, Kennedy argues that the UN system was never able to fully live up to the task of civilizing national governments in order to secure safe conditions for all inhabitants of the world. Rather pessimistically, Kennedy concludes that the UN has indeed been a global failure, yet normatively remains because there is no alternative to it.

There might be a general problem with creating universal narratives for humanity as such, however. Such narratives, which root in the Enlightenment epoch (see Herder, 1994 [1774]), have lost much of their plausibility under the new paradigm of global history informed by postcolonial studies (Conrad, 2016b). In view of the recent emergence of transnational structures of global governance, one possible avenue for research is to posit the political nation as simply one form of agent among others such as multinational corporations or globally active NGOs (Spruyt, 1994b). Another point arises with respect to moral stances. In the foreword to his *No Enchanted Palace*, Mark Mazower (2009) discusses the difficulty of composing critical historical accounts of global sociability. Attacks on the UN system have prevailed in the US domestic debate as well as elsewhere to such an extent that global historians tend to refrain from adopting an all-too-negative perspective in reconstructing its history. It is in that sense that the baseline of Kennedy's book is to uphold the Kantian vision and motivate international stakeholders to realize civility in global politics against all odds. Against this, Mazower highlights the extent to which the founding of the UN in 1945 also served the interests of Britain, as a vehicle for securing imperial influence, and the US, as a means to achieve a new hegemonic position on the world stage.

A further problem is that most historical scholarship is still wedded to a methodological nationalism (Chernilo, 2007). Several scholars have argued that, in studying the history of the UN system, the nation is not a helpful starting point (Amrith and Sluga, 2008). How can one deal historically with the metaphorical transfer from the individual to the state? Such a move was central to Kant's argument in 1785, but states are not human beings and their being in a constant state of war against each other is only a specific historical imagination that does not necessarily render an adequate picture of global political life. It makes seemingly rational agents out of the most complicated collective processes. How do nation states know their national interest? Though they may appear on the world stage as deliberate agents (Anghie, 2002), the inner life of states involves processes no less complicated than those the psyche of one human being might go through in bringing out a clear will. The argument is that statistical inquiries and numerical communications were crucial in defining national interests in the first place. These technologies made states believe that they knew what their interests were in confronting other states in the global arena.

The problem with the dominant account, as exemplified by Kennedy's book, is not that it misinterprets the UN's track record, which is indeed poor if measured against the initial promises, but that it takes the governmental experience of some highly industrialized political collectives as a template for assessing the governmental practice of the UN. Kennedy takes the rhetoric of 1945 at face value. Two questions are pertinent. First, what were the prerequisites for the Kantian rhetoric in 1945? More research is necessary in order for us to better understand the reasons why, at the founding moment of the UN system, it seemed necessary to make big promises. This has a lot to do with the logics and legacies of European imperial rule. Let us refer again to the analysis by Mazower, who linked the UN rhetoric to late imperial necessities. This is a promising avenue for research. In 1945 European colonialism was still very active. Research on the history of international organizations needs to be related far more closely the historiography of the late phase of imperialism. Only in the 1960s, two decades after the UN's founding, did imperial governance structures give way globally to a new dominant structure, which was the emergence of sovereign nation states across the globe. In 1960, when 17 African territories became independent states, the notion of a global 'family of nations' acquired a new plausibility, yet did so only in conflicting ways. What effectively emerged was, at best, a caricature of the Kantian vision.

The second question arises when the historian faces this new mode of structuring global politics in accordance with the concept of nations that are to be united in one organizational perspective – a united nations. How did the UN become one of the chief driving forces in a new mode of '*gouvernementalité*', (post-national) governance without government? Imagining the political world as a series of sovereign nation states implies overarching, that is transnational, key concepts. A non-national global framework had to be designed in order to create norms for the interaction between these nations and to somehow unite them. But a brief look at statistics bears witness to the lingering on of the nation in global connections.

Historians can endlessly debate the intricate power games in the Security Council or the General Assembly during the Cold War epoch. What did the Soviet Union want? What were the aims in Washington, Peking, New Delhi, Cairo or Accra? How well did this or that chief strategist or president perform? How strong was the impact of the global South through the Group of 77 that emerged out of the Non-Aligned Movement and gained considerable negotiating power in the United Nations Conference on Trade and Development (UNCTAD) Conference in Geneva in 1964 (Lüthi, 2008 is an excellent example of such an approach)? Such questions, however, seem to sidetrack the really hot issue of how a global political framework of communication emerged. Why not look more closely at those institutions that created statistically supported visions of gains in wealth all over the planet? Why not take a closer look at the Economic and Social Council as a core institution of the UN system? Why not investigate more thoroughly the collective mentality in this specific social context (Murphy, 1984)?

Too many historians have tended thus far to refrain from such an analysis because of methodological problems. However, methodological nationalism is only one issue here. Another is the difficulty of assembling the archival sources, most of them hard to get at and dispersed in many different places, for one narrative. Historical research in the archives of international organizations is not easy because these institutions tend to neglect their records. Not only at the UN Headquarters in New York, but also at the seats of technical UN bodies like the Food and Agriculture Organization (FAO) in Rome or the UN Economic Commission for Africa in Addis Ababa, Ethiopia, access to single documents is generally difficult because of a lack of finding tools and poor diligence on archival issues by the respective authorities. There is a telling difference between the way international organizations tend their archives and national archival practices. All modern nation states finance archives of their past decisions; international organizations are far less systematic in this respect.

Up to now historians of international organizations and international politics have tended to use statistical information as a largely unquestioned basis for their analysis. Existing historical scholarship shows a tendency to take all the statistics on the condition of the globe issued by UN authorities (and other international organizations such as the Organisation for Economic Co-operation and Development) as hard facts against which the adequacy of past political decisions can be judged. Area statistics (that is, cartographic and cadastral surveys), population censuses and GDP abstractions from economic life are regularly used to assess the historical abilities of individual national governments with respect to global political interaction. In a somewhat simplistic way, historians tend to reify a realist approach to international relations in their accounts. Questions as to which agents – under which conditions – collected these seemingly factual numerical data are rarely addressed. The very historicity of statistical knowledge of the global has so far received way too little attention. How and why did nation states come to learn what their interests were as opposed to the interests of other states?

Technical internationalism

Despite this criticism of the state of the art in international history, it is exciting to observe some of historians' recent fundamental questionings that use international organizations as a privileged field for global history (Kott, 2011). Over the last few years a number of studies have been published on single technical UN organizations, such as the International Labour Organization (ILO), the World Health Organization (WHO), the United Nations Educational Scientific and Cultural Organization (UNESCO) or the United Nations Development Programme (UNDP). In addition, the UN Intellectual History Project has produced oral history evidence on the technical mindset of key drivers. Most of them grew directly out of the British colonial service and shared a strong inclination to a modest form of socialism as evidenced in the records of the Fabian Society (Anstee, 2003; Hodge, 2007). These investigations show the great effect that the UN system has had upon world sociability in the broad realm of international economic development (for the state of the literature see Hodge, 2015).

Such findings fit observations in political science. In the late 1980s James Rosenau and Ernst-Otto Czempiel observed a new set of political problems that transcended the sphere of influence of existing national governments. They famously stated: 'The concept of governance without government is especially conducive to the study of world politics inasmuch as centralized authority is conspicuously absent from this domain of human affairs' (Rosenau and Czempiel, 1992: 24). They spoke of the problem of governance without government with respect to environmental management and poverty alleviation. The governing bodies they had in mind were international organizations as represented in the UN system. Neo-institutionalist world-society analysis has produced ample evidence of the emergence of a 'world culture' through sometimes small and unspectacular definitions of norms in almost all political fields (Krücken, 2009).

In international organizations a method of connecting enlightened rationality to power and a specific mode of fusing the social sciences with politics are at work that differ significantly from national and urban governance. The intensities and forms of governance are not the same at national and international level. This chapter's noting of the gathering of numbers on all possible instances of the social brings to the fore a historical record in which national governance figures as a 'deep' practice, whereas the use of statistics in international organizations is treated as a rather 'weak' or 'lean' form of global governance. This picture of the historical experience in global politics is quite distant from the Kantian approach. It builds on the observation by sociologists that something like a world society has emerged (Wobbe, 2000). It asks what the 'world' is in such a construct (Albert, 2016: 18–19), how it came into being and what the impact of statistics was in making it a plausible space of reference for social interaction across large distances.

As a matter of fact, bodies like the FAO, UNICEF or the United Nations Environment Programme run on a rather small labour force and a rather low level of finance compared to other governmental institutions. In contrast to running an international organization, ruling a city or nation requires considerably greater intensity of governmental intervention in many respects. Deep governance of this kind is today called for at a global level, but such calls do not match the culture of governance that has emerged there. Current understandings of governmentality include a strong presence by experts who bring specific knowledge claims and a modern rationality to bear on the problems of governing collective life. Governmental activity is generally being modelled to deal with activities as diverse as those of fire brigades, police forces or tax-collecting authorities, the provision of childcare and the organization of the disposal of waste. The root of modern statistics is in the aim to facilitate such tasks (Porter and Ross, 2003; Wagner, 2003).

International organizations are social organizations that engage to some extent in the practice of governance. They are collective governing bodies, just as national imperial governments are or were. But if they are compared to other social organizations engaged in governing collective life, peculiar anomalies appear. The United Nations system is a global network of agents engaged in the work of governance, but it has never been a world government. It has established global norms of governance, but it has never governed the globe in the way a national government or a city council governs a nation or a city. International organizations are peculiar governing bodies that cannot be assessed historically if one takes the history of the nation state as a model, since in that context governance without government must appear as a fundamental contradiction.

Those governmental practices that gained a normative status globally in the late twentieth century are closely related to the history of nations. More concretely, the democratically legitimized republican administrations of nation or city states have become the international norm. But the UN governs neither a city nor a state, and can never comply with this norm. It rules the world, however unsuccessfully, and rules it not by providing childcare, or by policing waste disposal, but in a much less costly and intrusive way. Since 1945 the UN system has diversified enormously. The governmental structure that has unfolded does not match those patterns of national or urban governance with which political historians are familiar. The UN has a parliament (the General Assembly) that seems to legitimize all governmental actions. It has a defence department (the Security Council) and a department of internal affairs – ECOSOC. But those are about all the parallels one can find in the UN system to the organization of politics on the national or urban scale. The closer one looks into UN history, the more diffuse familiar structures of governance become and the less helpful they seem for historical analysis. The UN is not a state and it rules the world differently from the way that national governments and city councils rule their territories. Judged by its practices, it is certainly not a candidate for what Kant once had in mind, even though self-assuring statements permanently claim that this was the original idea.

The history of statistics – that is, the quantification of all possible social instances through numbers – is an excellent avenue for clarifying the differences in governance between the local, national and international levels. Research on the history of statistics has largely focused on national contexts and has thus far not looked deeply enough into the function of statistics in the international realm. The most prominent work has been done by Alain Desrosières (1993), who focused on the process of 'adunation' – that is, the statistical computing of a nation. On the local and national levels, the advent of statistical techniques helped authorities to 'see like a state' (Scott, 1998). On this level, the rule of numbers made a public purpose visible and helped in legitimizing power at a centre where all the information came together (Porter, 1995; Bernstein, 2001). But despite the ubiquitous proliferation of statistics in the aftermath of World War II, no single centre of calculation emerged and as of today no single government has ruled the world through the power of numbers. Rather, we are confronted by an anonymous history of technical rule, as Sigfried Giedion (1946) postulated long ago with respect to the mega-process of mechanization. Historians of statistics to date have only rarely studied cases in which statistical apparatuses with a great social impact have emerged without being provided by central authorities. However, this is the main feature of global statistics when used as a mode of governance today by the UN (and other bodies like the OECD or international financial institutions).

By virtue of statistics, international organizations have deployed a new mode of governance that can be termed 'technical' or 'technocratic' internationalism. The term can be set against legal internationalism as postulated by legal scholars during the first decades of the twentieth century (see Huber, 1910). It is borrowed here from Wolfram Kaiser and Johan Schot (2014), who analysed European integration through experts, cartels and international organizations. Kiran Klaus Patel (2018: 167) has taken up this notion in his recent critical history of the European project, and this author has tried elsewhere to apply it to early UN history (Speich Chassé, 2014). The idea is to gain an analytical tool for understanding the historical trajectory of non-national knowledge- and information-gathering institutions that cover geographically wide territories but lack the executive authority of national governments and precisely do *not* use big data in order to strengthen a centre (of calculation and hence power). Instead they create a plethora of expert-based reports that generate an aura of objectivity with respect to all facts concerning the world. In this acentric process all agency becomes invisible, and accountability simply evaporates. Partisan interest is consequently replaced by the seemingly objectively good. Historically well-established forms of critique and the material that has fuelled political history globally since the Enlightenment epoch are simply drowned in a flood of data. By definition, technocratic rule has no author or dictator but assigns the task of governing to apparently objective truths as represented by the 'one best way' to solve each and every problem once and for all (Lübbe, 1971; Fischer, 1990).

In questioning the historical roots of this new form of global governance that is working without formal government structures it seems relevant to ask: which institutions issued those statistics, on what epistemic grounds, and what was the cost of such governance? The example might make clear that technical internationalism inadvertently activates the creation of data through statistics as one of the chief driving forces of global history. According to the French sociologist Georges Balandier, who was already studying global interaction in the 1950s, the production of knowledge must be considered one major factor in all the power games that structure the 'société globale' (global society; Balandier, 1966). Over the second half of the twentieth century and during the first decades of the twenty-first, numbers and statistics have gained an unprecedented importance in global political communication that needs to be discussed. Who can be held responsible for the way in which international organizations like the UN pretend to know what the most pressing issues are that world society needs to communicate – and hopefully solve?

The concept of a technical internationalism makes it quite clear that accounts of the history of global governance that attribute power to single national interests do not hold. After 1989 the legacy of a Pax Americana has gained ground in historical explanations (Latouche, 1989; Escobar, 1995; Hardt and Negri, 2000). But such analyses are overly simplifying. Statistical checking of the Millennium Development Goals depends on aerial surveys, censuses of populations and accounts of potentials for economic growth. Neither the Soviet Union nor the United States of America can be held responsible for an order of global knowledge that emerged in the period of the Cold War. Rather, a planetary statistical framework came into existence that put the comparison of national numbers at its core. It epistemically strengthened at the same time both the foreign policies of powerful industrialized countries and national self-determination against foreign domination in the new states of the global South.

The concept of a technical internationalism is also helpful in understanding why – with respect to global political processes – the nation cannot be an *explanans* but must rather be an *explanandum*. National interest shaped the world as it is today. But, at the same time, through the emergence of global frameworks of knowledge and statistics, nations emerged, and were constructed and objectified, as chief agents in a comparative view (Werron, 2015a). In the suggested perspective the nation is much more the effect of global political communication than a prime mover or agent. How states identify their own interests relative to others resulted historically from global (statistical) communication. National interest is not a helpful starting point for the analysis of the current global condition. The fact that national governance has become an international norm means that it cannot be used as a template for describing the historical process of which this norm is a part.

UN practices in technical internationalism

The compilation of territorial statistics through cadasters and maps, the counting of populations in censuses and the accounting for economic wealth are three main fields of technical internationalism. The following section relates world governmental activity by the UN to these practices.

With respect to cartography, the UN has never been very important. The mapping of the world grew, on the one hand, out of ordnance surveys that were rooted in the logic of national military defence and were crucial in the establishment of European nation states. On the other, armchair scientists in geography played an important role in achieving a global accord on geodesy. Such individual players, over the course of the nineteenth century, felt it adequate to coordinate scales and epistemic conventions and to agree on shared reference points in their sophisticated geodetic measurements with colleagues quite irrespective of the national political aims of their respective governments, whether Italian, Swiss, French, British, German, Danish, American or Siamese (Winichakul, 1994; Gugerli and Speich, 2002; Kramper, 2019). Learned men convened as individuals in associations like the International Meteorological Organization, for example, that was founded in Geneva as early as 1873. This is, in fact, one of the oldest international organizations. Only in the field of telecommunications are even older organizational innovations at international level on record, apart from in international humanitarian law (International Committee of the Red Cross). At the time of the founding of the UN (1945) all pressing issues in mapping had already been solved by other agents.

This was not the case with counting people. Even though population censuses historically go right back to the Roman Empire and belong among the oldest practices of technical rule that the written record bears witness to, debates on the subject became very intense after 1945. In contrast to the statistical appropriation of arable plots and national territories, the population census remained highly contested (Connelly, 2008). This chapter, however, does not follow the complicated history of pro-natalist and anti-natalist population politics that unfolded on a world scale, but focuses on a third practice, that is the role of macroeconomic calculus in accounting for material wealth, a practice in which the UN played a crucial part.

National income statistics were greatly advanced by authors such as Simon Kuznets in the US and Colin Clark and Richard Stone in Great Britain during the middle decades of the twentieth century. The instrument was initially designed to make visible the structure of economic wealth within a given national political entity according to the category of class. Modern estimates of gross or net national incomes are a result of the political constraints of the inter-war period, the Great Depression of the 1930s and World War II, an epoch of heightened nationalism. Statistically minded economists gained an interest in better understanding the respective importance of single sectors such as agriculture, industrial production or services to the sum total of national wealth. They delineated compartments of economic interaction for calculative purposes and – by the way – established historically important definitions of what could count as an economic activity in the first place and what could not. The 1930s gave rise to a new comparative framework of economic analysis. In order to gain an encompassing view, scholars compiled data from tax registers and other sources from their respective governments to add up the full activity of the nation's economy.

The measuring procedures for income accounting had to reflect the sociocultural structure of the entity that it wanted to depict. The issue was hotly debated. Simon Kuznets explained his conception in 1933 in an influential article in the *Encyclopedia of the Social Sciences* (Kuznets, 1933). He stressed the usefulness of computing gross economic totals as an instrument to 'appraise the prevailing economic organization in terms of its returns' (Kuznets, 1933: 205). Such an approach had to be grounded in local specificities and in the contingency of history.

In fact, it was Kuznets' conviction that one had to design a specific procedure for quantifying each entity in time and space. Inevitably, this rendered the compilation of global data rather problematic. Initially, Kuznets' cautionary remarks referred to the comparison of two or more industrialized countries that shared basic economic structures. The task was gigantic. All labour activities that were being performed by all members of one single nation's political collective had to be assessed with respect to their relevance to the full national total, with the important exception of persons who were not being reimbursed monetarily, such as women working in households in accordance with the dominant norm of the family in highly gendered social structures. The problems of accounting for economic wealth globally became fundamental when international comparisons based on national income were expanded into what was to become known as the global separation between the 'First' and the 'Third' World.

Kuznets' abstraction of a GDP for the US furthered an international comparative framework, and British colleagues took it up, which resulted in a new numerical total with a global meaning. To put it in the terms suggested by Bruno Latour, the procedure can be understood as the historical creation of an 'inscription device' that generated a new kind of visibility for the economic condition of the globe (see Latour, 1987). In very close cooperation with the Organisation for European Economic Co-operation (OEEC), from 1947 the statistical office of the United Nations invested considerable financial means and human resources in order to stabilize globally shared reference points and a general agreement on methodology for the distributive mapping of the world's wealth, accounting on the basis of a comparative national order (Speich Chassé, 2016).

Evidence for such inquiries could be gathered in principle through comparative investigations. By offering more or less stable inscriptions of the condition of one economic entity (always a nation) at one point in time, the accounting procedures made it possible to relate several such inscriptions to each other and thus create the basis for an economic theory of world development. To take up Bruno Latour's vocabulary again, 'cascades of inscriptions' could be arranged through which economic facts would move in the form of 'immutable mobiles' towards higher levels of truth and objectivity (Latour, 1990: 26). One important step in this upward direction was to take total income for a given year (as measured in terms of gross national income), divide it by the size of the population and then connect the resulting figure to estimates of earlier years, thus composing a time series from which yet another inscription could be derived, namely a rate of growth.

Estimating the end product of a country's economic activity according to the respective impact of single sectors and forms of activity gave rise to the question as to whether a change in economic organization would lead to a change in returns – that is, an increasing level of wealth for all inhabitants of the world.

The UN needed such a comparative framework in order to establish a fair share for each single member nation to contribute to the organization's budget. Nations were invited to compute national incomes according to a general System of National Accounts first published in 1952 (in cooperation with OEEC) in a rather slim volume that, over time and due to substantial revisions, grew into a thick book. Scholars at Penn State, at the University of Groningen and at other venues subsequently tackled the thorny issue of international comparison and further refined the statistical techniques (Groningen Growth and Development Centre, 2019).

Today, the Millennium Development Goals and the Sustainable Development Goals that were issued by the UN in 2000 and 2015 respectively represent excellent examples of this technical internationalism in global economic development. Macroeconomic calculus has gained even more importance in view of the pressing issue of climate change. The UN-hosted Intergovernmental Panel on Climate Change (IPCC), as well as the United Nations Framework Convention on Climate Change (UNFCCC), the World Bank and the International Monetary Fund strongly embrace statistical tools such as Wealth Accounting and the Valuation of Ecosystem Services (WAVE) that directly build on the historical GDP experience in global governance and strengthen the relevant stance of the UN. But sociological, historical and epistemic critique is still rather poor (Speich Chassé et al, 2015; WAVES, 2020).

Periodization in the history of technical internationalism

The UN's specific experience in technical governance can be transferred in a broader perspective onto statistics as a local, national and global tool for ruling polities. The suggestion is to study numerical statistics as a way of dealing with difference. Historically skin colour, religious belief or GDP per capita have worked largely unquestioned as the chief markers of difference in world polity. Whenever a large number of individual people turned into one collective, their respective differences became problematic. The anonymous statistical governance by the UN can be understood as an answer to this problem. Portraying definitional issues as technical – that is, assuming them to be non-political – has been a helpful device for securing political rule globally. Talking numbers is a political strategy and has been for a long time. Domestically as well as globally, the articulation of difference has generated violent conflict, even physical extermination in extreme cases. Technical procedures have had a strong influence within these contestations.

A technical history of the UN could be written along the lines of the administration of difference. It needs to be set against the Enlightenment epoch during which single scholars were important in standing up in opposition to monarchical rule, which they sought to turn republican by the power of reason (see Kant, 1977). Likewise, modern international rule as evidenced in the UN system also invites scholars to shed new light on European imperialism. It is quite astonishing to see how little interest colonial administrators assigned to comparative statistics on territory, people and economic potentials overseas. Statistics never were imperial, always distinctly national. The technical constraints of imperial rule over vast geographic realms were written into the way in which the technocrats of the UN system initially tried to govern the world. This mode of data creation belongs to a past epoch during which individual learned white men had a great impact. The founding of the UN around 1945 was largely informed by their advice. In the 1970s new forms of global sociability emerged through local grassroots initiatives and the advent of a neoliberal political economy; during the 1990s the very notion of economic development was detached from nation state authorities and reframed as an individual right under the banner of a new methodological individualism that was largely based on big data (Sen, 1999).

Over the past two centuries, a rich record of experience has been accumulated in producing knowledge about the social (Raphael, 1996) and creating seemingly objective frames of reference in order to be able to deal politically with the data within one nation. What is missing are similar accounts of these practices in the realm of the international. Such accounts, which look at global convergence on the goals of social change, would need to survey a process that has continued over a number of stages or epochs.

First came the practice of assessing a king's or an emerging nation's wealth through numbers. This practice extends back at least to the Renaissance, if not to the Roman Empire. Wealth statistics started with William Petty in the seventeenth century, and its record is rich in anecdotes of individual learned persons who envisioned a collective view on the *condition humaine* (human condition). States reacted slowly to the new technology (Behrisch, 2016). The history of the

International Statistical Institute that was founded during the middle decades of the nineteenth century shows how individual scientists connected across national boundaries in order to substantiate their enlightened claims. In the late nineteenth century, scholars such as Jacques Bertillon single-handedly defined categories of numerical classification that have ruled global political communication in fields like hygiene and health up to the present day.[2] In most cases, relations between these learned white men and the political nation were difficult. In order to single out social differences, they created categories that did not always correspond with political needs. This led, most famously, to the beheading of Johann Heinrich Waser in 1780 in the city state of Zurich because he published social statistics. We are not very well informed about this first epoch of numerical communication because scholarship in the history of statistics has focused on numbers as a mode of national state control, rarely on them as a mode of realizing a modern personal individuality by statistical scholars themselves. At this early stage in the history of international technical governance, the difference between critical individual scholars and a hegemon stood out.

In contrast to the monarchical tradition in Europe, over the nineteenth century city and national governments created powerful new answers to the problem of difference. A national mode of governance crystallized around the question of who belonged to the national body politic and who did not. The problem of difference moved from tension between statistically interested individuals and the state to the statistical creation of different groups within one political entity. The rise of the nation state to become the dominant form of governing collective political life was to a large extent connected to the search for, and the creation of, national unity. Scholars quickly connected with this new phenomenon of nationalism and produced ample evidence to support a quest for unity. In national discourse differences within the envisioned national body politic acquired the characteristics of anomalies that needed to be extinguished. As a matter of fact, most modern nation states defined their respective versions of national unity by oppressing difference through structural violence. Numerical communications on territory, population and economic potential were crucial in defining deviance and the norm in the process of nation building (Anderson, 1983).

This violent method of nationally governing difference gained momentum with the intensification of national governmental interventions around World War I. An interest in setting international norms became relevant that gave rise to international organizations in martial law, telecommunications and geodesy. When modern forms of national welfare states emerged in Europe during the last decades of the nineteenth and the first decades of the twentieth century, macroeconomic considerations began to loom large. Increasing amounts of wealth were to be distributed, and the question of who should pay for this and who would be allowed to profit gained importance. In the national experience of political rule, the problem of difference crystallized around the question of inclusion in or exclusion from systems of political participation and social security. The more the modern nation state had to offer to its citizens in material terms, the more pressing became the question of inclusion or exclusion, which meant that more energy was invested in the task of eradicating internal difference, and numerical statistics, thanks to experts, became more precise.[3]

Another way of dealing with difference, no less connected to violence, can be found in an alternative governmental experience, namely in empires. Jane Burbank and Frederick Cooper (2010) have produced evidence from the last 2,000 years of global history demonstrating that empires have always needed to find modes of accommodating and appropriating difference without eradicating it. Empires, by definition, encompass large geographical spaces that are inhabited by different peoples. They have never been able to ignore these differences, nor have they been in a position to simply overrule them. Since empires in world history were faced with the problem of ruling at a distance, they needed to design modes of managing difference other than those employed by national states. The problem of imperial governance has, according to Cooper and Burbank, always been the establishment of mechanisms to safeguard compliance at the peripheries at the least possible cost to the metropoles (Burbank and Cooper, 2010).

Frederick Cooper defined empires as global 'units of political and ethical debate' (Cooper, 2005: 172). His approach contrasts with more familiar accounts of imperial history that focus on exploitation and violence. Understanding empires as communicative engines does not mean neglecting violence. It means focusing on the historical stabilization of social codes that allowed for the oppression and violation of certain groups as opposed to others within one imagined social collective to be rendered legitimate in the eyes of relevant publics. Imperial powers have fought many wars and have shed an enormous amount of blood. But in keeping up imperial spheres of influence over centuries, no imperial power has ever felt the necessity – nor had the material means – to engage in a constant deployment of funds to secure old people's pensions, organize waste disposal or provide childcare on an empire-wide scale. Empires ruled through definitional authority, but they did not systematically apply modern numerical statistics because they did not need numerical data to uphold their rule – at least until the 1960s.

Enlarging European modernity to a global scale was closely connected to imperialism, but – somewhat surprisingly – the application of numerical statistics as a governmental tool remained very basic in this specific form of global governance. The application of statistics was much more conflictive and incomplete than recent postcolonial critique might suggest (Appadurai, 1996: 115–21). Most probably the promise of the modern welfare state fatally undermined the legitimacy of the late European empires after 1945 and eventually led to decolonization – and to a new concept first labelled in 1968 by the then West German minister for development, Hans-Jürgen Wischnewski (1968), as '*Weltinnenpolitik*' (world domestic politics).

Statistics could have helped colonial administrators in governing difference, but they also worked as an anti-imperial tool. Numerical statistics on territory, population and economy, the chief avenues of UN rule, were firmly attached to the national form and could not easily be applied to the imperial problem of governing difference with which the colonial authorities in European metropoles were confronted up to the 1960s. But then, in the age of imperial decline, global abstractions acquired strong political power. Indicators such as GDP per capita allowed material differences in wellbeing across the planet to be depicted in one universal language and thus strongly furthered the idea that all human beings were to be considered equal. Through international organizations like the Expanded Program for Technical Assistance (EPTA, later UNDP) or the World Bank and the International Monetary Fund, macroeconomic knowledge became a communicative device in the appropriation of difference, which it still is today.

It seems plausible to postulate the emergence of a new constellation in the connection of statistical expertise to political rule in the second half of the twentieth century, which could be termed technical internationalism. It is represented by the UN system in an exemplary fashion. It fused social science to governance globally in a historically unprecedented way that annihilated central authority in nations as in empires. Finally, it made use of the anonymity of numerical communication that allows for the execution of definitional – and hence political – authority without the necessity or even the possibility of localizing it anywhere.

Conclusion

A technical history of the UN can show how the social sciences have worked to use quantification as a unifying frame of reference thanks to the toil of thousands of individual scholars. They oriented their research interests according to globally established categorical systems that made differences visible and at the same time promised to eradicate them. Technical statistics created a vision of an economic machine that could generate wealth nationally anywhere on the planet and level inequality sometime in the future if it was well organized by international bodies such as the UN. It is not Kant's vision of a global republic, but numerous single acts succeeded in creating a statistical replica of the world that opened the way to the current state of global governance.

One main finding of the present chapter is that a specific form of governmental practice by international organizations such as the UN does exist, but it is not identical with the practice of governance by national governments. A technical history of the UN does not take the nation state as the norm, but rather shows it to be a historical effect of cooperation on a more abstract level. Measured against power politics on national levels, this specific form of global governance seems to be unspectacular in its mere technicality and to be quite toothless when it comes to enforcing compliance with resolutions by direct coercion. On the national and international levels, statistics have been used in different ways. On the national level, statistical apparatuses were applied in order to strengthen centres of power and make them visible. On the global level, their effect was to make agency invisible.

A further finding is that it would certainly be wrong to assume that the global governmental practice of statistical fact-finding is or was either apolitical or ineffective with respect to the shaping of global change. Rather, the separation of governmental tasks into the two categories – 'political' and 'technical' – is a political move in itself as it involves the definition of what is a general fact and what is a partisan opinion. Social and economic historians have long turned their attention to this complication in analysing national political strife and domestic institution building. But the historiography of international organizations still puts too much emphasis on a simplified notion of politics that categorically separates an assumed realm of pure political agency from all the technical work that creates the image of a rulable world in which national executive politicians might shape their foreign policy.

It seems to be a promising strategy for further research to study the various ways in which statistics dealing with large spaces (globally) were connected to political issues and to define the epochs in which such connections occurred. In analysing these conjectures historians might profit from an interdisciplinary debate with world society analysis, while sociologists and political scientists might be prompted to complicate their models with empirical evidence.

Notes

[1] More precisely, it starts with the US appropriation of the Kantian vision as transmitted by Alfred Lord Tennyson in the poem 'Locksley Hall' (1837). A copy of this is said to have been in Harry Truman's pocket long before he inherited the task of constructing the UN from Franklin D. Roosevelt (see Hilderbrand, 1990).

[2] The International Classification of Disease (ICD) that dates back to Bertillon is one example.

[3] It is no wonder that early scholars in the history of statistics focused on insurance as a core problem in establishing modern systems of social security (Krüger et al, 1987).

References

Abbott, Kenneth W. (1993) ' "Trust but Verify": The Production of Information in Arms Control Treaties and other International Agreements', *Cornell International Law Journal*, 26(1): 26–58.

Abbott, Kenneth W., Keohane, Robert O., Moravcsik, Andrew, Slaughter, Anne-Marie and Snidal, Duncan (2000) 'The Concept of Legalization', *International Organization*, 54(3): 401–19.

Abdelal, Rawi (2009) *Capital Rules: The Construction of Global Finance*, Cambridge, MA: Harvard University Press.

Abirafeh, Lina (2009) *Gender and International Aid in Afghanistan: The Politics and Effects of Intervention*, Jefferson, NC: McFarland.

Abu-Lughod, Lila (2002) 'Do Muslim Women Really Need Saving? Anthropological Reflections on Cultural Relativism and Its Others', *American Anthropologist*, 104(3): 783–90.

Adler-Nissen, Rebecca (ed) (2012) *Bourdieu in International Relations: Rethinking IR*, London: Routledge.

Ahrne, Göran and Brunsson, Nils (2011) 'Organization Outside Organizations: The Significance of Partial Organization', *Organization* 18: 83–104.

Ahvenainen, Jovma and Britton, John A. (2004) 'Showdown in South America', *Business History Review*, 78(1): 1–27.

Albert, Mathias (2016) *A Theory of World Politics*, Cambridge: Cambridge University Press.

Albert, Mathias and Buzan, Barry (2013) 'On the Subject Matter of International Relations', *Review of International Studies*, 43(5): 898–917.

Albert, Mathias and Stetter, Stephan (2015) 'Embedding Regional Integration in the Fabric of a Differentiated World Society and a Differentiated World Political System', in Boris Holzer, Fatima Kastner and Tobias Werron (eds) *From Globalization to World Society: Comparing Neo- Institutional and Systems Theoretical Perspectives*, London: Routledge, pp 61–82.

Albert, Mathias and Buzan, Barry (2017) 'International Relations Theory and the "Social Whole": Encounters and Gaps between IR and Sociology', *International Political Sociology*, 7(2): 117–35.

Albert, Mathias, Kessler, Oliver and Stetter, Stephan (2008) 'On Order and Conflict: International Relations and the "Communicative Turn"', *Review of International Studies*, 34(S1): 43–67.

Albert, Mathias, Buzan, Barry and Zürn, Michael (2013a) 'Introduction: Differentiation Theory and International Relations', in Mathias Albert, Barry Buzan and Michael Zürn (eds) *Bringing Sociology into International Relations*, Cambridge: Cambridge University Press, pp 1–26.

Albert, Mathias, Buzan, Barry and Zürn, Michael (eds) (2013b) *Bringing Sociology to International Relations: World Politics As Differentiation Theory*, Cambridge: Cambridge University Press.

Albrecht, Ulrich, Asbjorn, Eide, Kaldor, Mary, Leitenberg, Milton and Perry Robinson, Julian (1980) *A Short Research Guide on Arms and Armed Forces*, New York: Facts on File.

Alexandrowicz, Charles H. (1957) 'The Discriminatory Clause in South Asian Treaties in the Seventeenth and Eighteenth Centuries', in David Armitage and Jennifer Pitts (eds) *The Law of Nations in Global History*, Oxford: Oxford University Press, 2016, pp 140–52.

Alimento, Antonella and Stapelbroek, Koen (2018) *The Politics of Commercial Treaties in the Eighteenth Century: Balance of Power, Balance of Trade*, Palgrave London: Macmillan.

Amrith, Subil S. and Sluga, Glenda (2008) 'New Histories of the United Nations', *Journal of World History*, 19(3): 251–74.

Andersen, Neils A. (2003) *Discursive Analytical Strategies: Understanding Foucault, Koselleck, Laclau, Luhmann*, Bristol: Policy Press.

Anderson, Benedict (1983) *Imagined Communities: Reflections on the Origin and Spread of Nationalism*, London: Verso.

Anderson, Benedict (1998) 'Nationalism, Identity, and the Logic of Seriality', in Benedict Anderson (ed) *The Spectre of Comparisons*, London: Verso, pp 29–45.

Anderson, Benedict (2006) *Imagined Communities: Reflections on the Origin and Spread of Nationalism* (2nd edn), London: Verso.

Anderson, Jon W. (1982) 'Social Structure and the Veil: Comportment and the Composition of Interaction in Afghanistan', *Anthropos*, 77(3/4): 397–420.

Anghie, Anthony (2002) 'Colonialism and the Birth of International Institutions. Sovereignty, Economy, and the Mandate System of the League of Nations', *Cambridge Studies in International and Comparative Law*, X: 11–46.

Anghie, Anthony (2004) *Imperialism, Sovereignty and the Making of International Law*, Cambridge: Cambridge University Press.

Anghie, Anthony (2007) *Imperialism, Sovereignty, and the Making of International Law*, Cambridge: Cambridge University Press.

Anstee, Margaret J. (2003) *Never Learn to Type: A Woman at the United Nations*, Chichester: Wiley.

Appadurai, Arjun (1996) *Modernity at Large: Cultural Dimensions of Globalization*, Minneapolis, MN: University of Minnesota Press.

REFERENCES

Aradau, Claudia and Huysmans, Jef (2013) 'Critical Methods in International Relations: The Politics of Techniques, Devices and Acts', *European Journal of International Relations*, 20(3): 596–619.

Archer, Clive (2015) *International Organizations* (4th edn), New York: Routledge.

Arnold, John H., Hilton, Matthew and Rüger, Jan (eds) (2018) *History after Hobsbawm: Writing the Past for the Twenty-First Century*, Oxford: Oxford University Press.

Aron, Raymond (1951) *Les guerres en chaîne* (3rd edn), Paris: Gallimard.

Arrighi, Giovanni (1994) *The Long Twentieth Century: Money, Power and the Origins of Our Time*, London: Verso.

Auslin, Michael R. (2006) *Negotiating with Imperialism: The Unequal Treaties and the Culture of Japanese Diplomacy*, Cambridge, MA: Harvard University Press.

Aydin, Cemil (2016) 'Regionen und Reiche in der politischen Geschichte des langen 19. Jahrhunderts (1750–1924)', in Sebastian Conrad and Jürgen Osterhammel (eds) *1750–1870: Wege zur modernen Welt*, München: C.H. Beck, pp 35–253.

Badenoch, Alexander and Fickers, Andreas (eds) (2010) *Materializing Europe: Transnational Infrastructures and the Project of Europe*, Basingstoke: Palgrave Macmillan.

Bairoch, Paul and Burke, Susan (1989) 'European Trade Policy 1814–1914', in Peter Mathias and Sidnes Pollard (eds) *The Cambridge Economic History of Europe Since the Decline of the Roman Empire, Volume 8: The Industrial Economies: The Development of Economic and Social Policies*, Cambridge: Cambridge University Press.

Balandier, Georges (1966) 'The Colonial Situation: A Theoretical Approach', in Immanuel Wallerstein (ed) *Social Change: The Colonial Situation*, New York: John Wiley, pp 34–61.

Balbi, Gabriele, Calvo, Spa, Fari, Simone and Richeri, Guiseppe (2014) *Network Neutrality: Switzerland's Role in the Genesis of the Telegraph Union, 1855–1875*, Bern: Peter Lang.

Ballantyne, Tony and Burton, Antoinette M. (2014) *Empires and the Reach of the Global, 1870–1945*, Cambridge, MA: Harvard University Press.

Barnett, Michael and Finnemore, Martha (2004) *Rules for the World: International Organizations in Global Politics*, Ithaca, NY: Cornell University Press.

Bartelson, Jens (2010) 'The Social Construction of Globality', *International Political Sociology* 4(3): 219–35.

Barth, Fredrik (1978) 'Scale and Network in Urban Western Society', in Fredrik Barth (ed) *Scale and Social Organization*, Oslo: Universitetsforlaget, pp 163–83.

Bayly, Christopher A. (2004) *The Birth of the Modern World 1780–1914*, Oxford: Blackwell.

Bayly, Christopher A. (2005) 'From Archaic Globalization to International Networks, Circa 1600–2000', in Jerry H. Bentley, Renate Bridenthal and Anand A. Yang (eds) *Interactions: Transregional Perspectives on World History*, Honolulu, HI: University of Hawai'i Press, pp 14–29.

Bayly, Christopher A. (2018) *Remaking the Modern World 1900–2015: Global Connections and Comparisons*, Hoboken, NJ: John Wiley.

Beckfield, Jason (2010) 'The Social Structure of the World Polity', *American Journal of Sociology*, 115(4): 1018–68.

Behrisch, Lars (2016) *Die Berechnung der Glückseligkeit. Statistik und Politik in Deutschland und Frankreich im späten Ancien Régime*, Ostfildern: Jan Thorbecke Verlag.

Bell, Duncan (ed) (2007) *Victorian Visions of Global Order: Empire and International Relations in Nineteenth-Century Political Thought*, Cambridge: Cambridge University Press.

Bell, Duncan and Sylvest, Casper (2006) 'International Society in Victorian Political Thought: T.H. Green, Herbert Spencer, and Henry Sidgwick', *Modern Intellectual History*, 3(2): 207–38.

Benton, Lauren and Ford, Lisa (2016) *Rage for Order: The British Empire and the Origins of International Law, 1800–1850*, Cambridge, MA: Harvard University Press.

Bernhard, Stefan and Schmidt-Wellenburg, Christian (2020) *Charting Transnational Fields*, New York: Routledge.

Bernstein, Michael A. (2001) *A Perilous Progress: Economists and Public Purpose in Twentieth-Century America*, Princeton, NJ: Princeton University Press.

Bethell, Leslie (ed) (1987) *The Independence of Latin America*, Cambridge: Cambridge University Press.

Bigo, Didier (2011) 'Pierre Bourdieu and International Relations: Power of Practices, Practices of Power', *International Political Sociology* 5(3): 225–58.

Bilgin, Pinar (2012) 'Globalization and In/Security: Middle Eastern Encounters with International Society and the Case of Turkey', in Stephan Stetter (ed) *The Middle East and Globalization: Encounters and Horizons*, New York: Palgrave Macmillan, pp 59–75.

Billaud, Julie (2013) 'Visible under the Veil: Dissimulation, Performance and Agency in an Islamic Public Space', *Journal of International Women's Studies*, 11(1): 120–35.

Billig, Michael (1995) *Banal Nationalism*, London: Sage.

Birtsch, Günter and Rüsen, Jörn (eds) (1972) *Texte zur Geschichtstheorie: Mit ungedruckten Materialien zur Historik*, Göttingen: Vandenhoeck & Ruprecht.

Bluntschli, Johann C. (1863) *Allgemeines Staatsrecht* (3rd edn), München: J.G. Cotta.

Bluntschli, Johann C. (1866) *Die Bedeutung und die Fortschritte des modernen Völkerrechts*, Berlin: C.G. Lüderitz.

Bluntschli, Johann C. (1873) *Das Moderne Völkerrecht der Civilisierten Staaten als Rechtsbuch Dargestellt*, Berlin: C.G. Lüderitz.

Blyth, Mark (2013) *Austerity*, Oxford: Oxford University Press.

Böckenförde, Ernst-W. and Dorn-Van Rossum, Gerhard (1978) 'Organ, Organismus, Organisation, politischer Körper', in Otto Brunner, Werner Conze and Reinhart Koselleck (eds) *Geschichtliche Grundbegriffe: Historisches Lexikon zur politisch-sozialen Sprache in Deutschland, Band 4*, Stuttgart: Klett-Cotta, pp 519–622.

Bogusz, Tanja (2018) *Experimentalismus und Soziologie: Von der Krisen- zur Erfahrungswissenschaft*, Frankfurt am Main: Campus.

Boltanski, Luc (1999) *Distant Suffering: Morality, Media and Politics*, Cambridge: Cambridge University Press.

Boltanski, Luc (2007) *La souffrance à distance: Morale humanitaire, médias et politique*, Paris: Gallimard.

Booth, Ken and Wheeler, Nicholas J. (2008) *The Security Dilemma: Fear, Cooperation and Trust in World Politics*, Basingstoke: Palgrave Macmillan.

Borch, Christian (2016) 'High-frequency Trading, Algorithmic Finance and the Flash Crash: Reflections on Eventalization', *Economy and Society*, 45(3–4): 350–78.

Bordo, Michael D., Taylor, Alan M. and Williamson, Jeffrey G. (eds) (2003) *Globalization in Historical Perspective*, Chicago, IL: University of Chicago Press.

Borger, Julian (2020) 'CIA Controlled Global Encryption Company for Decades, Says Report', *The Guardian*. www.theguardian.com/us-news/2020/feb/11/crypto-ag-cia-bnd-germany-intelligence-report [Accessed 13 February 2020].

Bourdieu, Pierre (1977) *Outline of a Theory of Practice*, Cambridge: Cambridge University Press.

Bourdieu, Pierre (1989) 'Social Space and Symbolic Power', *Sociological Theory*, 7(1): 14–25.

Bourdieu, Pierre (1991a) 'Epilogue: On the Possibility of a Field of World Sociology', in Pierre Bourdieu and James S. Coleman (eds) *Social Theory for a Changing Society*, Boulder, CO: Westview Press, pp 373–87.

Bourdieu, Pierre (1991b) 'Genesis and Structure of the Religious Field', *Comparative Social Research*, 13(1): 1–44.

Bourdieu, Pierre (1992) *The Rules of Art*, Stanford, CA: Stanford University Press.

Bourdieu, Pierre and Wacquant, Loïc J.D. (1992) *An Invitation to Reflexive Sociology*, Chicago, IL: University of Chicago Press.

Bousquet, Antoine (2018) *The Eye of War: Military Perception from the Telescope to the Drone*, Minneapolis, MN: University of Minnesota Press.

Boyce, D. George (1999) *Decolonisation and the British Empire, 1775–1997*, London: Palgrave Macmillan.

Brassey, Thomas A. (1986 [1897]) 'Relative Strength', in Bryan Ranft (ed) *Ironclad to Trident: 100 Years of Defence Commentary: Brassey's 1886–1986*, London: Brassey's Defence Publishers, pp 30–1.

Braudel, Fernand (1977) *Afterthoughts on Material Civilization and Capitalism*, Baltimore, MD: Johns Hopkins University Press.

Bregman, Rutger (2017) *Utopia for Realists*, London: Bloomsbury.

Brendebach, Jonas (2018) 'Towards a New International Communication Order? UNESCO, Development and "National Communication Policies" in the 1960s and 1970s', in Jonas Brendebach, Martin Herzer and Heidi J. Tworek (eds) *Exorbitant Expectations: International Organizations and the Media in the Nineteenth and Twentieth Centuries*, New York: Routledge, pp 158–81.

Bright, Charles and Geyer, Michael (2007) 'Globalgeschichte und die Einheit der Welt im 20. Jahrhundert', in Sebastian Conrad, Andreas Eckert and Ulrike Freitag (eds) *Globalgeschichte: Theorien, Ansätze, Themen*, Frankfurt am Main: Campus, pp 53–80.

Britton, John A. (2013) *Cables, Crises, and the Press: The Geopolitics of the New International Information System in the Americas, 1866–1903*, Albuquerque, NM: University of New Mexico Press.

Brooks, Richard (1997) 'Fred T Jane and Fighting Ships', in Bernard Ireland and Eric Grove (eds) *Jane's War at Sea, 1897–1997*, New York: Harper Collins, pp 6–7.

Broome, André and Quirk, Joel (2015) 'Governing the World at a Distance: The Practice of Global Benchmarking', *Review of International Studies*, 41(5): 819–41.

Brubaker, Rogers (1996) *Nationalism Reframed: Nationhood and the National Question in the New Europe*, Cambridge: Cambridge University Press.

Brunkhorst, Hauke (2014) *Critical Theory of Legal Revolutions*, New York: Bloomsbury Academic.

Brussels Tariff Union (1890) 'Convention Concerning the Formation of an International Union for the Publication of Customs Tariffs', in Charles I. Bevans (ed) *Treaties and Other International Agreements of the United States of America 1776–1949*, Vol 1. Washington, DC: Government Publishing Office. 1968, pp 172–83.

BSR (Business for Social Responsibility) (2018) *Human Rights Impact Assessment: Facebook in Myanmar*. https://fbnewsroomus.files.wordpress.com/2018/11/bsr-facebook-myanmar-hria_final.pdf [Accessed 6 August 2020].

Bull, Hedley and Watson, Adam (1984) *The Expansion of International Society*, Oxford: Clarendon Press.

Bull, Malcolm (2013) 'Help Yourself', *London Review of Books*, 35(4): 15–17.

Bultmann, Daniel (2014) 'Analyzing the Cambodian Insurgency as a Social Field', *Small Wars & Insurgencies*, 25 (2): 457–78.

Bundesministerium für Wirtschaft und Energie (2019) 'Bericht der Bundesregierung über ihre Exportpolitik für konventionelle Rüstungsgüter im Jahre 2018'. www.bmwi.de/Redaktion/DE/Publikationen/Aussenwirtschaft/ruestungsexportbericht-2018.html [Accessed 28 February 2020].

Burbank, Jane and Cooper, Frederick (2010) *Empires in World History: Power and the Politics of Difference*, Princeton, NJ: Princeton University Press.

Burckhardt, Jacob (1992) 'Wirtschaft IV–VIII (1983)', in Otto Brunner, Werner Conze and Reinhart Koselleck (eds) *Geschichtliche Grundbegriffe*, Stuttgart: Klett-Cotta, pp 550–92.

Buzan, Barry (2004) *From International to World Society? English School Theory and the Social Structure of Globalisation*, Cambridge: Cambridge University Press.

Buzan, Barry (2014) 'The "Standard of Civilization" as an English School Concept', *Millennium: Journal of International Studies*, 42(3): 576–94.

Buzan, Barry and Lawson, George (2014a) 'Rethinking Benchmark Dates in International Relations', *European Journal of International Relations*, 20(2): 437–62.

Buzan, Barry and Lawson, George (2014b) 'Capitalism and the Emergent World Order', *International Affairs*, 90(1): 71–91.

Buzan, Barry and Lawson, George (2015) *The Global Transformation: History, Modernity and the Making of International Relations*, Cambridge: Cambridge University Press.

Buzan, Barry and Little, Richard (2000) *International Systems in World History: Remaking the Study of International Relations*, Oxford: Oxford University Press.

Buzan, Barry and Little, Richard (2001) 'Why International Relations Has Failed as an Intellectual Project and What To Do about It', *Millennium: Journal of International Studies*, 30(1): 19–39.

Buzan, Barry and Wæver, Ole (2004) *Regions and Powers: The Structure of International Security*, Cambridge: Cambridge University Press.

Calhoun, Craig J. (1997) *Nationalism*, Buckingham: Open University Press.

Calhoun, Craig J. (2004) 'A World of Emergencies: Fear, Intervention, and the Limits of Cosmopolitan Order', *Canadian Review of Sociology/Revue canadienne de sociologie*, 41(4): 373–95.

Calhoun, Craig J. (2010) 'The Idea of Emergency: Humanitarian Action and Global (Dis)Order', in D. Fassin and M. Pandolfi (eds) *Contemporary States of Emergency: The Politics of Military and Humanitarian Interventions*, New York: Zone Books, pp 29–58.

Campbell, W. Joseph (2010) *Getting It Wrong: Ten of the Greatest Misreported Stories in American Journalism*, Berkeley, CA: University of California Press.

Carnegie, Allison and Carson, Austin (2019) 'The Disclosure Dilemma: Nuclear Intelligence and International Organizations', *American Journal of Political Science*, 63(2): 269–85.

Carse, Ashley (2017) 'Keyword: Infrastructure – How a Humble French Engineering Term Shaped the Modern World', in Penelope Harvey, Caspar B. Jensen and Atsuro Morita (eds) *Infrastructures and Social Complexity: A Routledge Companion*, London: Routledge, pp 27–39.

Case, Holly (2018) 'The Quiet Revolution: Consuls and the International System in the Nineteenth Century', in Timothy Snyder and Katherine Younger (eds) *The Balkans as Europe, 1821–1914*, Rochester, NY: University of Rochester Press, pp 110–38.

Cassel, Pär Kristoffer (2012) *Grounds of Judgement: Extraterritoriality and Imperial Power in Nineteenth-Century China and Japan*, Oxford: Oxford University Press.

Central Commission for Navigation on the Rhine (1966) *150 Years Central Commission for Rhine-Navigation*, Duisburg-Ruhrort: Binnenschiffahrts-Verlag.

Cerny, Phillip G. (1997) 'Paradoxes of the Competition State: The Dynamics of Political Globalization', *Government and Opposition*, 32(2): 251–74.

Chakrabarty, Dipesh (2000) *Provincializing Europe: Postcolonial Thought and Historical Difference*. Princeton, NJ: Princeton University Press.

Chang, Ha-Joon (2002) *Kicking Away the Ladder: Development Strategy in Historical Perspective*, London: Anthem Press.

Chase-Dunn, Christopher, Yukio, Kawano and Brewer, Benjamin D. (2000) 'Trade Globalization since 1795: Waves of Integration in the World-System', *American Sociological Review* 65(1): 77–95.

Chernilo, Daniel (2006a) 'Methodological Nationalism and Its Critique', in Gerard Delanty and Krishan Kumar (eds) *The Sage Handbook of Nations and Nationalism*, London: Sage, pp 129–40.

Chernilo, Daniel (2006b) 'Social Theory's Methodological Nationalism: Myth and Reality', *European Journal of Social Theory*, 9(1): 5–22.

Chernilo, Daniel (2007) *A Social Theory of the Nation-State: The Political Forms of Modernity Beyond Methodological Nationalism*, London: Routledge.

Chishti, Maliha and Farhoumand-Sims, Cheshmak (2011) 'Transnational Feminism and the Women's Rights Agenda in Afghanistan', in Zubeda Jalalzai and David Jefferess (eds) *Globalizing Afghanistan: Terrorism, War, and the Rhetoric of Nation Building*, Durham, NC: Duke University Press, pp 117–44.

Choudhury, Deep K.L. (2010) *Telegraphic Imperialism: Crisis and Panic in the Indian Empire, c1830–1920*, Basingstoke: Palgrave Macmillan.

Claude, Inis L. (1959) *Swords into Plowshares: The Problems and Progress of International Organization* (2nd edn), New York: Random House.

Clavin, Patricia (2013) *Securing the World Economy: The Reinvention of the League of Nations, 1920–46*, Oxford: Oxford University Press.

Clavin, Patricia and Sluga, Glenda (eds) (2017) *Internationalisms: A Twentieth-Century History*, Cambridge: Cambridge University Press.

Cohn, Theodore H. (2016) *Global Political Economy: Theory and Practice*, London: Routledge.

Commission for Global Governance (1995) *Our Global Neighbourhood*, Oxford: Oxford University Press.

Connelly, Matthew (2008) *Fatal Misconception: The Struggle to Control World Population*, Cambridge, MA: Harvard University Press.

Conrad, Sebastian (2016a) 'Eine Kulturgeschichte globaler Transformation', in Sebastian Conrad and Jürgen Osterhammel (eds) *Geschichte der Welt: Vol 4. 1750–1870: Wege zur modernen Welt*, München: C.H. Beck, pp 411–625.

Conrad, Sebastian (2016b) *What Is Global History?* Princeton, NJ: Princeton University Press.

Conrad, Sebastian and Osterhammel, Jürgen (2016) 'Einleitung', in S. Conrad and J. Osterhammel (eds) *1750–1870: Wege zur modernen Welt*, München: C.H. Beck, pp 9–34.

Conrad, Sebastian and Randeria, Shalini (eds) (2002) *Jenseits des Eurozentrismus: Postkoloniale Perspektiven in den Geschichts- und Kulturwissenschaften*, Frankfurt am Main: Campus Verlag.

Cooper, Frederick (2005) *Colonialism in Question: Theory, Knowledge, History*, Oakland, CA: University of California Press.

Coulter, Ann (2015) *Adios America: The Left's Plan to Turn Our Country into a Third World Hellhole*, Washington, DC: Regnery.

Coutain, Bryan (2009) 'The Unconditional Most-Favored-Nation Clause and the Maintenance of the Liberal Trade Regime in the Postwar 1870s', *International Organization*, 63(1): 139–75.

Cox, Robert W. (1981) 'Social Forces, State and World Orders: Beyond International Relations Theory', *Millennium: Journal of International Studies*, 10(2): 126–55.

Cullather, Nick (2002) 'Damming Afghanistan: Modernization in a Buffer State', *The Journal of American History*, 89(2): 512–37.

Davies, Hannah C. (2016) 'Spreading Fear, Communicating Trust: Writing Letters and Telegrams During the Panic of 1873', *History and Technology*, 32(2): 159–77.

Davies, Hannah C. (2018) *Transatlantic Speculations: Globalization and the Panics of 1873*, New York: Columbia University Press.

Davies, Michael and Woodward, Richard (2014) *International Organizations: A Companion*, Cheltenham: Edward Elgar.

Davies, Thomas R. (2014) *NGOs: A New History of Transnational Civil Society*, New York: Oxford University Press.

Davies, William (2014) *The Limits of Neoliberalism: Authority, Sovereignty and the Logic of Competition*, London: Sage Publications.

Davis, John R. (1997) 'The British Sonderweg: The Peculiarities of British Free Trade, 1845–80', *Diplomacy & Statecraft*, 8(3): 68–90.

Davis, Nathalie Z. (2011) 'Decentering History: Local Stories and Cultural Crossings in a Global World', *History and Theory*, 50(2): 188–202.

De Courcel, Geoffroy C. (1988) 'The Berlin Act of 26 February 1885' in S. Forster, W. Mommsen and R. Robinson (eds) *Bismarck, Europe and Africa: The Berlin Africa Conference 1884–5 and the Onset of Partition*, Oxford: Oxford University Press.

De Zwart, Pim and van Zanden, Jan L. (2018) *The Origins of Globalisation: World Trade in the Making of the Global Economy, 1500–1800*, Cambridge: Cambridge University Press.

Decorzant, Yann (2011) *La societé des nations et la naissance d'une conception de la régulation économique internationale*, Berlin: Peter Lang.

Deitelhoff, Nicole (2009) 'The Discursive Process of Legalization: Charting Islands of Persuasion in the ICC Case', *International Organization*, 63(1): 33–65.

Desan, Mathieu H. (2013) 'Bourdieu, Marx, and Capital: A Critique of the Extension Model', *Sociological Theory*, 31(4): 318–42.

Desrosières, Alain (1993) *La Politique des Grands Nombres: Histoire de la Raison Statistique*, Paris: La Découverte.

Deutsch, Karl W. (1963) *The Nerves of Government: Models of Political Communication and Control*, New York/London: Free Press/Collier-Macmillan.

Devresse, Maria-S. and Scalia, Damien (2016) 'Hearing Tried People in International Criminal Justice: Sympathy for the Devil', *International Criminal Law Review*, 16(5): 796–825.

Dickinson, Edward R. (2018) *The World in the Long Twentieth Century: An Interpretive History*, Oakland, CA: University of California Press.

Dodd, Adam (2017) 'The Crisis of Humanity: Or What If We Have Never Been Human?', *History and Theory*, 56(1): 138–45.

Doe, Helen (2010) 'Waiting for Her Ship to Come In? The Female Investor in Nineteenth-Century Sailing Vessels', *Economic History Review*, 63(1): 85–106.

Dorsch, Sebastian (2013) 'Space/Time Practices and the Production of Space and Time. An Introduction', *Historical Social Research/Historische Sozialforschung*, 38(3): 7–21.

Droysen, Johann G. (1897) *Outline of the Principles of History* (trans Elisha B. Andrews), Boston, MA: Ginn & Co.

Droysen, Johann G. (1972) *Texte zur Geschichtstheorie: Mit ungedruckten Materialien zur Historik* (ed G. Birtsch and J. Rüsen), Göttingen: Vandenhoeck & Ruprecht.

Duara, Prasenjit (2011) 'The Cold War as a Historical Period: An Interpretive Essay', *Journal of Global History*, 6(3): 457–80.

DuBois, W.E.B. (1915) 'The African Roots of the War', *Atlantic Monthly*, 115(May): 707–14.

Dugard, John (2013) 'Palestine and the International Criminal Court: Institutional Failure or Bias?', *Journal of International Criminal Justice*, 11(3): 563–70.

Duncan, Richard (2012) 'A New Global Depression', *New Left Review*, 77 (Sept/Oct): 5–33.

Dunne, Tim and Reus-Smit, Christian (eds) (2017) *The Globalization of International Society*, Oxford: Oxford University Press.

Dunne, Tim, Hansen, Lene and Wight, Colin (2013) 'The End of International Relations Theory?', *European Journal of International Relations*, 19(3): 405–25.

Eckel, Jan (2018) '"Alles hängt mit allem zusammen": Zur Historisierung des Globalisierungsdiskurses der 1990er und 2000er Jahre', *Historische Zeitschrift*, 307(1), 42–78.

Edensor, Tim (2002) *National Identity, Popular Culture and Everyday Life*, Oxford: Berg.

Edwards, Paul N., Bowker, Geoffrey C., Jackson, Steven J. and Williams, Robin A. (2009) 'Introduction: An Agenda for Infrastructure Studies', *Journal of the Association for Information Systems*, 10(5): 364–74.

Edwards, Zophia and Go, Julian (2019) 'The Forces of Imperialism: Internalist and Global Explanations of the Anglo-European Empires, 1750–1960', *The Sociological Quarterly*, 60(4): 628–53.

Eichengreen, Barry (1996) *Globalizing Capital: A History of the International Monetary System*, Princeton: Princeton University Press.

Eisenstadt, Shmuel N. (2000) *Multiple Modernities*, Cambridge: Cambridge University Press.

Eisenstein, Zillah R. (2002) 'Feminisms in the Aftermath of September 11', *Social Text*, 20(3) 79–99.

Engel, Alexander (2015) 'Buying Time: Futures Trading and Telegraphy in Nineteenth-Century Global Commodity Markets', *Journal of Global History*, 10(2): 284–306.

Engels, Franziska, Wentland, Alexander and Pfotenhauer, Sebastian M. (2019) 'Testing Future Societies? Developing a Framework for Test Beds and Living Labs as Instruments of Innovation Governance', *Research Policy*, 48(9): article no 103826.

Epple, Angelika (2010) *Das Unternehmen Stollwerck: Eine Mikrogeschichte der Globalisierung (1839–1932)*, Frankfurt am Main: Campus.

Epple, Angelika (2015) 'Globale Machtverhältnisse, lokale Verflechtungen: Die Berliner Kongokonferenz, Solingen und das Hinterland des kolonialen Waffenhandels', in Christof Dejung and Martin Lengwiler (eds) *Ränder der Moderne – Neue Perspektiven auf die Europäische Geschichte (1800–1930)*, Köln: Böhlau-Verlag, pp 65–91.

Epple, Angelika and Schaser, Angelika (2009) *Gendering Historiography: Beyond National Canons*, Frankfurt am Main: Campus.

Epple, Angelika, Erhart, Walter and Grave, Johannes (eds) (2020) *Practices of Comparing: Towards a New Understanding of a Fundamental Human Practice*, Bielefeld: Bielefeld University Press.

Escobar, Arturo (1995) *Encountering Development: The Making and Unmaking of the Third World*, Princeton, NJ: Princeton University Press.

Evans, Richards (2016) *The Pursuit of Power: Europe 1815–1914*, London: Penguin.

Fabian, Johannes (1983) *Time and the Other*, New York: Columbia University Press.

Farrell, Theo (2005) 'World Culture and Military Power', *Security Studies*, 14(3): 448–88.

Fearon, James D. (1995) 'Rationalist Explanations for War', *International Organization*, 49(3): 379–414.

Ferguson, Niall, Maier, Charles, Manela, Erez and Sargent, Daniel J. (eds) (2010) *The Shock of the Global: The 1970s in Perspective*, Cambridge, MA: Harvard University Press.

Finnemore, Martha (1996) *National Interest in International Society*, Ithaca, NY: Cornell University Press.

Fischer, Frank (1990) *Technocracy and the Politics of Expertise*, Newbury Park, CA: SAGE.

Fitzmaurice, Andrew (2014) *Sovereignty, Property and Empire, 1500–2000*, Cambridge: Cambridge University Press.

Flüchter, Antje and Schöttli, Jivanta (2015) *The Dynamics of Transculturality*, Wiesbaden: Springer.

Fox, Jon E. (2017) 'The Edges of the Nation: A Research Agenda for Uncovering the Taken-for-Granted Foundations of Everyday Nationhood', *Nations and Nationalism*, 23(1): 26–47.

Freije, Vanessa (2019) 'The "Emancipation of Media": Latin American Advocacy for a New International Information Order in the 1970s', *Journal of Global History*, 14(2): 301–20.

Fried, Alfred H. (1908) *Das internationale Leben der Gegenwart*, Leipzig: B.G. Teubner.

Frieden, Jeffry A. (2006) *Global Capitalism*, New York: Norton.

Friedman, Milton (1962) *Capitalism and Freedom*, Chicago, IL: University of Chicago Press.

Friedman, Thomas L. (2005) *The World Is Flat*, New York: Farrar, Straus and Giroux.

GATT Secretariat (1986) 'Text of the *General Agreement on Tariffs and Trade (1947)*', Geneva: GATT Secretariat.

Geiss, Immanuel (1988) 'Free Trade, Internationalization of the Congo Basin, and the Principle of Effective Occupation', in Stig Förster, Wolfgang J. Mommsen and Ronald Robinson (eds) *Bismarck, Europe and Africa: The Berlin Africa Conference 1884–5 and the Onset of Partition*, Oxford: Oxford University Press, pp 263–80.

Gellner, Ernest (1983) *Nations and Nationalism*, Oxford: Basil Blackwell.

German Foreign Office (2012) 'Aufzeichnung des Vortragenden Legationsrats I. Klasse Hofmann, 22. Oktober 1981', in Horst Möller, Gregor Schöllgen and Andreas Wirsching (eds) *Akten zur Auswärtigen Politik der Bundesrepublik Deutschland: 1981*, München: Oldenbourg Verlag, pp 1613–20.

Getachew, Adom (2019) *Worldmaking after Empire: The Rise and Fall of Self-Determination*, Princeton, NJ: Princeton University Press.

Geyer, Michael and Bright, Charles (1995) 'World History in a Global Age', *American Historical Review*, 100(4): 1034–60.

Giddens, Anthony (1985) *The Nation-State and Violence*, Cambridge: Polity.

Giedion, Sigfried (1946) *Mechanization Takes Command: A Contribution to Anonymous History*, New York: Oxford University Press.

Glaser, Charles L. (2010) *Rational Theory of International Politics: The Logic of Competition and Cooperation*, Princeton, NJ: Princeton University Press.

Go, Julian (2008) 'Global Fields and Imperial Forms: Field Theory and the British and American Empires', *Sociological Theory*, 26(3): 201–29.

Go, Julian (2011) *Patterns of Empire: The British and American Empires, 1688 to the Present*, Cambridge: Cambridge University Press.

Go, Julian (2014): 'Capital, Containment, and Competition: The Dynamics of British Imperialism, 1730–1939', *Social Science History*, 38(1/2): 43–69.

Go, Julian (2016) *Postcolonial Thought and Social Theory*, New York: Oxford University Press

Go, Julian and Krause, Monika (2016): 'Fielding Transnationalism: An Introduction', in J. Go and M. Krause (eds) *Fielding Transnationalism*, Oxford: Wiley-Blackwell, pp 6–30.

Go, Julian and Lawson, George (eds) (2017a) *Global Historical Sociology*, Cambridge: Cambridge University Press.

Go, Julian and Lawson, George (2017b) 'Introduction: For a Global Historical Sociology', in Julian Go and George Lawson (eds) *Global Historical Sociology*, Cambridge: Cambridge University Press, pp ix–xii.

Go, Julian and Watson, Jake (2019) 'Anticolonial Nationalism: From Imagined Communities to Colonial Conflict', *European Journal of Sociology*, 60(1): 31–68.

Goldblat, Jozef (2002) *Arms Control: The New Guide to Negotiations and Agreements*, London: Sage Publications.

Goldgar, Anne (2007) *Tulipmania: Money, Honor, and Knowledge in the Dutch Golden Age*. Chicago, IL: University of Chicago Press.

Gorski, Philip S. (2000) 'The Mosaic Moment: An Early Modernist Critique of Modernist Theories of Nationalism', *American Journal of Sociology*, 105(5): 1428–68.

Gorski, Philip S. (ed) (2013) *Bourdieu and Historical Analysis*, Durham, NC: Duke University Press.

Goswami, Manu (2002) 'Rethinking the Modular Nation Form: Toward a Sociohistorical Conception of Nationalism', *Comparative Studies in Society and History*, 44(4): 770–99.

Green, Brendan R. and Long, Austin (2020) 'Conceal or Reveal? Managing Clandestine Military Capabilities in Peacetime Competition', *International Security*, 44(3): 48–83.

Grimm, Jacob and Grimm, Wilhelm (1854) *Deutsches Wörterbuch von Jacob Grimm und Wilhelm Grimm*, Leipzig: Hirzel.

Groningen Growth and Development Centre (2019) *Penn World Table Version 9.1*. www.rug.nl/ggdc/productivity/pwt/ [Accessed 9 March 2020].

Gruber, Richard G. (1919) *Internationale Staatenkongresse und Konferenzen: Ihre Vorbereitung und Organisation*, Berlin: Puttkammer & Mühlbrecht.

Gugerli, David and Speich, Daniel (2002) *Topografien der Nation*, Zürich: Chronos.

Habermas, Jürgen (1989) *The Structural Transformation of the Public Sphere: An Inquiry into a Category of Bourgeois Society*, Cambridge, MA: MIT Press.

Hall, Peter A. and Soskice, David (eds) (2001) *Varieties of Capitalism*, Oxford: Oxford University Press.

Hall, Stuart (1992) 'The West and the Rest: Discourses and Power', in Stuart Hall and Bram Gieben (eds) *Formations of Modernity*, Cambridge: Polity Press, pp 185–227.

Hanke, Lewis (1974) *All Mankind Is One: A Study of the Disputation between Bartolome de Las Casas and Juan Gines de Sepulveda in 1550 on the Intellectual and Religious Capacity of the American Indians*, DeKalb, IL: Northern Illinois University Press.

Haraway, Donna (1988) 'Situated Knowledges: The Science Question in Feminism and the Privilege of Partial Perspective', *Feminist Studies*, 14(3): 575–99.

Hardt, Michael and Negri, Antonio (2000) *Empire*, Cambridge, MA: Harvard University Press.

Headrick, Daniel (2010) 'A Double-Edged Sword: Communications and Imperial Control in British India', *Historical Social Research*, 35(1): 51–65.

Hearn, Jonathan (2018) 'How to Read the Wealth of Nations (or Why the Division of Labor Is More Important than Competition in Adam Smith)', *Sociological Theory*, 36(2): 162–84.

Hegel, Georg W.F. (1821) *Grundlinien der Philosophie des Rechts*, Berlin: Nicolaische Buchhandlung.

Helleiner, Eric and Pickel, Andreas (eds) (2005) *Economic Nationalism in a Globalizing World*, Ithaca, NY: Cornell University Press.

Herder, Johann G. (1994 [1774]) *Auch eine Philosophie der Geschichte zur Bildung der Menschheit*, Riga: Hartknoch.

Herren, Madeleine (2009) *Internationale Organisationen seit 1865*, Darmstadt: Wissenschaftliche Buchgesellschaft.

Hewitson, Mark (2010) *Nationalism in Germany, 1848–1866: Revolutionary Nation*, Basingstoke: Palgrave.

Heywood, Andrew (2017) *Political Ideologies: An Introduction* (6th edn), London: Palgrave.

Hieronymi, Otto (ed) (1980) *The New Economic Nationalism*, London: Macmillan.

Hilderbrand, Robert C. (1990) *Dumbarton Oaks: The Origins of the United Nations and the Search for Postwar Security*, Chapel Hill, NC: University of North Carolina Press

Hilgers, Mathieu and Mangez, Eric (eds) (2015) *Bourdieu's Theory of Social Fields*, New York: Routledge.

Hill, Christopher L. (2008) *National History and the World of Nations: Capital, State, and the Rhetoric of History in Japan, France, and the United States*, Durham, NC: Duke University Press.

Hironaka, Ann (2017) *Tokens of Power: Rethinking War*, New York: Cambridge University Press.

Hirschkind, Charles and Mahmood, Saba (2002) 'Feminism, the Taliban, and Politics of Counter-Insurgency', *Anthropological Quarterly*, 75(2): 339–54.

Hobbes, Thomas (1651) *Leviathan*, London: Green Dragon.

Hobsbawm, Eric J. (1994) *The Age of Extremes: The Short Twentieth Century*, London: Penguin Books.

Hobsbawm, Eric J. (2004) 'The World Unified [1975]', in Frank J. Lechner and John Boli (eds) *The Globalization Reader* (2nd edn), Malden, MA: Blackwell, pp 58–62.

Hobson, John A. (1915) *Towards International Government*, London: G. Allen & Unwin.

Hobson, John M. (2012) *The Eurocentric Conception of World Politics: Western International Theory, 1760–2010*, Cambridge: Cambridge University Press.

Hodge, Joseph M. (2007) *Triumph of the Expert: Agrarian Doctrines of Development and the Legacies of British Colonialism*, Athens, OH: Ohio University Press.

Hodge, Joseph M. (2015) 'Writing the History of Development', *Humanity: An International Journal of Human Rights, Humanitarianism, and Development*, 6(3): 429–63 and 6(4): 125–74.

Hofmeyr, Isabel (2013) *Gandhi's Printing Press: Experiments in Slow Reading*, Cambridge, MA: Harvard University Press.

Holzer, Boris (2011) 'Netzwerke', in Andreas Niederberger and Philipp Schink (eds) *Globalisierung*, Stuttgart: J.B. Metzler, pp 339–45.

Holzer, Boris, Kastner, Fatima and Werron, Tobias (eds) (2015a) *From Globalization to World Society: Comparing Neo-Institutional and Systems Theoretical Perspectives*, London: Routledge.

Holzer, Boris, Kastner, Fatima and Werron, Tobias (2015b) 'Introduction: From Globalization to World Society', in Boris Holzer, Fatima Kastner and Tobias Werron (eds) *From Globalization to World Society: Neo-Institutional and Systems-Theoretical Perspectives*, New York: Routledge, pp 1–21.

Hont, Istvan (2005) *Jealousy of Trade: International Competition and the Nation-State in Historical Perspective*, Cambridge, MA: Harvard University Press.

Hopkins, Tom (2015) 'The Limits of "Cosmopolitical Economy": Smith, List and the Paradox of Peace through Trade', in Thomas Hippler and Milos Vec (eds) *Paradoxes of Peace in Nineteenth-Century Europe*, Oxford: Oxford University Press, pp 77–91.

Howe, Anthony (1997) *Free Trade and Liberal England, 1846–1946*, Oxford: Oxford University Press.

Howe, Anthony (2007) 'Free Trade and Global Order: The Rise and Fall of a Victorian Vision', in D. Bell (ed) *Victorian Visions of Global Order*, Cambridge: Cambridge University Press, pp 24–46.

Howse, Robert (2016) 'The World Trade Organization 20 Years On: Global Governance by Judiciary', *European Journal of International Law*, 27(1): 1–77.

Hroch, Miroslav (2005) *Das Europa der Nationen: Die moderne Nationsbildung im europäischen Vergleich*, Göttingen: Vandenhoeck & Ruprecht.

Huber, Max (1910) 'Die soziologischen Grundlagen des Völkerrechts', *Archiv für Rechts- und Wirtschaftsphilosophie*, 4: 1–35.

Huntington, Samuel P. (1971) 'The Change to Change: Modernization, Development, and Politics', *Comparative Politics*, 3(3): 283–322.

Hutchinson, John (2004) *Nations as Zones of Conflict*, London: Sage.

Hutchinson, John (2006) 'Hot and Banal Nationalism: The Nationalization of "the Masses"', in Gerard Delanty and Krishnan Kumar (eds) *The Sage Handbook of Nations and Nationalism*, London: Sage, pp 295–306.

Hutchinson, John (2017) *Nationalism and War*, Oxford: Oxford University Press.

Innis, Harold A. (1972) *Empire and Communications*, Toronto: University of Toronto Press.

Irwin, Douglas A. (1996) *Against the Tide: An Intellectual History of Free Trade*, Princeton, NJ: Princeton University Press.

Irwin, Douglas A. (2009) *Free Trade under Fire* (3rd edn), Princeton, NJ: Princeton University Press.

Irwin, Douglas A. (2017) *Clashing over Commerce: A History of US Trade Policy*, Chicago, IL: University of Chicago Press.

ISS (Institute for Strategic Studies) (1958) *Memorandum and Articles of Association of the Institute for Strategic Studies. Incorporated the 20th day of November, 1958*, London: Denion, Hall & Burgin.

ISS (Institute for Strategic Studies) (1959) *The Soviet Union and the NATO Powers: The Military Balance*, London: ISS.

Jackson, Ben (2011) 'An Ideology of Class: Neoliberalism and the Trade Unions, c.1930–1979', in Clare V. J. Griffiths, James J. Nott and William Jr. Whyte (eds) *Classes, Cultures and Politics: Essays for Ross McKibbin*, Oxford: Oxford University Press, pp 282–304.

Jackson, Robert H. (1993) 'The Weight of Ideas in Decolonization: Normative Change in International Relations', in Judith Goldstein and Robert O. Keohane (eds) *Ideas and Foreign Policy*, Ithaca, NY: Cornell University Press, pp 111–38.

Jensen, Steven (2016) *The Making of International Human Rights: The 1960s, Decolonization, and the Reconstruction of Global Values*, New York: Cambridge University Press.

Jervis, Robert (1978) 'Cooperation under the Security Dilemma', *World Politics*, 30(2): 167–214.

Jochum, Georg (2017) *'Plus Ultra' oder die Erfindung der Moderne: Zur neuzeitlichen Entgrenzung der okzidentalen Welt*, Bielefeld: transcript.

John, Richard R. (2010) *Network Nation: Inventing American Telecommunications*, Cambridge, MA: Belknap Press of Harvard University Press.

John, Richard R. and Tworek, Heidi (2019) 'Global Communications', in Maria T. da Silva Lopes, Christina Lubinski and Heidi Tworek (eds) *The Routledge Handbook to the Makers of Global Business*, London: Routledge, pp 315–31.

Jones, Geoffrey (2005) *Multinationals and Global Capitalism: From the Nineteenth to the Twenty First Century*, Oxford: Oxford University Press.

Kaiser, Wolfram and Schot, Johan W. (2014) *Writing the Rules of Europe: Experts, Cartels and International Organisation*, Basingstoke: Palgrave Macmillan.

Kamber, Peter (2004) 'Hitler als "Charismatiker" – "Zweiter Dreissigjähriger Krieg": Zur Kritik an Hans-Ulrich Wehlers "Deutscher Gesellschaftsgeschichte"', *traverse*, 2004/2: 119–29.

Kant, Immanuel (1977) *Zum ewigen Frieden: Ein philosophischer Entwurf* (Kant-Werke Vol 11), Frankfurt am Main: Suhrkamp.

Kant, Immanuel (1984 [1795]) *Zum ewigen Frieden. Ein philosophischer Entwurf*, Stuttgart: Reclam.

Karl, Kailah M. (2012) 'The Other Fifty Percent: Psychological Operations and Women in Eastern Afghanistan', *American Intelligence Journal*, 30(2): 28–33.

Karns, Margaret P. and Mingst, Karen A. (2010) *International Organizations: The Politics and Processes of Global Governance* (2nd edn), Boulder, CO: Lynne Rienner Publishers.

Kaukiainen, Yrjö (2001) 'Shrinking the World: Improvements in the Speed of Information Transmission, c. 1820–1870', *European Review of Economic History*, 5(1): 1–28.

Kayaoğlu, Turan (2010) *Legal Imperialism: Sovereignty and Extra-Territoriality in Japan*, Cambridge: Cambridge University Press.

Keene, Edward (2012) 'The Treaty-Making Revolution of the Nineteenth Century', *International History Review*, 34(3): 475–500.

Kelley, Judith G. and Simmons, Beth A. (2019) 'Introduction: The Power of Global Performance Indicators', *International Organization*, 73(3): 491–510.

Kennedy, David (1987) 'The Move to Institutions', *Cardozo Law Review*, 8: 841–988.

Kennedy, Paul M. (2007) *The Parliament of Man: The United Nations and the Quest for World Government*, London: Allen Lane.

Kindleberger, Charles P. (1975) 'The Rise of Free Trade in Western Europe, 1820–1875', *Journal of Economic History*, 35(1): 20–55.

Kleinschmidt, Jochen (2018) 'Differentiation Theory and the Global South as a Metageography of International Relations', *Alternatives: Global, Local, Political*, 43(2): 59–80.

Kohn, Hans (1950) *Die Idee des Nationalismus: Ursprung und Geschichte bis zur französischen Revolution*, Heidelberg: Lambert Schneider.

Koselleck, Reinhart (2004) *Futures Past: On the Semantics of Historical Time*, New York: Columbia University Press.

Koskenniemi, Martti (2001) *The Gentle Civilizer of Nations: The Rise and Fall of International Law 1870–1960*, Cambridge: Cambridge University Press.

Koskenniemi, Martti (2008) 'Into Positivism: Georg Friedrich von Martens (1756–1821) and Modern International Law', *Constellations*, 15(2): 189–207.

Kott, Sandrine (2011) *Les Organisations Internationales – Terrains d'Étude pour une Histoire Globale*. www.zeithistorische-forschungen.de/site/40209186/default.aspx#fr [Accessed 9 March 2020].

Kramper, Peter (2019) *The Battle of the Standards: Messen, Zählen und Wiegen in Westeuropa 1660–1914*, Berlin: De Gruyter Oldenbourg.

Krause Hansen, Hans, Christensen, Lars T. and Flyverbom, Mikkel (2015) 'Introduction: Logics of Transparency in Late Modernity: Paradoxes, Mediation and Governance', *European Journal of Social Theory*, 18(2): 117–31.

Krause, Monika (2014) *The Good Project: Humanitarian Relief NGOs and the Fragmentation of Reason*, Chicago, IL: University of Chicago Press.

Krause, Monika (2016) 'How Fields Vary', *British Journal of Sociology*, 69(1): 3–22.

Krippner, Greta R. (2011) *Capitalizing on Crisis*, Cambridge, MA: Harvard University Press.

Krohn, Wolfgang and Weyer, Johannes (1989) 'Gesellschaft als Labor: Die Erzeugung sozialer Risiken durch experimentelle Forschung', *Soziale Welt*, 40(3): 349–73.

Krohn, Wolfgang and Weyer, Johannes (1994) 'Society as a Laboratory: The Social Risks of Experimental Research', *Science and Public Policy*, 21(3): 173–83.

Krücken, Georg (ed) (2009) *World Society: The Writings of John W. Meyer*, Oxford: Oxford University Press.

Krüger, Lorenz, Gigerenzer, Gerd and Morgan, Mary S. (eds) (1987) *The Probabilistic Revolution*, Cambridge, MA: MIT Press.

Kuznets, Simon S. (1933) 'National Income', in Edwin Seligman (ed) *Encyclopedia of the Social Sciences*, New York: Macmillan, pp 205–24.

Laborie, Léonard (2015) 'Global Commerce in Small Boxes: Parcel Post, 1878–1913', *Journal of Global History*, 10(2): 235–58.

Lacher, Hannes and Germann, Julian (2012) 'Before Hegemony: Britain, Free Trade, and Nineteenth-Century World Order Revisited', *International Studies Review*, 14(1): 99–124.

Lampe, Markus (2009) 'Effects of Bilateralism and the MFN Clause on International Trade: Evidence for the Cobden–Chevalier Network, 1860–1875', *Journal of Economic History*, 69(4): 1012–40.

Lampe, Markus (2011) 'Explaining Nineteenth-Century Bilateralism: Economic and Political Determinants of the Cobden–Chevalier Network', *Economic History Review*, 64(2): 644–68.

Lanchester, John (2018) 'After the Fall', *London Review of Books*, 40(13): 3–8.

Lang, Andrew (2014) *World Trade Law after Neoliberalism*, Oxford: Oxford University Press.

Lapid, Yosef (1989) 'The Third Debate: On the Prospects of International Theory in a Post-Positivist Era', *International Studies Quarterly*, 33(3): 235–54.

Lasson, Adolf (1871) *Princip und Zukunft des Völkerrechts*, Berlin: Verlag von Wilhem Hertz.

Latouche, Serge (1989) *L'Occidentalisation du Monde*, Paris: La Découverte.

Latour, Bruno (1987) *La Science en Action: Introduction à la Sociologie des Sciences*, Paris: La Découverte.

Latour, Bruno (1990) 'Drawing Things Together', in Michael Lynch and Steve Woolgar (eds) *Representation in Scientific Practice*, Cambridge, MA: MIT Press, pp 19–68.

Law, John (1994) *Organizing Modernity*, Oxford: Blackwell.

Law, John and Urry, John (2004) 'Enacting the Social', *Economy and Society*, 33(3): 390–410.

Lawson, George, Armbruster, Chris and Cox, Michael (eds) (2010) *The Global 1989*, Cambridge: Cambridge University Press.

League of Nations (1920) 'The Covenant of the League of Nations', *Official Journal*, Feb 1920: 3–16.

Lechner, Frank. J. and Boli, John (2005) *World Culture*, Malden, MA: Blackwell.

Lincove, David (2018a) 'Key Sources of Multinational Data on Conventional and Nuclear Armaments', *Reference & User Services Quarterly*, 58(1): 11–5.

Lincove, David (2018b) 'Data for Peace: The League of Nations and Disarmament 1920–40', *Peace & Change*, 43(4), 498–529.

Link, Stefan (2018) 'How Might 21st Century De-Globalization Unfold? Some Historical Reflections', *New Global Studies*, 12(3): 343–65.

List, Friedrich (1922) *Das nationale System der politischen Oekonomie, erster Band, Der internationale Handel, die Handelspolitik und der deutsche Zollverein* (Neudruck nach der Ausgabe letzter Hand), Jena: Gustav Fischer.

Lorca, Arnulf B. (2015) *Mestizo International Law*, Cambridge: Cambridge University Press.

Lord, Kristin M. (2006) *The Perils and Promise of Global Transparency: Why the Information Revolution May Not Lead to Security, Democracy, or Peace*, Albany, NY: State University of New York Press.

Lorenz, Chris (2017) '"The Times They Are A-Changin": On Time, Space and Periodisation in History', in Mario Carretero, Stefan Berger and Maria Grever (eds) *Palgrave Handbook of Research in Historical Culture and Education*, London: Palgrave Macmillan, pp 109–31.

Lorimer, James (1883) *The Institutes of the Law of Nations. A Treatise of the Jural Relations of Separate Political Communities – Vol 1*, Edinburgh: Blackwood and Sons.

Lorimer, James (1884) *The Institutes of the Law of Nations: A Treatise of the Jural Relations of Separate Political Communities – Vol 2*, Edinburgh: Blackwood and Sons.

Lübbe, Hermann (1971) 'Technokratie, Politische und wirtschaftliche Schicksale einer philosophischen Idee', *WeltTrends*, 18: 39–62.

Lübbe, Hermann (1996) 'Netzverdichtung: Zur Philosophie industriegesellschaftlicher Entwicklungen', *Zeitschrift für philosophische Forschung*, 50(1–2): 133–50.

Luckmann, Thomas (1970) 'On the Boundaries of the Social World', in Maurice Natanson (ed) *Phenomenology and Social Reality: Essays in Memory of Alfred Schutz*, The Hague: Martinus Nijhoff, pp 73–100.

Luhmann, Niklas (1972) *Rechtssoziologie* (2 vols), Reinbek: Rowohlt.

Luhmann, Niklas (1975a) 'Die Weltgesellschaft', in *Soziologische Aufklärung, Vol 2*, Opladen: Westdeutscher Verlag, pp 51–71.

Luhmann, Niklas (1975b) 'Einführende Bemerkungen zu einer Theorie symbolisch generalisierter Kommunikationsmedien', in *Soziologische Aufklärung, Vol 2*, Opladen: Westdeutscher Verlag, pp 170–92.

Luhmann, Niklas (1975c) 'Interaktion, Organisation, Gesellschaft', in *Soziologische Aufklärung, Vol 2*, Opladen: Westdeutscher Verlag, pp 9–20.

Luhmann, Niklas (1975d) 'Weltzeit und Systemgeschichte: Über Beziehungen zwischen Zeithorizonten und Strukturen gesellschaftlicher Systeme', in *Soziologische Aufklärung, Vol 2*, Opladen: Westdeutscher Verlag, pp 128–66.

Luhmann, Niklas (1979) *Trust and Power*, Chichester: John Wiley.

Luhmann, Niklas (1981) 'Veränderungen im System gesellschaftlicher Kommunikation und die Massenmedien', in *Soziologische Aufklärung, Vol 3*, Opladen: Westdeutscher Verlag, pp 309–20.

Luhmann, Niklas (1995a) *Social Systems*, Stanford, CA: Stanford University Press.

Luhmann, Niklas (1995b) 'Die Behandlung von Irritationen: Abweichung oder Neuheit?', in *Gesellschaftsstruktur und Semantik, Vol 4*, Frankfurt am Main: Suhrkamp, pp 55–100.

Luhmann, Niklas (1995c) 'Kultur als historischer Begriff', in *Gesellschaftsstruktur und Semantik, Vol 4*, Frankfurt am Main: Suhrkamp, pp 31–54.

Luhmann, Niklas (1996) *Die Realität der Massenmedien* (2nd edn), Opladen: Westdeutscher Verlag.

Luhmann, Niklas (1997a) 'Globalization or World Society: How to Conceive of Modern Society?', *International Review of Sociology*, 7(1): 67–79.

Luhmann, Niklas (1997b) *Die Gesellschaft der Gesellschaft*, Frankfurt am Main: Suhrkamp.

Luhmann, Niklas (2000) *Die Politik der Gesellschaft*, Frankfurt am Main: Suhrkamp.

Luhmann, Niklas (2012/13) *Theory of Society* (2 vols), Stanford, CA: Stanford University Press.

Luhmann, Niklas (2017) *Systemtheorie der Gesellschaft*, Berlin: Suhrkamp.

Lunn, Simon (1989) 'The East–West Military Balance: Assessing Change', in François Heisbourg (ed) *The Changing Strategic Landscape*, *Adelphi Papers*, London: Palgrave, pp 49–71.

Lüthi, Lorenz M. (2008) *The Sino-Soviet Split: Cold War in the Communist World*, Princeton, NJ: Princeton University Press.

Maddison, Angus (2001) *The World Economy*, Paris: Development Centre of the OECD.

Maier, Charles S. (2014) *Leviathan 2.0*, Cambridge, MA: Belknap Press of Harvard University Press.

Maier, Charles S. (2016) *Once Within Borders: Territories of Power, Wealth, and Belonging since 1500*, Cambridge, MA: Harvard University Press.

Mallet, Louis (1891) 'The Policy of Commercial Treaties' [1865], in Louis Mallet (ed) *Free Exchange*, London: Kegan Paul, Trench, Trübner & Co, pp 72-94.

Manchanda, Nivi (2017) 'The Imperial Sociology of the "Tribe" in Afghanistan', *Millennium*, 46(2): 165–89.

Mann, Michael (1997) 'Has Globalization Ended the Rise and Rise of the Nation-State?', *Review of International Political Economy*, 4(3): 472–96.

Mann, Michael (2013) *The Sources of Social Power, Vol 4*, Cambridge: Cambridge University Press.

Mann, Michael (2017) *Wiring the Nation: Telecommunication, Newspaper-Reportage, and Nation Building in British India 1850–1930*, Oxford: Oxford University Press.

Maoz, Zeev (2010) *Networks of Nations: The Evolution, Structure, and Impact of International Networks, 1816 2001*, Cambridge: Cambridge University Press.

Marsh, Peter T. (1999) *Bargaining on Europe: Britain and the First Common Market, 1860–1892*, New Haven, CT: Yale University Press.

Martinez-Robles, David (2016) 'Constructing Sovereignty in Nineteenth-Century China: The Negotiation of Reciprocity in the Sino-Spanish Treaty of 1864', *International History Review*, 38(4): 719–40.

Mason, Daniel S., Thibault, Lucie and Misener, Laura (2006) 'An Agency Theory Perspective on Corruption in Sport: The Case of the International Olympic Committee', *Journal of Sport Management*, 20(1): 52–73.

Mattern, Janice B. and Zarakol, Ayşe (2016) 'Hierarchies in World Politics', *International Organization*, 70(3): 623–54.

Mattli, Walter (1999) *The Logic of Regional Integration: Europe and Beyond*, Cambridge: Cambridge University Press.

Mauelshagen, Franz (2017) 'Bridging the Great Divide: The Anthropocene as a Challenge to the Social Sciences and Humanities', in Celia Deane-Drummond, Sigurd Bergmann and Markus Vogt (eds) *Religion and the Anthropocene*, Eugene, OR: Cascade Books, pp 87–102.

Mayall, James (1984) 'Reflections on the "New" Economic Nationalism', *Review of International Studies*, 10(4): 313–21.

Mayall, James (1990) *Nationalism and International Society*, Cambridge: Cambridge University Press.

Mazower, Mark (2009) *No Enchanted Palace: The End of Empire and the Ideological Origins of the United Nations*, Princeton, NJ: Princeton University Press.

McCarthy, Daniel R. and Fluck, Matthew (2017) 'The Concept of Transparency in International Relations: Towards a Critical Approach', *European Journal of International Relations*, 23(2): 416–40.

McVety, Amanda K. (2018) 'Wealth and Nations: The Origins of International Development Assistance', in Stephen J. Macekura and Erez Manela (eds) *The Development Century: A Global History*, New York: Cambridge University Press, pp 21–39.

Merchant, Brian (2017a) 'Were the Raw Materials in Your iPhone Mined by Children in Inhumane Conditions?', *Los Angeles Times*, 23 July. www.latimes.com/opinion/op-ed/la-oe-merchant-iphone-supplychain-20170723-story.html [Accessed 27 January 2019].

Merchant, Brian (2017b) *The One Device: The Secret History of the iPhone*, New York: Little, Brown.

Messmer, Heinz (2003) *Der soziale Konflikt: Kommunikative Emergenz und systemische Reproduktion*, Stuttgart: Lucius & Lucius.

Messmer, Heinz (2007) 'Contradiction, Conflict, and Borders', in Stephan Stetter (ed) *Territorial Conflicts in World Society: Modern Systems Theory, International Relations and Conflict Studies*, London: Routledge, pp 90–110.

Meyer, John W. (1994) 'Rationalized Environments', in John W. Meyer and W. Richard Scott (eds) *Institutional Environments and Organizations: Structural Complexity and Individualism*, Thousand Oaks, CA: Sage, pp 28–54.

Meyer, John W. (2000) 'Globalization: Sources and Effects on National States and Societies', *International Sociology*, 15(2): 233–48.

Meyer, John W. and Jepperson, Ronald L. (2000) 'The "Actors" of Modern Society: The Cultural Construction of Social Agency', *Sociological Theory*, 18(1): 100–20.

Meyer, John W., Boli, John, Thomas, George M. and Ramirez, Fransisco O. (1997) 'World Society and the Nation-State', *American Journal of Sociology*, 103(1): 144–81.

Mignolo, Walter D. (2013) 'On Comparison: Who Is Comparing What and Why?', in Rita Felski and Susan Stanford Friedman (eds) *Comparison: Theories, Approaches, Uses*, Baltimore, MD: Johns Hopkins University Press, pp 99–119.

Milanovic, Branko (2016) *Global Inequality: A New Approach for the Age of Globalization*, Cambridge, MA: Harvard University Press.

Miller, Manjari C. (2013) *Wronged by Empire: Post-Imperial Ideology and Foreign Policy in India and China*, Palo Alto, CA: Stanford University Press.

Milward, Alan (1982) 'Tariffs as Constitutions', in Susan Strange and Roger Tooze (eds) *The International Politics of Surplus Capacity*, London: Routledge, pp 43–50.

Mitrany, David (1948) 'The Functional Approach to World Organization', *International Affairs*, 24(3): 350–63.

Modelski, George (1996) 'Evolutionary Paradigm for Global Politics', *International Studies Quarterly*, 40(3): 321–42.

Molla, Rani (2018) 'In Just Five Years, Facebook, Apple, Amazon, Netflix and Google Have Doubled Their Effect on the S&P 500', *Recode*, 20 March. www.recode.net/2018/3/30/17180932/facebook-apple-amazon-netflix-google-doubled-sp500-index [Accessed 27 January 2019].

Mügge, Daniel (2016) 'Studying Macroeconomic Indicators as Powerful Ideas', *Journal of European Public Policy*, 23(3): 410–27.

Mulgan, Geoff (2013) *The Locust and the Bee*, Princeton, NJ: Princeton University Press.

Müller, Norbert (2000) *Pierre De Coubertin 1863–1937. Olympism: Selected Writings*, Lausanne: International Olympic Committee.

Müller, Simone M. (2015) 'Beyond the Means of 99 Percent of the Population: Business Interests, State Intervention, and Submarine Telegraphy', *Journal of Policy History*, 27(3): 439–64.

Müller, Simone M. (2016) *Wiring the World: The Social and Cultural Creation of Global Telegraph Networks*, New York: Columbia University Press.

Müller, Simone M. and Tworek, Heidi J.S. (2015) '"The Telegraph and the Bank": On the Interdependence of Global Communications and Capitalism, 1866–1914', *Journal of Global History*, 10(2): 259–83.

Muñiz, Manuel (2017) 'Populism and the Need for a New Social Contract', in Henning Meyer (ed) *Understanding the Populist Revolt*, Brussels: Social Europe, pp 10–13.

Murphy, Craig (1984) *The Emergence of a NIEO Ideology*, Boulder, CO: CR Press.

Murphy, Craig (1994) *International Organization and Industrial Change: Global Governance since 1850*, New York: Oxford University Press.

Murray, Williamson and Millett, Allan R. (1992) *Calculations: Net Assessment and the Coming of World War II*, New York: The Free Press.

NATO (1972a) *Allied Defense in the Seventies*, Brussels: NATO Information Service.

NATO (1972b) Memorandum 'NATO Pamphlet "Allied Defense in the Seventies"', NATO Archives, IMSM-0005-72-ENG.

NATO (1982) '"Economist" Article 31st July 1982. Note by the Chairman. Defence Review Committee', NATO Archives, DRC-N(82)40-ENG.

Nayak, Meghana and Selbin, Eric (2010) *Decentering International Relations*, London: Zed.

Nelson, Travis and Cottrell, M. Patrick (2015) 'Sport without Referees? The Power of the International Olympic Committee and the Social Politics of Accountability', *European Journal of International Relations*, 22(2): 437–58.

Neumann, Iver (2005) 'Sublime Diplomacy: Byzantine, Early Modern, Contemporary', *Millennium: Journal of International Studies*, 34(3): 865–88.

Neumann, Iver and Wigen, Einar (2018) *The Steppe Tradition in International Relations: Russians, Turks and European State-Building 4000 BCE–2017 CE*, Cambridge: Cambridge University Press.

Norris, Robert S. and Kristensen, Hans M. (2015) 'Counting Nuclear Warheads in the Public Interest', *Bulletin of Atomic Scientists*, 71(1): 85–90.

O'Brien, Patrick (2018) 'Foreword', in Manuel Perez Garcia and Lucio de Sousa (eds) *Global History and New Polycentric Approaches: Europe, Asia and the Americas in a World Network System*, London: Palgrave, pp xi–xiii.

O'Connor Witter, Maureen (2005) 'Sanctioned Spying: The Development of the Military Attaché in the Nineteenth Century', in Peter Jackson and Jennifer Siegel (eds) *Intelligence and Statecraft: The Use and Limits of Intelligence in International Society*, Westport, CT: Praeger, pp 87–107.

O'Riley, Michael F. (2007) 'Postcolonial Haunting: Anxiety, Affect, and the Situated Encounter', *Postcolonial Text*, 3(4): 1–15.

Ogle, Vanessa (2014) 'State Rights against Private Capital: The "New International Economic Order" and the Struggle over Aid, Trade, and Foreign Investment, 1962–1981', *Humanity: An International Journal of Human Rights, Humanitarianism, and Development*, 5(2): 211–34.

Ogle, Vanessa (2015) *The Global Transformation of Time 1870–1950*, Cambridge, MA: Harvard University Press.

Ohmae, Kenichi (1995) *The End of the Nation State: The Rise of Regional Economies*, New York: The Free Press.

Olcott, Jocelyn (2017) *International Women's Year: The Greatest Consciousness-Raising Event in History*, New York: Oxford University Press.

Oncken, Auguste (1891) 'L'article onze du traité du paix de Francfort et l'expiration des traités de commerce: le 1er Fevrier 1892', *Revue d'économie politique*, 5(7): 585–603.

OSCE (Organisation for Security and Cooperation in Europe) (1994) 'Global Exchange of Military Information'. https://www.osce.org/fsc/41384?download=true [Accessed 28 February 2020].

OSCE (Organisation for Security and Cooperation in Europe) (2011) 'Vienna Document 2011 on Confidence- and Security-Building Measures'. www.osce.org/fsc/86597?download=true [Accessed 28 February 2020].

Osterhammel, Jürgen (1999) *Colonialism: A Theoretical Overview*, Princeton, NJ: Markus Wiener Publishers.

Osterhammel, Jürgen (2009) *Die Verwandlung der Welt: Eine Geschichte des 19. Jahrhunderts*, München: C.H. Beck.

Osterhammel, Jürgen (2014) *The Transformation of the World: A Global History of the Nineteenth Century*, Princeton, NJ: Princeton University Press.

Osterhammel, Jürgen (2016a) 'Global History and Historical Sociology', in James Belich, John Darwin, Margret Frenz and Chris Wickham (eds) *The Prospect of Global History*, Oxford: Oxford University Press, pp 23–43.

Osterhammel, Jürgen (2016b) 'Hierarchien und Verknüpfungen: Aspekte einer globalen Sozialgeschichte', in Sebastian Conrad and Jürgen Osterhammel (eds) *Geschichte der Welt: Vol 4. 1750–1870: Wege zur modernen Welt*, München: C.H. Beck, pp 627–836.

Osterhammel, Jürgen (2017) 'Globalisierungen', in *Die Flughöhe der Adler: Historische Essays zur globalen Gegenwart*, München: C.H. Beck, pp 12–41.

Osterhammel, Jürgen (2018) 'Geschichte des Freihandels', *Aus Politik und Zeitgeschichte*, 68(4–5): 11–7.

Otis, Laura C. (2001) *Networking: Communicating with Bodies and Machines in the Nineteenth Century*, Ann Arbor, MI: University of Michigan Press.

Özkirimli, Umut (2010) *Theories of Nationalism* (2nd edn), Basingstoke: Palgrave.

Pahre, Robert (2007) *Politics and Trade Cooperation in the Nineteenth Century*, Cambridge: Cambridge University Press.

Palen, Marc-William (2016) *The 'Conspiracy' of Free Trade: The Anglo-American Struggle Over Empire and Economic Globalisation, 1846–1896*, Cambridge: Cambridge University Press.

Panitch, Leo and Gindin, Sam (2012) *The Making of Global Capitalism*, London: Verso.

Pascal, Blaise (1910) *Thoughts, Letters, and Minor Works* (trans W.F. Trotter, M.L. Booth and O.W. Wight), New York: P.F. Collier & Son.

Patel, Kiran K. (2018) *Projekt Europa: Eine kritische Geschichte*, München: C.H. Beck.

Peacock, Byron (2010) '"A Virtual World Government unto Itself": Uncovering the Rational-Legal Authority of the IOC in World Politics', *Olympika: The International Journal of Olympic Studies*, 19: 41–58.

Pedersen, Susan (2007) 'Back to the League of Nations', *American Historical Review*, 112(4): 1091–117.

Petersmann, Ernst-Ulrich (1988) 'Strengthening GATT Procedures for Settling Trade Disputes', *The World Economy*, 11(1): 51–90.

Petzke, Martin (2016) 'Taken in by the Numbers Game: The Globalization of a Religious "Illusio" and "Doxa" in Nineteenth-Century Evangelical Missions to India', *Sociological Review*, 64(2): 124–45.

Piketty, Thomas (2014) *Capital in the Twenty-First Century*, Cambridge, MA: Harvard University Press.

Pitts, Jennifer (2018) *Boundaries of the International: Law and Empire*, Cambridge, MA: Harvard University Press.

Pollack, Andrew (1984) 'Bell System Breakup Opens Era of Great Expectations and Great Concern', *New York Times*, 1 January. www.nytimes.com/1984/01/01/us/bell-system-breakup-opens-era-of-great-expectations-and-great-concern.html [Accessed 27 January 2019].

Porter, Michael E. (1990) *The Competitive Advantage of Nations*, New York: Free Press.

Porter, Theodore M. (1995) *Trust in Numbers: The Pursuit of Objectivity in Science and Public Life*, Princeton, NJ: Princeton University Press.

Porter, Theodore M. and Ross, Dorothy (eds) (2003) *The Cambridge History of Science, Volume 7: The Modern Social Sciences*, Cambridge: Cambridge University Press.

Potter, Pitman B. (1945) 'Origin of the Term International Organization', *American Journal of International Law*, 39(4): 803–6.

Pryke, Sam (2009) *Nationalism in a Global World*, Basingstoke: Palgrave.

Ranft, Bryan (1986) 'General Introduction', in Bryan Ranft (ed) *Ironclad to Trident: 100 Years of Defence Commentary: Brassey's 1886–1986*, London: Brassey's Defence Publishers, pp xv–xx.

Rantanen, Terhi (2009) *When News Was New*, Malden, MA: Wiley-Blackwell.

Raphael, Lutz (1996) 'Die Verwissenschaftlichung des Sozialen als methodische und konzeptionelle Herausforderung für eine Sozialgeschichte des 20. Jahrhunderts', *Geschichte und Gesellschaft*, 22(2): 165–93.

Rathbun, Brian C. (2007) 'Uncertain about Uncertainty: Understanding the Multiple Meanings of a Crucial Concept in International Relations Theory', *International Studies Quarterly*, 51(3): 533–57.

Regev, Motti (2011) 'Pop-Rock Music as Expressive Isomorphism: Blurring the National, the Exotic, and the Cosmopolitan in Popular Music', *American Behavioral Scientist*, 55(5): 558–73.

Reid, Anthony (2015) *A History of Southeast Asia: Critical Crossroads*, Hoboken, NJ: John Wiley & Sons.

Reinhard, Wolfgang (2015) 'Introduction', in Wolfgang Reinhard (ed) *Empires and Encounters 1350–1750*, Cambridge, MA: Belknap Press of Harvard University Press, pp 3-52.

Reinhard, Wolfgang (2016) *Die Unterwerfung der Welt: Globalgeschichte der Europäischen Expansion 1415–2015*, München: C.H. Beck.

Reinsch, Paul S. (1911) *Public International Unions: Their Work and Organization*, Boston, MA: Athenaeum Press.

Reus-Smit, Christian (1997) 'The Constitutional Structure of International Society and the Nature of Fundamental Institutions', *International Organization*, 51(4): 555–89.

Reus-Smit, Christian (1999) *The Moral Purpose of the State: Culture, Social Identity, and Institutional Rationality in International Relations*, Princeton, NJ: Princeton University Press.

Reus-Smit, Christian (2001) 'Human Rights and the Social Construction of Sovereignty', *Review of International Studies*, 27(4): 519–38.

Rieger, Bernhard (2005) *Technology and the Culture of Modernity in Britain and Germany, 1890–1945*, Cambridge: Cambridge University Press.

Rittberger, Volker, Zangl, Bernhard and Kruck, Andreas (2011) *International Organization* (2nd edn), Basingstoke: Palgrave Macmillan.

Robertson, Roland (1992) *Globalization: Social Theory and Global Culture*, London: Sage.

Robertson, Roland (1993) 'Globalization and Sociological Theory', in Herminio Martins (ed) *Knowledge and Passion: Essays in Honour of John Rex*, London: I.B. Tauris, pp 175–96.

Robertson, Roland (1995) 'Glocalization: Time–Space and Homogeneity–Heterogeneity', in Mike Featherstone, Scott Lash and Roland Robertson (eds) *Global Modernities*, London: Sage, pp 25–44.

Rodrik, Dani (2018) *Straight Talk on Trade: Ideas for a Sane World Economy*, Princeton, NJ: Princeton University Press.

Rosanvallon, Pierre (2013) *The Society of Equals*, Cambridge, MA: Harvard University Press.

Rosenau, James N. and Czempiel, Ernst-Otto (eds) (1992) *Governance without Government: Order and Change in World Politics*, Cambridge: Cambridge University Press.

Rosenberg, Justin (1994) *The Empire of Civil Society*, London: Verso.

Rosenboim, Or (2017) *The Emergence of Globalism*, Princeton, NJ: Princeton University Press.

Ruggie, John G. (1982) 'Embedded Liberalism in the Post-War Economic Order', *International Organization*, 36(2): 379–415.

Sachsenmaier, Dominic (2011) *Global Perspectives on Global History: Theories and Approaches in a Connected World*, Cambridge: Cambridge University Press.

Sassen, Saskia (2001) *The Global City: New York, London, Tokyo* (2nd edn), Princeton, NJ: Princeton University Press.

Saull, Richard (2017) 'Hegemony and the Global Political Economy', *Oxford Research Encyclopedias*, December. https://oxfordre.com/internationalstudies/view/10.1093/acrefore/9780190846626.001.0001/acrefore-9780190846626-e-208 [Accessed 4 January 2019].

Schermers, Henry G. and Blokker, Niels (2011) *International Institutional Law: Unity within Diversity* (5th edn), Boston, MA: Martinus Nijhoff Publishers.

Schipper, Frank and Schot, Johan (2011) 'Infrastructural Europeanism, or the Project of Building Europe on Infrastructures: An Introduction', *History and Technology*, 27(3): 245–64.

Schlichte, Klaus (2015) 'Herrschaft, Widerstand und die Regierung der Welt', *Zeitschrift für Internationale Beziehungen*, 22(1): 113–27.

Schücking, Walther (1908) 'Die Organisation der Welt', in W. van Calker (ed) *Festgabe für Paul Laband*, Tübingen: J.C.B. Mohr, pp 533–614.

Schwartz, Hermann (2000) *States versus Markets*, Basingstoke: MacMillan.

Scott, James C. (1998) *Seeing Like a State: How Certain Schemes to Improve the Human Condition Have Failed*, New Haven, CT: Yale University Press.

Sen, Amartya (1999) *Development as Freedom*, Oxford: Oxford University Press.

Sending, Ole J. (2015) *The Politics of Expertise: Competing for Authority in Global Governance*, Ann Arbor, MI: University of Michigan Press.

Sewell, William H., Jr (2005) *Logics of History: Social Theory and Social Transformation*, Chicago, IL: University of Chicago Press.

Sharman, Jason C. (2018) 'Myths of Military Revolution: European Expansion and Eurocentrism', *European Journal of International Relations*, 24(3): 491–513.

Shulman, Peter (2015) 'Ben Franklin's Ghost: World Peace, American Slavery, and the Global Politics of Information before the Universal Postal Union', *Journal of Global History*, 10(2): 212–34.

Silberner, Edmund (1939) *La guerre dans la pensée économique du 16. au 18. siècle*, Paris: Sirey.

Simmel, Georg (1958 [1908]) *Soziologie: Untersuchungen über die Formen der Vergesellschaftung* (4th edn), Leipzig: Duncker & Humblot.

Simmel, Georg (1978 [1900]) *The Philosophy of Money*, London: Routledge.

Sinn, Hans-Werner (2003) *The New Systems Competition*, Oxford: Blackwell.

SIPRI (Stockholm International Peace Research Institute) (1969) *SIPRI Yearbook of World Armaments and Disarmament 1968/69*, Stockholm: SIPRI.

Skocpol, Theda (1979) *States and Social Revolutions: A Comparative Analysis of France, Russia, and China*, Cambridge: Cambridge University Press.

Slauter, Will (2009) 'Forward-Looking Statements: News and Speculation in the Age of the American Revolution', *Journal of Modern History*, 81(4): 759–72.

Slobodian, Quinn (2015) 'How to See the World Economy: Statistics, Maps, and Schumpeter's Camera in the First Age of Globalization', *Journal of Global History*, 10(2): 307–32.

Slobodian, Quinn (2018) *Globalists: The End of Empire and the Birth of Neoliberalism*, Cambridge, MA: Harvard University Press.

Slotten, Hugh R. (2015) 'International Governance, Organizational Standards, and the First Global Satellite Communication System', *Journal of Policy History*, 27(3): 521–49.

Smith, Anthony D. (1983) 'Nationalism and Classical Social Theory', *British Journal of Sociology*, 34(1): 19–38.

Smith, Anthony D. (1998) *Nationalism and Modernism: A Critical Survey of Recent Theories of Nations and Nationalism*, London: Routledge.

Smith, Bonnie G. (1995) 'Gender and the Practices of Scientific History: The Seminar and Archival Research in the Nineteenth Century', *American Historical Review*, 100(4): 11–66.

Sossai, Mirko (2013) 'Transparency as a Cornerstone of Disarmament and Non-Proliferation Regimes', in Andrea Bianchi and Anne Peters (eds) *Transparency in International Law*, Cambridge: Cambridge University Press, pp 392–416.

Spaulding, Robert M. (2018) 'The Central Commission for the Navigation of the Rhine and European Media, 1815–1848', in Jonas Brendebach, Martin Herzer and Heidi Tworek (eds) *Exorbitant Expectations: International Organizations and the Media in the Nineteenth and Twentieth Centuries*, New York: Routledge, pp 17–37.

Speich Chassé, Daniel (2014) 'Technical Internationalism and Economic Development at the Founding Moment of the UN System', in Mark Frey, Sönke Kunkel and Corinna R. Unger (eds) *International Organisations and Development, 1945–1990*, Basingstoke: Palgrave Macmillan, pp 23–45.

Speich Chassé, Daniel (2016) 'The Roots of the Millennium Development Goals: A Framework for Studying the History of Global Statistics', *Historical Social Research*, 41(2): 218–37.

Speich Chassé, Daniel, Moreno, Camila and Fuhr, Lili (2015) *Carbon Metrics: Global Abstractions and Ecological Epistemicide*, Berlin: Heinrich Böll Stiftung.

Spivak, Gayatri C. (1994) 'Can the Subaltern Speak?', in Patrick Williams and Laura Chrisman (eds) *Colonial Discourse and Post-Colonial Theory: A Reader*, London: Routledge, pp 66–111.

Spruyt, Hendrik (1994a) 'Institutional Selection in International Relations: State Anarchy as Order', *International Organization*, 48(4): 527–57.

Spruyt, Hendrik (1994b) *The Sovereign State and Its Competitors: An Analysis of Systems Change*, Princeton, NJ: Princeton University Press.

Standage, Tom (1998) *The Victorian Internet: The Remarkable Story of the Telegraph and the Nineteenth Century's On-Line Pioneers*, New York: Walker.

Stanziani, Alessandro (2018) *Eurocentrism and the Politics of Global History*, Cham: Palgrave Macmillan.

Stedman Jones, Daniel (2012) *Masters of the Universe*, Princeton, NJ: Princeton University Press.

Steinmetz, George (1998) 'Critical Realism and Historical Sociology: A Review Article', *Comparative Studies in Society and History*, 39(4): 170–86.

Steinmetz, George (2007) *The Devil's Handwriting: Precoloniality and the German Colonial State in Qingdao, Samoa, and Southwest Africa*, Chicago, IL: University of Chicago Press.

Steinmetz, George (2013) 'Major Contributions to Sociological Theory and Research on Empire, 1830s–Present', in George Steinmetz (ed) *Sociology and Empire. The Imperial Entanglements of a Discipline*, Durham, NC: Duke University Press, pp 1–52.

Steinmetz, George (2014) 'The Sociology of Empires, Colonialism, and Postcolonialism', *Annual Review of Sociology*, 40: 77–103.

Steinmetz, Willibald (2015) '"Vergleich" – eine begriffsgeschichtliche Skizze', in Angelika Epple and Walter Erhart (eds) *Die Welt beobachten: Praktiken des Vergleichens*, Frankfurt am Main: Campus, pp 85–134.

Steller, Verena (2011) *Diplomatie von Angesicht zu Angesicht: Diplomatische Handlungsformen in den Deutsch–Französischen Beziehungen 1870–1919*, Paderborn: Schöningh.

Stetter, Stephan (2008) *World Society and the Middle East: Reconstructions in Regional Politics*, Basingstoke: Palgrave Macmillan.

Stetter, Stephan (2014) 'World Politics and Conflict Systems: The Communication of a "No" and Its Effects', *Horizons of Politics*, 5(12): 43–67.

Stetter, Stephan (2016) 'Middle East Diplomacy', in Costas Constantinou, Pauline Kerr and Paul Sharp (eds) *SAGE Handbook of Diplomacy*, London: Sage, pp 385–98.

Stichweh, Rudolf (2000) *Die Weltgesellschaft: Soziologische Analysen*, Frankfurt am Main: Suhrkamp.

Stichweh, Rudolf (2001) 'Scientific Disciplines, History of', in Neil J. Smelser and Paul B. Baltes (eds) *International Encyclopedia of the Social & Behavioral Sciences*, Amsterdam: Elsevier, pp 13727–31.

Stichweh, Rudolf (2002) 'Politik und Weltgesellschaft', in Kai-Uwe Hellmann and Rainer Schmalz-Bruns (eds) *Theorie der Politik: Niklas Luhmanns politische Soziologie*, Frankfurt am Main: Suhrkamp, pp 287–96.

Stichweh, Rudolf (2003) 'Genese des globalen Wissenschaftssystems', *Soziale Systeme*, 9(1): 3–26.

Stichweh, Rudolf (2007) 'Evolutionary Theory and the Theory of World Society', *Soziale Systeme*, 13(1–2): 528–42.

Stiegler, Bernd and Werner, Sylwia (eds) (2016) *Laboratorien der Moderne: Orte und Räume des Wissens in Mittel- und Osteuropa*, Paderborn: Wilhelm Fink.

Subrahmanyam, Sanjay (1997) 'Connected Histories: Notes towards a Reconfiguration of Early Modern Eurasia', *Modern Asian Studies*, 31(3): 735–62.

Subramanian, Arvind and Kessler, Martin (2013) 'The Hyperglobalization of Trade and its Future', *Peterson Institute for International Economics, Working Paper 13–6*. www.piie.com/publications/wp/wp13-6.pdf [Accessed 14 March 2019].

Sumpter, Caroline (2006) 'The Cheap Press and the Reading Crowd', *Media History*, 12(3): 233–52.

Swartz, David (1997) *Culture & Power: The Sociology of Pierre Bourdieu*, Chicago, IL: University of Chicago Press.

Taylor, Alan (2003) 'Foreign Capital in Latin America in the Nineteenth and Twentieth Centuries', *NBER Working Paper Series No 9580*, March. www.nber.org/papers/w9580 [Accessed 1 May 2020].

The American Presidency Project (2001) 'The Weekly Address Delivered by the First Lady, Laura Bush, November 17, 2001', 17 November. https://georgewbush-whitehouse.archives.gov/news/releases/2001/11/20011117.html [Accessed 16 April 2020].

Therborn, Göran (2012) 'Class in the 21st Century', *New Left Review*, 78(Nov–Dec): 5–29.

Thomas, George (2013) 'Rationalized Cultural Contexts of Functional Differentiation', in Matthias Albert, Barry Buzan and Michael Zürn (eds) *Bringing Sociology to International Relations: World Politics as Differentiation Theory*, Cambridge: Cambridge University Press, pp 27–49.

Tian, Nan and Wezeman, Pieter D. (2017) 'Increased International Transparency in Military Spending Is Possible', *SIPRI*, 19 October. www.sipri.org/commentary/topical-backgrounder/2017/increased-international-transparency-military-spending-possible [Accessed 28 February 2020].

Tilly, Charles (1994) 'States and Nationalism in Europe 1492–1992', *Theory and Society*, 23(1): 131–46.

Todd, David (2015) *Free Trade and its Enemies in France, 1814–1851*, Cambridge: Cambridge University Press.

Todorov, Tzvetan (1985) *Die Eroberung Amerikas: Das Problem des Anderen*, Frankfurt am Main: Suhrkamp.

Tomlinson, John (1994) 'A Phenomenology of Globalization? Giddens on Global Modernity', *European Journal of Communication*, 9(2): 49–172.

Topik, Steven C. and Wells, Allen (2012) 'Commodity Chains in a Global Economy', in Emily S. Rosenberg (ed) *A World Connecting*, Cambridge, MA: Belknap, pp 593–812.

Topik, Steven C. and Wells, Allen (2014) *Global Markets Transformed: 1870–1945*, Cambridge, MA: Harvard University Press.

Torp, Cornelius (2014) *The Challenges of Globalization: Economy and Politics in Germany 1860–1914*, Oxford: Berghahn Books.

Trachtenberg, Marc (1977) 'A New Economic Order: Etienne Clementel and French Economic Diplomacy during the First World War', *French Historical Studies*, 10(2): 315–41.

Trentmann, Frank (2008) *Free Trade Nation: Commerce, Consumption, and Civil Society in Modern Britain*, Oxford: Oxford University Press.

Trueblood, Benjamin F. (1899) *The Federation of the World*, Boston, MA: Houghton, Mifflin.

Tully, John (2009) 'A Victorian Ecological Disaster: Imperialism, the Telegraph, and Gutta-Percha', *Journal of World History*, 20(4): 559–79.

Tworek, Heidi J.S. (2014) 'Magic Connections: German News Agencies and Global News Networks, 1905–1945', *Enterprise & Society*, 15(4): 672–86.

Tworek, Heidi J.S. (2019) *News from Germany: The Competition to Control World Communication, 1900–1945*, Cambridge, MA: Harvard University Press.

Tworek, Heidi J.S. (2020) 'A Union of Nations or Administrations? Representation, Rights, and Sovereignty at the Creation of the International Telecommunications Union', in Gabriele Balbi and Andreas Fickers (eds) *The International Telegraph Union*, Berlin: De Gruyter, pp 243–64.

Tworek, Heidi J.S. and Müller, Simone (2015) 'Introduction: The Governance of International Communications: Business, Politics, and Standard-Setting in the Nineteenth and Twentieth Centuries', *Journal of Policy History*, 27(3): 405–15.

Tworek, Heidi J.S. and Hamilton, John M. (2017) 'The Natural History of the News: An Epigenetic Study,' *Journalism: Theory, Criticism, Practice*, 18(4): 391–407.

UN (United Nations) (2018) 'Securing our Common Future: An Agenda for Disarmament'. https://front.un-arm.org/documents/SG+disarmament+agenda_1.pdf [Accessed 28 February 2020].

UN (United Nations) (2019) 'Military Expenditures: United Nations Report on Military Expenditures'. www.un.org/disarmament/convarms/milex/ [Accessed 28 February 2020].

UN General Assembly (1980) 'Reduction of Military Budgets' (= Resolution 35/142). https://undocs.org/A/RES/35/142 [Accessed 28 February 2020].

USSR Ministry of Defence (1982) *Whence the Threat to Peace*, Moscow: Military Publishing House, USSR Ministry of Defense.

Verran, Helen (2002) 'A Postcolonial Moment in Science Studies', *Social Studies of Science*, 32(5–6): 729–62.

Verter, Bradford (2003) 'Spiritual Capital: Theorizing Religion with Bourdieu against Bourdieu', *Sociological Theory*, 21(2): 150–74.

Viner, Jacob (1950) *The Customs Union Issue*, Oxford: Oxford University Press. 2014.

Von Liszt, Franz (1898) *Das Völkerrecht: Systematisch dargestellt*, Berlin: J. Springer.

Von Ranke, Leopold (2010) *The Theory and Practice of History* (ed with intro by Georg G. Iggers), London: Routledge.

Vrba, Elisabeth S. and Gould, Stephan J. (1986) 'The Hierarchical Expansion of Sorting and Selection: Sorting and Selection Cannot Be Equated', *Paleobiology*, 12(2): 217–28.

Wagner, P. (2003) 'The Uses of the Social Sciences', in Theodore M. Porter and Dorothy Ross (eds) *The Modern Social Sciences*, Cambridge: Cambridge University Press, pp 537–52.

Wallerstein, Immanuel (1974–89) *The Modern World System* (3 vols), New York: Academic Press.

Wallerstein, Immanuel (2011) *The Modern World-System IV: Centrist Liberalism Triumphant, 1789–1914*, Berkeley, CA: University of California Press.

Walter, Ben (2017) *Gendering Human Security in Afghanistan: In a Time of Western Intervention*, London: Routledge.

Walter-Busch, Emil (1996) *Organisationstheorien von Weber bis Weick*, Amsterdam: G + B Verlag Fakultas.

Ward, Michael (2004) *Quantifying the World: UN Ideas and Statistics*, Bloomington, IN: Indiana University Press.

Wardhaugh, Jessica (2013) 'Crowds, Culture and Power: Mass Politics and the Press in Interwar France', *Journalism Studies*, 14(5): 743–58.

Warner, Michael (2014) *The Rise and Fall of Intelligence: An International Security History*, Washington, DC: Georgetown University Press.

WAVES (Wealth Accounting and Value of Ecosystem Services) (2020) www.wavespartnership.org [Accessed 9 March 2020].

Weber, Albrecht (1983) *Geschichte internationaler Wirtschaftsorganisationen*, Wiesbaden: Steiner.

Webster, Andrew (2005) 'The Transnational Dream: Politicians, Diplomats and Soldiers in the League of Nations' Pursuit of International Disarmament, 1920–1938', *Contemporary European History*, 14(4): 493–518.

Wehler, Hans-Ulrich (2008) *Deutsche Gesellschaftsgeschichte 1914–1949*, München: C.H. Beck.

Wendt, Alexander (2003) 'Why a World State is Inevitable', *European Journal of International Relations*, 9(4): 491–542.

Wenzlhuemer, Roland (2007) 'The Dematerialization of Telecommunication: Communication Centres and Peripheries in Europe and the World, 1850–1920', *Journal of Global History*, 2(3): 345–72.

Wenzlhuemer, Roland (2010) 'Editorial: Telecommunication and Globalization in the Nineteenth Century', *Historical Social Research*, 35(1): 7–18.

Wenzlhuemer, Roland (2013) *Connecting the Nineteenth-Century World: The Telegraph and Globalization*, Cambridge: Cambridge University Press.

Werron, Tobias (2010) *Der Weltsport und sein Publikum: Zur Autonomie und Entstehung des modernen Sports*, Weilerswist: Velbrück.

Werron, Tobias (2012a) 'Schlüsselprobleme der Globalisierungs- und Weltgesellschaftstheorie', *Soziologische Revue*, 35(2): 99–118.

Werron, Tobias (2012b) 'Worum konkurrieren Nationalstaaten? Zu Begriff und Geschichte der Konkurrenz um "weiche" globale Güter?', *Zeitschrift für Soziologie*, 41(5): 338–55.

Werron, Tobias (2015a) 'What Do Nation-States Compete for? A World-Societal Perspective on Competition for "Soft" Global Goods', in Boris Holzer, Fatima Kastner and Tobias Werron (eds) *From Globalization to World Society: Comparing Neo-Institutional and Systems Theoretical Perspectives*, London: Routledge, pp 85–106.

Werron, Tobias (2015b) 'Why Do We Believe in Competition? A Historical-Sociological View of Competition as an Institutionalized Modern Imaginary', *Distinktion: Scandinavian Journal of Social Theory*, 16(2): 186–210.

Werron, Tobias (2016) 'Gleichzeitigkeit unter Abwesenden: Zu Globalisierungseffekten elektrischer Telekommunikationstechnologien', in Bettina Heintz and Hartmann Tyrell (eds) *Interaktion–Organisation–Gesellschaft Revisited: Anwendungen, Erweiterungen, Alternativen* (special issue of *Zeitschrift für Soziologie*), Stuttgart: Lucius & Lucius, pp 251–70.

Werron, Tobias (2018) *Der globale Nationalismus*, Berlin: Nicolai.

Werron, Tobias (2019) 'The Social Construction of National Reputation', in Diana Ingenhoff, Candace White, Alexander Buhmann and Spiro Kiousis (eds) *Bridging Disciplinary Perspectives of Country Image, Reputation, Brand, and Identity*, New York: Routledge, pp 150–67.

Werron, Tobias (2020a) 'Global Publics as Catalysts of Global Competition: A Sociological View', in Valeska Huber and Jürgen Osterhammel (eds) *The Global Public and Its Limits*, Cambridge: Cambridge University Press, pp 343–66.

Werron, Tobias (2020b) 'Knappheitsnationalismus: Globale Vergleiche als Instrumente partikularistischer Weltauffassungen', in Hannah Bennani, Martin Bühler, Andrea Glauser and Sophia Kramer (eds) *Globale Beobachtungen und Vergleiche*, Hamburg: Campus, pp 113–39.

Werron, Tobias and Ringel, Leopold (2020) 'Pandemic Practices, Part One: How to Turn "Living Through the COVID-19 Pandemic" into a Heuristic Tool for Sociological Theorizing', *Sociologica*, 14(2): 55–72.

Westad, Odd A. (2017) *The Cold War: A World History*, New York: Basic Books.

White, Hayden (1980). 'The Value of Narrativity in the Representation of Reality', *Critical Inquiry*, 7(1): 5–27.

White, Hayden (2002) 'The Historical Text as Literary Artifact', in Brian Richardson (ed) *Narrative Dynamics: Essays on Time, Plot, Closure, and Frames*, Columbus, OH: Ohio State University Press, pp 191–210.

White, John A. (1995) *Transition to Global Rivalry: Alliance Diplomacy and the Quadruple Entente, 1895–1907*, Cambridge: Cambridge University Press.

Wilson, Woodrow (1919) *The League of Nations*, 65 Congress, 3rd Session. Senate Document No 389.

Wimmer, Andreas (2002) *Nationalist Exclusion and Ethnic Conflict: Shadows of Modernity*, Cambridge: Cambridge University Press.

Wimmer, Andreas (2013) *Waves of War: Nationalism, State Formation, and Ethnic Exclusion in the Modern World*, Cambridge: Cambridge University Press.

Wimmer, Andreas (2018) *Nation Building: Why Some Countries Come Together While Others Fall Apart*, Princeton, NJ: Princeton University Press.

Wimmer, Andreas and Glick Schiller, Nina (2002) 'Methodological Nationalism and Beyond: Nation-State Building, Migration and the Social Sciences', *Global Networks*, 2(4): 301–34.

Wimmer, Andreas and Min, Brian (2006) 'From Empire to Nation-State: Explaining Wars in the Modern World, 1816–2001', *American Sociological Review*, 71(6): 867–97.

Wimmer, Andreas and Feinstein, Yuval (2010) 'The Rise of the Nation-State across the World, 1816 to 2001', *American Sociological Review*, 75(5): 764–90.

Winichakul, Thongchai (1994) *Siam Mapped: A History of the Geo-Body of a Nation*, Honolulu, HI: University of Hawaii Press.

Winseck, Dwayne R. and Pike, Robert M. (2007) *Communication and Empire: Media, Markets, and Globalization, 1860–1930*, Durham, NC: Duke University Press.

Wischnewski, Hans-Jürgen (1968) *Nord-Süd-Konflikt: Beiträge zur Entwicklungspolitik*, Hannover: Verlag für Literatur und Zeitgeschehen.

Wobbe, Theresa (2000) *Weltgesellschaft*, Bielefeld: Transcript Verlag.

Wobring, Michael (2005) *Die Globalisierung der Telekommunikation im 19. Jahrhundert: Pläne, Projekte und Kapazitätsausbauten zwischen Wirtschaft und Politik*, Frankfurt am Main: Peter Lang.

Wohlforth William C. (1993) *The Elusive Balance: Power and Perception during the Cold War*, Ithaca, NY: Cornell University Press.

Wolf, Eric (1982) *Europe and the People without History*, Berkeley, CA: University of California Press.

Wolf, Eric (1997) *Europe and the People without History*, Berkeley, CA: University of California Press.

Woolf, Leonard S. (1916) *International Government: Two Reports* (2nd edn), London: Allen & Unwin.

Wörterbuch Der Französischen Revolutionssprache (1799) Paris (no author or publisher given).

Wright, Robert (2001) *Nonzero: The Logic of Human Destiny*, New York: Vintage.

WTO (World Trade Organization) (2018) 'Members and Observers'. www.wto.org/english/thewto_e/whatis_e/tif_e/org6_e.htm [Accessed 3 April 2020].

Yang, Daqing (2010) *Technology of Empire: Telecommunications and Japanese Expansion in Asia, 1883–1945*, Cambridge, MA: Harvard University Asia Center.

Yellen, Jeremy (2019) *The Greater East Asia Co-Prosperity Sphere: When Total Empire Met Total War*, Cornell, NY: Cornell University Press.

Zahedi, Ashraf (2011) 'When the Picture Does Not Fit the Frame: Engaging Afghan Men in Women's Empowerment', in Jennifer Heath and Ashraf Zahedi (eds) *Land of the Unconquerable: The Lives of Contemporary Afghan Women*, Berkeley, CA: University of California Press, pp 293–305.

Zeiler, Thomas W. (2013) 'Offene Türen in der Weltwirtschaft', in Akira Iriye (ed) *Die globalisierte Welt, 1945 bis heute*, Munich: Beck, pp 183–356.

Zeiler, Thomas W. (2014) 'Opening Doors in the Global Economy', in Akira Iriye (ed) *Global Interdependence*, Cambridge, MA: Belknap Press, pp 203–361.

Zerubavel, Eviatar (1982) 'The Standardization of Time: A Sociohistorical Perspective', *American Journal of Sociology*, 88(1): 1–23.

Zhao, Yuezhi (2012) 'Understanding China's Media System in a World Historical Context', in Daniel Hallin and Paolo Mancini (eds) *Comparing Media Systems beyond the Western World*, New York: Cambridge University Press, pp 144–76.

Index

A

Afghanistan 16, 117–37, 229
Africa 57–8, 63–5, 88, 109, 189–90, 205, 209, 216, 219, 249
America
   the Americas 46, 57, 63, 103, 164, 181, 216
   Central America 188–9
   Latin America 109, 181–4, 186, 201, 208–9
   North America 47, 109, 115, 199, 201
   South America 65, 183–4, 189, 201, 209, 214–19
   see also United States
anthropology 48
anticolonialism 86, 92
arms control 229–30, 235–41
Asia 63, 87–8, 109, 120, 137, 181–9, 201–19
   East 181, 201, 214
   South 205, 219
   South East 44, 189, 209
Asian Tigers 183–5
Australia 65, 207, 216, 220
authoritarianism 184, 189

B

balance of power 146, 149, 153, 214, 217
Barings Bank 179–80
Barth, Fredrik 71
Bayly, Christopher 14, 45, 58, 171
benchmark dates 37–8, 147
Berlin Conference 153, 219
Berne 206
Bluntschli, Johann Caspar 103–14
Bourdieu, Pierre 14–15, 81–9, 94–7
Bretton Woods 182, 185, 215
Britain (Great Britain, United Kingdom) 85, 89, 106, 133, 166, 180–5, 190, 205, 214–20, 226, 232, 247, 255
British Empire 9, 89, 150, 198, 206, 208, 211, 215, 219–20
Burbank, Jane 14, 44, 58–9, 260
bureaucratic rationality 32
business history 200
Buzan, Barry 37, 44, 145

C

Canada 133, 201–7
capital 17, 83–97, 145, 154, 178–80, 184–7, 200–1, 212–13, 219–20, 224, 226
   colony 85–6, 89
   cultural 83–4, 88, 92, 220
   economic 83–5, 88–9, 92
   political 84–5, 92–3
   symbolic 22, 84–5, 92
capitalism 47, 72, 103, 166, 180–91, 200, 244
   global capitalism 181, 184, 187, 214–15
capitalist crisis 179, 187
capitalist governance 17, 20, 177, 188–92
Central America *see* America
Central Commission for the Navigation on the Rhine (CCNR) 101, 105, 108
centre–periphery differentiation 144–8
Chakrabarty, Dipesh 3, 46, 48–50
China 59, 65, 75, 79, 86, 144, 148, 150, 153, 158, 184, 188–91, 200, 209, 216, 219
Cold War 9, 60, 86, 99, 101, 114–15, 126, 152, 190, 215, 234, 237–8, 241, 248, 253
colonialism 9, 11, 17, 28, 59, 85, 90, 92–3, 149, 197, 229, 248
   anticolonialism 86, 92
   postcolonialism 8–9, 154
coloniality 7, 12
communication 14, 17–20, 28, 30–1, 36, 45, 58, 60, 63–78, 82, 94–5, 105, 108–12, 141–9, 160, 165–9, 174–9, 195–213, 235, 240, 243–4, 247–8, 253–4, 259–61
   global communication 19–21, 66, 160, 165, 169, 174–5, 240, 243

communication technology 67, 69, 71–2, 141, 198
communication theory 65–6, 141, 149
community of states 101, 108–11, 115, 213–14, 224
comparison 7, 14, 18, 20–22, 43, 48–61, 64, 93, 165, 175, 188, 196, 228, 231, 236, 240, 253, 256–7
  comparative practices 46, 49
  global comparisons 2, 168
complexity 13, 26, 30–1, 38, 40, 92, 139–46, 154, 209, 223
cooperation 100, 108–13, 133–4, 169, 205–6, 214–7, 221–5, 229, 231, 244, 256–7, 262
Congress of Vienna 15, 99–102, 246
Cooper, Frederik 14, 44–9, 58–9, 260

D

decolonization 60, 72, 89–90, 154, 212, 261
differentiation 6, 14–7, 21, 29–41, 63–95, 107, 111, 140–9, 155, 178, 187–8, 197
  see also functional differentiation
differentiation theory 6, 14–7, 21, 29–34, 39–41, 65, 73–87, 94–5, 140–4, 149, 197
diplomacy 113, 148–9, 161, 201, 213, 218, 222
disciplines 1–6, 12, 19, 22, 52, 71, 157, 224
Droysen, Johann Gustav 14, 52–6

E

East Asia *see* Asia
embedded liberalism 151, 183–87, 222
empire 9–15, 28, 38, 46, 57–9, 72–3, 81–95, 124–5, 140–53, 182, 198, 206–8, 211–20, 244, 255, 258, 260–1
  see also British Empire
English School 42, 149, 152
entanglements 5–7, 13, 17, 25–9, 35–7, 41, 48, 121, 146, 178–9, 191–2, 204
epochal shifts 32–4
epochs 4–5, 10–14, 20, 29, 32–4, 43–46, 50–61, 258, 263
ethnography/ethnographic 15, 21, 82, 117–20, 132–6
Eurasia 57, 148
Eurocentrism 4–9, 14, 43–9, 53, 74, 151
Europe 2–3, 8–11, 28, 33–4, 43, 46–59, 63–7, 72–8, 81, 87–9, 103–11, 120, 130, 143, 147, 152–3, 158, 161–2, 176–7, 181–9, 197, 199, 202, 206, 214–21, 226, 229, 231, 237–8, 240, 244–61

European expansion 10, 64, 66–7, 73, 152
event history 38
evolution 6–10, 13–16, 21, 26, 28, 31, 35–40, 46, 63–81, 95, 139–47, 154, 192, 220, 228, 232, 235, 237, 240
evolution theory 16, 65, 81, 95, 139, 154
evolutionary theory 65, 95
Expanded Program for Technical Assistance (EPTA) 261

F

field theory 14–15, 21, 79, 81–9, 93–7
First World War 15, 17, 35, 60, 81, 89, 99–101, 151, 153, 178, 181, 214, 220–1, 259
France 106, 116, 158, 164, 176, 181, 217–19, 226, 233
free labour 177
free trade 18, 111, 150, 170–6, 213–26
functional differentiation 32–3, 40, 69, 73–8, 95, 143–9, 155

G

gender relations 129, 132, 136
General Agreement on Tariffs and Trade (GATT) 182, 214, 222–5
Germany 51–3, 60, 68, 106, 133, 158, 165, 180–1, 208, 216, 218, 226
Geschichtsphilosophie *see* philosophy of history
Giddens, Anthony 159, 178
global, the 4, 6, 12, 16, 27, 33, 41, 45, 136, 210, 220
global capitalism *see* capitalism
global communication *see* communication
global historical sociology 1, 5, 16–17, 139, 177–9, 192
global history 1–19, 25–36, 39–50, 53, 56–7, 60, 79, 178, 192, 195, 197, 210, 215, 246, 249, 253, 260
global public 37, 112, 122, 133, 224
  see also public
Global South 141, 147, 150, 154, 209–10, 223, 248, 254
globalisation 2–4, 10–11, 14–21, 31, 45, 51, 58–9, 63–78, 157–67, 173–87, 196, 201–3, 211–12, 217, 221, 225–6
globality 10–2, 27–9, 36–7, 41
Great Britain *see* Britain
Great Depression, the 182, 215, 255

H

Habermas, Jürgen 67, 143, 197
habitus 15, 82–3, 96

INDEX

Hegel, Georg Wilhelm Friedrich 53–4, 103, 107, 112
hegemony 20, 152, 208, 212–20
historicism 14, 43, 46, 54
historiography 4, 19, 46–8, 53, 88, 215, 243–8, 262
Hobsbawm, Eric 47, 63
human rights 68, 82, 85, 92, 121, 146, 149–54, 199, 223
humanitarian intervention 15, 117, 120–4, 140
Hume, David 170

I

imperialism (high imperialism) 15, 58, 77, 81–2, 87–97, 150–4, 168, 205–6, 219–20, 248
India 65, 86, 166, 183, 189, 199, 205–6
Indonesia 209
industrialization 33, 36, 50–2, 64, 78, 180–4
institutionalization 6, 22, 68, 71, 101–4, 147, 153, 165–7, 174–5, 206, 227, 230–1, 239
intergovernmental organizations (IGOs) 72–3, 84
Intergovernmental Panel on Climate Change (IPCC) 256
international, the 29, 31, 38, 64, 66, 73–4, 79, 81–2, 87, 91, 101–4, 107–19, 123, 134–5, 141, 145–52, 154, 167–8, 186, 191–6, 201, 206–8, 212–13, 218–26, 234, 249–52, 256, 258, 262
International Atomic Energy Agency (IAEA) 228
International Committee of the Red Cross 110, 246, 255
International Criminal Court (ICC) 112, 123, 147
international history 1–5, 245, 249
International Institute for Strategic Studies (IISS) 18, 228, 231–41
International Labour Organisation (ILO) 101, 249
international law 101, 103, 107–8, 111–14, 146, 149, 161, 213, 217, 221, 225–6
International Monetary Fund (IMF) 182, 235, 257, 261
International Olympic Committee (IOC) 110
international organization/international organizations 11, 15, 18, 82, 85, 99–102, 105–8, 111–16, 146, 152, 167, 169, 174, 186, 206–7, 212–13, 220–1, 227–35, 239–40, 243–55, 259–61
international politics 16, 22, 108, 139–41, 146–54, 157
international political system 16, 28, 139–40, 145–9
international relations 1–5, 17, 37–44, 72, 97, 100, 139, 146–54, 161, 178, 196–7, 214, 233, 244, 246
international society 28, 103, 149, 161, 196, 208, 216, 219, 223
International Telegraph Union (ITU) 101, 108, 206–7
Italy, Italian 106, 165, 190, 200, 205, 226, 254

J

Japan 53, 57, 75, 77, 153, 180–4, 189, 205, 208, 216, 219

K

Kabul 117, 119, 128, 137
Kant, Immanuel 114, 243, 245–7, 252, 258, 262
Keynesianism 182–3, 185, 215
Kindleberger, Charles 215–16
Koselleck, Reinhart 48, 58
Kuznets, Simon 255–6

L

Latin America *see* America
Latour, Bruno 103, 256
League of Nations 73, 99, 101, 110, 114, 153, 214, 221, 233, 235
liberal internationalism 217, 219
List, Friedrich 170–6
long nineteenth century 10–14, 26–7, 34–9, 58, 60
long twentieth century 10–11, 14, 18, 20, 37, 44, 47, 58, 64–6, 73–4, 77–9, 81, 166, 174, 211–12, 226
Luhmann, Niklas 42, 66–79, 82, 95, 140–4, 167, 213

M

methodological nationalism 1–2, 23, 157–8, 164, 168, 247
Mexico 200
Millennium Development Goals (MDGs) 253, 257
modernity 2–17, 28, 32–3, 40, 46, 48, 52, 57, 64, 72, 77, 85, 103, 124–5, 129, 139, 141, 144, 150–4, 159, 161, 168, 173, 192–3, 211, 261
  European modernity 3, 261
  multiple modernities 10, 33
modernization 8, 43, 45, 51, 125, 173
multinational enterprises (MNEs) 200–1, 203–4, 207–9, 244

N

narrative objective 14, 20, 43, 56–60
nation state 2, 11–12, 15, 22–3, 27, 31, 40, 64, 70–3, 79, 81–2, 85–6, 90, 93–4, 121, 157–9, 161, 167, 169, 174, 204–6, 213, 223, 244, 247–9, 251, 254, 258–62
nationalism 1–2, 12, 16–17, 20, 36, 70, 90, 92, 97, 157–76, 181, 247, 249, 255, 259
  conflict nationalism 160, 163–6
  identity nationalism 160, 163–6
  institutionalized nationalism 160, 163–4, 166–8, 173–4
  scarcity nationalism 160, 163–4, 168–74
neo-institutionalism 29, 31, 93, 121, 132, 141, 167, 250
neoliberalism 150, 184–7, 223–4
network compression 66, 78
New World Information and Communication Order (NWICO) 196, 208
news agencies 65–7, 166, 208
non-governmental organizations (NGOs) 7, 84, 92, 110, 116, 125, 146–7, 230, 239, 244, 247
North America *see* America

O

Organization for Security and Cooperation in Europe (OSCE) 231–2, 235
Osterhammel, Jürgen 14, 27–9, 34–6, 44, 57–8, 64–8, 74–5, 79, 91, 102, 146, 153, 165, 176, 195, 200, 215–16, 220
Ottoman Empire 57, 153, 214–19

P

particular/universal 2–3, 5–6, 16–17, 21, 26–7, 30–5, 40, 43–5, 53, 64–8, 70–2, 77–8, 81–5, 93–101, 107, 115, 117–37, 126–9, 135–6, 140–8, 152–3, 160–2, 165, 167, 179, 192, 199–200, 207, 209, 244, 246, 261
periodization 2, 4, 10–12, 14, 19–22, 34, 40, 43–61, 64, 174, 226, 257
philosophy of history 3, 7, 26, 38–9, 53
Poland, Polish 182
postcolonial studies 1, 246
postcolonialism *see* colonialism
postcoloniality 7, 12
primary institutions 82, 148–9, 152–3
print media 65–6, 103, 144, 166–7, 208, 235, 240
protectionism 18, 158, 171–3, 182, 189, 213, 215, 220
Prussia 105, 116, 220

public/publics 22, 37, 47, 67, 74, 102–4, 112–13, 120–2, 128–9, 133, 168–70, 177, 181, 185, 192, 197–205, 213, 215, 228–40, 252, 260
  global public, global public sphere 37, 112, 122, 133, 165–6
  global public goods 224
public opinion 199, 238–40

R

Ranke, Leopold von 14, 51, 53–4
rational actorhood 6, 32
rationalized others 121, 123, 127
regionalism 181
restabilization 39, 142–6, 154–5
revolutions 14, 28, 35–6, 46, 64, 68, 104, 143, 175–6, 179, 195, 226
  American Revolution 35
  French Revolution 35, 46, 64, 175
Ricardo, David 169–70
Russia 109, 112, 150, 158, 188–9, 200, 208–9, 216, 232

S

Sattelzeit 11, 58
Saudi Arabia 189
Second World War 9, 50–1, 97, 150–3, 171, 183, 202, 211, 233, 244, 246, 252
secularization 45–6, 51
Smith, Adam 159, 169–170, 176
social field 6, 16, 81, 140–5, 151–4
  global field 93
South America *see* America
South Asia *see* Asia
South East Asia *see* Asia
South Korea 183–4, 189
sovereignty 86, 93, 107, 109, 111, 148–9, 160–1, 177, 214, 225
Spain, Spanish 85, 161
Stockholm International Peace Research Institute (SIPRI) 18, 228, 231, 234–9, 241
Sustainable Development Goals (SDGs) 257
Sweden, Swedish 200
symbolic capital *see* capital
symbolically generalized media of communication 66, 69–70
System of National Accounts 257
systems theory 7, 11, 14, 16, 21, 29–33, 39, 93, 139–44

T

tariffs 108, 172, 182–3, 214–15, 217–22
telecommunication 20, 68, 72, 74, 78, 165, 199–203, 207, 254, 260

INDEX

telegraph, telegraphy 37, 63–8, 72, 108, 145, 165, 195–210, 212
telos, teleology 13–14, 41, 45, 54–6
temporalities 8, 36, 40, 178
The Transformation of the World 34, 44, 57
third-party actors 18–19, 22, 96, 114, 121, 227–40
transparency 18, 227–36
transport infrastructure 36, 64
turning points 13, 15, 20, 26, 37–40, 81–2, 114, 181

U

uncertainty 51, 106, 228, 230
United Kingdom *see* Britain
United Nations (UN) 18–19, 73, 85, 228, 233, 243–63
United Nations Charter 85, 126, 136
United Nations Development Program 250, 261
United Nations Economic and Social Council (ECOSOC) 126, 251
United Nations Educational, Scientific and Cultural Organization (UNESCO) 208, 250
United Nations Framework Convention on Climate Change (UNFCCC) 257
United Nations General Assembly 234, 248, 251
United Nations Security Council 153, 244, 248, 251
United States 85, 89, 106, 150, 171, 180–9, 199–201, 205–6, 211, 214, 219–20, 253
universal, universalism, universalization 2, 9, 12, 14, 15–16, 22, 27, 65–7, 68–70, 82, 111, 121, 135, 165, 167–8, 188, 190, 244, 261

specific universalism 69–70, 73
universal history 44–5, 46, 246
Universal Postal Union (UPU) 101, 108, 206–7, 221

V

variation/selection 38–40, 76–7, 140–4, 146, 154
Vietnam 189, 215

W

Wallerstein, Immanuel 11, 36, 169
Wealth Accounting and the Valuation of Ecosystem Services (WAVE) 257
Weber, Max 23, 142
women's rights 119–20, 126–32, 136
world, the 2–6, 9, 12, 15–22, 28–9, 35, 41–50, 52–3, 58, 63–8, 72–5, 77, 90–2, 99–116, 120, 123, 126, 139, 147, 150–4, 160–75, 179–83, 186, 189–91, 197–210, 215–16, 221, 233, 243–7, 251–8, 262
World Bank 182, 235, 257, 261
world economy 11, 18, 59, 84, 195–9, 212–16, 221–6
world politics (system of) 2, 11, 15–19, 37, 60, 70, 100–2, 112–17, 122, 140–1, 146–51, 190–2, 213, 216, 225–32, 239–41, 246, 250
world society theory 3–7, 13, 25–42, 65, 93–7
world system 36, 65, 88, 211–12
world trade 18, 111, 113, 182, 184, 211–26
World Trade Organization (WTO) 182, 188, 214–16, 222, 224–6

www.ingramcontent.com/pod-product-compliance
Lightning Source LLC
Chambersburg PA
CBHW070910030426
42336CB00014BA/2357